Kentucky Marriages

1797-1865

Compiled by

G. GLENN CLIFT

✳

Reprinted From

THE REGISTER OF

THE KENTUCKY HISTORICAL SOCIETY

Excerpted and reprinted from
THE REGISTER OF THE KENTUCKY HISTORICAL SOCIETY
April, July, October, 1938;
January, April, July, October, 1939;
January, April, July, October, 1940.

Reprinted with special permission from
THE KENTUCKY HISTORICAL SOCIETY
Genealogical Publishing Co., Inc.
Baltimore, 1966, 1974, 1978, 1983, 1987, 1995, 2000

Library of Congress Catalogue Card Number 66-27027
International Standard Book Number 0-8063-0076-0

INTRODUCTION

The marriage notices following were taken from the Lexington, Kentucky, Public Library's 1787-1865 files of Lexington newspapers. Gaps in the inclusive dates reflect years missing in those files.

The original purpose of the work was to make these records available only to users of the library's newspaper holdings in an effort to minimize usage of the rare collection for genealogical research. The compilation was made available to the general public when it was published in eleven numbers of *The Register of the Kentucky Historical Society* beginning with the issue of April, 1938, and ending with the issue of October, 1940.

Kentucky Marriages, 1797-1865, represents the first volume of the original two-volume compilation. The second volume, *Kentucky Obituaries, 1787-1854*, was also published in *The Register of the Kentucky Historical Society* beginning in January, 1941, and ending in April, 1943. Complete sets of *The Register* containing the two volumes are no longer in print.

The present reprinting marks the first time that *Kentucky Marriages, 1797-1865*, has been fully indexed as a separate publication.

For purposes of bibliography an abbreviation of the name of the newspaper from which a notice or story was taken is given with that notice or story.

The abbreviations used denote:

I   —*Lexington Intelligencer*
KG—*Kentucky Gazette*
M —Married
O —(Lexington) *Observer*
OR—*Lexington Observer and Reporter*
P —*Lexington Public Advertiser*
R —*Reporter* or *Kentucky Reporter*
S —*Kentucky Statesman*

G. GLENN CLIFT
Frankfort, Kentucky
March 7, 1966

KENTUCKY MARRIAGES
1787-1860

1797

John Price to Miss Susannah Gano, daughter of the Rev. John Gano. Married near Frankfort, Jan. 1, 1797. KG 1/7.

Dr. F. Ridgley, of Lexington, to Miss Short, sister of Major Short, of Woodford county. Married Mar. 16, 1797. KG 3/22.

1799

Hon. John Brown, U. S. Congressman from Kentucky, to Miss Margaret Mason, daughter of the late Rev. John Mason, of New York City. Married Feb. 21, 1799. KG 4/4.

1800

Dr. Samuel Stoy, to Miss Coons, daughter of John Coons, both of Lexington. Married Dec. 9, 1800. KG 12/9.

1802

William Hays, of Mercer county, to Miss Lucy Gatewood, of Fayette county. Married Nov. 2, 1802. KG 12/7.

Robert Bradley, of Lexington, to Miss Elizabeth Lytle, of the North Western Territory. Married Nov. 21, 1802. KG 11/30.

Capt. Henry Marshall, of Lexington, to Miss Catherine Allen, of Clarke county. Married Nov. 1802. KG 11/30.

Mann Satterwhite, to Miss Charlotte Ashby, both of Fayette county. Married Dec. 22, 1802. KG 12/28.

1803

John Tompkins, to Miss Abigain Watson, both of Fayette county. Married May 3, 1803. KG 5/10

Dr. Walter Brashier, to Miss Margaret Barr. Married May 5, 1803. KG 5/10.

James Haggin, of Mercer county, to Miss Henrietta Humphreys, of near Lexington. Married May 26, 1803. KG 6/7.

Dr. John Goodlett, of Fayette county, to Miss Rebeckah Patterson, daughter of Col. Robert Patterson, of Lexington. Married June 1, 1803. KG 6/7.

Henry Purviance, to Miss Margaret Ross, both of Lexington. Married June 2, 1803. KG 6/7.

William Todd, of Lexington, to Miss Elizabeth LeGrand, of the neighborhood of Lexington. Married July 6, 1803. KG 7/12.

Joseph H. Daveiss, attorney of the United States for the Kentucky District, to Miss Nancy Marshall, sister of Gen. John Marshall, Chief Justice of the United States. Married at the home of Mr. H. Marshall, July 16, 1803. KG 7/14.

Cornelius Coyle, of Lexington, to Miss Rebecca Allen, of Clarke county. Married July 21, 1803. KG 7/26.

David Sutton, to Miss Juliet May, both of Lexington. They were married Sept. 4, 1803. KG 9/6.

Philemon B. Price, to Miss Polly Mansell, both of Fayette county. Married Oct. 6, 1803. KG 10/11.

Rev. William Rainey, to Miss Margaretta Fisher, daughter of Major Fisher, of Fayette county. Married Dec. 15, 1803. KG 12/20.

1804

Samuel H. Woodson, to Miss Nancy Meede, both of Jessamine county. Married Jan. 1, 1804. KG 1/17.

John Smith, to Miss Matilda Sheley, both of Fayette county. Married Jan. 1, 1804. KG 1/17.

Robert McGrath, to Miss Peggy Dougherty. Married Jan. 10, 1804. KG 1/17.

Joseph Cleneay, merchant, to Miss Eliza Green, daughter of Capt. John Green. Married at Washington, Ky., Feb. 18, 1804. KG 2/21.

Thomas D. Owings, to Miss Maria Nicholas, daughter of the late Col. George Nicholas. Married Mar. 17, 1804. KG 3/20.

John Walker Baylor, of Lexington, to Miss Sophia Weidner, of Pittsburg. Married Apr. 2, 1804. KG 4/10.

John McDowell, to Miss Lucy LeGrand, both of Fayette county. Married Apr. 12, 1804. KG 4/17.

Porter Clay, to Miss Sophia Grosh, both of Lexington. Married Apr. 12, 1804. KG 4/17.

Robert Wickliffe, of Bardstown, to Miss Margaretta Howard, of Fayette county. Married May 1, 1804. KG 5/8.

William Henry, to Miss Rubena Lake, both of Lexington. Married May 30, 1804. KG 6/5.

John Clifford, of Philadelphia, to Miss Molly Morton, daughter of William Morton, of Lexington. Married June 17, 1804. KG 6/19.

Capt. William Smith, to Miss Jane Mallory, both of Fayette county. Married July 1, 1804. KG 7/3.

Thomas C. Howard, of Richmond, Ky., to Miss Amelia Patrick, of Fayette county. Married Aug. 16, 1804. KG 8/28.

Alfred Wallis, of North Carolina, to Miss Polly Hargy, of Lexington. Married Sept. 27, 1804. KG 10/2.

Alfred Grayson, of Washington, Ky., to Miss Letitia Breckinridge, daughter of John Breckinridge, of Fayette county. Married Oct. 26, 1804. KG 10/20.

Andrew Price, of Lexington, to Miss Polly Lee, of Woodford county. Married November 11, 1804. KG 11/13.

Dr. Samuel G. Mitchell, of Millersburg, to Miss Nancy Henderson, of Bourbon county. Married Dec. 3, 1804. KG 12/11.

Alexander Frazer, of Lexington, to Miss Nancy Oliver, of Jessamine county. Married Dec. 20, 1804. KG 12/25.

Willis Price, to Miss Peggy Payne, daughter of Sanford Payne, all of Fayette county. Married Dec. 20, 1804. KG 12/25.

1805

Dr. Elisha Warfield, of Lexington, to Miss Maria Barr, of the vicinity of Lexington. Married Jan. 15, 1805. KG 1/29.

Dr. James Wardlow, of Shelbyville, to Miss Lucinda B. Hopkins, daughter of Gen. Samuel Hopkins, of Henderson county. Married in January, 1805. KG 2/5.

Major George Trotter, to Miss Eliza Pope, both of Lexington. Married Jan. 30, 1805. KG 2/5.

James Marshall, of Brooke county, Va., to Miss Mary W. Marshall, daughter of Capt. Henry Marshall, of Lexington, Ky. Married Feb. 19, 1805. OR 2/26.

Ebenezer Sharpe, professor of Languages at Transylvania University, to Miss Eliza Lake, both of Lexington. Married Apr. 4, 1805. OR 4/9.

Samuel Postlethwait, formerly a merchant of Lexington, to Miss Anne Dunbar. Married at Natchez, Mar. 9, 1805. KG 4/9.

Thomas C. Lewis, attorney-at-law, to Miss Lucinda Barlow, of Scott county. Married Apr. 3, 1805. KG 4/16.

Capt. Samuel Williams, of Paris, to Miss Agatha Bryan, daughter of Capt. George Bryan, of Fayette county. Married Apr. 18, 1805. (This marriage was denied by the parties concerned in KG 4/30.)

George Yellot, of Baltimore, to Miss Bethia Burrell, late of New York. Married at the Bourbon Furnace, May 18, 1805. KG 5/7.

Elihu Stout, a printer at Vincennes, to Miss Lucy Sullivan, of Jefferson county. Married Apr. 25, 1805. KG 5/14.

John M. Garrard, son of Governor Garrard, to Miss Ship, daughter of Laban Ship, of Bourbon county. This announcement appeared under a Paris, Ky., heading of Thursday May 29, 1805. Reprint in KG 6/11.

Thomas Redd, of Woodford County, to Miss Elizabeth Bullock, of Fayette county. Married June 30, 1805. KG 7/2.

John Tilford, to Miss Polly Trotter, daughter of George Trotter, all of Lexington. Married Aug. 6, 1805. KG 8/13.

William Creighton, Secretary of the State of Ohio, to Miss Eliza Meade, daughter of Col. David Meade, of Jessamine county. Married Sept. 7, 1805. KG 9/10.

Z. Moore, to Miss Patton, daughter of Mr. Patton, Post Master at Paris. Married Sept. 12, 1805. OR 8/17.

Francis Downing, of Lexington, to Miss Peggy Gardner, daughter of Capt.

7

Gardner, of Fayette county. Married Sept. 20, 1805. KG 8/24.

John Starks, to Miss Elizabeth Price, daughter of Byrd Price, both of Fayette county. Married Oct. 5, 1805. OR 10/7.

James Kelly, merchant of Paris, to Miss Elizabeth Clarke, daughter of John Clarke, of Bourbon county. Married Oct. 10, 1805. KG 10/17.

Dr. Coleman Rogers, of Danville, to Miss Jane Farrar, of Fayette county. Married Nov. 3, 1805. KG 11/7.

Woodson Wrenn, merchant of Lexington, to Miss Polly Grant, daughter of Col. John Grant, of Boone county. Married Nov. 5, 1805. KG 11/14.

Willis Field, of Bourbon county, to Miss Buck, of Woodford county. Married Nov. 7, 1805. KG 11/14.

Thomas Sandford, Representative in Congress, to Miss Peggy Bell, of Woodford county. Married Nov. 10, 1805. KG 11/14.

Samuel Redd, of Lexington, to Miss Dorothy Bullock, of Fayette county. Married Nov. 11, 1805. KG 11/14.

Dr. R. Warfield, of Barbourville, to Miss Polly Woodson, daughter of Henry Woodson, of Knox county. Married Nov. 3, 1805. KG 11/28.

William T. Barry, to Miss Lucy Overton, daughter of Waller Overton, all of Fayette county. Married Nov. 26, 1805. KG 11/28.

William Brown, of Paris, to Miss Harriet Warfield, of Fayette county. Married Nov. 26, 1805. KG 12/12.

Jephthah Dudley, merchant of Frankfort, to Miss Elizabeth Lewis, daughter of Thomas Lewis, of Fayette county. Married Dec. 5, 1805. KG 12/12.

Dr. Amasa Delano, of Woodford county, to Miss Judith Garth, of Scott county. Married Dec. 11, 1805. KG 12/19.

George Craig, of Frankfort, to Miss Elizabeth Morton, of Clarke county. Married Dec. 22, 1805. KG 12/26.

Pugh Price, of Fayette county, to Miss Letitia Tinsley. Married Dec. 22, 1805. KG 12/26.

Joel Scott, of Scott county, to Miss Bebecca Wilmot, of Bourbon county Married Dec. 24, 1805. KG 1/9/06.

1806

John Bell, to Miss Rachael Stout, both of Lexington. Married Dec. 12, 1806. KG 2/19.

Nugent Gardiner, of Frankfort, to Miss Polly Van Pelt, of Lexington. Married Feb. 18, 1806. KG 2/22.

Mordecai Gist, of Frederick county, Maryland, to Miss Patsy Clarke, of Clarke county, Ky. Married Feb. 19, 1806. KG 2/26.

Dr. Walter Warfield, to Mrs. Margaret Wilson, both of Lexington. Married Feb. 27, 1806. KG 3/1.

Capt. William Hamilton, to Miss Pricilla C. Manor, both of Fayette county. Married Feb. 25, 1806. KG 3/1.

William Murphy, of Washington, Ky., to Miss Mary Morton, daughter of George Morton, of Mason county. Married Mar. 6, 1806. KG 3/12.

Fayette Posey, to Miss Eliza Pendleton Davis, second daughter of Col. Charles Davis, of Henderson county. Married Feb. 21, 1806. KG 3/19.

Daniel Thornbury, of Bullitt county, to Miss Agatha Bryon, of Fayette county. Married Mar. 19, 1806. KG 3/26.

John A. Grimes, of Fayette county, to Miss Lucy S. Broaddus, of Jessamine county. Married Mar. 25, 1806. KG 3/29.

Will Ward, of Lexington, to Miss Margaret McClanahan, of Bourbon county. Married Apr. 10, 1806. KG 4/16.

Capt. George Howard, of Mt. Sterling, to Miss Cassandra Hukill, of Montgomery county. Married Apr. 22, 1806. KG 5/6.

Capt. William Pollock, of Cynthiana, to Miss Rebecca Warfield, of Fayette county. Married Apr. 29, 1806. KG 5/6.

Christopher Tompkins, of Muhlenberg county, to Miss Theodocia Logan, daughter of Col. John Logan, Treasurer of Kentucky. Married in Frankfort, May 10, 1806. KG 5/17.

Benjamin Park, Delegate to Congress from the Indiana Territory, to Miss Eliza Barton, of Lexington. Married June 5, 1806. KG 6/7.

William Cahill, to Miss Mary Walsh, both of Lexington. Married June 22, 1806. KG 6/24

Samuel Long, to Miss Harriott Prentiss, both of Lexington. Married July 17, 1806. KG 7/19.

Joseph Woods, of Smithland, Livingston county, Ky., to Miss Jane West, daughter of Edward West, of Lexington. Married Aug. 25, 1806. KG 9/18.

William Todd, of Lexington, to Miss Polly LeGrand, daughter of Peter LeGrand, of Fayette county. Married Sept. 18, 1806. KG 9/25.

John R. Young, of Woodford county, to Miss Nancy Woolridge, of Versailles. Married Oct. 2, 1806. KG 10/6.

Mark Hardin, Register of the Land Office, to Mary Adair, daughter of Gen. John Adair, Senator in Congress. Married Oct. 4, 1806. KG 10/27.

Hugh Payne, to Miss Matilda Brown of Fayette county. Married Nov. 20, 1806. KG 11/24.

Benjamin Moseby, of Boone county, to Miss Tabitha Price, daughter of Byrd Price, of Fayette county. Married Nov. 25, 1806. KG 11/27.

Nelson Turner, to Miss Sarah E. Shaw, both of Fayette county. Married Dec. 4, 1806. KG 12/11.

Joseph H. Stevenson, to Miss Polly Tribble, daughter of the Rev. A. Tribble, both of Madison county. Married Dec. 23, 1806. KG 12/29.

1808

Joseph Hawkins, attorney-at-law, to Miss George Ann Nicholas, daughter of the late Col. George Nicholas. Married July 3, 1808. R 7/9.

Benjamin Reynolds, of Pennsylvania, to Miss Milly S. Allen, daughter of Isham Allen, of Clarke county, Ky. Married Sept. 12, 1808. R 9/26.

Davis Hardin, of Madison county, to Miss Eliza Williams Simpson, of Fayette county, daughter of Col. Richard Simpson, late of North Carolina. Married Oct. 16, 1808. R 10/31.

1809

Joseph L. Downing, to Miss Molly Ann Richardson, daughter of Marquis Richardson, of Lexington. Married Jan 3, 1809. KG 1/10.

Major Charles Jouette, to Miss Susan R. Allen, daughter of Isham Allen, of Clarke county. Married Jan. 15, 1809. KG 1/17.

Charles Gilkey, Jr., of Montgomery county, to Miss Anthret Daniel of Clark county. Married Jan. 12, 1809. KG 1/17.

Spencer Alsop, to Miss Judith Carter. Married Jan. 22, 1809. KG 1/24.

Lewis Haller, to Miss Fanney Alsop. Married Jan. 22, 1809. KG 1/24.

David Megowen, to Miss Nancy Foster, both of Lexington. Married Jan. 25, 1809. KG 1/31.

William Shrieve, of Jessamine county, to Mrs. Ann Wake, of Woodford county. Married Feb. 5, 1809. KG 2/13.

Jonas Huffman, of Harrison county, to Miss Sophia Drox, of Millersburg. Married Feb. 22, 1809. KG 2/27.

Robert Buster, of Montgomery county, to Miss Sally Brown, of Clarke county. Married Mar. 9, 1809. KG 3/14.

Clement A. Smith, to Miss Martha W. Mansel, daughter of George Mansel, of Fayette county. Married Mar. 23, 1809. KG 3/28.

Nathaniel G. S. Hart, of Lexington, to Miss Ann Gist, of Frankfort. Married Apr. 6, 1809. KG 4/11.

Elijah Noble, to Miss Louisa Platt, both of Lexington. Married Mar. 30, 1809. KG 4/11.

Blackhall Stevens, to Miss Helen Kelly, both of Lexington. Married May 14, 1809. KG 5/16.

Abner LeGrand, merchant, to Miss Jane Morton, daughter of William Morton, all of Lexington. Married July 10, 1809. KG 7/18.

Dr. Arthur Campbell, of Smithland, to Miss Catherine West, daughter of Edward West, of Lexington. Married July 11, 1809. KG 7/18.

John Jordan, Jr., Post Master, to Miss Sarah Van Phul, both of Lexington. Married July 22, 1809. KG 7/25.

James Wilson, Woodford county, to Miss Jane Smith, of Fayette county Married July 26, 1809. KG 8/1.

Joseph McCord, of New York, to Miss Molly Logan, daughter of D. Logan, of Fayette county. Married July 25, 1809. KG 8/8.

Absalom Cavens, to Miss Sally Goreham, both of Fayette county. Married Aug. 17, 1809. KG 8/29.

William Carles, to Miss Dolley Emily, both of Scott county. Married Aug. 17, 1809. KG 8/29.

Reuben Stevenson, of Mason county, to Miss Cassandra Jones, of Georgetown. Married Aug. 20, 1809. KG 8/29.

Sandford Wilson, to Miss Rachel Holland, of Scott county. Married Tuesday, Aug. 22, 1809.   KG 8/29.

Robert H. Grayson, of Mason county, to Miss Sophonisba Cabell, daughter of the late Joseph Cabell, of Virginia.   Married at Cablesdale, Sept. 3, 1809. KG 9/12.

John Marshall, of Frankfort, to Miss Ann Birney, of Danville.   Married Sept. 15, 1809.   KG 8/19.

William Pruitt, to Miss Margaret Edmiston, both of Fayette county. Married Sept. 13, 1809.   KG 8/19.

James W. Coburn, to Miss Susan S. Doniphan, daughter of Dr. A. Doniphan, all of Mason county.   Married Sept. 6, 1809.   KG 8/19.

Henry Daniel, of Mount Sterling, to Miss Louise Thompson, daughter of Clifton Thompson, of Fayette county.   Married Oct. 11, 1809.   KG 10/24.

John Marsh, to Miss Elizabeth Hull, daughter of the late John Hull, all of Lexington.   Married Nov. 23, 1809.   KG 12/5.

John Hull, to Miss Rebecca Cook, daughter of John Cook, all of Lexington. Married Nov. 28, 1809.   KG 12/5.

Jacob Hall, of Lexington, to Miss Martha McGowan, daughter of Charles McGowan, of Fayette county.   Married Nov. 30, 1809.   KG 12/5.

1810

Hon. John Pope, United States Senator, to Miss Eliza J. D. Johnson, daughter of the late Joshua Johnson, of Lexington.   Married Feb. 11, 1810.   KG 3/6.

Dr. Edward Dorsey, of Flemingsburg, to Miss Juliet McDowell, daughter of Col. James McDowell, of Fayette county.   Married May 15, 1810.   KG 5/22.

Thomas Berryman, of Lexington, to Miss Elizabeth Keen, daughter of Francis Keen, of Fayette county.   Married May 21, 1810.   KG 5/22.

Major Edward P. Long, to Miss Tabitea A. Russell, daughter of Gen. Robert S. Russell, both of Fayette county.   Married May 29, 1810.   KG 6/12.

James Weir, of Frankfort, to Miss Joanna T. Parrish, daughter of Capt. James Parrish, of Woodford county.   Married May 6, 1810.   KG 6/12.

Samuel Price, to Miss Maria West, daughter of Edward West, of Lexington. Married Oct. 4, 1810.   KG 10/9.

William Hart, to Miss Diana Bradford, daughter of John Bradford, of Lexington.   Married Nov. 1, 1810.   KG 11/6.

William Bain, to Miss Louisa Mansell.   Married in Fayette county, Oct. 28, 1810.   KG 11/6.

Doctor R. Witherspoon, of Williamsburg, South Carolina, to Miss Mary Ann Todd, eldest daughter of Gen. Robert Todd.   Married in the vicinity of Lexington, Nov. 13, 1810.   KG 11/20.

Samuel T. Davenport, of the Orleans Territory, to Miss Susan Garrett, of Lexington, Ky.   Married Nov. 16, 1810.   KG 11/20.

John Wilson, of Washington, to Miss Rachel Deweese, of Lexington Married Nov. 20, 1810.   KG 11/27.

Presley Edwards, of Russellville, to Miss Hester Pope, of Lexington. Married Nov. 22, 1810.   KG 11/27.

11

Dr. Maximilian W. Owens, of Washington, Ky., to Miss Eliza Durrett Married in November, 1810. KG 11/27.

Matthew Duncan, editor of the *Farmer's Friend,* to Miss Susan C. Slaughter Married in Nelson county, in November, 1810. KG 11/27.

1811

Abraham Bowman, to Miss Nancy Gatewood, both of Fayette county Married Feb. 7, 1811. KG 2/19.

Benjamin Howard, Governor of the Louisiana Territory, to Miss Mary Thompson Mason, daughter of Stephen Thompson Mason, dec'd. They were married in Virginia Feb. 14, 1811. KG 3/5.

William D. Young, of Lexington, to Miss Maria C. Jackson, daughter of John Jackson, of Woodford county. Married in Versailles, Feb. 28, 1811. KG 3/5.

Peter C. Buck, of Versailles, to Miss Miriam Price, daughter of Samuel Price, of Lexington. Married Apr. 14, 1811. KG 4/16.

James Tilford, of Russellville, to Miss Mary MacCoun, of Lexington. Married May 2, 1811. KG 5/17.

William T. Turner, to Miss Lucy Ann Cochran, both of Lexington. Married May 5, 1811. KG 5/7.

William Coleman, of Virginia, to Miss Ann Hawes, eldest daughter of Richard Hawes, of the vicinity of Lexington. Married May 29, 1811. KG 6/4.

Robert Bywater, of Lexington, to Miss Ann Beard, daughter of Joseph Beard, of Lexington. Married May 29, 1811. KG 6/4.

Pleasant Baird, of Lexington, to Miss Mary McCall, of Louisville. Married May 28, 1811. KG 6/4.

John J. Crittenden, to Miss Sarah O. Lee, of Woodford county. Married May 27, 1811. KG 6/4.

Philip Quniton, to Miss Eliza Grayson, daughter of Benjamin Grayson, all of Bairdstown. Married May 23, 1811. KG 6/4.

Benjamin Johnson, attorney-at-law, to Miss Matilda Williams, daughter of Charles Williams, of Scott county. Married Sept. 8, 1811. KG 9/10.

John Henry Vos, Tragedian of the Lexington Theater, to Miss Scotland Greer, of Lexington. Married at Paris, Sept. 18, 1811. KG 9/24.

Capt. Littleberry Ellis, to Miss Susan Shoot, daughter of William John Shoot, all of Fayette county. Married Oct. 6, 1811. KG 10/8.

John T. Johnson, of Scott county, to Miss Sophia Lewis, daughter of Mrs. Elizabeth Lewis, of Fayette county. Married Oct. 9, 1811. KG 10/15.

Hon. Gabriel Slaughter, to Mrs. Rhodes, of Scott county. Married Oct. 3, 1811. KG 10/15.

Thomas Grant, to Miss Margaret Greer, both of Lexington. Married Oct. 31, 1811. KG 11/5.

Carnville Agniel, of Fayette county, to Miss Louisa Gex, of Ohio. Married Oct. 3, 1811. KG 11/5.

John C. Bartlett, of New Orleans, to Miss Margaretta G. Nicholas, of Lexington. Married Nov. 4, 1811. KG 11/5

James Gabriel Trotter, to Miss Elizabeth Nicholas, daughter of the late Col. George Nicholas. Married at Lexington, Nov. 10, 1811. KG 11/12.

Benjamin Young, to Miss Nancy Moore, daughter of Capt. William Moore. Married in Fayette county, Nov. 5, 1811. KG 11/12.

1812

Capt. Robert Edwards, of Jessamine county, to Miss Rebecca Sodowsky, daughter of Jacob Sodowsky, of Jessamine county. Married Jan. 28, 1812. KG 2/4.

Bertrand Gurin, professor of the French language at Transylvania University, to Miss Frances Hickey, both of Lexington. Married Feb. 10, 1812, by the Rev. Robert Angier, a Catholic clergyman of Scott county. KG 2/18.

David Todd, to Miss Eliza Barr, daughter of Robert Barr. Married Apr. 7, 1812. KG 4/7.

Thomas Todd, one of the Supreme Court Judges of the United States, to Mrs. Lucy Washington, sister of Mrs. Madison. Married Mar. 28, 1812, at the residence of the President of the United States. KG 4/14.

Ben Taylor, of Georgetown, to Miss Theodocia Payne, of Fayette county. Married Apr. 1, 1812. KG 4/14.

Capt. James Dougherty, of Fayette county, to Miss Jane Robinson, daughter of Jonathan Robinson, of Scott county. Married May 7, 1812. KG 5/12.

John Bull, to Mary Foster, both of Lexington. Married May 7, 1812. KG 5/12.

James Boardman, of Lexington, to Miss Polly Smith, daughter of Alexander Smith, of Fayette county. Married May 7, 1812. KG 5/12.

Gabriel Tompkins, of Fayette county, to Miss Mary Lacy, daughter of Capt Elijah Lacy, of Woodford county. Married May 13, 1812. KG 5/19.

Abraham S. Barton, cashier of the Kentucky Insurance Bank, to Miss Sarah Merrell, daughter of Major Benjamin Merrell, of Fayette county. Married May 14, 1812. KG 5/19.

Dr. A. I. Mitchell, of Frankfort, to Miss Elizabeth Allen, daughter of Capt William Allen, of Fayette county. Married May 25, 1812. KG 6/2.

Matthew H. Jouett, of Frankfort, to Miss Margaret Allen, daughter of Capt. William Allen, of Fayette county. Married May 25, 1812. KG 6/2.

Samuel Tilford, of Lexington, to Miss Ruth H. Clopper, of Philadelphia. Married at the latter place, May 2, 1812. KG 6/9.

Benjamin M. Brook, of Fairfax county, Va., to Miss Paulina Ann Satterwhite, daughter of Capt. M. Satterwhite, of Fayette county. Married July 26, 1812. KG 8/4.

Ezra Woodruff, of Lexington, to Miss Martha Henry, daughter of John Henry, of Fayette county. Married Nov. 12, 1812. KG 11/17.

Thomas Robinson, of Natchez, to Miss Mary McConnel, of Woodford county. Married Feb. 8, 1813. KG 2/16.

Dr. Joseph Crockett, of Jessamine county, to Miss Elizabeth Bullock, of Green county. Married at the Woodford county residence of Charles Railey, Apr. 2, 1813. KG 4/6.

Thomas Railey, to Miss Sarah Railey, daughter of William Railey, all of Woodford county. Married Mar. 22, 1813. KG 4/6.

William McCalla, of Lexington, to Miss Martha Finley, only daughter of General Finley, of Chillicothe. Married Mar. 31, 1813. KG 4/6.

Dr. Joseph Buchanan, to Miss Nancy Gath, of Madison county. Married Mar. 31, 1813. KG 4/20.

John G. Gamble, of Richmond, Va., to Miss Nancy P. Greenup, of Kentucky, eldest daughter of Christopher Greenup, former Governor of Kentucky. Married at Richmond, Va., Mar. 11, 1813. KG 4/20.

Daniel Talbott, to Miss Amy Stout, daughter of David Stout, all of Lexington. Married Apr. 8, 1813. KG 4/20.

Capt. John Hamilton, of Fayette county, to Miss Patsey Gaines, of Bourbon county. Married May 6, 1813. KG 5/11.

Capt. Levi L. Todd, to Miss Sarah Ashby, of Lexington. Married May 6, 1813. KG 5/11.

William Tegarden, to Miss Margaret Gatewood, both of Fayette county. Married May 3, 1813. KG 5/11.

Benjamin Wyne, to Miss Mary Doyle, both of Lexington. Married May 20, 1813. KG 5/25.

John Fry, to Miss Nancy Carson, both of Lexington. Married June 10, 1813. KG 6/15.

Pollard Keene, merchant of Nicholasville, to Miss Catherine Robards, daughter of William Robards, of Jessamine county. Married July 24, 1813. KG 8/3.

Francis Walker, to Miss Nancy Comstock, both of Lexington. Married Sept. 2, 1813. KG 9/7.

Thomas J. Crittenden, to Miss Nancy Parker, of Lexington. Married Sept. 6, 1813. KG 9/21.

George Shannon, to Miss Rosette Price. Married Sept. 19, 1813. KG 9/21.

1814

Ichabod Woodruff, of Lexington, to Miss Mary C. Williams, of Elizabethtown, N. J. Married Jan. 25, 1814. KG 2/28.

Samuel Patterson, of Lexington, to Miss Rachel Willgus, of Fayette county. Married Mar. 3, 1814. KG 3/7.

Moses Norvell, of the *Nashville Whig*, to Miss Hannah West, of Lexington, Ky. Married in Nashville, Mar. 1, 1814. KG 3/14.

Joseph H. Hervey, to Miss Anne Agnew. Married in Lexington, Apr. 28,

1814. KG 5/2.

Samuel Mount, to Miss Mary Stout. Married Apr. 28, 1814. KG 5/2.

G. B. P. Gaston De L'Orme, to Miss Rebecca Warfield, of Lexington. Married May 28, 1814. KG 6/6.

Henry Baber, of Va., to Miss Letitia White, daughter of Daniel White, of Fayette county, Ky. Married June 11, 1814. KG 6/20.

Robert Warden, to Miss Catherine Lewis, both of Lexington. Married June 12, 1814. KG 6/20

James A. Canon, of Richmond, Ky., to Miss Frances Royle, of Fayette county. Married July 7, 1814. KG 7/11.

John A. Cock, of Lexington, to Miss Sarah H. Bosworth, of Fayette county. Married July 7, 1814. KG 7/11.

Dr. J. Poston, to Miss Kitty H. Wooren, both of Winchester, Ky. Married July 15, 1814. KG 7/18.

H. Boswell, of Cynthiana, to Miss Rachel Desha, of Mason county, daughter of the Hon. Joseph Desha, Representative in Congress. Married Dec. 6, 1814. KG 12/19.

John C. Richardson, to Miss Mary Ann Parker, both of Lexington. Married Dec. 22, 1814. KG 12/26.

Samuel Wilron, of Forest Hill, to Miss Sophia Anderson, daughter of Capt. W. Anderson, of Jessamine county. Married Dec. 22, 1814. KG 12/26.

1915

Dudley Shipp, to Miss ———— Ellis, daughter of William Ellis, dec'd., of Fayette county. Married Feb. 14, 1815. KG 2/20.

Samuel McMeekin, to Miss Henrietta Todd, daughter of William Todd, all of Lexington. Married Mar. 19, 1815. KG 3/27.

John Shore, to Miss Eliza Woolfolk, both of Fayette county. Married May 4, 1815. KG 5/13.

Dr. J. R. Witherspoon, to Miss Sophia Graham, daughter of General Joseph Graham, of North Carolina. Married June 2, 1815. KG 6/12.

Farmer Dewees, to Miss Maryanne Holmes, niece of Col. James Morrison, all of Lexington. Married Oct. 16, 1815. KG 10/30.

William Graves, merchant of Lexington, to Miss Mary Graves, daughter of Col. John Graves, of Fayette county. Married Oct. 26, 1815. KG 10/30.

John Hawkins, to Mrs. Margaret Singleton, both of Jessamine county. Married Oct. 22, 1815. KG 10/30.

1816

James Nutter, of Nicholasville, to Miss Mary Lewis, of Jessamine county. Married Feb. 13, 1816. R 2/14.

David Montgomery, of Lexington, to Miss Catherine McKinney, daughter of Capt. Gerard McKinney, of Fayette county. Married Mar. 5, 1816. R 3/6.

Robert P. Kenny, to Miss Eliza Boggs, daughter of Robert Boggs, both of Fayette county. Married Mar. 29, 1816. R 4/10.

Henry Johnson, of Scott county, to Miss Betsey Julia Flournoy, daughter of Matthews Flournoy, of Fayette county. Married Apr. 2, 1816. R 4/10.

Major Henry Beard, of Lexington, to Mrs. Martha Beard, daughter of John McCreery, of Allegheny county, Penn., and relict of William Beard, of Fayette county, Ky. Married Apr. 10, 1816. KG 4/15.

Rev. Mr. Wallace, to Mrs. Margaret Purviance, both of Lexington. Married July 12, 1816. KG 7/29.

Thomas A. Marshall, of Paris, to Miss Eliza P. Price, of Lexington. Married Nov. 26, 1816. KG 12/2.

Nathaniel Barbee, of Lexington, to Miss Catherine Bradford, of Scott county. Married Nov. 26, 1816. KG 12/2.

Major William Bradford, of the U. S. Army, to Miss Frances Smith, daughter of Capt. Robert Smith, of Scott county. Married Tuesday evening Dec. 3, 1816. KG 12/9.

John M. Rice, to Miss Eliza A. Grugett, of Richmond. Married in December, 1816. R 12/25.

Alexander Logan, to Miss Varlinda Offutt, of Scott county. Married in December, 1816. R 12/25.

Milton King, to Miss Susan T. Wales, of Woodford county. Married in December, 1816. R 12/25.

Dr. Rudd, of Bardstown, to Miss Ann Palmer. Married in December, 1816. R 12/25.

Andrew M. January, to Miss Sarah Huston, daughter of William Huston, all of Lexington. Married Dec. 31, 1816. KG 1/6/1817.

Francis Hostetter, to Miss Catherine Lonkard, both of Lexington. Married Dec. 28, 1816. KG 1/6/1817.

1817

Thomas P. Hart, to Miss Mary Ann Gardner, both of Lexington. Married Mar. 13, 1817. KG 3/24.

Jacob Steele, to Miss Deborah Owings, both of Owingsville. Married Mar. 20, 1817. KG 3/24.

Major William O. Butler, to Miss Eliza Todd, of Lexington. Married Apr. 17, 1817. KG 4/28.

George Neal, to Miss Lucy Singleton, both of Jessamine county. Married June 29, 1817. R 7/9.

Joseph I. Lemon, of Lexington, to Miss Margaretta Ann Leatherer, only daughter of the Rev. John Leatherer, of Scott county. Married June 30, 1817. R 7/9.

Thomas Duke, of Washington, Ky., to Miss Eliza Taylor, of Lexington. Married July 3, 1817. R 7/9.

George Woodward, to Miss Nancy Whitney, both of Lexington. Married July 20, 1817. R 7/30.

Charles Bradford, cashier of the Kentucky Insurance Bank, to Miss Mary Ann Corlis, of Bourbon county. Married in Sept., 1817. R 9/17.

Major Uriel Sebree, of Lexington, to Miss Elizabeth Payne, of Scott county. Married in September, 1817. R 9/17.

Isaac Shelby, Jr., son of Governor Isaac Shelby, to Miss Maria Warren, of Lincoln county. Married in Sept., 1817. R 9/17.

Peyton R. Pleasants, of Frankfort, to Miss Nancy C. Humphreys, of Lexington. Married Oct. 14, 1817. R 10/15.

Jeremiah Rogers, to Miss Polly Clark, of Clarke county. Married in October, 1817. R 10/15.

Dr. Burr Harrison, to Miss Catharine Camp, of Bardstown. Married in November, 1817. R 11/12.

John S. Snead, merchant, to Miss Martha Anne Postlethwait, daughter of Capt. John Postlethwait, of Lexington. Married Nov. 4, 1817. R 11/12.

Archibald McCullough, to Miss Helvia Bruce. Married Dec. 11, 1817. R 12/17.

Thomas Kane, to Miss Charlotte Kelly, daughter of Henry Kelly, all of Lexington. Married Dec. 14, 1817. R 12/12.

James Barrett, of Tennessee, to Miss Mary L. Barret, of Greensburg, Ky Married Dec. 8, 1817. R 12/24.

Thomas Essex, to Miss Anne Essex, daughter of Dr. Essex, of Tennessee. Married in Lexington, Ky., Dec. 28, 1817. R 12/31.

1818

John P. Aldridge, to Miss Ann Dickinson, both of Lexington. Married Jan. 8, 1818. R 1/14.

Dr. John C. Grosjean, to Miss Julia Ann Allen, of Bourbon county. Married in January, 1818. R 1/28.

Thomas R. West, to Miss Matilda Booth. Married at Louisville, in January, 1818. R 1/28.

John H. Branham, to Miss Ann James. Married at Frankfort, in January, 1818. R 1/28.

John L. Bevis, to Miss Elizabeth Watson. Married at Frankfort, in January, 1818. R 1/28.

Major John Wyatt, Fayette county, to Mrs. Patsy Harris. They were married in Hanover county, Va., in January, 1818. R 1/28.

M. D. Richardson, of Lexington, to Miss Ann Dougherty. Married in Fleming county, in January, 1818. R 2/4.

Dr. George Rogers, to Miss Sarah Gorin, daughter of Colonel John Gorin. Married in Glasgow, Ky., Mar. 10, 1818. R 3/18.

Harvey Gregg, to Miss Nancy Payne, both of Lexington. Married Mar. 17, 1818. R 3/18.

John W. Wayne, to Miss Eliza Talbott, daughter of Major Hugh Talbott, of Millersburg. Married March 1, 1818. R 3/25.

Price Prewitt, of Missouri Territory, to Miss Patsey Thompson, daughter of Asa Thompson, of Fayette county. Married Mar. 2, 1818. R 3/25.

Thomas M. Allen, of Virginia, to Miss Rebecca W. Russell, daughter of Gen. Robert S. Russell, of Fayette county. Married Mar. 24, 1818. R 1/1.

William How, to Miss Nancy Simpson, both of Fayette county. Married Apr. 2, 1818. R 4/8.

Cumberland Wilson, of Lexington, to Miss Mary Harper, of Woodford county. Married Apr. 2, 1818. R 4/8.

Simeon Schwitzler, to Miss Elizabeth Cornelius, daughter of Abner Cornelius, of Lexington. Married Apr. 9, 1818. R 4/5.

James Gregg, of Fayette county, to Miss Susan McCampbell, daughter of James McCampbell, of Jessamine county. Married Apr. 9, 1818. R 4/15.

William W. Blair, Counsellor at Law, of Lexington, to Miss Anna H. Warfield, daughter of Dr. Walter Warfield. Married in Lexington, Apr. 15, 1818. R 4/22.

Anthony Gaunt, to Miss Mary Campbell, daughter of Archibald Campbell, both of Lexington. Married Apr. 13, 1818. R 4/22.

Lewis C. Ellis, late of Lexington, to Miss Mary D. Parish, of Clarke county. Married Apr. 7, 1818. R 4/22.

James C. Rodes, of Lexington, to Miss Martha Thompson, daughter of Clifton Thompson, of Fayette county. Married in April or May, 1818. R 5/6.

Wilson Merrill, of Lexington, to Miss Sophia Hanna, of Frankfort. Married in April or May, 1818. R 5/6.

William Wood, to Miss Helen Julian, both of Frankfort. Married May 27, 1818. R 9/2.

James Holloway, to Miss Anne Morin, of Union county. Married in April, 1818. R 5/6.

Capt. D. M. Hickman, of Paris, to Miss Eliza Johnson, of Bourbon county. Married in April or May, 1818. R 5/6.

Capt. Thomas P. Moore, to Miss Mary McAfee, of Harrodsburg. Married in Apr. or May, 1818. R 5/6.

Walker Sanders, of Lexington, to Miss Louisa Flournoy, daughter of M. Flournoy. Married May 7, 1818.

James Wyatt, to Miss Sally Stevenson, both of Fayette county. Married May 7, 1818. R 5/13.

John Regis Alexander, of Woodford county, to Miss Marian F. Campbell. Married in Lexington, May 14, 1818. R 5/20.

Dr. John F. Henry, of Georgetown, to Miss Mary Duke. Married in Washington, Ky., in May, 1818. R 5/20.

Henry Crittenden, of Frankfort, to Miss Allen, daughter of the late Col. John Allen. Married in Shelby county in May, 1818. R 5/20.

Capt. John Hathaway, of Baltimore, to Miss Tabitha Ann S. Jackson, of Alexandria. Married in Lexington, Ky., May 17, 1818. R 5/20.

Robert Woods, to Mrs. Sarah B. West, daughter of Edward West, of Lexington. Married in Nashville, in May, 1818. R 6/3.

Joshua Norvell, to Miss Maria Craig. Married at the Port of Arkansas in

May, 1818. R 6/3.

William Richardson, of New Orleans, to Miss Sinia Higgins. Married in Lexington, Ky., May 28, 1818. R 6/3.

Abraham Spears, of Bourbon county, to Miss Nancy T. Walton, of Harrison county. Married in May, 1818. R 6/3.

James W. Palmer, bookseller of Lexington, to Miss Mary Breen. Married in Philadelphia, May 19, 1818. R 6/10.

Henry Brothers, to Miss Patsey Sallee. Married in Mt. Sterling, June 31, 1818. R 6/10.

Robert H. McNair, merchant, to Miss Margaret Mercer, both of Lexington. Married June 16, 1818. R 6/17.

Thomas Wooly, of Brookville, Ind., to Miss Mary Craven, of Cincinnati. Married May 21, 1818. R 6/24.

Capt. Robeson DeHart, to Miss Sarah Castleman. They were married in Frankfort, July 14, 1818. R 7/22.

William Cirode, to Miss Jane White, daughter of Daniel White, of Fayette county. Married Aug. 2, 1818. R 8/12.

James Mason, of Edwardsville, to Mrs. Jordan, of Lexington. Married in St. Louis, Mo., Aug. 15, 1818. R 9/16.

Col. Thomas Fletcher, of Bath county, to Mrs. Margaret Bartlett, of Lexington. Married in Aug., 1818. R 8/26.

John T. Hawkins, to Miss Mary Rigg, daughter of Jonathan Rigg, of Fayette county. Married Aug. 31, 1818. R 9/9.

Capt. Leslie Combs, to Miss Margaret Trotter, daughter of George Trotter, Sr., all of Lexington. Married Tuesday, Sept. 1, 1818. R 9/2.

Dr. Walter New, to Miss Courtney Baylor. Married in Logan county, in September, 1818. R 9/30.

Philip C. Slaughter, to Miss Elizabeth Payne. Married in Logan county, in Sept., 1818. R 9/30.

William Comfort, to Miss Eleanor Whitsitt. Married in Logan county, in Sept., 1818. R 9/30.

Robert Poor, to Miss Herndon. Married in Logan county in September, 1818. R 9/30.

Samuel P. Orr, to Miss Eliza Bane. Married in Logan county, in September, 1818. R 9/30. Note: All above marriages in Logan county were solemnized the same evening.

James L. Hickman, of Frankfort, to Miss Maria Shackelford. Married in Fleming county, in Sept., 1818. R 9/30.

John M. Robinson, to Miss Lucy Ann Butler. Married in Bourbon county in Sept., 1818. R 9/30.

Amos Kendall, editor of the *Argus*, to Miss Mary B. Woolfolk. Married in Jefferson county, in Oct., 1818. R 10/14.

Frank J. Allen, to Miss Eliza T. Gayle. Married at Paris, in Oct., 1818. R 10/14.

William G. Warham, of Charleston, S. C., to Miss Sarah P. Hunt. Married in Lexington in Oct., 1818. R 10/14.

Lewis Vance, to Miss Lydia Ahull, both of Paris. Married Oct. 15, 1818. R 10/21.

John Alexander, to Miss Susan Moore, both of Fayette county. Married in Oct., 1818. R 10/21.

Wesley Roberts, to Miss Eliza Stout, daughter of Jedia Stout, all of Fayette county. Married in October, 1818. R 10/21.

Major General Peter B. Porter, of New York, to Mrs. Letitia P. Grayson, of Kentucky, daughter of the late John Breckinridge, former Attorney General of the U. S. Married at Princeton, N. J., Oct. 16, 1818. R 11/11.

Franklin Gorin to Miss Louisa Underwood. Married at Glasgow, Ky., in October, 1818. R 11/11.

John Howard, to Miss Martha Wells. Married in Oct. or Nov., 1818. R 11/11.

Thomas Shreve, to Miss Mary Scott, daughter of John Scott, of Jessamine county. Married Nov. 9, 1818. R 11/18.

Simon Bradford, to Miss Eliza M. West, daughter of Edmund West. Married in Lexington, Nov. 15, 1818. R 11/18.

Capt. Richard Hawes, Jr., to Miss Hetty Nicholas, daughter of the late Col. George Nicholas. Married Nov. 13, 1818. R 11/18.

Capt. Samuel Spotts, of the U. S. Army, to Miss Mary Hanna, of Frankfort. Married Dec. 21, 1818. R 12/30.

1819

Jacob Stout, to Miss Harriett Kay, both of Fayette county. Married Jan. 7, 1819. R 1/13.

Henry Guibert, to Miss Susan Arcambal. Married in Lexington, Jan. 25, 1819. R 1/27.

Augustus F. Hawkins, of Versailles, to Miss Harriet Leavy, daughter of William Leavy, of Lexington. Married Feb. 28, 1819. R 3/3.

Thomas Burbridge, of Clarke county, to Miss Elizabeth C. Ferguson, of Fayette county. Married Mar. 10, 1819. R 3/17.

Joseph M. Gregg, to Miss Matilda Hamilton, daughter of Samuel Hamilton. Married in Bracken county, Mar. 28, 1819. R 4/14.

Samuel Bayles, printer, to Miss Mary Carty. Married in Mason county, April 3, 1819. R 4/14.

Platt Stout to Miss Margaret Chambers, daughter of James Chambers. Married at Maysville, Mar. 25, 1819. R 4/14.

Capt. Bowling Starke, of Hanover county, Va., to Miss Eliza C. New, daughter of Col. Anthony New, of Kentucky. Married Mar. 25, 1819. R 4/28.

William Challem, Jr., to Miss Sarah E. Cock, both of Lexington. Married April 29, 1819. R 5/5.

James G. Taliaferro, of Louisiana, to Miss Elizabeth M. B. Williamson, of Versailles, Ky. Married May 1, 1819. R 5/5.

Robert W. January, of Russellville, to Miss Harriet Postlethwait, of Lexington. Married May 13, 1819. R 5/19.

Jacob Swing, of Lebanon, Ohio, to Miss Emily Postlethwait, daughter of Joseph Postlethwait, of Lexington, Ky. Married May 16, 1819. R 5/19.

John Grimes, of Fayette county, to Miss Rachel Magnom, of Tennessee. Married May 12, 1819, in Lexington. R 5/19.

Jacob Piatt, of Kentucky, to Miss Martha Perry, of Cincinnati. Married in May, 1819. R 5/19.

Lieut. Charles Ward, to Miss Catherine T. Lindsay. Married in Newport, in May, 1819. R 5/19.

Lieut. W. Brunot, to Miss Ann T. Reville. Married in Newport, in May, 1819. R 5/19.

Dr. J. B. Bowling, of Clarksville, Tenn., to Miss Sophronia Ewing, daughter of Gen. Robert Ewing, of Logan county, Ky. Married May 13, 1819. R 5/19.

George Lyne, to Miss Martha Hopkins, daughter of Gen. Hopkins, all of Henderson. Married Apr. 20, 1819. R 5/19.

Presley Davis, of Nelson county, Ky., to Miss Ann Milton, of Frederick county, Virginia. Married May 1, 1819. R 5/26.

George W. Hardin, of Georgetown, to Mrs. Paulina V. McMillin, daughter of Capt. William Sutton, of Scott county. Married May 16, 1819. R 6/2.

Capt. Hawes Graves, of Fayette county, to Miss Ann B. White, only daughter of John White, of Spottsylvania county, Va. Married Apr. 8, 1819. R 5/2.

Major James W. Denny, of Louisville, to Miss Alice Talbot, daughter of Capt. Cyrus Talbot, of Nelson county. Married May 20, 1819. R 6/2.

Daniel Breck, of Richmond, Ky., to Miss Jane B. Todd, of Fayette county. Married June 2, 1819. R 6/9.

Samuel Thompson, of Lexington, to Miss Margaret Woorley. Married June 3, 1819. OR 6/9.

John Gorin, to Miss Eliza Wilson. Married in Logan county, in June, 1819. R 6/9.

Burgess Gilbert, to Miss Louisa Turner. Married in Logan county in June, 1819. R 6/9.

David McIlvain, to Miss Susan Allen. Married in Shelbyville in June, 1819. R 6/9.

Randolph Railey, of Woodford county, casier of the Bank of Versailles, to Miss Caroline Crittenden. Married July 6, 1819. This was Randolph Railey, Jr. R 7/14.

Capt. Henry Wingate, to Miss Penelope Anderson. Married at Frankfort, July 9, 1819. R 7/14.

James B. Huie, of Virginia, to Miss Malinda C. M. Thompson, daughter of Col. John Thompson, dec'd., of Jefferson county, Ky. Married July 19, 1819. R 7/28.

Francis Carr, to Miss Sarah Brenton. Married in Lexington, July 30, 1819. R 8/4.

Peter January, of Woodford county, to Miss Nancy January, of Maysville. Married Aug. 2, 1819. R 8/25.

David Stout, to Mrs. Jerusha Drake. Married in Lexington, Aug. 21, 1819. R 8/25.

John H. Stewart, to Miss Catharine Ross, daughter of William Ross. Married in Fayette county, Aug. 17, 1819. R 8/25.

Wilson Parker, to Mrs. Charlotte Satterwhite. Married in Fayette county, Aug. 12, 1819. R 8/25.

Thomas Joyes, of Louisville, to Miss Judeth M. Venable. Married in Shelby county, in Sept., 1819. R 9/8.

Nelson Burdett, of Garrard county, to Miss America Samuel. Married in Franklin county, in Sept., 1819. R 9/8.

John H. Hanna, of Frankfort, to Miss Mary S. Hunt, eldest daughter of J. W. Hunt. Married at Lexington, Sept. 19, 1819. R 9/22.

Joseph Bruen, to Miss Margery Parker. Married in Lexington, Sept. 19, 1819. R 9/22.

William Davenport, to Miss Eliza Major. Married in Christian county in September, 1819. R 9/22.

Edgcomb P. Suggett, to Miss Maria Nash. Married at Georgetown in September, 1819. R 9/22.

Thomas Fowler, of Washington, Mason county, to Miss Polly Barbour. Married in September, 1819. R 9/22.

Alexander McNees, to Miss Elizabeth Adams. Married in Harrison county in September, 1819. R 9/22.

James Armstrong, editor of the *Kentucky Advertiser,* to Mrs. Jane Price Ridgely. Married at Lexington, Sept. 22, 1819. R 9/29.

Thomas J. Hamilton, to Miss Martha Sanderson. Married in Fayette county in September, 1819. R 9/29.

Lewis Thornton to Miss Eliza Curry. Married at Paris, in September, 1819. R 9/29.

James Lewis, to Miss Sarah Nall. Married in Nelson county in September, 1819. R 9/29.

Micajah W. Sharp, to Miss Nancy Sharp. Married in Shelby county in September, 1819. R 9/29.

John Slaughter, son of the acting governor of Kentucky, to Miss Mary Bell Weisiger. Married in Franklin county in September, 1819. R 10/6.

Henry Spence, to Miss Ann Peyton. Married at Frankfort in October, 1819. R 10/6.

Martin Marshall, of Washington, Mason county, to Miss Eliza Marshall, daughter of the late Capt. Thomas Marshall. Married in October, 1819. R 10/6.

Major George Thompson, of Mercer county, to Miss Salley Hart, eldest daughter of Nathaniel Hart. Married in Woodford county, Oct. 1, 1819. R 10/6.

Thomas A. Palmer, to Miss Nancy F. Wood. Married in Mason county in October, 1819. R 10/6.

R. Asberry, of Mason county, to Miss Malinda Threlkeld. Married in Fleming county in October, 1819. R 10/6.

Edward Furr, to Miss Elizabeth Lightfoot. Married in Fleming county in October, 1819. R 10/6.

George Ballard, to Miss Lavina Moberly. Married in Madison county in October, 1819. R 10/6.

Orvie Collins, to Miss Mary Christy. Married in Clarke county in October, 1819. R 10/13.

Capt. Enoch Briton, of Madison county, to Miss Edith Jackson. Married in October, 1819. R 10/13.

James H. Gentry, to Miss Ann Campbell. Married in Madison county, in October, 1819. R 10/13.

George Tyler, to Miss Elizabeth Ann Brown. Married in Fayette county in October, 1819. R 10/13.

Clark Dennis, of Fayette county, to Miss Elizabeth Scott, of Scott county. Married in October, 1819. R 10/13.

J. C. S. Harrison, to Miss Clarisa B. Pike, daughter of the late General Pike. Married in Boone county in October, 1819. R 10/13.

Chester B. Powell, merchant of New Orleans, to Miss Mary Ann Tompkins, daughter of R. G. Tompkins. Married in Fayette county, Oct. 7, 1819. R 10/20.

Robert Tilford, of Lexington, to Miss Mary Ann Dougherty, daughter of Thomas Dougherty, of Washington City. Married in Flemingsburg in October, 1819. R 10/20.

Levin L. Shreve, of Lexington, to Miss Hannah D. Andrews, daughter of Capt. John Andrews. Married in Flemingsburg in October, 1819. R 10/20.

William Murrell, to Miss Elizabeth Garnett. Married in Hopkinsville in October, 1819. R 10/20.

Thomas Ross, to Miss Charlotte Offutt. Married in Christian county in October, 1819. R 10/20.

David Talley, to Miss Bradley. Married in Christian county in October, 1819. R 10/20.

————— Wood, to Miss Elizabeth Kay. Married in Christian county in October, 1819. R 10/20.

Daniel Browning, to Miss Polly Hart. Married in Fleming county in October, 1819. R 10/20.

William Smith, of New Castle, to Miss Harriet Herndon. Married in Henry county in October, 1819. R 11/3.

Hugh A. Blevens, to Mrs. Emily King, widow of William King. Married in Cumberland county in October, 1819. R 11/3.

Robert Burbridge, of Scott county, to Miss Elizabeth Barnes. Married near Port Gibson, Miss., in October, 1819. R 11/3.

Thomas B. Martin, of Frankfort, to Miss Susan Resor. Married in Scott county, in October, 1819. R 11/3.

Dr. John M. Talbot, to Miss Sarah Basey. Married at Louisville in November, 1819. R 11/10.

John B. Wigginton, of Bowling Green, to Miss Angelina T. Shepherd. Married in Christian county in November, 1819. R 11/10.

Rev. Mr. Grinstead, of Maysville, to Miss Marianne Lane. Married in Montgomery county in November, 1819. R 11/10.

William Rodes, to Miss Paulina G. Clay, daughter of Green Clay. Married in Madison county, in Nov., 1819. R 11/10.

William H. Caperton, of Richmond, Ky., to Miss Eliza Estill, daughter of James Estill. Married in Madison county in November, 1819. R 11/10.

Samuel Denham, to Miss Sarah Colter. Married in Madison county in November, 1819. R 11/10.

James Anderson, to Miss Mary Wrigglesworth. Married in Lexington, Nov. 10, 1819. R 11/17.

John C. Andrews, Jr., editor of the *Weekly Recorder,* Chillicothe, to Miss Mary B. Orr, daughter of Col. A. D. Orr. Married in Mason county in November, 1819. R 11/17.

Benjamin Gratz, of Philadelphia, to Miss Maria C. Gist. Married at Cane Wood, in Clarke county, Wednesday, Nov. 24, 1819. R 12/1.

Alvaraz Fisk, of New Orleans, to Mrs. Eliza W. Major. Married in Woodford county in November, 1819. R 12/1.

Robert Scroggin, of Bourbon county, to Miss Nancy Ward. Married in Harrison county in Nov., 1819. R 12/1.

Lewis Day, Jr., to Miss Eleanor Hawkins. Married in Harrison county in November, 1819. R 12/1.

Richard Blanton, to Miss Maria Snead, daughter of Achilles Snead. Married at Frankfort in Dec., 1819. R 12/8.

Thomas P. Wilson, of Shelbyville, to Miss Elizabeth R. Greathouse. Married in Nov. or Dec., 1819. R 12/8.

C. Wooldridge, to Miss Mary Ewing, of Logan county. Married in December, 1819. R 12/5.

John D. Thomas, merchant of Winchester, to Miss Maria K. Graves. Married at Winchester in Dec., 1819. R 12/15.

John P. Taylor, to Miss Rachel P. Martin. Married in Winchester in December, 1819. R 12/15.

Richard Jones, to Miss Lydia Greening. Married in Clarke county in December, 1819. R 12/15.

Thomas Royle, to Miss Elizabeth Bryan. Married in Lexington in December, 1819. R 12/22.

Sandy Holton, to Miss Caroline Allen, daughter of Richardson Allen, of Fayette county. Married Dec. 23, 1819. R 12/31.

John Stringfeller, to Miss Lucy Tandy, both of Fayette county. Married Dec. 16, 1819. R 12/31

1820

Hiram Bledsoe, to Miss Susan Hughes. Married in Bourbon county in January, 1820. R 1/12.

John Combs, to Miss Marinda Vivion. Married in Clarke county in January, 1820. R 1/12.

John Arnold, to Miss Polly Walls. Married in Clarke county in January, 1820. R 1/12.

Benjamin Vance, of Bowling Green, to Miss Catherine Morton. Married in Logan county in January, 1820. R 1/12.

Lowman L. Hawes, attorney-at-law, Maysville, to Miss Charlotte Brown, daughter of John Brown. Married at Maysville in January, 1820. R 1/19.

Joseph Freeland, of Mason county, to Miss Elizabeth Russell, daughter of Gen. Robert Russell, of Fayette county. Married Jan. 9, 1820. R 1/19.

William Breckinridge, of Fayette county, to Miss Deborah M. Russell, daughter of Gen. Robert Russell, of Fayette county. Married Jan. 9, 1820. R 1/19.

James Strode, of Winchester, to Miss Mary Parish, of Lexington. Married Feb. 21, 1820. R 2/23.

Abraham B. Morton, of Lexington, to Miss Martha Fletcher, daughter of James Fletcher, of Jessamine county. Married Feb. 3, 1820. R 2/16.

Benjamin Goode, to Miss Nancy Daniel, daughter of Capt. Elijah Daniel. Married in Christian county in February, 1820. R 3/1.

.... McKeever, to Miss Ellen Johnson. Married in Christian county in February, 1820. R 3/1.

Edward Peers, to Miss Margaret Lowrey. Married at Limestone (Maysville ?) in March, 1820. R 3/15. Note: At this late date newspapers rarely called Maysville by her old name.

Dr. Joseph W. Knight, of Shelbyville, to Mrs. Ann Pleasants. Married in Lexington Mar. 16, 1820. R 3/22.

Israel B. Grant, to Miss Letitia Warren, daughter of Thomas Warren. Married in Scott county in March, 1820. R 4/5.

William Ward, to Miss Nancy M. Smith. Married in Greenup county in April, 1820. R 5/19.

Robert T. Campbell, to Miss Eliza Postlethwaite, daughter of Joseph Postlethwaite. Married in Lexington, Thursday evening, Apr. 13, 1820. R 4/19.

Col. Richard Maston, of Missouri, to Miss Didemma Vardeman, daughter of the Rev. Jeremiah Vardeman. They married in Fayette county in April, 1820. R 4/19.

John Pope, to Mrs. Frances Walton. Married in Washington county in May, 1820. R 5/17.

Robert Hough, to Miss Emmeline E. Robert. Married in Lexington, May 18, 1820. R 5/24.

David Cochran Slaughter, to Miss Louisa Ann Young, of Jessamine county, daughter of the late Abner Young. Married Sunday, May 14, 1820. R 5/24.

Daniel Ford, to Miss Mary Randolph, both of Fayette county. Married May 11, 1820. R 5/24.

John W. Ball, to Miss Mary Wickliffe, daughter of Charles Wickliffe.

Married in Lexington, June 12, 1820. R 6/14.

Marquis Barnett, editor of the Bardstown *Repository*, to Miss Matilda Gault Thomas, daughter of Major Edward S. Thomas, of Bardstown. Married in June, 1820. R 6/14.

John B. Harbin, to Miss Eliza Coons, daughter of George Coons, of Fayette county. Married June 29, 1820. R 7/5.

Dr. B. F. Bedinger, son of Major Bedinger, of Blue Licks, to Miss Sarah Wade, daughter of David Wade. They were married at Cincinnati, in July, 1820. R 7/12.

Thomas Ludwell Lee, of Woodford county, to Miss Mary Davidson, niece of Dr. Alexander Patrick, also of Woodford county. Married Aug. 8, 1820. R 8/16.

William Hopkins, to Miss Eliza Carson. Married in Lexington, Sept. 5, 1820. R 9/13.

William Kirkwood, of Louisville, to Miss Nancy Adams. Married in Jefferson county in September, 1820. R 9/13.

John M. Heran, of Louisville, to Miss Neomi Challen. Married at Lexington in September, 1820. R 9/13.

Capt. Jonathan Hunt, to Miss Ann A. Johnson. Married in Franklin county in September, 1820. R 9/13.

William G. Hunt, editor of the *Monitor,* to Miss Fanny Wigglesworth. Married in Lexington in October, 1820. R 10/4.

James Lemon, Sr., of Lexington, to Mrs. Proctor. Married in Jessamine county in October, 1820. R 10/4.

1821

David Martin, to Miss Ephia Webster, daughter of Roy Webster, of Fayette county. Married Oct. 5, 1820. R 10/17.

William P. Nicholson, of Bath county, to Miss Mary T., daughter of Isaac Webb, of Fayette county. Married Oct. 19, 1820. R 10/23.

Joseph M. White, to Miss Ellen K. Adair, daughter of Governor (John) Adair. Married at Frankfort, Tuesday evening Dec. 5, 1820. R 12/11.

Capt. Frederick Yeiser, to Miss Lucy Bradford. Married in Danville in December, 1820. R 12/11.

Rev. Jeremiah Vardeman, to Miss Elizabeth Bryan. Married in Fayette county Dec. 21, 1820. R 12/25.

George Boswell, merchant of Lexington, to Miss Mary Keen, daughter of Oliver Keen. Married Feb. 6, 1821. R. 2/12.

Andrew McClane, formerly of Lancaster, Pa., to Miss Elizabeth Price. Married at Lexington, Ky., in February, 1821. R 2/12.

Dr. R. L. Wiley, of Salem, Ind., to Miss Tabitha A. Russell, daughter of Col. William Russell. Married in Fayette county, Ky., Feb. 8, 1821. R 2/12.

Lewis Sanders, Jr., to Miss Margaret Price. Married in Franklin county in February, 1821. R 2/12.

James McDonald, of Frankfort, to Miss Ann Alexander Taylor, daughter of Major Edmund H. Taylor, of Jefferson county. Married in March, 1821. R 4/2.

Hugh Stevenson, to Miss Sidney McDaniel, both of Lexington. Married in March, 1821. R 4/2.

Dr. H. George Doyle, of Louisville, to Mary Ann Elizabeth, daughter of the late William Todd, of Lexington. Married April 24, 1821. R 4/30.

S. I. M. Major, of Frankfort, to Miss Martha Bohannon, of Lexington. Married May 10, 1821. R 5/21.

Rev. Mr. Ward, of St. Louis, to Miss Sarah Clifford, of Lexington, Ky. Married May 17, 1821. R 5/21.

———— Randolph, of Virginia, to Miss Mary Bird. Married at Chaumere, the residence of D. Meade, May 23, 1821. R 5/28.

Benjamin Dudley, M. D., to Miss Anna Short, daughter of Peyton Short. Married at the Episcopal Church, at Lexington, Sunday June 10, 1821. R 6/11.

Charles M. Davenport, to Miss Mary Harrison, both of Jessamine county. Married June 11, 1821. R 6/18.

George Washington Anderson, to Miss Eleanor Murdock Hart, daughter of Thos. Hart, Jr., dec'd. Married in Fayette county, Aug. 2, 1821. R 8/6.

John Painter, of Frankfort, to Miss Amanda Williams, daughter of Caleb Williams, of Lexington. Married July 31, 1821. R 8/6.

James Wheeler, to Miss Sarah Deal, of Fayette county. Married Aug. 2, 1821. R 8/6.

William Washington, to Miss Margaret Fletcher, daughter of General Thomas Fletcher, of Bath county. Married in Lexington, Aug. 3, 1821. R 8/13.

Daniel D. Smith, to Miss Elizabeth Todd. Married at Kaskaskia, in August 1821. R 8/20.

Elijah Morton, of Arkansas, to Miss Nancy W. Stewart, daughter of Major William Stewart. Married at Russellville, Ky. in August, 1821. R 8/20.

Pollard Simmonds, of Neville, Ohio, to Miss Harriet Ritter. Married at Rittersville, Ky., in Aug., 1821. R 8/20.

Ephraim M. Ewing, to Miss Jane McIntire. Married in Russellville in Sept., 1821. R 9/24.

James L. McKoin, to Miss Fanny Wade. Married in Russellville in Sept., 1821. R 9/24.

Capt. Samuel Thurston, to Miss Dorcas Kimball. Married in Edwardsville, in Sept., 1821. R 9/24.

Joseph Towler, to Mrs. Julia S. Megowan. Married in Lexington, Sept. 20, 1821. R 10/1.

James Tingle, to Miss Ann Hughes. Married in Lexington in September, 1821. R 9/24.

Dr. Lewis G. Mullins, of Lancaster, Ky., to Miss America Eastin, daughter of the Rev. A. Eastin. Married in Bourbon county, in Sept., 1821. R 10/1.

Thomas Palmer, to Miss Mary McMunn. Married in Louisville. in Sept., 1821. R 10/1.

Nathaniel Sawyier, to Mrs. Pamela Bacon. Married in Frankfort, in Sept.,

27

1821. R 10/1.

James McKensey, to Miss Lucintha Roundtree. Married in Bowling Green in Sept., 1821. R 10/1.

Thomas Webb, to Miss Catharine Springle. Married in Lexington in Oct., 1821. R 10/8.

Thomas Rankin, to Miss Sarah T. Robb, daughter of Major Joseph Robb. Married in Fayette county in Oct., 1821. R 10/8.

Thomas Nuttall, to Miss Nancy Pollard. Married in Jessamine county in Oct., 1821. R 10/8.

John H. Martin, to Miss Emily Kerr. Married at Glasgow, Ky., Sept. 26, 1821. R 10/8.

John M. Foster, to Miss Marcia White, daughter of Col. Phillip White. Married in Franklin county in Oct., 1821. R 10/15.

Charles Buford, of Scott county, to Miss Henrietta P. Adair, daughter of General John Adair, Governor of Kentucky. Married at Frankfort, Tuesday Evening, Nov. 13, 1821. R 11/19.

Henry Boyer, to Miss Agnes Wallace. Married in Fayette county in Nov., 1821. R 12/3.

Dr. Lloyd Warfield, of Paris, to Miss Mary Barr. Married in Lexington in Nov., 1921. R 12/3.

Thomas Marshall, of Washington, Ky., to Miss Juliana Whetcroft. Married in Washington City, in Nov., 1821. R 12/3.

Major David Irvine, to Miss Susanna H. McDowell, daughter of Dr. E. McDowell. Married in Danville in Nov., 1821. R 12/3.

Joseph B. Lancaster, of Springfield, to Miss Ann America Blair, daughter of Samuel Blair, of Fayette county. Married Nov. 26, 1821. R 12/3.

Charles Alexander, of Hopkinsville, to Miss Martha M. Madison, of Fayette county. Married Dec. 4, 1821. R 12/10.

Dr. James Humphries, to Miss Johanna Hickey, daughter of Simon Hickey. Married in Lexington in Dec., 1821. R 12/10.

Elijah W. Craig, to Miss Almira Grosvenor. Married in Lexington Dec. 25, 1821. R 12/31.

J. F. Robinson, to Miss Susan Mansell, both of Georgetown. Married Dec. 29, 1821. R 1/7/1822.

John Miller, to Miss Jane Holmes. Married in Scott county, in Dec., 1821. R 1/7/1822.

Horace Carpenter, of Port Gibson, Miss., to Miss Martha Matilda Green, daughter of the late Henry Green. Married in Fayette county, Dec. 20, 1821. R 1/7/1822.

1822

James K. Duke, of Mason county, to Miss Mary Buford. They were married in Scott county in Feb., 1822. R 2/18.

Dr. Samuel Gregg, to Miss Cassa Pitts. Married in Scott county in Feb., 1822. R 2/18.

Vincent Cromwell, to Miss Nancy Todd, both of Fayette county. Married in Feb., 1822. R 2/18.

Henry Lyter, to Miss Mary Hotsell. Married in Bourbon county in Feb., 1822. R 2/18.

James Withers, to Miss Mary Graves. Married in Fayette county in Feb., 1822. R 2/18.

Buford Allen to Miss ———————— Graves. Married in Fayette county in Feb., 1822. R 2/18.

Major George Shackelford, of Richmond, Ky., to Miss Susan Rankin. Married in Henderson county in Feb., 1822. R 2/25.

Duke W. Simpson, to Miss Sally Chenault. Married in Madison county in Feb., 1822. R 2/25.

Samuel Taylor Brashear, to Miss Susan Leake. Married in Scott county in Feb., 1822. R 2/25.

William Leake, to Miss Catherine Brashear. Married in Scott county in Feb., 1822. R 2/25.

Rev. William Warfield, to Miss Rachel Edwards, daughter of Benjamin Edwards. Married in Christian county in Feb., 1822. R 3/4.

John H. Moore, of Boone county, to Miss Emily Rogers, daughter of John Rogers. Married in Fayette county in Mar., 1822. R 3/4.

Peleg Barker, to Miss Sarah Doneghy. Married in Danville in Feb., 1822. R 3/4.

Richard D. Bradburn, of Springfield, to Miss Susan Ellis. Married in Mercer county in Feb., 1822. R 3/4.

John Hall, to Miss Mary Walker. Married in Maysville in February, 1822. R 3/4.

Jacob Rohrer, to Miss Artimesa Patterson, both of Logan county. Married in Tennessee, in Feb., 1822. R 3/4.

Robert Thompson, to Miss E. Bryant, daughter of Jesse Bryant. Married in Fayette county in March, 1822. R 3/11.

Dr. Joseph McMurtry, to Miss Lucy L. Madison. Married in Jessamine county in March, 1822. R 3/11.

Gen. William Rector, of St. Louis, to Miss Eliza, daughter of Thomas January of Lexington, Ky. Married in former place Feb. 29, 1822. R 3/18.

John F. Jenkins, Professor at Transylvania University, to Miss Mary Ann Pike, daughter of Capt. Job H. Pike, of Lexington. Married Thursday, March 14, 1822. R 3/18.

W. L. Thompson to Miss Elizabeth Massie. Married in Jefferson county in March, 1822. R 3/25.

Dr. Matthews W. Flournoy, of Nicholasville, to Henrietta Blackburn, daughter of W. B. Blackburn, of Versailles. Married latter place in April, 1822. R 4/15.

John McCabe, to Miss Maria Sale. Married in Nicholasville in April, 1822. R 4/15.

Thomas H. Clements to Miss Mary McConnell. Married in Nicholasville in April, 1822. R 4/15.

Joseph Smith, of Frankfort, to Miss Sarah Taylor, daughter of the Rev. John Taylor, of Franklin county. Married April 9, 1822. R 4/15.

Capt. Stephenson Irvine, of Fayette county, to Miss Frances Brook. Married in Frankfort, April 9, 1822. R 4/15.

Dr. J. N. Bybee to Mrs. Roane. Married at Harrodsburg in April, 1822. R 4/15.

Martin Durald, of New Orleans, to Miss Susan H. Clay, eldest daughter of Henry Clay. Married Monday, April 22, 1822, by the Rev. G. T. Chapman. R 4/29.

Theoderick Jenkins, to Miss Eliza Duncan. Married at Paris in April, 1822 R 4/29.

David A. Russell to Miss Eleanor Alsop. Married at Danville in May, 1822. R 5/6.

Andrew Alexander to Miss Mira L. Madison, daughter of the late Governor Madison. Married in Woodford county in May, 1822. R 5/6.

Francis Murphy to Miss Jane Reese. Married at Maysville in May, 1822. R 5/6.

William Garrett to Miss Ann McConathy, of Lexington. They were married in May, 1822. R 5/27.

———————— Henderson, of the Lexington Theater, to Miss Jane Calender, lately of Baltimore. Married in Lexington, Ky., in May, 1822. R 5/27.

F. Smith, of Boone county, to Miss Lucy Rice. Married in Cincinnati in May, 1822. R 5/27.

Genl Jessup to Miss Ann Croghan, eldest daughter of Major Croghan. Married in Jefferson county in May, 1822. R 5/27.

John W. Coleman to Miss Louisa Sutton. Married in Lexington in June, 1822. R 6/3

Virgil McKnight, of Versailles, to Miss Anne Logan. Married in Shelby county in May, 1822. R 6/3.

Charles S. Bibb to Miss Rebecca Mitchell. Married in Frankfort in May, 1822. R 6/3.

Richard Clarke to Miss Mary Gordon. Married in Madison county in May, 1822. R 6/3.

Dudley Webster to Miss Mary Clarke. Married in Madison county in May, 1822. R 6/3.

Harrison Daniel, of Nicholasville, to Miss Lucy Ann Curd, of Fayette county. Married latter place in June, 1822. R 6/10.

Moses Wallace to Miss Rebecca Thompson. Married in Lexington in June, 1822. R 6/10.

Dr. John Tenant, of Virginia, to Miss Sarah Gardner, of Lexington, Ky Married June 12, 1822. R 6/17.

Thomas Leaming Caldwell to Miss Mary Jane Clifford, daughter of the late

John Clifford, of Lexington. Married in Cincinnati in June, 1822. R 6/17.

John R. Carter, of Pike county, Mo., to Miss Nancy Jeanes, of Montgomery county. Married in June, 1822. R 6/17.

James Devore, of Mo., to Miss Elizabeth L. Harrison, daughter of Robert C. Harrison, of Fayette county, Ky. Married June 20, 1822. R 6/24.

John W. White to Miss Sarah Vaughan. Married in Lexington July 21, 1822. R 7/22.

Capt. Samuel McDowell to Miss Marcia Bell. Married in Mercer county in September, 1822. R 9/9.

William Lotspeich, aged 82 years, to Mrs. Sprake, aged 52 years, both of Lexington. Married in September, 1822. R 9/9.

Rev. Mr. Hall, of Springfield, to Mrs. Elizabeth Trotter, of Lexington. Married Sept. 4, 1822. R 9/9.

William Satterwhite to Mrs. Sophia Norman, of Fayette county. Married in September, 1822. R 9/9.

——————— Alexander, to Miss Nancy Downton, daughter of Richard Downton. Married in Fayette county in Sept., 1822. R 9/9.

Major John McDowell to Miss Jane Lyle. Married in Fayette county in September, 1822. R 9/9.

Lewis Barbee to Miss Mary Goodwin. Married in Fayette county in September, 1822. R 9/9.

Rev. Eli Smith, of Frankfort, to Miss Mary Brown, of Newburyport, Mass. Married Aug. 21, 1822. R 9/30.

William Hubbell, of Georgetown, to Miss Elizabeth Price. Married in Franklin county in September, 1822. R 9/30.

John A. Gano, of Cincinnati, to Miss Catherine Hubbell. They were married in Georgetown, Ky., in September, 1822. R 9/30.

Robert Crittenden, Secretary of the Arkansas Territory, to Miss Ann Morris, daughter of John Morris. Married in Franklin county, Ky., in September, 1822. R 10/7.

John Thompson to Miss Russia Oldham. Married in Madison county in September., 1822. R 10/7.

Sidney P. Clay, of Madison county, to Miss Ann Keen, daughter of John Keen, of Fayette county. Married in October, 1822. R 10/7.

John J. Allen to Miss Cynthia McAfee, daughter of John McAfee, all of Mercer county. Married Oct. 16, 1822. R 10/21.

Hugh W. Patten, a professor in the Southern College, to Jane M. Barclay, daughter of Samuel Barclay. Married in Warren county in October, 1822. R 10/28.

Alexander K. Marshall, of Mason county, to Mrs. Eliza Ball. Married in November, 1822. R 11/11

Dr. B[asil] Duke, of Washington, Mason county, to Miss Margaret Chinn, of Mason county. Married in Oct., 1822. R 11/11.

Capt. Robert R. Buchanan, of the steam boat *Maysville*, to Miss Harriet Browning, of Mason county. Married in Oct., 1822. R 11/11.

John Gaunt, of Lexington, to Miss Letitia Pullem, of Fayette county Married in November, 1822. R 11/18.

George McDaniel of Fayette county, to Miss Patsey Kenton, of Mason county. Married in November, 1822. R 11/18.

Percival Butler, of Woodford county, to Miss Eliza Allen, daughter of the late Col. John Allen. Married in Franklin county in November, 1822. R 12/2.

Col. Joseph Pollard, of Frankfort, to Mrs. Ann Daveiss, widow of Col. Joseph Hamilton Daveiss. Married in Henderson county in November, 1822. R 12/2.

Edmond W. Rootes to Mrs. Mary Anne Bell. Married in Richmond, Va., in December, 1822. R 12/23.

Dr. Luke Munsel, of Louisville, to Miss Eliza Sneed, daughter of Achilles Sneed. Married at Frankfort in December, 1822. R 12/23.

Maurice L. Miller, of Jefferson county, to Miss Kitty J. Thomas, daughter of Rowland Thomas. Married in New Castle, Ky., in December, 1822. R 1/6/1823.

1823

William Croghan, of Louisville, to Miss O'Hara. Married at Pittsburg in January, 1823. R 2/10.

Joseph Ficklin, editor of the *Kentucky Gazette,* to Mrs. Polly Campbell. Married in the vicinity of Hopkinsville in January, 1823. R 1/13.

Samuel Laird, of Fayette county, to Mrs. Catherine Logan. Married in Woodford county Jan. 16, 1823. R 1/27.

Clear Oxley to Miss Philadelphia Oliver. Married in Fayette county Jan. 16, 1823. R 1/27.

Benjamin Dunn to Miss Clarissa Burnsides. Married in Garrard county Jan. 30, 1823. R 2/3.

Richard Ashton to Miss Diana Hoagland. Married in Lexington in March, 1823. R 3/10.

Dr. Joel C. Frazer to Miss R. T. Warfield. Married at Cynthiana in March, 1823. R 3/10.

Robert S. Barr, of Franklin, Mo., to Miss Mary Duncan. They were married at Paris, Ky., in March, 1823. R 3/10.

Samuel Smith, M. D., formerly of Lexington, to Miss Anna Wykoff. Married at Baton Rouge in February, 1823. R 3/10.

Robert Breckinridge, of Kentucky, to Miss Ann Sophonisba, daughter of General Preston of Abington, Va. Married at latter place March 11, 1823. R 3/31.

Lewis Collins, editor of the *Maysville Eagle* to Miss Mary Eleanor Peers, daughter of Valentine Peers, all of Maysville. Married Tuesday evening, April 1, 1823, by the Rev. J. T. Edgar. R 4/7.

Dr. Urbin C. Ewing, of Russellville, to Miss Sarah R. L. Moore. Married in Lexington April 20, 1823. R 4/21.

Dr. Charles Edwin Williams, of Erie, Ala., to Miss Arabella Ann Dodge.

Married in Winchester, Ky., in April, 1823. R 4/28.

James R. Turnbull to Miss Eliza Patrick, both of Winchester. Married in April, 1823. R 4/28.

William W. Tate, of Hanover, Va., to Miss Ann L., daughter of Col. Anthony New, of Kentucky. Married former place in April, 1823. R 4/28.

Richard A. Curd to Miss Eleanor Hunt, daughter of J. W. Hunt, of Lexington. Married May 8, 1823. R 5/12.

Dr. J. L. Maxwell, of Lexington, to Miss Sinai M. Rowan, daughter of William Rowan, of Fayette county. Married May 1, 1823. R 5/12.

John Higbee, Jr., to Miss Paulina D. Caldwell. Married in Fayette county in June, 1823. R 6/23.

Charles S. Morehead, of Russellville, to Miss Amanda Leavy, daughter of William Leavy, of Lexington. Married July 10, 1823. R 7/14.

Thomas H. Smith to Miss Belary Moss. Married in Clarke county July 17, 1823. R 7/21.

Mr. John B. Overton, of Virginia, to Miss Susan Mary Overton, of Lexington, Ky. Married Aug. 28, 1823. R 9/1.

Jacob Shotts to Miss Mary Ewing, both of Fayette county. Married July 31, 1823. R 9/1.

Albert G. Irvine, of Madison county, to Miss Eliza Coleman, daughter of Col. James Coleman. Married in Lexington in September, 1823. R 9/15.

J. J. Polk to Miss Eliza Todd, daughter of William Todd. Married in September, 1823. R 9/15.

Jefferson T. Vimont, of Millersburg, to Miss Babet Mentelle, of Fayette county. Married Sept. 18, 1823. R 9/22.

Hon. Thomas Reynolds, Chief Justice of the State of Illinois, to Miss Eliza Ann, daughter of Ambrose Young, of Fayette county, Ky. Married Sept. 5, 1823. R 9/29.

William W. Whitney to Miss Emily Satterwhite, both of Lexington. Married Sept. 15, 1823. R 9/29.

Col. Calvin C. Morgan, of Huntsville, Ala., to Miss Henrietta, daughter of John W. Hunt. Married Sept. 24, 1823. R 9/29.

Alexander G. Morgan, of Huntsville, Ala., to Miss America, daughter of Richard Higgins. Married Sept. 25, 1823. R 9/29.

Major Thomas Biddle to Miss Ann Mulanphy, of Florisant. Married in Mo., in September, 1823. R 9/29.

Adam C. Keenon, of Frankfort, to Miss Elizabeth Clarke. Married in Franklin county in September, 1823. R 9/29.

James Erwin, of Cahawba, Ala., to Miss Ann B. Clay, second daughter of Henry Clay. Married at Ashland, Tuesday Evening, October 23, 1823. R 10/27.

Francis B. Fogg to Miss Mary Rutledge, daughter of Major Henry M. Rutledge. Married at Nashville in Oct., 1823. R 10/27.

John C. Self to Miss America Morton, daughter of Thomas Morton. Married in Woodford county, Nov. 20, 1823. R 11/24.

John B. Craighead to Mrs. Lavina Beck, relict of John E. Beck. Married at Nashville in November, 1823. R 11/24.

U. B. Chambers to Miss Sophia Mahoney. Married at Georgetown in November, 1823. R 11/24.

John T. Cleveland, editor of the *Missouri Intelligence*, to Miss Louisiana Hughes, daughter of William Hughes, formerly of Jessamine county, Ky. Married in Howard county, Mo., Oct. 30, 1823. R 12/8.

Henry Hogland, son of Governor William Hogland, west of the Ohio, to Elizabeth Carpenter, eldest daughter of John Carpenter, land lord of Norris Town, west of the Ohio. They were married at the Governor's hall, Friday, May 27, 1787. KG 11/17.

Major John Fitzpatrick to Miss Mary Cavandish. Married at Norris Town, west of the Ohio, June 7, 1787. KG 11/17.

John Muckledroy to Miss Easter Brindley. Married June 23, 1787. KG 11/17.

William Mackey, merchant of Mayslick, to Miss Jane Pogue, daughter of General R. Pogue, of Mason county. Married in Nov., 1823. R 12/8.

Isaac Desha to Miss Cornelia Pickett, daughter of Col. John Pickett, of Mason county. Married in Nov., 1823. R 12/8.

Benjamin Keiser to Miss Catherine Hull. Married at Lexington, Dec. 7, 1823. R 11/22.

Major Benjamin O'Fallon to Miss Sophia Lee, daughter of Patrick Lee Married at St. Charles, Mo., in December, 1823. R 12/22.

Hugh Briton, of Lexington, to Miss Agnes Ingles, of Fayette county Married Dec. 16, 1823. R 12/22.

David Logan to Miss Margaret Biship, both of Fayette county. Married December 16, 1823. R 12/22.

Robert Brown to Mrs. Pamelia Prewett. Married at Frankfort in December, 1823. R 12/30.

General John Edgar, of Kaskaskia, an officer in the Revolution, aged 90 years, to Miss Eliza Stevens, aged 14 years. Married December 25, 1823, in Williamsburg township, Ill., by John W. Gilliss. R 1/5/1824.

1824

Rev. Mr. Graham, of Cincinnati, to Miss Jane S. W. Ridgely, daughter of Dr. F. Ridgely, of Lexington. Married Jan. 7, 1824. R 1/12.

John P. Morris to Miss Mary J. Hughes, both formerly of Jessamine county, Ky. Married in Howard county, Mo., Nov. 21, 1823. R 1/12/1824.

Clifton Rodes, of Madison county, to Miss Amanda Owsley, daughter of Judge Owsley. Married in Garrard county, Dec. 23, 1823. R 1/12/1824.

Cyrus C. Tevis to Miss Elizabeth Stone, daughter of John Stone. Married in Madison county Dec. 23, 1823. R 1/12/1824.

George P. Ross to Miss Sophia Bennett, daughter of Moses Bennett. Married in Madison county Dec. 23, 1823. R 1/12/1824.

Joseph Searcy to Miss Nancy Todd, daughter of John Todd (of Madison county(?). Married latter place Dec. 16, 1823. R 1/12/1824.

Elias Brown to Miss Susan Mauze. Married in Madison county Dec. 25, 1823. R 1/12/1824.

Samuel Gentry to Miss Susan Rankle. Married in Madison county Dec. 25, 1823. R 1/12/24.

Elias Epperson to Miss Elizabeth Dalton. Married in Madison county, Dec. 25, 1823. R 1/12/1824.

Pearow Epperson to Miss Nancy Dalton. Married in Madison county Dec. 25, 1823. R 1/12/1824.

Rial B. English to Miss Polly Fowler. Married Madison county Jan. 1, 1824. R 1/12.

Thomas Right to Miss Margaret Harris. Married in Madison county Jan. 1, 1824. R 1/12.

Peter Coty to Miss Eliza Payne, of the Equestrian Company of Messrs. Pepin and Barnet, and pupils of Mr. Pepin. Married in Lexington, Sunday, Jan. 18, 1824. R 1/19.

Isaac Lewis, of Mason county, to Miss Sarah Brent, daughter of Hugh Brent. Married at Paris in January, 1824. R 1/26.

James F. Bradley, of Lexington, to Miss Nancy Kellar, daughter of Jacob Kellar. Married Feb. 11, 1824. R 2/16.

Joseph Love, aged 71 years, to Mrs. Mary Marshall, aged 61 years. Married in Warren county in February, 1824. R 3/1.

Major Joseph Lecompt, of Henry county, to Miss Margaret Mitchell, daughter of William Mitchell, dec'd, of Shelby county. Married Feb. 17, 1824. R 3/1.

William Tanner, of the *Western Monitor,* to Miss Julia Dedman. Married in Lexington March 23, 1824. R 4/5.

James Jameson, of Montgomery county, to Miss Mary Ann Stout. Married in Lexington in March, 1824. R 4/5.

Charleton Hunt, of Paris, to Miss Rebecca Warfield, daughter of Dr. Elisha Warfield. Married Apr. 13, 1824. R 4/19.

Major William Jones, of Richmond, to Miss Elizabeth Field, daughter of Willis Field, of Woodford county. Married April 20, 1824. R 4/26.

Richard Henry Lee, of Mason county, to Miss Eliza A. Luke. Married at Frankfort, in April, 1824. R 4/26.

William L. Breckinridge, to Miss Frances C. Prevost. They were married in Lexington May 12, 1824. R 5/17.

David Harris, of Woodford county, to Mrs. Eleanor Stout, of Lexington. Married May 15, 1824. R 5/17.

James Shannon, of Wheeling Va., to Mrs. Susan McDowell. Married Thursday, May 20, 1824, in Lincoln county, Ky., at the residence of Governor Shelby. R 5/24.

Philip Swigert, of Frankfort, to Miss Jane Watson, of Woodford county. Married May 18, 1824. R 5/24.

James Taylor, Jr., of Newport, to Miss Susan Barry, daughter of William T. Barry. Married May 20, 1824. R 5/24.

Dr. William Price to Miss Elizabeth Haggin, daughter of James Haggin. Married May 13, 1824. R 5/24.

Hon. W. P. Roper, of Flemingsburgh, to Miss Lucy Price Weisiger. Married in Frankfort, June 2, 1824. R 6/7.

B. R. McIlvaine, of Louisville, to Catherine, daughter of Anthony Dumensil, of Lexington. Married June 10, 1824. R 6/14.

Alphius Lewis, of Clarke county, to Miss Theodosia A. Turner, of Fayette county. Married June 2, 1824. R. 6/21.

Jephthah D. Garrard, of Frankfort, to Miss Sarah Bella Ludlow, of Cincinnati. Married at Col. A. Dudley's, near Lexington June 25, 1824. R 6/28.

Simeon Anderson, of Lancaster, to Miss Amelia Owsley, daughter of Judge Owsley. Married in Garrard county in Sept., 1824. R 9/13.

Richard Martin to Miss Sarah Ann Harrison, daughter of Mrs. Jane Harrison. Married in Jessamine county Sept. 8th, 1824. R 9/27.

Charles T. Marshall to Miss Jane Luke. Married in Mason county in September, 1824. R 9/27.

Rev. Andrew Todd, of Bourbon county, Ky., to Miss Catherine Wilson. Married in Washington, Pa., in September, 1824. R 9/27.

Major John Chamblin, of Bourbon county, to Miss Isabella Richardson. Married in Clarke county in Sept., 1824. R 10/4

Henderson Bell, of Fayette county, to Miss Frances Brown, daughter of John Brown. Married in Madison county Oct. 19, 1824. R 10/25.

Williamson Ware Bacon to Miss Ann Maria, daughter of the Rev. Silas M. Noel, all of Franklin county. Married Nov. 3, 1824. R 11/8.

O. Grimes, of Fayette county, to Miss Eliza Matson, daughter of Capt. Thomas Matson. Married in Bourbon county in Nov., 1824. R 11/15.

David Castleman to Miss Virginia Harrison, daughter of Robert C. Harrison, Sr., all of Fayette county. Married on Thursday Nov. 11, 1824. R 11/22

Franklin B. Vimont, of Millersburg, to Miss Susan W. Throckmorton, daughter of Thomas Throckmorton, (of Nicholas county?). Married latter place Nov. 25, 1824. R 11/29.

Dr. Joseph D. Roberts to Miss Martha Ann, daughter of George Todd, all of Frankfort. Married Nov. 16, 1824. R 11/29.

Gen. James Dudley, of Fayette county, to Mrs. Mourning Royster. Married in Madison county in Nov., 1824. R 11/29.

Ambrose W. Dudley, of Frankfort, to Miss Eliza Talbott, daughter of Isham Talbott. Married in Paris in Nov., 1824. R 11/29.

Dr. John W. Long to Miss Jane Stephenson. Married in Woodford county Nov. 22, 1824. R 12/6.

John R. Gay, of Versailles, to Miss Catherine Hall, daughter of Major Charles W. Hall. Married in Scott county Dec. 9, 1824. R 12/13.

William Wright Southgate, of Newport, to Miss Adelize Keen, of Lexington.

Married Dec. 7, 1824. R 12/20.

H. Davenport to Miss Cassander Ward. Married at Winchester in December, 1824. R 12/20.

John Hutchcraft to Miss Margaret McIlvain. Married at Paris in December, 1824. R 12/20.

Thompson Finnell to Miss Penelope W. Williamson. Married in Scott county in December, 1824. R 1/10/1825.

John W. Tibbatts to Miss Ann Taylor, daughter of General James Taylor. Married in Newport in December, 1824. R 1/10/1825.

Matthew Hersman to Miss Lucy Kiser. Married in Lexington Dec. 30, 1824. R 1/10/1825.

1825

Orville Shelby to Miss Caroline E., daughter of Gen. James Winchester. Married in Tenn., Jan. 30, 1825. KG 2/24.

Frederick Beckman to Miss Eliza, youngest daughter of Col. Shaumburg, all of New Orleans. Married Jan. 6, 1825. KG 2/10.

Jacob Kizer, of Fayette county, to Mrs. Sarah Self, formerly of Lexington. Married in New Albany, Ind., Jan. 30, 1825. K 2/14.

Harvey McGuire to Miss Eliza Randolph. Married in Fayette county in Jan., 1825. R 1/31.

William D. Payne, of Louisville, to Miss Emeline Ward, daughter of David L. Ward. Married Jan. 20, 1825. R 1/31.

Col. Benjamin Estill, of Abingdon, Va., to Mrs. Patsey Sproule. Married in Frankfort, Jan. 20, 1825. R 1/31.

Thomas Layton to Miss Amanda Keiser. Married Jan. 15, 1825. R 1/17.

Hugh Dewlin to Miss Anna Sampson, both of Lexington. They were married Jan. 15, 1825. R 1/17.

George Cranmer to Miss Catherine Winter. Married in Lexington Jan. 13, 1825. R 1/17.

Thomas Jefferson Payne, of Fayette county, to Miss ―――――― Craig. Married in Woodford county in January, 1825. R 1/17.

Thomas Woolfolk, of Woodford county, to Miss Charlotte McClung. Married in Mason county in January, 1825. R 1/17.

William M. Brand to Miss Harriet W., daughter of President Holley. Married in Lexington Jan. 8, 1825. R 1/10.

John Buford, of Versailles, to Mrs. Ann B. Watson, daughter of the late Capt. Edward Howe. Married in Woodford county Jan. 4, 1825. R 1/10.

James E. Christian to Miss Elizabeth Kizer, daughter of Jacob Kizer. Married in Fayette county Feb. 13, 1825. R 2/21.

Henry Machir, merchant of Maysville, to Miss Clementina E. January, daughter of Samuel January, of Limestone (Maysville). Married Feb. 17, 1825. R 2/21.

Albert G. Harrison to Miss Virginia L. Bledsoe. Married in Mt. Sterling in

February, 1825. R 2/28.

Dr. William R. Jennings, of Tenn., to Miss Nancy Calmes, daughter of Gen. Marquis Calmes. Married in Woodford county, Ky., in February, 1825. R 2/28.

Clement Dunkin to Miss Catherine Ann Woodruff, both of Lexington. Married Feb. 10, 1825. KG 2/17.

Waller Rodes, of Lexington, to Miss Rogers, daughter of James Rogers. Married in Fayette county in March, 1825. R 3/14.

James Paxton, of Columbus, O., to Miss Mary, daughter of the late Capt. Thomas Marshall. Married in Washington, Ky., in March, 1825. R 3/14.

Mason Brown, of Maysville, to Miss Judith Ann, daughter of Judge Bledsoe, of Lexington. Married Mar. 10, 1825. R 3/14.

William B. Kilgore, editor of the *Richmond* (Ky.) *Republican,* to Miss America, daughter of Major Thomas C. Howard. Married in Richmond in March, 1825. R 3/14.

Presley Athey to Miss Melinda Armstrong, both of Lexington. Married March 15, 1825. KG 3/17.

James I. Miller, of Shelby county, to Miss Harriet, daughter of Capt. Wall, of Lexington. Married March 4, 1825. KG 3/17.

Samuel Taylor to Miss Melissa, daughter of Mrs. Scroggin, all of Lexington. Married April 28, 1825. KG 5/5.

Bennet P. Sanders, M. D., to Miss Eleanor, daughter of Luther Stephens, all of Lexington. Married April 19, 1825. R 4/25.

Capt. Patterson Bain to Miss Maria Hurt. Married May 10, 1825. KG 5/12.

Francis Withers to Mrs. Sarah P. Warham. Married in Georgetown, S. C., April 11, 1825. R 5/16.

Col. George F. Strother, of St. Louis, to Miss Theodocia L., daughter of John W. Hunt, of Lexington. Married June 1, 1825. R 6/6.

Samuel D. Everett, merchant of Mt. Sterling, to Miss Henrietta, daughter of Marquis Richardson, of Fayette county. Married June 21, 1825. R 6/27.

William McChesney, of New Jersey, to Miss Rebecca G. Ashton. Married in Lexington, Ky., in June, 1825. R 6/27.

Capt. James B. Payne to Miss Eliza Ann, daughter of Henry Churchill, all of Jefferson county. Married June 15, 1825. R 6/27.

John McIlvain, of Paris, to Miss Charlotte, eldest daughter of Louis Vimont, of Millersburg. Married June 23, 1825. R 6/27.

John Carrell, Jr., to Miss Sarah Ann, daughter of the late John Cauffman, of Philadelphia, all of them. Married June 25, 1825. R 7/11.

Benjamin C. Wood to Miss Ferguson, daughter of Nathaniel Ferguson. Married in Fayette county in August, 1825. R 8/15.

David A. Sayre to Miss Abby V. Hammond, both of Lexington. Married in the Lexington Episcopal Church, Thursday, Aug. 18, 1825. R 8/22.

John H. James to Miss Abbey Bailey, both of Cincinnati. Married in August, 1825. R. 8/22.

John Ford, of Va., to Mrs. Nancy Ford, daughter of Mr. C. Self. Married in Fayette county, Ky., in Aug., 1825. R 8/22.

Dr. James Conquest Cross, of Lexington, to Miss Agnes, daughter of David Flournoy, of Scott county. Married Sept. 1, 1825. R 9/5.

Capt. A. Stephens to Miss Roman, daughter of William Roman. Married Sept. 1, 1825. R 9/5.

George Washington Brown to Miss Matilda Chrisman, daughter of Capt. Hugh Chrisman, all of Jessamine county. Sept. 14, 1825. R 9/26.

F. R. Richardson to Miss Sarah M., daughter of Mr. B. Magoffin, of Harrodsburgh. Married Sept. 22, 1825. Mrs. Richardson was from Mississippi. R 9/26.

Nelson C. Johnson, of Oldham county, to Miss Fanny Smith, daughter of Henry Smith, dec'd. Married in Shelby county in September, 1825. R 10/3.

John F. Anderson, of Lexington, to Miss Nancy O. Martin, eldest daughter of John L. Martin. Married Sept. 29, 1825. R 10/3.

James H. Birch, of Cynthiana, to Miss Sarah C., daughter of Daniel Halstead, of Lexington. Married in Oct., 1825. R 10/10.

John S. Spratswell to Miss Elizabeth Broun. Married in Lexington Sept. 29, 1825. R 10/10

John Rootes Thornton to Mrs. Eliza Owings, both of Paris. Married in Lexington Oct. 5, 1825. R 10/10

Joseph N. Hudson, merchant of Danville, to Miss Matilda B. Munford, daughter of William Munford, of Lincoln county. Married Oct. 6, 1825. R 10/17.

David C. Humphreys, of Frankfort, to Miss Sarah Scott, daughter of Dr. Joseph Scott, of Chillicothe, O. Married Oct. 6, 1825. R 10/31.

Frederick Rutledge, of Charleston, S. C., to Miss Henrietta M. Rutledge, of Nashville. Married Oct. 15, 1825. R 10/31.

Henry Leake, of Woodford county, to Miss Cynthia Alexander, daughter of Jonathan Alexander, of Scott county. Married Oct. 22, 1825. R 10/31.

Dr. William S. Ridgley, of Lexington, to Miss Sarah H. Graham, daughter of Thomas Graham, of Cincinnati. Married Oct. 25, 1825. R 11/7.

John Handy, of Georgetown, to Miss Mary Watkins, of Woodford county. Married Oct. 30, 1825. R 11/7.

William Hurst, of Lexington, to Miss Sarah P. Daulton, of Mason county. Married in November, 1825. R 11/21.

Julius M. Clarkson, of Bourbon county, to Miss Lucy Ann Slaughter, daughter of George Slaughter, of Lexington. Married Oct. 27, 1825. R 12/5.

Joseph Parkes to Miss Elizabeth Frank, both of Nicholas county. Married Nov. 8, 1825. R 12/5.

John A. McClung to Miss Eliza Johnston, daughter of Dr. John Johnston, all of Mason county. Married Nov. 24, 1825. R 12/5.

Major Richard S. Wheatley, of Burlington, Ky., to Miss Eleanor M. Green, daughter of William Green, of Belleview, Boone county, Ky. Married Nov. 22, 1825. R 12/5.

Mr. A. Latapie to Miss Sophia Martin, both of Nashville. Married Dec. 15, 1825. R 12/26.

William Shannon to Miss Elizabeth Ellis, daughter of Ezer Ellis. Married in December, 1825. R 1/2/1826.

1826

Luther Stephens to Miss Ann Skillman. Married in Lexington Jan. 11, 1826. R 1/16.

Joseph Milward to Miss Eliza Young. Married in Lexington Jan. 11, 1826. R 1/16.

Thomas T. Shreve, of Greenupsburgh, to Miss Eliza Ann Rogers. Married in Bath county in Jan., 1826. R 1/16.

John Rankin, of Aberdeen, Ohio, to Miss Margaret Bickley, daughter of Capt. William Bickley, (of Mason county?). They were married in latter place in January, 1826. R 1/16.

Amos Kendall, one of the editors of the *Argus,* to Miss Jane Kyle. Married in Franklin county in Jan., 1826. R 1/16.

Edmund A. Bacon to Miss Rebecca Hawkins, daughter of E. Hawkins. Married in Franklin county in Jan., 1826. R 1/16.

Joseph W. Allen to Miss Lucinda Anderson, daughter of Reuben Anderson. Married at Frankfort in Jan., 1826. R 1/16.

Abraham P. Maury, editor of the *Nashville Republican,* to Miss Mary Claiborne. Married Jan. 19, 1826. R 1/23.

Frederick A. M. Davis, M. D., of Augusta, to Miss Julia E. Briggs. Married in Lexington Jan. 19, 1826. R 1/30.

Anthony Rosell to Miss Nancy Happy. Married in Fayette county in January, 1826. R 1/30.

G. G. Skipworth to Miss Mary Ann Newsom, daughter of Major William Newsom, of Maury county, Tenn. Married in Jan., 1826. R 1/30.

Gen. Henry Atkinson, of the U. S. Army, to Miss Mary Ann, eldest daughter of the late Thomas Bullitt. Married in Louisville in January, 1826. R 1/30.

Capt. George Kennerly, of St. Louis, to Miss Elziere, Danghter of Col. Pierre Menard, of Kaskaskia. Married Dec. 27, 1825. R 1/30/1826.

Dr. James Taggart to Miss ————— Chiles. Married in Clarke county Feb. 2, 1826. R 2/6.

Hugh Brent, merchant of Paris, to Mrs. Susan Lewis, of Fayette county. Married January 31, 1826. R 2/6.

Bird Smith, merchant of Lexington, to Miss Elvira Price, of Woodford county. Married Feb. 1, 1826. R 2/6.

Albert G. Hodges, printer of the *Kentucky Whig,* to Miss Elizabeth Todd. Married at Frankfort Feb. 2, 1826. R 2/6.

John Hall to Miss Elizabeth Rutherford. Married in Logan county in Jan., 1826. R 2/13.

James Proctor to Miss Sally Blakey. Married in Logan county in Jan., 1826. R 2/13.

W. P. Wright, of Russellville, to Miss Sarah Ragsdale. Married in Logan county in Jan., 1826. R 2/13.

Nathan Mixer, of Keene, N. H., to Mrs. Eleanora Chamberlain. Married in Lexington, Ky., Feb. 9, 1826. R 2/13.

Gideon Kirk to Miss Sally Duff, daughter of William Duff. Married in Mason county in February, 1826. R 2/20.

James Watts, of Fayette county, to Miss Sally Hulett. Married in Jessamine county in Feb.. 1826. R 2/20.

Thomas Duke, of Texas, to Miss Nancy Ashby. Married in Lexington in Feb., 1826. R 2/20.

Charles Berryman to Miss Nancy Hudson. Married in Fayette county in February, 1826. R 2/20.

Christopher Veltineer, of Lexington, to Miss Mary Ann Moyers. Married in Woodford county in Feb., 1826. R 2/20.

Robert Enders to Miss Amanda Barbee. Married in Union county in Feb., 1826. R 2/20.

Ezra Webb, merchant of Florence, Ala., to Miss Louisa Terrass, daughter of H. Terrass. Married in Feb., 1826. R 2/20.

Ephraim Deer to Miss Nancy Henderson. Married in Danville in Feb., 1826. R 2/20.

E. L. Shackelford, of Richmond, Ky., to Miss Margaret, daughter of Major Daniel Miller. Married in Madison county in February, 1826. R 2/20.

Stephen Cox to Miss Sally Hieatt. Married in Madison county in Feb., 1826. R 2/20.

Robert Cox to Mrs. Elly Ballard. Married in Madison county in Feb., 1826. R 2/20.

Dr. Thomas J. Garden, of Charlotte, to Miss Robina Scott, of Campbell county. Married in Virginia in February, 1826. R 2/27.

Major Charles F. Burton, of Perryville, to Miss Sophia, daughter of General John King. Married in Cumberland county in Feb., 1826. R 2/27.

Amos P. Balch, of Indiana, to Miss Polly Sawyer. Married in Warren county, Ky., in Feb., 1826. R 2/27.

William Sawyer, of Logan county, to Miss Lucinda Sawyer, daughter of Benjamin Sawyer. Married in Warren county in Feb., 1826. R 2/27.

Moses Campbell to Miss Surilda Parrish. Married in Logan county in Feb., 1826. R 2/27.

William Bradley, of Franklin county, to Miss Mahala Kirkpatrick. Married in Harrison county in Feb., 1826. R 2/27

Joshua Sidwell to Miss Mary, daughter of Thomas McLauglin. Married in Bourbon county in Feb., 1826. R 2/27.

Charles Gilkey, of Richmond, Ky., to Mrs. Agnes Barnett. Married in Fayette county, Ky., in Feb., 1826. R 2/27.

Bowling Embry, of Richmond, Ky., to Miss Louisa, daughter of George Howard. Married in Mt. Sterling in Feb., 1826. R 2/27.

Dr. Samuel S. Porter, of Sumptersville, N. C., to Miss Jane W. Moore, daughter of the late Rev. James Moore. Married in Fayette county Feb. 23, 1826. R 2/27.

Robert Ellis, of Todd county, Ky., to Mrs. Ann Williamson, of Montgomery county, Tenn. Married Mar. 2, 1826. R 3/27.

Jonathan Brown to Miss Elizabeth Beauchamp. Married in Fayette county Mar. 16, 1826. R 3/27.

William Loudon to Miss Elizabeth Ford. Married in Fayette county March 16, 1826. R 3/27.

Thomas C. O'Rear, merchant, to Miss Susan G. Norton, daughter of G. Norton. Married in Lexington Mar. 16, 1826. R 3/27.

Stephen Cook to Miss Rebecca Baxter. Married in Frankfort in Mar., 1826. R 3/27.

Thomas L. Metcalf to Mrs. Elizabeth Carey. Married in Louisiana in March, 1826. R 3/27.

Franklin Wharton, formerly of Washington City, to Miss Mary Jane, eldest daughter of Dr. J. W. Baylor, formerly of Paris, Ky. Married at Cantonment, Arkansas Territory, in March, 1826. R 3/27.

Richard Rowland Cuney, M. D., of Alexandria, La., to Miss Millisent Fowler Coyle, of Lexington, Ky. Married April 10, 1826. R 4/17.

Col. James Madison Parker, of the Northern Neck of Virginia, to Miss Modoline Barbary Myers, of Lexington. Married April 13, 1826. R 4/17.

Dr. H. T. Lewis, of Hardinsburgh, Ky., to Miss Letitia Downing, daughter of Mr. F. Downing, of Lexington. Married April 24, 1826. R 5/1.

Dr. Ferdinand Flournoy, of Fayette county, to Miss Amanda Wall, daughter of Capt. Garrett Wall. Married in Scott county in April, 1826. R 5/1.

1826 AND MISCELLANEOUS

James Royle to Miss Martha Price. Married Feb. 13, 1821. LPA 2/14.

Thomas Hickey, formerly of Lexington, to Miss Susan Young, of Winchester. Married May 25, 1821. LPA 6/2.

Thomas M. Hickey, attorney, to Miss Paulina Keen, daughter of O. Keen. Married in Lexington May 31, 1821. LPA 6/2.

Jacob H. Holeman, editor of the *Commonwealth,* to Miss Mary Ann Wake, of Nicholasville. Married in May, 1821. LPA 6/9.

Joseph Appleton, to Miss Holly True, both of Lexington. They were married June 3, 1821. LPA 6/9.

Col. J. J. Monroe, brother of the President of the U. S., to Miss Huldah Hubbard, daughter of Rev. Hubbard. Married at Chariton, Mo., July 19, 1821. LPA 8/29.

George Rogers to Miss Jane Austin. Married in Scott county in April, 1826 R 5/1.

Major Rodes Thompson to Mrs. Mildred Leathers. Married in Scott county in April, 1826. R 5/1

John Roe, Jr., of Mason county, to Miss Louisa Everett, daughter of John D Everett, of Lewis county. Married April 14, 1826. R 5/1.

Barnard P. Gash, of Mason county, to Miss Ibbey Barr, of Lewis county

Married April 25, 1826. R 5/1.

John Keating to Mrs. Mary R. Wheelwright. M* in Cincinnati in April, 1826.

Dr. Benjamin Gray, of Tuscumbia, Ala., to Miss Mary Young, daughter of Ambrose Young. M in Fayette county, April 11, 1826. R 5/8.

Dr. Dorsey to Miss Jane Whittington. M in Flemingsburg, in May, 1826. R 5/15.

Robert Wash, one of the Judges of the Supreme Court, to Mrs. Berry, daughter of Major William Christy. M in St. Louis in April, 1826. R 5/15.

John Gordon to Miss Elizabeth Howe, daughter of Mr. E. Howe. M in Lexington May 11, 1826. R 5/22.

Lewis A. Thompson to Miss Margaret H. Ashton, daughter of Richard Ashton, all of Lexington. M May 18, 1826. R 5/22.

John Lagras to Miss Louisa Bridwell, both of Lexington. M May 5, 1826. R 5/22.

John Christian, a blind Almanac seller, to Nelly Palmer, aged 65 years. He was 75 years of age. They were m in the Fayette co. poor-house, May 25, 1826. A decent dinner was given by Mr. Thornton, the overseer. R 5/29.

William Frost, formerly of Boston, to Mrs. Elizabeth Wells. M in Frankfort May 21, 1826. R 5/29.

Oswald Kidd to Miss Sarah Hazelrigg. M in Clarke county in May, 1826 R 6/5.

Frances Talbot to Miss Eliza Donoho. M in Clarke county in May, 1826. R 6/5.

John W. Smith to Miss Nancy Vawter. M in Jessamine county in May, 1826. R 6/5.

Maslin Smith to Miss Mary A. R. Smith, both of Lexington. M June 1, 1826. R 6/12.

William Frazer to Miss Ann Overton, both of Lexington. M June 20, 1826. R 6/26.

Robert Nelson, merchant of Nicholasville, to Miss Jane Ann Lee, daughter of General Henry Lee, of Mason county. M June 20, 1826. R 7/3.

Dr. Anderson Campbell, of Madison county, to Miss Mary Jane LeGrand, of Lexington. M June 27, 1826. R 7/3.

Orville B. Martin, of Lexington, to Miss Sarah Ann Sneed, daughter of Achilles Sneed, dec'd., of Frankfort. M June 29, 1826. R 7/3.

Garnett Duncan, of Louisville, to Miss Patsey W. Martin, daughter of John L. Martin. M in Fayette county July 6, 1826. R 7/10.

Joseph Reynes to Miss Polixene Mazureau, both of New Orleans. M in July, 1826. R 7/17.

Jonathan Jenkins, aged 74 years, to Ann Hancock, aged 73 years, both of Garrard county. M Aug. 4, 1826. R 8/21.

Henry Clay, Jr., to Miss Elizabeth Scott. M in Bourbon county Aug. 4,

1826. R 8/21.

Silas Newland to Miss Emily Broaddus. M in Madison county in Aug., 1826. R 8/28.

John F. Crutchfield to Miss Sarah Jerman. M in Madison county in Aug., 1826. R 8/28.

Matthew Jenkins to Miss Elizabeth Hughes, late of Lexington, Ky. M at St. Augstine, July 17, 1826. R 8/28.

John Hawkins, of Bourbon county. He died in August, 1826. R 8/28.

Philip Byandywine Hockaday to Miss Maria, daughter of Samuel Hanson. M in Winchester Aug. 31, 1826. R 8/28.

Henry Eddy, editor of the *Illinois Gazette*, to Miss Mary Jane, daughter of John Marshall, all of Shawneetown. Married in August, 1826. R 9/11.

Achille Murat, formerly of Italy, eldest son of the late Majesty King Joachim, of Naples, to Mrs. Catherine Dangerfield Gray, lately of Fredericksburg, Va. She was a daughter of Major Byrd C. Willis. M at Tallahassee, Fla., in August, 1826. R 9/11.

Major Notly Flournoy, of Georgetown, to Miss Margaret G. Keen, of Lexington. M Sept. 12, 1826. R 9/18.

———— Price, of Nashville, to Miss E. Robinson, daughter of George Robinson, of Lexington, Ky. M Sept. 13, 1826. R 9/18.

Hugh I. Brent, merchant of Paris, to Miss Margaret Chambers, daughter of John Chambers, of Washington, Ky. M in September, 1826. R 9/18.

Garett Davis to Miss Rebecca, daughter of Judge Robert Trimble. M in Bourbon county in September, 1826. R 9/25.

William Sparks to Miss Eliza, daughter of David Barton. M in Bourbon county in Sept., 1826. R 9/25.

Joseph Collier, of Harrison county, to Miss Hannah Mountjoy. M in Bourbon county in Sept., 1826. R 9/25.

Benjamin Bell to Miss Lucinda Abbot. M in Bourbon county in Sept., 1826. R 9/25.

Matthew Harrison to Miss Eliza, daughter of Nicholas Grimes. M in Bourbon county in Sept., 1826. R 9/25.

Egbert Mallory to Miss Catherine Spawl. M in Paris in Sept., 1826. R 9/25.

W. H. Allen, of New Castle, to Miss Susan D. Owen. M in Shelby county in Sept., 1826. R 9/25.

W. F. Birch, editor of the Cynthiana *Advertiser,* to Harriett Ann Campbell. M in Mt. Sterling in Sept., 1826. R 9/25.

Rev. Joseph P. Cunningham, of Alabama, to Miss Elizabeth Frances, daughter of Capt. Isaac Webb, of Fayette county, Ky. M Sept. 27, 1826. R 10/2.

Francis Hord, of Mason county, to Miss Elizabeth, daughter of Kendall Moss. M in Fleming county in Oct., 1826. R 10/9.

Thomas Shanklin to Miss Mary Smith. M in Fleming county in October,

1826. R 10/9.

John W. Waggoner to Miss Entima Bivings, of Flemingsburg. M in Fleming county in Oct., 1826. R 10/9.

James Triplett to Miss Eleanor Triplett. M in Fleming county in October, 1826. R 10/9

Charles Bridges to Miss Jane, daughter of Henry Pickerell. M in Fleming county in Oct., 1826. R 10/9.

Thomas Yates, of Fleming county, to Miss Malinda Small. M in Mason county in Oct., 1826. R 10/9.

Jacob Planck, of Fleming county, to Miss Mary Rogers. M in Bath county in Sept., 1826. R 10/9.

John Milton, of Kentucky, to Miss Louisa T., daughter of Bushrod Taylor. M near Winchester, Va., in Sept., 1826. R 10/9.

William Rowan, of Nelson county to Miss Eliza, daughter of R. Boice. M in Mercer county in Sept., 1826. R 10/9.

John Polard, of Alabama, to Miss Nancy, daughter of Edward Hayden. M in Bardstown in Oct., 1826. R 10/9.

James Hewitt to Miss Clarissa Grant. M in Maysville in Oct., 1826 R 10/9.

Vachel Weldin to Miss Margaret Armstrong. M in Augusta in Sept., 1826. R 10/9.

William Respass to Miss Susan Corlis. M in Bourbon county in Oct., 1826. R 10/9.

Reason V. Sowards, of Georgetown, to Miss Alice Barnet. M in Harrison county in Sept., 1826. R 10/9.

Jesse M. Riely to Miss Mary, daughter of Capt. James Lampton. M in Winchester in Oct., 1826. R 10/9.

H. Pettitt, of Fayette county, to Miss Julia G., daughter of John Atchison. M in Warren county in Oct., 1826. R 10/16.

James P. Weems to Miss Martha Ann Andrews. M in Todd county in October, 1826. R 10/16,

Henry G. Slaughter, of Hopkinsville, Ky., to Miss Sarah E. Carter. M in Montgomery county, Tenn., in Sept., 1826. R 10/16.

William Pully to Miss Elizabeth, daughter of Joseph Jones. M in Madison county in Oct., 1826. R 10/16.

Abel G. Elkins, of Richmond, Ky., to Miss Elizabeth, daughter of William Hogan. M in Madison county in Oct., 1826. R 10/16.

Capt. Harvey T. Gorman to Miss Mahala Grimes. M in Bourbon county in Oct., 1826. R 10/16.

Mrs. Lucinda Newton, of Mercer county. She died in October, 1826, aged 63 years. R 10/16.

Mrs. Sarah Turner, of Madison county. She died in October, 1826, aged 58 years. R 10/16.

Robert Wickliffe to Mrs. Mary O. Russell, of Lexington. M Oct. 16, 1826. R 10/23.

Charles Humphries to Miss Elizabeth, daughter of Jonathan Rigg, of Fayette county. M Oct. 19, 1826. R 10/23.

Dr. Joseph A. Moore to Miss Eliza, daughter of Dr. John Watson, dec'd. M in Versailles in October, 1826. R 10/23/1826.

Dr. William L. Richards to Miss Elonora, daughter of Dr. Keen. M in Georgetown in October, 1826. R 10/23.

William S. Cleaveland to Miss Mary, daughter of Rev. James Elmore. M in Jessamine county in Oct., 1826. R 10/23.

William Bryson, of Greenup county, to Miss Susan Plummer, of Fleming county. M in Oct., 1826. R 10/30.

Edward Hinds, of Mo., to Mrs. Elizabeth Wilson, widow of Thomas Wilson. M in October, 1826. R 10/30.

Col. John Ewing to Miss Jennings, daughter of Col. Jennings. M in Christian county in Oct., 1826. R 10/30.

Samuel D. Lockwood to Mary Virginia Stith Nash, both of Illinois. M in Oct., 1826. R 10/30.

William Patton McKee to Miss Sarah Hillery West, both of Illinois. M in Oct., 1826. R 10/30.

Nicholas D. Coleman, of Cynthiana, to Miss Lucy A., daughter of Capt. Thomas Marshall, dec'd, of Washington. M in Mason county in Oct., 1826. R 10/30.

John Mitchell to Miss Ball. M in Maysville in Oct., 1826. R 10/30.

James Cochran to Miss Mary Eldridge. M in Bourbon county in Oct., 1826. R 10/30.

George Thomas, of Bourbon county, aged 70 years, to Miss P. Bartlett. M in Clarke county in Oct., 1826. R 10/30.

Wesley Broadwell to Miss Elizabeth Timberlake. M in Cynthiana in October, 1826. R 11/6.

Levi Prewitt to Miss Margaret Boyce. M in Fayette county in Nov., 1826. R 11/6.

Ebenezer Tingle to Miss Mary Wheeler. M in Fayette county in Nov., 1826. R 11/6.

Phenix Burns to Miss Ann, daughter of Capt. Newbold Crockett. M in Fayette county in Nov., 1826. R 11/6.

Joseph Logan to Miss Minerva Campbell, of Jessamine county. M in Lexington, at the Episcopal Church, Nov. 1, 1826. R 11/6.

Henry T. Duncan to Miss Eliza, daughter of Samuel Pike. M in Paris in Nov., 1826. R 11/6.

William C. Goodloe, of Richmond, to Miss Almira, daughter of Judge Owsley. M in Garrard county in Oct., 1826. R 11/6.

John J. Crittenden to Mrs. Maria R. Todd. M in Frankfort Nov. 13, 1826. R 11/20.

Rev. Simon N. Crane, late of New Jersey, to Miss Amanda Taylor. M in Lexington, Ky., in Nov., 1826. R 11/20.

W. H. Stockdell, of Georgetown, to Miss Rachel Kincaid. M in Madison county in Nov., 1826. R 11/20.

Thomas B. Hickman to Miss Elizabeth Shryock. M in Lexington in Nov., 1826. R 11/27.

Henry Innes Bodley to Miss Sarah Gist Bledsoe, daughter of Judge Bledsoe. M Nov. 22, 1826, in Lexington. R 11/27.

Edwin Upshaw Berryman, of Lexington, Ky., to Miss Maria M., daughter of John G. Coster. M in New York City in Nov., 1826. R 11/27.

W. M. Tompkins, of Versailles, to Miss Mary, daughter of Major James Blain, dec'd. M in Franklin county in Nov., 1826. R 11/27.

John Roche, Professor of Languages at Transylvania University, to Miss Sarah Ann Elizabeth Smith, daughter of John Smith, dec'd. M in Lexington Nov. 30, 1826. R 12/4.

Samuel Cochran to Miss Mary Bland. M in Maysville in Nov., 1826. R 12/4.

William Chancellor to Miss Nancy, daughter of Robert Glenn. M in Mason county in Nov., 1826. R 12/4.

William Hawkins, of Georgetown, to Miss Jane Butler. M at Port Williams in Nov., 1826. R 12/4.

Daniel McCarty Payne, of Lexington, to Miss Zelinda Ann, daughter of Capt. John Smith. M in Harrison county in Nov., 1826. R 12/4.

Robert P. Stout, of Meade county, to Miss Sally Maria Price, daughter of John Price. M in Fayette county Nov. 30, 1826. R 12/11.

Oliver Hukell to Miss Hetty Ball. M in Maysville in Dec., 1826. R 12/11.

John Gault to Miss Lavina, daughter of Peter Digman. M in Mason county in Nov., 1826. R 12/11.

Thomas H. Bradford, of Georgetown, to Sarah C., daughter of Col. William Steele, dec'd. M in Woodford county in Nov., 1826. R 12/11.

1827

Robert Hamilton to Miss Sarah, daughter of Alexandria Curry. M in Scott county in Nov., 1826. R 12/11.

Dr. Thomas B. Pinckard to Miss Catharine, daughter of Capt. Vance. M in Lawrenceburgh, Ind., in Nov., 1826. R 12/11.

Owen D. Winn to Miss Amanda Robinson. M in Lexington Dec. 7, 1826. R 12/18.

William Dickinson, of Lexington, to Miss Eleanor Murdock. M in Fayette county Dec. 12, 1826. R 12/18.

Noah C. Summers, of Shepherdsville, to Miss Margaret C., daughter of Mrs. Jane Harrison, of Jessamine county. M Dec. 21, 1826. R 12/25.

Thomas Tucker Whittlesey, of Salisbury, Conn., to Caroline, only daughter of L. Holley, dec'd., and sister of the President of Transylvania University (1826). M Nov. 29, 1826. R 1/6/1827.

George F. Barnes to Miss Elizabeth H. Dudley. M in Fleming county in Jan., 1827. R 1/13.

Wesley Knight, of Pickaway county, Ohio, to Miss Sarah, daughter of John Gallagher. M in Fleming county, Ky., in Jan., 1827. R 1/13.

Charles Triplett to Miss Clarissa Dawkins. M in Fleming county in Jan., 1827. R 1/13.

Reason Williams to Miss Jane, daughter of James Buchanon. M in Fleming county in Jan., 1827. R 1/13.

Joseph Belt Faris to Miss Betsy Ann, daughter of Major John Finley. M in Fleming county in Jan., 1827. R 1/13.

Andrew McClure, merchant of Lexington, to Miss Rachel, daughter of John Barton. M Jan. 24, 1826, in Fayette county. R 1/27.

Samuel Parish to Miss ———— Garrett. M in Hopkinsville in Jan., 1827. R 1/27.

B. Griffith, of Harrison county, to Miss Harriet, daughter of John King, of Bourbon county. M Jan. 30, 1827. R 2/7.

John Henderson Bell to Miss Elizabeth Ann, daughter of Major John McDowell, of Fayette county. M Jan. 24, 1827. R 2/7.

Capt. Fielding E. Dickey to Miss Elizabeth Breckinridge. M in Georgetown Feb. 8, 1827. R 2/14.

Y. Moore, Jr., to Miss Lucinda Rutherford. M in Fayette county March 1, 1827. R 3/3.

Thomas Haines to Miss Nancy Merrill. Married in Fayette county Feb. 21, 1827. R 3/3

Alfred Edmondson, of Scott county, to Kitty Ann Burton, of Fayette county. M Feb. 26, 1827. R 3/10.

Col. Alexander Tilford, of Scott county, to Mrs. Agnes Prewitt, of Mercer county. M Feb. 21, 1827. R 3/10.

James McKane to Miss Margaret Smith. M in Lexington on Apr. 18, 1827. R 4/25.

John Murphy, of Lexington to Miss Julia Fry. M in Clarke county Apr. 19, 1827. R 4/25.

Joseph N. McDowell, M. D., of Fayette county, to Miss Amanda V. Drake, of Cincinnati. M in latter place Mar. 27, 1827. R 4/25.

Henry Dulany to Miss Frances A. Carter, daughter of Landon Carter, dec'd., of Sabine Hall. M in Fredericksburgh, Va., in April, 1827. R 4/25.

Thomas H. Hubbard, of Madison county, to Miss Elizabeth W. Reid. M in Laurel county in Apr., 1827. R 4/25.

Col. John O'Fallon to Miss Caroline, daughter of Thomas O. Sheets, late of Baltimore. M in St. Louis in Mar., 1827. R 4/25.

George W. Washington, of Frankfort, to Miss Gabrilla A., daughter of Thomas W. Hawkins. M in Bourbon county in May, 1827. R 5/9.

George R. Smith to Miss Mileta, daughter of Gen. David Thomson. M in Scott county in May, 1827. R 5/9

David S. Chambers, of Louisville, to Miss Emily Postlethwaite, daughter of Capt. John Postlethwaite, of Lexington. M May 28, 1827. R 6/2.

Robert S. Russell, of Fayette county, to Miss Sarah, daughter of Col. T.

Ware, of Bourbon county. M May 29, 1827. R 6/6.

James Rucks to Miss Louisa V., daughter of Dr. Preston W. Brown, of Louisville. M at Nashville in May, 1827. R 6/6.

Rev. James Challen, of Cincinnati, to Miss Eliza Bradford, of St. Francisville. M June 9, 1827. R 6/9.

Edmund H. Hopkins to Miss Mary Ann Hamilton. M at Henderson May 29, 1827. R 6/9.

John Keizer, grocer of Lexington, to Miss Jane B. Fleming, of Fayette county. M June 14, 1827. R 6/16.

Major Maurice Langhorne, of Maysville, to Mrs. P. Brooks. M June 14, 1827. R 6/16.

Alfred Shelby, of Lincoln county, to Miss Virginia H. Hart, daughter of Nathaniel Hart, of Woodford county. M June 14, 1827. R 6/16.

Tobias Gibson, of Miss., to Miss Louisiana B. Hart, daughter of Nathaniel Hart, of Woodford county. M June 14, 1827. R 6/16.

James Paton to Miss Catharine Trundell, both of Paris. M June 1, 1827. R 7/11.

Dr. Aylett Hawes, of Ky., to Miss Mary, daughter of Walker Hawes, of King William county, Va. M in July, 1827. R 7/23.

Thomas Bell, of Cincinnati, to Miss Joanna M., eldest daughter of Joseph C. Homblower, of Newark, N. J. M in July, 1827. R 7/25.

James Millar to Miss Mary Reed. M Aug. 4, 1827. R 8/18.

M. V. Harrison, clerk of the Montgomery Circuit Court, to Miss Dulcinea M. Bledsoe, daughter of Rev. Moses Bledsoe, dec'd. M near Mt. Sterling Aug. 21, 1827. R 8/29.

William Watson to Mrs. Elizabeth Cobb, both of Lexington. M Aug. 30, 1827. R 9/1.

James K. Marshall, of Mason county, to Miss Catharine C. Hickman, daughter of J. L. Hickman. M in Bourbon county in Sept., 1827. R 9/19.

Thomàs Kirkpatrick to Miss Elizabeth Miller. M in Bourbon county in Sept., 1827. R 9/19.

——————— Loofborough to Miss ——————— Haggin, daughter of James Haggin. M in Woodford county in Sept., 1827. R 9/19.

Dr. A. W. Scales, of Virginia, to Miss Eleanor C. Coyle, of Lexington. M Oct. 7, 1827. R 10/10.

Peter Camper to Miss Rebecca Crosthwait. M in Bourbon county in Oct., 1827. R 10/10.

Charles Lander to Mrs. Elizabeth Irvine. M in Paris in Oct., 1827. R 10/10.

Isaac Stephens to Miss Berthena Stephens. M in Paris in October, 1827. R 10/10.

Preston H. Griffing to Miss Paulena Ashurst. M in Paris in Oct., 1827. R 10/10.

John Allen Gano, of Georgetown, Ky., to Miss Catharine Conn, daughter of William Conn. M in Paris in Oct., 1827. R 10/10.

Andrew Mitchell, of Maysville, to Miss Lavenia Digman. M in Mason county in Oct., 1827. R 10/10.

Rev. S. E. Blackburn to Miss Sarah Glass, daughter of Dr. Glass. M in Louisville in Oct., 1827. R 10/10.

Aaron K. Wooley, of Miss., to Miss Sally Howard Wickliffe, eldest daughter of Robert Wickliffe, of Lexington. M latter place Oct. 9, 1827. R 10/12.

Thomas Woods, of Bourbon county, to Miss Lucretia Fry, daughter of the Widow Fry, of Fayette county. M Oct. 11, 1827. R 10/13.

Benjamin Finnell, of Georgetown, to Miss Margaret Sutfin, daughter of Low Sutfin. M in Scott county, in Oct., 1827. R 10/24.

William Woods to Miss Sarah Parrish, daughter of Capt. James Parrish. M in Woodford county in Oct., 1827. R 10/24.

William Swift, of Lexington, to Miss Virja Vimont. M in Millersburg in Oct., 1827. R 10/24.

Jesse Bunnell to Miss Spicey May. M in Lexington in Oct., 1827. R 10/27.

Augustus G. Herndon to Miss Eliza G. Herndon. M in Bourbon county Oct. 25, 1827. R 10/27.

James Henry Wallace to Miss Eliza Bosworth, both of Fayette county. M Nov. 1, 1827. R 11/3.

John Thompson to Miss Sarah Taylor. M in Lexington Nov. 8, 1827. R 11/10.

George Starkey to Miss Eleanor E. Ferguson, daughter of Dr. Ferguson. M in Louisville in Nov., 1827. R 11/10.

Rev. Charles Clinton Beatty, of Steubenville, to Miss Hetty Elizabeth Davis. M in Maysville in Nov., 1827. R 11/28.

John Hutchings, of Paris, Ky., to Miss Eliza Holtzman. M in Georgetown. D. C., in Oct., 1827. R 12/8.

Watson Sinclair to Miss Eliza Morrison, both of Lexington. M Dec. 12, 1827. R 12/15.

Dr. Robert Holland, of Russellville, Ala., to Miss Margaret Trotter, daughter of Samuel Trotter, of Lexington, Ky. M Dec. 11, 1827. R 12/15.

A. G. Meriwether, editor of the *Kentucky Gazette*, to Miss Eliza Jane Sharp. M in Fayette county Dec. 11, 1827. R 12/15.

Robert McMurtry to Miss Betsey Ann Netherland. M in Nicholasville Nov. 27, 1827. R 12/15.

William W. Fleming to Miss Sophia Robinson, both of Fayette county. M Dec. 19, 1827. R 12/22.

Thomas Peyton, of Georgetown, to Miss Rebecca Keatey, of Lexington. M Dec. 24, 1827. R 12/29.

Thomas Gibbons to Mrs. Matilda Smithers. M in Lexington Dec. 25, 1827.

R 12/29.

Horatio F. Blanchard to Miss Sarah Gill. M in Louisville Dec. 5, 1827. R 12/29.

1828

Sydney P. Clay, of Bourbon county, Ky., to Miss Isabella Eliza Jane Reed, late of Danville, Ky. M in Nashville in Dec. 1827. R 1/5/1828.

Dr. John F. Henry, of Hopkinsville, to Miss Lucy E. S. Ridgely. M in Lexington in Jan., 1828. R 1/5.

——————— White, of Middletown, Jefferson county, to Miss ——————— Bridwell. M in Lexington in Jan., 1828. R 1/5.

George W. Morton to Miss Elizabeth Scott. M in Lexington in Jan., 1828. R 1/5.

John Bates to Miss Nancy Adams, both of Fayette county. M Feb. 6, 1828. R 2/13.

Capt. Francis G. West to Miss Nancy Williams, both of Lexington. M Feb. 1, 1828. R 2/13.

Harrison Lock to Miss Rebecca Mosby, both of Fayette county. M. Feb. 14, 1828. R 2/20.

George Washington Sutton, of Fayette county, to Miss Laura C. Grosvenor, of Lexington. M Feb. 13, 1828. R 2/20.

Thomas B. Johnson to Miss Harriet, daughter of James Patterson, all of Fayette county. M Feb. 11, 1828. R 2/20.

Major A. McClintick, of Carlisle, Nicholas county, to Miss Mary Ann E. Freeland, daughter of James Freeland, of Fayette county. M Feb. 28, 1828. R 3/5.

Gabriel Martin to Miss Elizabeth Kenney, both of Fayette county. M Mar. 16, 1828. R 3/19.

Dr. Henry Morehead, late of Bowling Green, to Mrs. Ann Stuart, of Jessamine county. M Feb. 28, 1828. R 3/19.

Western Berkley Thomas, formerly of Frankfort, Ky., to Miss Emeline Few Howard, daughter of John Howard. M in Augusta, Ga., in Mar., 1828. R 4/9.

Dr. Azra Offut, of Jessamine county, to Miss Antoinette Caroline Hale, daughter of the late Smith Hale, of Woodford county. M in Apr., 1828. R 4/16.

Dr. James Johnson, of Louisville, to Miss Sophia Zane, daughter of Noah Zane. M at Wheeling in Apr., 1828. R 4/23.

N. S. Thomas, to Miss Mary C. Bedford. M in Bourbon county in May, 1828. R 5/7.

Isaac Clinkenbeard to Miss Ivea Allen. M in Bourbon county in May, 1828. R 5/7.

Hon. Joseph Duncan, of Illinois, to Miss Elizabeth Caldwell Smith, of New York City. M at Washington City in May, 1828. R 5/28.

Thomas H. Waters, of Washington county, to Miss Caroline Virginia Higgins, of Lexington. M latter place May 28, 1828. R 6/4.

Samuel P. Devore to Miss Mary E. Johnson, both of Fayette county. M June 5, 1828. R 6/11.

Hugh McDaniel to Miss Sarah Robinson, both of Fayette county. M June 9, 1828. R 6/11.

John H. Robb to Miss Nancy S. Smith, both of Lexington. M June 24, 1828. R 6/25.

Thomas H. Bartlett, of New Castle, Henry county, to Miss Lucy Frazer, of Lexington. M latter place July 15, 1828. R 7/16.

James W. McCann to Miss Amanda F. Downing, daughter of John Downing, all of Nicholasville. M Aug. 17, 1828. R 8/27.

Daniel Virden to Miss Caroline Barnet, both of Lexington. M Sept. 13, 1828. R 9/17.

Samuel G. Henry to Miss Mary Haden, both of Versailles. M in Cincinnati, Ohio, in Sept., 1828. R 9/17.

John S. Van de Graff, of Scott county, to Miss Mary H. Simpson, of Fayette county. M Oct. 2, 1828. R 10/15.

Dr. J. B. Duke, of Paris, to Miss Caroline A. Thomas. M at Frankfort in Sept., 1828. R 10/15.

Samuel D. Walker, of New Orleans, to Miss Ann Eliza Campbell, daughter of John R. Campbell, of Shelby county, Ky. M Oct. 14, 1828. R 10/22.

Samuel Hicks, of Spotsylvania county, Va., to Miss Maria, daughter of William Pollard, of Jessamine county, Ky. M Oct. 9, 1828. R 10/22.

Major Isaac L. Baker, of La., to Miss Margaret H. Crozier. M in Miss., in Oct., 1828. R 10/29.

Matthew Hume, of Bourbon county, to Miss Maria, daughter of Robert Cunningham, of Clarke county. M Nov. 6, 1828. R 11/12.

Dr. Owen C. Blount, of La., to Miss Maria N. Stedman, of Lexington, Ky. M Nov. 6, 1828. R 11/12.

Thomas Witherspoon, of Ala., to Mrs. Sarah W. Lapsley. M in Paris, Ky., in Nov., 1828. R 11/12.

James L. Peek to Miss Mary Francis. M in Jessamine county, Nov. 4, 1828. R 11/12.

Charles Henry Talbott, formerly of Jessamine county, now of Garrard county, to Miss Elizabeth Owsley, daughter of Judge Owsley. M Nov. 6, 1828. R 11/19.

Dr. James P. Parker to Miss Mary Millikin, daughter of Major John Millikin. M at Burlington, Oct. 23, 1828. R 11/19.

Samuel Rankin, of Maysville, to Miss Nancy M., daughter of the Rev. William H. Rainey. M Nov. 18, 1828. R 11/26.

John Brand, Jr., of Lexington, to Miss Priscilla W. Downing, of Fayette county. M Nov. 19, 1828. R 11/26.

Pierce B. Anderson, of East Tennessee, to Miss Ann M. Luke. M in Mason county in November, 1828. R 11/26.

W. G. Bakewell to Miss Alicia A. Matthews. M in Louisville in November,

1828.   R 11/26.

Ashton Garrett to Miss Mary M. Spangler.   M in Lexington in Nov., 1828.
R 11/26.

Lieut. A. Drane, of the U. S. Army, to Miss Elizabeth Rebecca, daughter of
Dr. Ferguson.   M in Louisville in Nov., 1828.   R 12/3.

Capt. Thomas P. Hart, to Miss Sarah D. Postlethwaite, daughter of Capt.
John Postlethwaite.   M in Lexington Dec. 9, 1828.   R 12/17.

Isaac T. Preston to Miss Catharine, daughter of Robert Layton.   M in New
Orleans in Dec., 1828.   R 12/17.

Rev. Samuel Steele to Miss Ann Jane Russell.   M in Clarke county in
Dec., 1828.   R 12/17.

John N. Smith to Miss Jane Oden.   M in Paris in Dec., 1828.   R. 12/17.

Madison B. Johnson, of Lexington, to Mrs. Sally Ann Irvine.   M in Madison
county, at the residence of the late Gen. Green Clay, in Dec., 1828.   R 12/31.

1829

Dr. Lemuel Sanders to Miss Sarah, daughter of H. M. Winslow.   M in Lexington in Jan., 1829.   R 1/21.

Capt. Samuel Davis McCullough, of Lexington, to Miss Christiana Wallace.
M in Columbia, Tenn., in Jan., 1829.   R 1/21.

James Hutchcraft to Miss Eliza Ann, daughter of Gen. S. M. Williams.
M in Montgomery county in Jan., 1829.   R 1/21.

Matthew Culbert to Miss Prudence F. Lilly.   M in Paris in Jan., 1829.
R 1/21.

Julius C. Bristow to Miss Mary Pew.   M in Bourbon county in Jan., 1829.
R 1/21.

William V. Loving to Miss Amanda, daughter of Alexander Graham.   M in
Bowling Green in Jan., 1829.   R 1/21.

Preston Hay, of Nashville, to Miss Sarah Work.   M in Warren county in
Jan., 1829.   R 1/21.

Charles D. Morehead to Miss Eliza Loving.   M in Warren county in Jan.,
1829.   R 1/21.

Sanderson Robert, merchant of Philadelphia, formerly of Lexington, Ky.,
to Miss Sarah, eldest daughter of Abraham Barker, of Philadelphia.   M in Jan.,
1829.   R 1/28.

Leonard Coffman, Jr., to Miss Nancy, daughter of Asa Wilgus.   M in Logan
county in Jan., 1829.   R 1/28.

Samuel Wilson, of Versailles, to Miss Jane, youngest daughter of the late
Col. William Steele.   M in Woodford county Jan. 21, 1829.   R 1/28.

James Heathman to Miss Elizabeth Hailey, both of Fayette county.   M Jan.
22, 1829.   R 2/4.

Lieut. Albert S. Johnston, of the U. S. Infantry, to Miss Henrietta, daughter
of the late Major William T. Preston.   M in Louisville in Jan. 20, 1829.   R 2/11.

Daniel D. Jones, editor of the *Bardstown Herald*, to Miss Nancy M., daughter of Gen. Simpson. M in Bardstown in Feb., 1829. R 2/11.

Hon. Samuel Houston, Governor of Tennessee, to Miss Eliza Allen, daughter of John Allen. M in Summer county, Tenn., in Jan., 1829. R 2/11.

Franklin D. Pettitt to Miss Elizabeth Zook. M in Frankfort in Feb., 1829. R 2/11.

Thomas L. Moore, of Fayette county, to Miss Mary Ann A. Higgins, of Bourbon county. M Jan. 29, 1829. R 2/11.

William Henderson to Miss Nancy Steward, daughter of William Steward, of Cynthiana. M Feb. 3, 1829. R 4/18.

William Lynn to Miss Malinda Keizer. M in Fayette county Feb. 12, 1829. R 2/18.

Robert C. Harrison, Jr., to Miss Theodosia Tompkins, daughter of G. R. Tompkins. M Feb. 19, 1829. R 2/25.

Richard Shackelford to Miss Celia Hubbard, daughter of Major George Hubbard. M in Madison county in Feb., 1829. R 3/4.

Benjamin Tevis to Miss Mary Ann Lanham, daughter of William Lanham M in Madison county in Feb., 1829. R 3/4.

Hon. James Clark, Representative in Congress from this (Fayette county, Ky.) District, to Mrs. Margaret E. Thornton, daughter of A. Buckner, of Virginia. M in Washington City Mar. 3, 1829. R 3/18.

John W. Cook, of Springfield, to Miss Elizabeth T. Pope, daughter of John Pope. M in Frankfort in Mar., 1829. R 3/18.

William E. Lightfoot, of Jefferson county, to Miss Amelia Eldridge, of Bourbon county. M. Mar. 10, 1829. R 3/18.

Joseph G. Norwood, printer, to Miss Louisa Taylor. M in Lexington Mar. 12, 1829. R 3/18.

James I. Lemmon to Miss Fayette Taylor. M in Lexington, Mar. 12, 1829. R 3/18.

George W. Brown to Miss Elizabeth, daughter of Elijah Cartmell. M in Fayette county Mar. 29, 1829. R 4/8.

Thomas Hemingway to Miss Jane Hilton, of Lexington. M Apr. 9, 1829 R 4/15.

Joseph Masterson to Miss Sarah Webster, both of Fayette county. M Apr. 7, 1829. R 4/15.

Benjamin Webster to Miss Ruth Webster. M Apr. 18, 1829. R 4/22.

George Bealer to Miss Nancy Fitzgerald, of Fayette county. M Apr. 14, 1829. R 4/22.

Nelson Prewitt to Miss Ann Mary Coleman, both of Fayette county. M Apr. 16, 1829. R 4/22

Worden P. Churchill to Miss Mary J. Prather. M at Louisville in Apr., 1829. R 5/6

William F. Bullock, of Louisville, to Miss Sophia, daughter of Hon. John P. Oldham. M in Jefferson county in May, 1829. R 5/13.

Hon. Pryor Lea to Miss Minerva Ann Hearb. M in Tenn., in May, 1829. R 5/27.

Albert Hickman to Miss Harriet Grimes. M May 22, 1829. R 5/27.

———— Harney to Miss Eliza Keizer. M in Fayette county May 19, 1829. R 5/27.

Ignatius T. Cavins, printer, to Miss Sarah O. Caudry. M in Lexington Tuesday, May 19, 1829. R 5/27.

Hon. Henry Pirtle to Miss Jane Ann, eldest daughter of Fr. Rogers. M in Louisville in May, 1829. R 5/27.

George W. Weisinger, of Tuscumbia, Ala., to Miss Amanthus Bullitt, daughter of Cuthbert Bullitt, dec'd. M in Louisville, Ky., in May, 1829. R 5/27.

Samuel S. Nicholas, to Miss Matilda Prather, daughter of Thomas Prather, dec'd. M in Louisville in May, 1829. R 5/27.

Hardin N. Riley, of Clarke county, Ky., to Miss Fanny Tate. M in Batavia, Ohio, in May, 1829. R 6/3.

C. W. Hall to Miss Caroline Myers. M in East Tenn., in May, 1829. R 6/3.

Goodrich E. Lightfoot, of Jefferson county, to Miss Jane, daughter of John G. Martin, of Bourbon county. M June 4, 1829. R 6/17.

David Cline to Miss Louisa Speaks, both of Bourbon county. M June 7, 1829. R 6/17.

Ormsby Hite to Miss Amelia P. Matthews. M in Louisville in June, 1829. R 6/17.

Hon. George McDuffie to Miss Mary Rebecca Singleton, daughter of Richard Singleton, of Sumter District, N. C. M May 27, 1829. R 6/24.

Capt. Thomas A. Russell, of Fayette county, to Miss Sarah L., daughter of Gen. James Garrard, of Bourbon county. M June 17, 1829. R 6/24.

David Murray to Miss Eliza Zimmerman, both of Lexington. M June 21, 1829. R 6/24.

John McChord to Miss Polly Peacocke, both of Fayette county. M June 29, 1829. R 7/1.

Rev. Samuel Y. Garrison to Miss Ann Poage, daughter of Gen. Robert Poage. M in Mason county in June, 1829. R 7/8.

James C. Slaughter to Miss Amanda P. Morton, daughter of William J. Morton. M in Russellville in June, 1829. R 7/8.

Merryman Bradshaw to Miss Eliza Price. M in Jessamine county June 30, 1829. R 7/8

William A. Leavy to Miss Mary Ann, second daughter of Samuel Trotter, all of Lexington. M July 2, 1829. R 7/8.

John Coburn to Miss Ann Chambers, both of Maysville. M June, 1829. R 7/8.

Dr. J. Charleton Beatty to Miss Charlotte Reid, daughter of Walker Reid, of Washington. M in Mason county in June, 1829. R 7/8.

Hartwell Boswell, of Arkansas Territory, to Mrs. Frances Ann Drake, widow of Capt. Robt. M. Desha, of the U. S. Marine Corps. M at residence of the late

Governor Desha, July 1, 1829. R 7/8.

Gideon Shryock to Miss Elizabeth Bacon. M at Frankfort, in July, 1829. R 7/15.

William Fellowes, of Louisville, to Miss Caroline Davis. M at Roxbury, Mass., in July, 1829. R 7/15.

John Sampson to Miss Sarah Moore. M in Lexington July 20, 1829. R 7/22.

John R. Clary to Miss Mary Ann Connell. M in Lexington on Thursday, July 18, 1829. R 7/22.

Harrison Currens, aged 15 years, to Miss Eliza Plough, aged 11 years, 11 months and 11 days. M in Mercer county in July, 1829. R 7/22.

Rev. James G. Barnett to Miss Elizabeth H. Usher. M in Christian county in July, 1829. R 7/29.

Thomas Jefferson Brown to Miss Mary Jane Wallace. M in Jessamine county in July, 1829. R 7/29.

George Harrison to Miss Pamelia Curtis. M in Winchester in July, 1829. R 7/29.

John D. Gosset to Miss Cynthia Corn. M in Clarke county in July, 1829. R 7/29.

Joseph Jones, Sr., to Miss Mary Schooler. M in Clarke county in July, 1829. R 7/29.

Charles Chowning, of Nicholasville, to Miss Nancy Patterson, of Fayette county. M July 23, 1829. R 7/29.

Capt. William P. Hume, of Bourbon county, to Miss Matilda, daughter of George Rennick, of Clarke county. M July 14, 1829. R 7/29.

Wesley Hill to Miss Elizabeth Keplinger, both of Bourbon county. M July 23, 1829. R 8/5.

Thomas Blackwell, of Madison county, to Miss Sarah Ann Robinson, of Fayette county. M July 30, 1829. R 8/5.

Thomas Hope to Miss Sarah S. Buford, daughter of Simon Buford. M in Shelby county in Aug., 1829. R 8/12.

James C. Todd to Miss Maria W. Blair, both of Fayette county. M Aug. 6, 1829. R 8/12.

John Hutchison to Miss Alley Parker, both of Fayette county. M Aug. 13, 1829. R 8/19.

John G. Talbot, of Jessamine county, to Miss Elizabeth Smith, daughter of Edmund Smith. M in Garrard county Aug. 11, 1829. R 8/19.

Woodson H. Gentry, editor of the *Winchester Republican,* to Miss Mary-Ann Winn. M in Clarke county in Sept., 1829. R 9/16.

George C. Winn to Miss Frances Jones. M in Madison county in Sept., 1829. R 9/16.

Solomon Park to Miss Eliza Jerman. M in Madison county in Sept., 1829. R 9/16.

Joseph Johnson to Miss Sally Mills. M in Madison county in Sept., 1829.

R 9/16.

A. H. Curry to Miss Amanda Hall. M in Russellville in Sept., 1829. R 9/16.

Dr. Robert O'Brien, of New Castle, to Miss Adaline K. Young, daughter of James L. Young. M in Oldham county in Sept., 1829. R 9/16.

James W. Simpson, of Mo., to Miss Sarah Taylor, daughter of the Rev. P. W. Taylor. M in Spencer county in Aug., 1829. R 9/16.

Calvin Webb to Miss Susan Bibb. M in Greensburg, Ky., in Sept., 1829. R 9/16.

William Triplett, merchant of Mayslick, to Miss Mary Ann Hodge. M in Maysville in Sept., 1829. R 9/16.

George Timberlake, of Harrodsburg, to Miss Emeline Reed, of Lexington. M Sept. 17, 1829. R 9/23

Victor M. Flournoy to Miss Elizabeth J. Johnson, daughter of John T. Johnson. M in Scott county in Sept., 1829. R 9/23.

John Bell to Miss Marian Young. M in Fayette county in Sept., 1829. R 9/30.

John A. Holderby to Miss Sarah Ann Hardin, daughter of Gen. William Hardin. M in Frankfort in Sept., 1829. R 9/30.

Silas King to Miss Jane Breckinridge. M in Sept., 1829. R 9/30.

George W. Gwin, of Louisville, to Miss Catharine Graham, daughter of George Graham. M in Sept., 1829. R 9/30.

James H. Allen to Miss Sarah McDowell, daughter of Major John McDowell, all of Fayette county. M Oct. 13, 1829. R 10/14.

Henry Bedford to Miss Lucy C. Ware, daughter of Col. Thompson Ware, of Bourbon county. M in Oct., 1829. R 10/14.

W. Green Clay to Miss P. P. Bedford, both of Bourbon county. M Oct. 8, 1829. R 10/14.

Obadiah Calvert to Miss Elizabeth Lindsay, daughter of Anthony Lindsay. M in Scott county in Oct., 1829. R 10/14.

William Goss to Miss Mary Hervey. M in Fayette county Oct. 8, 1829. R 10/14.

Elijah H. Drake, of Lexington, to Miss Emerine Thompson, daughter of Clifton Thomson, of Fayette county. M Oct. 7, 1829. R 10/21.

Samuel A. Atchison, editor of the *Bowling Green Advertiser,* to Miss Octavia Morehead. M in Warren county in Oct., 1829. R 10/21.

James B. Marshall, of Frankfort, to Miss Mary Ann S. Moore, daughter of Capt. Hugh Moore. M in Cincinnati in Oct., 1829. R 10/21.

Capt. A. S. Lewis, of the U. S. Army, to Miss Mary A. Mayo, daughter of Daniel Mayo. M in New Port, Ky., in Oct., 1829. R 10/21.

Hon. Crittenden Lyon to Mrs. Fanny Jones. M in Eddyville in Oct., 1829. R 10/28.

Robert Fleming, of Lexington, to Miss Jane Wilson, of Bourbon county. M Oct. 22, 1829. R 10/28.

Matthew Harrison to Miss Susan T. Mason, of Bourbon county. M Oct. 20, 1829. R 11/4.

Winslow Tolle to Miss Elizabeth Bradley, of Fayette county. M Oct. 20, 1829. R 11/4.

Rev. John C. Young, pastor of the Second Presbyterian Church of Lexington, to Miss Frances A., eldest daughter of the late J. Cabell Breckinridge. M Tuesday evening, Nov. 3, 1829, at Cabelldale. R 11/11.

Augusta W. Pinkard to Miss Margaret, daughter of E. Yeiser. M in Lexington, Oct. 27, 1829. R 11/11.

Simpson Gorham to Miss Letitia Boyd. M in Fayette county in Nov., 1829. R 11/11.

Henry H. Ferguson, of Jessamine county, to Miss Margaret K. Hurst. M in Woodford county Nov. 5, 1829. R 11/11.

Samuel Smith, of Carlisle, to Miss Serena, daughter of Samuel Hanson, of Winchester. M in Nov., 1829. R 11/11.

Orville Shelby, of Tenn., to Miss Ann Maria Boswell, eldest daughter of Dr. Jos. Boswell. M in Lexington, Nov. 12, 1829. R 11/18.

Rev. Zebulon Butler, of Miss., to Miss Mary Ann Murdock, daughter of the late John Murdock, of Cane Mount, Miss. M Nov. 11, 1829. R 11/18.

Scott Brown, of Frankfort, to Miss Celinda Henry, daughter of the late Zachariah Henry. M in Woodford county in Nov., 1829. R 11/18.

Richard H. Southgate, of Newport, Ky., to Miss Julia F. Sneed, daughter of the late Achilles Sneed. M in Frankfort in Nov., 1829. R 11/18.

John D. McClure to Miss Agnes H. Todd, daughter of George Todd. M in Frankfort in Nov., 1829. R 11/18.

Dr. Alexander Marshall, of Woodford county, to Miss Eliza Gillespie, of Danville. M in Nov., 1829. R 11/18.

Abraham Jonas, of Grant county, to Miss Louisa Block, daughter of Simon Block, late of Mo. M in Cincinnati in Nov., 1829. R 11/18.

Hon. John McLean, Senator in Congress from Illinois, to Miss Eliza M. Bayless. M in Union county, Ky., in Nov., 1829. R 11/18.

John E. Cromwell to Miss Harriett Ford. M in Fayette county Nov. 20, 1829. R 11/25.

William Ford to Miss Sarah Loudon, both of Fayette county. M Nov. 19, 1829. R 11/25.

Joseph H. Bledsoe, to Miss Mary Jane Baylor, of Bourbon county, daughter of the late G. W. Baylor M Nov. 18, 1829. R 11/25.

Robert T. Smith to Miss Ann, daughter of Jacob Sidnor, of Fayette county. M Nov. 19, 1829. R 11/25

Bryan Barbee to Miss Elizabeth Fisher, daughter of S. Fisher. M in Lincoln county in Nov., 1829. R 11/25.

James Spencer to Miss Elizabeth Chevis. M in Clarke county Nov. 10, 1829. R 11/25.

Solomon Buzzard to Mrs. Nancy Walker, both of Lexington. M Sunday Dec. 7, 1829. R 12/9.

John H. Pleasants, editor of the *Richmond* (Va.) *Whig*, to Miss Mary L. Massie, daughter of Henry Massie, of Alleghany county, Va. M at Falling Spring in above county Dec. 15, 1829. R 1/13/1830.

1830

William P. Curd, of Jessamine county, to Miss Mary A. Megowan, daughter of David Megowan, of Lexington. M Jan. 14, 1830. R 1/20.

Nathaniel Offutt, of Scott county, to Miss Mary Ann, daughter of Nathan Payne, of Fayette county. M Jan. 12, 1830. R 1/20.

Abraham Smith, of Fayette county, to Miss Mary E. B., daughter of Osborn Hendley, of Lexington. M Jan. 17, 1830. R 1/20.

Preston M. Brown, of Fayette county, to Miss Eliza Jane, daughter of William Geers, of Lexington. M Jan. 21, 1830. R 2/3.

Cornelius Coghlan to Miss Lavinia Fouke, both of the town of Illinois. M Jan. 11, 1830. R 2/3.

William G. Johnson to Miss Eliza Jane, daughter of Jacob Cassel, all of Lexington. M Feb. 4, 1830. R 2/10.

William W. Happy to Miss Mary Jane Graves, both of Lexington. M Feb. 3, 1830. R 2/10.

Richard Graves to Miss Catharine, daughter of Thomas Francis. M in Jessamine county Jan. 28, 1830. R 2/10.

Rev. John P. Trotter to Miss Pamela Brashear, of Mercer county. M in Franklin county Feb. 10, 1830. A 2/17.

John P. Cammack, of Frankfort, to Miss Nancy C. Sharp, of Lexington. M Jan. 23, 1830. A. 3/3.

Daniel Hockersmith, of Franklin county, to Miss Eliza Cummins, daughter of John Cummins, of Anderson county. M Feb. 4, 1830. A 3/10.

Joel Tilly, of Shelby county, to Miss Mary Cummins, daughter of John Cummins, of Anderson county. M Feb. 4, 1830. A 3/10.

James Weir, Jr., of Woodford county, to Miss Frances Jane Berry, of Fayette county. M Apr. 1, 1830. R 4/14.

William B. Shanks, of Bowling Green, to Miss Ann Eliza Lawton. M in Barren county in May, 1830. R 6/2.

Rev. Richard Fryer to Miss Elizabeth Curtis. M in Warren county in May, 1830. R 6/2.

Hamilton Atchison, Sr., aged about 65 years, to Miss Kitty Harrison, aged about 55 years, both of Fayette county. M May 23, 1830. R 6/2.

Jonathan D. Hager to Miss Sarah Springle, both of Lexington M. June 17, 1830. R 6/23.

George Boswell, of Lexington, to Miss Mary R. Berryman, of Fayette county. M June 20, 1830. R 6/23.

Archibald C. Bedford, of Bourbon county, to Miss Susan Byrns, daughter of the late Mr. Byrns, of Fayette county. M July 1, 1830. R 7/7.

Samuel P. Weisiger, of Frankfort, to Miss Jane Stokes. M at Carlisle in July, 1830. R 7/14.

John H. Randolph to Miss Nancy T. Moore. M in Fayette county in July, 1830. R 7/14.

Peter Gordon Hunt to Miss Mary Ann, daughter of Waller Bullock, both of Fayette county. M July 7, 1830. R 7/14.

James O. Harrison to Miss Margaretta Ross. M July 27, 1830. R 7/28.

Bushrod Jenkins, of Fayette county, to Miss Elizabeth Maria, daughter of Lewis Grigsby, all of Clarke county. M July 21, 1830. R 7/28.

Joseph Rush to Miss Elizabeth Jane Gardiner. M July 22, 1830. R 7/28.

Dr. Robert C. Palmer, of Springfield, to Miss Emily Hardin, daughter of Benjamin Hardin. M at Bardstown in July, 1830. R 7/28.

John Stettinius, of Washington, D. C., to Miss Mary, eldest daughter of Nicholas Longworth, of Cincinnati. M Tuesday July 20, 1830. R 7/28.

Leaven Bramble to Miss Mary Dobyns. M in Fleming county in Aug., 1830. R 8/18.

Robert R. Rose to Miss Mary Williams. M in Fleming county in Aug., 1830. R 8/18.

Angus L. Donovan to Miss Mary Beall. M in Maysville in Aug., 1830. R 8/18.

John L. Helm, of Elizabethtown, to Miss Lucinda B. Hardin, daughter of Benjamin Hardin. M at Bardstown in Aug., 1830. R 8/18.

Samuel Williams, of Paris, to Miss Benedicta Holloway. M in Bourbon county in Aug., 1830. R 8/18.

Alexander Mitchell to Miss Eveline Trundell, of Paris. M in Bourbon county in Aug., 1830. R 8/18.

John Kemper, of Garrard county, to Miss Frances Ann Doggett, of Mercer county. M Aug. 11, 1830. R 8/25.

Gen. E. W. Ripley to Mrs. Aurelia Davis. M at St. Francisville, La., in Aug., 1830. R 8/25.

James Parrish to Miss Margaret Shipp. M in Woodford county in Aug., 1830. R 9/8.

Absolom Faulconer, of Harrison county, to Miss Clarissa Perkins, daughter of Reuben Perkins, of Fayette county. M Aug. 26, 1830. R 9/8.

William M. Lee, of Lincoln county, to Miss Eliza Ann Jenkins, of Fayette county. M Sept. 2, 1830. R 9/8.

Capt. William Bryan to Miss Susan Gano Innes, daughter of the late Col. James Innes, all of Fayette county. M Sept. 8, 1830. R 9/15.

William Flatford, a soldier of the Revolution, aged 85 years, to Miss Chloe Allen, aged 45. M Sept. 5, 1830, at Summerfield, Prince William county, Va. "Another Revolutionary Soldier gone." R 9/15.

W. P. Bain to Miss Elizabeth Harrison, daughter of Dr. Burr Harrison, of Bardstown. M in Sept., 1830. R 9/29.

Charles Hayden to Miss Matilda R. Smith. M at Bardstown in Sept., 1830.

R 9/29.

Charles M. Cunningham, to Miss H. M. Magoffin, daughter of Beriah Magoffin. M in Harrodsburgh in Sept., 1830. R 9/29.

Samuel M. Lewis, of Harrodsburgh, to Miss Susan Taylor, daughter of Col. John Taylor. M in Mercer county in Sept., 1830. R 9/29.

Thomas L. Wiley to Miss Louisa Perry, of Dallas county, Ala. M near Cahawba, in Sept., 1830. R 9/29.

J. F. McCaleb, of Miss., to Miss Sophia Moore. M in Mercer county in Sept., 1830. R 10/6.

Rev. William H. Forsythe, pastor of Mount Pleasant Church, to Miss Louisa T. Moore. M in Cynthiana in Sept., 1830. R 10/6.

James D. McCoy, late editor of the *Reporter,* to Miss Mary S., daughter of John Dunwoody, of the vicinity of Cheneyville, La. M Oct. 7, 1830. R 10/13.

Charles E. Beynroth, of Louisville, to Miss Aminta Howard. M in Jefferson county in Oct., 1830. R 10/20.

Major John R. Henry to Mrs. Barbara F. Todd. M in Louisville in Oct., 1830. R 10/20.

Henry B. Oldham to Miss Fauchier. M in Louisville in Oct., 1830. R 10/20.

Joseph Pickering to Miss Elizabeth Fleming. M in Louisville in Oct., 1830. R 10/20.

Benjamin B. Johnson to Mrs. Jane B. Lewis. M in Frankfort in Oct., 1830. R 10/20.

Isaac Worthington, of Miss., to Miss Margaret Higgins, youngest daughter of Richard Higgins. M in Lexington Oct. 21, 1830. R 10/27.

William James to Miss Judith B. Haney, both of Fayette county. M Oct. 21, 1830. R 11/3.

Grant Allen, of Mercer county, to Miss Catharine Ware, daughter of Col. T. Ware, of Bourbon county. M Oct. 24, 1830. R 11/3.

John H. Phelps, of Hopkinsville, to Miss Elizabeth Morehead. M in Bowling Green Oct. 26, 1830. R 11/3

Henry Baldwin, Jr., to Miss Mary Florida Dickson. M near Nashville in Nov., 1830. R 11/17.

Charles Wilson to Miss Josephine Tarascon. M in Louisville in Nov., 1830. R 11/17.

Philip Vacaro to Miss Nancy Hoit. M in Louisville in Nov., 1830. R 11/17.

Martin G. Green to Miss Polly Huguely. M in Madison county in Nov., 1830. R 11/17.

Wiatt Hendron to Miss Matilda Coats. M in Madison county in Nov., 1830. R 11/17.

Joel Elkin to Miss Celia Crews. M in Madison county in Nov., 1830. R 11/17.

Uriah Jennings to Miss Sally Jennings. M in Madison county in Nov., 1830. R 11/17.

Thompson M. Arnold to Miss Sarah J. Stevenson. M in Madison county in Nov., 1830. R 11/17.

Daniel Moberly to Miss Milly Stagner. M in Madison county in Nov., 1930. R 11/17.

Silas Cawthan to Miss Mary Jarman. M in Madison county in Nov., 1830. R 11/17.

Dr. Henry Hopson, of Clarksville, Tenn., to Miss Catharine Cooke, daughter of Prof. John E. Cooke. M Nov. 17, 1830. R 11/24.

George Sidnor to Miss Ann Smith, both of Fayette county. M Nov. 11, 1830. R 11/24.

Asa Foster, of Bourbon county, to Miss Mary Ann Woods, of Lexington. M Nov. 18, 1830. R 11/24.

Joseph Brown to Miss Nancy McMains, both of Fayette county. M Nov. 18, 1830. R 11/24.

Levy Ragan to Miss Mary F. Miller, both of Lexington. M Nov. 20, 1830. R 11/24.

Chapman Coleman to Miss Ann Mary Crittenden, daughter of John J. Crittenden. M in Frankfort in Nov., 1830. R 11/24.

James Hedge to Miss Maria T. Branham. M in Bourbon county in Nov., 1830. R 11/24.

James Thornton, of Springfield, Ohio, to Miss Mary N. Elliott, daughter of John Elliott. M in Scott county in Nov., 1830. R 11/24.

Thomas J. Shepherd to Miss Amanda Smith. M in Scott county in Nov., 1830. R 11/24.

Henry H. Ready to Miss Williametta Sutton. M in Scott county in Nov., 1830. R 11/24.

William Nutter to Miss Pamelia Pitts. M in Scott county in Nov., 1830. R 11/24.

William Fowler to Miss Mary Cannon. M in Scott county in Nov., 1830. R 11/24.

Rev. Timothy Boot to Miss Lucy Jane Patton, of Lincoln county, Ky. M at Belle Fonte, Ala., in Nov., 1830. R 11/24.

Dr. Thomas J. Moore, of Bowling Green, to Miss Mary Amner Thompson, daughter of Richard Thompson. M in Mercer county in Nov., 1830. R 12/1.

John J. Hardin to Miss Eleanor Tolly. M in Mercer county in Nov., 1830. R 12/1.

Garland Christy to Miss Margaret Hickey, daughter of Simon Hickey. M Dec. 2, 1830. R 12/8.

Lemuel Bennett to Miss Nancy Jones, daughter of Col. Humphrey Jones. M in Madison county in Dec., 1830. R 12/8.

Thomas W. Boyd, of Richmond, Ky., to Miss Elizabeth Wherritt. M in Knox county in Nov., 1830. R 12/8.

Thomas J. Pickett, of Mason county, to Miss Margaret Campbell. M in Fleming county in Nov., 1830. R 12/8.

Isaac Cunningham to Miss Malinda S. Donaldson, daughter of the late Gen.

Donaldson, of Clarke county. M Nov. 25, 1830. R 12/8.

William Bailey to Miss Frederica Jacoby, both of Bourbon county. M in Nov., 1830. R 12/8.

Dr. John T. Cassel to Mrs. Sarah Weagley, both of Fayette county. M Dec. 11, 1830. R 12/22.

Courtney Talbot, of Bourbon county, to Miss Elizabeth, daughter of John Harp, of Fayette county. M Dec. 16, 1830. R 12/22.

George Bryan to Mrs. J. Miller. M in Bourbon county in Dec., 1830. R 12/22.

P. C. Morehead to Miss Eveline Larsh. M in Bowling Green in Dec., 1830. R 1/5/1831.

Rev. D. R. Harris to Miss Mary Ann McCutchen. M in Simpson county in Dec., 1830. R 1/5/1831.

James Williams, of Mercer county, to Miss Cassandra Briscoe. M in Washington county in Dec., 1830. R 1/5/1831.

William May to Miss Stewart. M in Mercer county in Dec., 1830. R 1/5/1831.

John Shields to Miss Martha Denny. M in Mercer county in Dec., 1830. R 1/5/1831.

Elisha Fitch to Miss Delilah Barnes. M in Fleming county in Dec., 1830. R 1/5/1831.

John Palmer to Mrs. McGee, of Harrison county. M in Fleming county in Dec., 1830. R 1/5/1831.

Douglass P. Lewis to Miss Elizabeth Clay, daughter of Col. H. Clay. M in Bourbon county in Dec., 1830. R 1/5/1831.

Rev. Walter Warder to Mrs. Dobyns, widow of Col. Charles Dobyns. M in Washington county in Dec., 1830. R 1/5/1831.

Samuel Fuqua to Miss Baker. M in Logan county in Dec., 1830. R 1/5/1831.

1831

Augustus Hall to Miss Sarah Henderson. M in Fayette county Jan. 7, 1831. R 1/12.

T. A. McGrath, of Louisville, to Mary Ann Roper, of Lexington. M Jan. 7, 1831. R 1/12.

David Wood to Miss Cerinda Step. M in Mercer county in Jan., 1831. R 1/12.

Dr. Henry Morehead to Mrs. Mary H. Hughes, daughter of S. Craig, all of Jessamine county. M Jan. 6, 1831. R 1/19.

A. G. Carter, of Kentucky, to Miss Elizabeth L. Carter. M Fairfax county, Va., in Jan., 1831. R 1/19.

Albert Gallatin Talbot, of Jessamine county, to Miss Elizabeth Caldwell, daughter of Capt. William Caldwell, of Jessamine county. M Jan. 12, 1831. R 1/26.

G. P. Bryant, of Oldham county, to Miss Nancy Bedford, of Bourbon county. M Jan. 18, 1831. R 1/26.

Joseph George to Miss Mary-Ann Kay, both of Fayette county. M Jan. 27, 1831. R 2/2.

William Summers to Miss Ruth Wood. M in Mason county in Jan., 1831. R 2/2.

Joseph Perkins, of Garrard county, to Miss Mary Ellen Thomas. M in Mercer county in Jan., 1831. R 2/2.

Dr. Samuel Hatch, of Georgetown, to Miss Julia Matilda Bradford, daughter of Daniel Bradford. M in Lexington Tuesday Feb. 8, 1831. R 2/9.

Joseph Madden to Miss Martha Mills. M in Fleming county in Feb., 1831. R 2/9.

John J. Hardin, of Franklin county, to Miss Sarah Smith. M in Mercer county in Jan., 1831. R 2/9.

Enoch S. Pepper to Miss Sarah R. Tebbs. M in Mason county in Jan., 1831. R 2/9.

George Doyle to Miss Elizabeth Strode. M in Clarke county in Jan., 1831. R 2/9.

John Quissenberry to Miss Sarah Ann Lindsay. M in Madison county in Feb., 1831. R 2/9.

Dr. John O. Hodges, of Harrison county, to Miss Eglentine Miller, daughter of Col. Isaac Miller, of Cynthiana. M Feb. 6, 1831. R 2/6.

John Bateman, of Fleming county, to Miss Elizabeth Lewis. M in Lewis county in Feb., 1831. R 2/23.

Brutus J. Clay to Miss Amelia J. Fields, daughter of E. H. Fields. M in Richmond, Madison county, in Feb., 1831. R 2/23.

George Jones to Miss Sarah Ann Dodd. M in Mercer county in Feb., 1831. R 2/23.

George T. Williamson to Miss Jane M. Taylor, daughter of Gen. James Taylor. M in Newport in Feb., 1831. R 2/23.

Sinclair Kirtley to Miss Mary Ann Peebles. M in Frankfort in Feb., 1831. R 3/2.

Capt. Francis Lockett, of Henderson county, to Miss Lydia Hickman, daughter of the Rev. William Hickman, Jr. M in Franklin county in Feb., 1831. R 3/2.

P. Wherrett to Miss Zerilda A. Morrison, both of Cynthiana. M Feb. 24, 1831. R. 3/16.

John Harp, of Fayette county, to Miss Jane Wallace, of Bourbon county. M Mar. 3, 1831. R 3/16.

Hon. Powhatan Ellis, Senator from Miss., to Miss Eliza Winn. M in Washington, D. C., in Feb., 1831. R 3/16.

Clabourne Kennedy to Miss Sidney Taylor. M in Nicholas county in Feb., 1831. R 3/16.

L. G. Johnson, of Louisville, to Miss Margaret Ann Sanders, of Lexington. M Mar. 20, 1831. R 3/23

Waller Lewis to Miss Emily Washington, daughter of John Washington.

M in Logan county in Mar., 1831. R 3/30.

Nathaniel Hardy to Miss Charlotte Howard. M in Louisville in Mar., 1831. R 3/30.

John V. Webb, of Scott county, to Miss Almira M. J. Bradford. M in Frankfort in Mar., 1831. R 3/30.

Ignatius Mattingly to Miss Rachel Barnes. M in Fayette county in Apr., 1831. R 4/6.

L. Rogers to Miss Minerva Bronson. M in Louisville in Apr., 1831. R 4/6.

G. Tinely to Miss Polly Mullikin. M in Louisville in Mar., 1831. R 4/6.

G. W. Hite, of Bardstown, to Miss Martha Ann Motley. M in Greensburgh in Mar., 1831. R 4/6.

James Isbel to Miss Betsy Ammerman. M in Bourbon county in Mar., 1831. R 4/6.

Zephariah Johnson to Miss Jane Rogers. M in Bourbon county in Mar., 1831. R 4/6.

James Nelson to Miss Charlotte Cook. M in Richmond, Ky., in Mar., 1831. R 4/6.

James Rowland to Miss Caroline Porter. M in Madison county in Mar., 1831. R 4/6

Thompson R. Ballard to Miss Charlotte Wood. M in Madison county in Mar., 1831. R 4/6.

Dr. S. S. Alexander, of Shepherdsville, to Miss Fatura W. Oldham. M in Jefferson county in Mar., 1831. R 4/6.

Robert Walker, of Bourbon county, the "Fiddler." Died in Mar., 1831. R 4/6.

Samuel R. Beckett, of Pendleton county, to Miss Martha G. Rannels. M in Bourbon county in Apr., 1831. R 4/13.

Robert Frazer, Jr., to Miss Catharine E. Coleman. M in Louisville in Apr., 1831. R 5/4.

Coleman Duncan, of Louisville, to Miss Mary S. Postlethwait, daughter of John Postlethwait. M in Lexington Apr. 19, 1831. R 4/20.

James Penny to Miss Jane W. Megowan, daughter of David Megowan. M Apr. 13, 1831. R 4/20.

Rev. William Warfield to Miss Joyce Deugued. M in Todd county in Apr., 1831. R 4/20.

Jepthah Dudley, of Frankfort, to Mrs. Sally Clay, widow of Gen. Green Clay. M in Madison county in Apr., 1831. R 4/20.

Dillis Dyer, of Ohio county, to Miss Elizabeth Chambers, of Miss. M Mar. 22, 1831. R 4/20.

Camden M. Ballard to Miss Lavinia H. Railey. M in Oldham county in Mar., 1831. R 4/20.

George R. Robertson, of Stanford, Ky., to Miss Maria Louisa Macurdy. M in Frankfort in Apr., 1831. R 5/14.

William P. Holloway to Miss Rhoda H. Oliver. M in Lexington May 3, 1831. R 5/4.

William Chiles to Miss Susannah H. Irwin. M in Clarke county in May, 1831. R 5/11.

Ellis Lancaster to Miss Susannah Perkins. M in Fayette county in May, 1831. R 5/11.

John W. Simrall, of Shelbyville, to Miss Mary D. Bartow, of Darien, Ga. M May 10, 1831. R 5/18.

Dr. B. W. Chamberlain, of Bourbon county, to Miss Margaret McClanahan. M in Fayette county in May, 1831. R 5/18.

Robert Ormsby, merchant of Louisville, to Miss Mary Jane Churchman. M in Baltimore in May, 1831. R 5/18.

James S. Irwin, of Pittsburgh, to Miss Ann E. Duncan. M in Louisville in May, 1831. R 5/18.

James Southgate to Miss Cornelia S. T. Brigham. M in Cincinnati in May, 1831. R 5/18.

Henry Ritchie to Miss E. Snedes, daughter of A. K. Snedes. M in Lexington Wednesday May 18, 1831. R 5/25.

Daniel Blake, of S. Carolina, to Miss Emma P. M. Rutledge. M at Nashville in June, 1831. R 6/29.

William Armstrong, of Louisville, to Miss Lucretia, daughter of Charles G. Dorsey. M in Jefferson county in June, 1831. R 6/29.

John Grimes to Miss Maria Hukell, both of Fayette county. M June 29, 1831. R 7/6.

James Mullens to Miss Ann Lewis. M in Mercer county in June, 1831. R 7/6.

Benjamin Duncan to Miss Nancy Anderson. M in Danville in June, 1831. R 7/6.

Samuel Wharton, of Danville, to Mrs. Vance. M in Lincoln county in June, 1831. R 7/6.

William Smedley, of Illinois, to Miss Nancy Robinson, daughter of the late Joseph Robinson, of Fayette county, Ky. M July 5, 1831. R 7/13.

J. M. C. Irwin to Miss Elizabeth G., daughter of Rev. Robert Marshall, all of Fayette county. M July 7, 1831. R 7/13.

William Brown to Miss Martha Nesbit. M in Paris in July, 1831. R 7/13.

James E. Cable to Miss Hanna Anderson. M in Louisville in July, 1831. R 7/13.

Joseph Pierce, Jr., to Miss Mary Shrieve, daughter of Thomas Shrieve, Sr. M in Louisville in June, 1831. R 7/13.

Moses Alexander, aged 93, to Mrs. Frances Tompkins, aged 105. They were married in Bath, Steuben county, N. Y., June 11, 1831. They were both taken out of bed dead the following morning. R 7/13.

Richard Henry Lee, late editor of the Maysville *Eagle*, to Miss Eliza Armstrong, daughter of John Armstrong. M in Maysville in July, 1831. R 7/20/1831.

Richard A. Bohannon to Miss Josephine A. Gray. M in Frankfort in July, 1831. R 7/20.

Capt. Edwin A. Turpin to Miss Eliza J. Satterwhite. M in Louisville in July, 1831. R 7/20.

Richard T. Keiningham, of Paris, to Miss Louisa A. Thomas. M in Frankfort in July, 1831. R 7/20.

William Chapman, of Lincoln county, to Miss Emily Morrison, of Bourbon county. M July 31, 1831. R 8/17.

Abner G. Daniel, of Madison county, to Mrs. Sally Smith. M in Garrard county Aug. 23, 1831. R 8/31.

George T. Underwood to Miss Eliza E. Shane, daughter of George Shane. M in Shelby county in Aug., 1831. R 8/31.

Col. John Cunningham, of Jessamine county, to Miss Agnes L. Wilson, daughter of Singleton Wilson. M in Shelby county in Aug., 1831. R 8/31.

Ephraim Drake, of Jessamine county, to Miss Esther M. Wilson, youngest daughter of Singleton Wilson. M in Shelby county in Aug., 1831. R 8/31.

John Scott Harrison to Miss Elizabeth R. Irwin, daughter of Archibald Irwin, of Pa. M at North Bend, Ohio, in Aug., 1931. R 8/31.

Col. James S. Wood, of Ind., to Mrs. Phebe Hymen. M in Mason county, Ky., in Aug., 1831. R 9/7.

W. L. Underwood to Miss Lucy C. Henry. M in Bowling Green in Aug., 1831. R 9/7.

A. W. P. Parker, of Lexington, to Miss Camilla L. Brashear. M in Bowling Green in Aug., 1831. R 9/7.

Lucian Murat, second son of Joachim Murat, late King of Naples, to Caroline Georgiana, youngest daughter of the late Thomas Frazier, of S. Carolina. M in Trenton, N. J., in Aug., 1831. R 9/7.

John B. Coleman, of Lexington, to Miss Catharine M. Ellis, daughter of the late Armstrong Ellis, of Miss. M Sept. 13, 1831, at Martin Grove, the residence of John L. Martin. R 9/14.

Charles S. Morehead, of Frankfort, to Miss Margaret Leavy, daughter of William Leavy. M in Lexington Sept. 6, 1831. R 9/14.

James Haun, of Scott county, to Miss Patsy Hurst, daughter of Capt. John Hurst, of Fayette county. M Sept. 1, 1831. R 9/14.

Col. Joseph Williams, of Montgomery county, to Miss Louisa Caroline Morrow. M in Bath county in Sept., 1831. R 9/14.

James Bridgford to Miss Arabella Hanson. M in Shelby county in Sept., 1831. R 9/14.

William J. N. Stevens to Miss Elizabeth Hilton. M in Lexington Sept. 13, 1831. R 9/21.

Rev. Jacob Creath, Jr., late of Mecklenburg county, Va., to Mrs. Susan Bedford. M in Fayette county, Ky., Sept. 15, 1831. R 9/21.

B. J. Peters, of Owingsville, to Miss Elizabeth Ann Farrow. M in Mt. Sterling in Sept., 1831. R 9/21.

Hall Anderson to Miss Emily Aldridge. M in Garrard county in Sept, 1831. R 9/21.

Ephraim Osborne to Miss Marg S. Megowan. M in Lexington in Sept., 1831. R 9/21.

Sydenham Talbott to Miss Nancy Smelser. M in Bourbon county in Sept., 1831. R 9/21.

Uriah Taylor, of Christian county, to Miss Ann America Taylor. M in Warren county in Sept., 1831. R 9/21.

Elias Simpson to Miss Nancy Briggs. M in Warren county in Sept., 1831. R 9/21.

Charles Lawton to Miss Lucy Ann Perkins. M in Warren county in Sept., 1831. R 9/21.

James Lowrey to Miss Elizabeth Shirley. M in Warren county in Sept., 1831. R 9/21.

Edward C. Payne, of Fayette county, to Miss Paulina C. Harbinson, daughter of the late David Harbinson, of Shelby county. M Sept. 13, 1831. R 9/21.

Edgar M. Crutchfield to Miss Eliza Berryman. M in Lexington in Sept., 1831. R 9/28.

R. C. Thompson to Miss Sarah Wrigglesworth. M in Louisville in Sept., 1831. R 9/28.

John Joyce to Miss Harriet Martin. M in Louisville in Sept., 1831. R 9/28.

John Thorn to Miss Mary Estes. M in Lincoln county in Sept., 1831. R 9/28.

Abraham M. Van Arsdall to Miss Dorinda Bohon. M in Mercer county in Sept., 1831. R 9/28.

Daniel Henderson to Miss Pamilia Cook. M in Mercer county in Sept., 1831. R 9/28.

Dr. Warren Frazer, of Athens, to Miss Laura S. Brooking, daughter of Robert E. Brooking, of Clarke county. M Sept. 29, 1831. R 10/5.

John M. Garth, of Scott county, to Miss Eliza Ann Graves, daughter of Col. Graves, of Fayette county. M Sept. 20, 1831. R 10/5.

John McCarny, of Paris, to Miss Elizabeth Debruler. M in Cynthiana in Sept., 1831. R 10/5.

Col. Achilles Chinn to Mrs. Betsey D. Baylor. M in Bourbon county in Sept., 1831. R 10/5.

Garnett Duncan, of Louisville, to Miss Caroline E. Shipman. M in New Haven, Conn., in Sept., 1831. R 10/5.

Waterson Sherrit, of Scott county, to Miss Maria W. Dorsey, daughter of R. Dorsey, of Fayette county. M Oct. 6, 1831. R 10/12.

Col. Edmund H. Taylor, of Frankfort, to Miss Martha S. Taylor, daughter of the late Edmund Taylor. M in Newport, Ky., in Oct., 1831. R 10/12.

Madison D. Stone to Miss Charlotte Embry. M in Madison county in Oct., 1831. R 10/12.

Jacob Huguely to Miss Florina White. M in Madison county in Oct., 1831. R 10/12.

William Marshall to Miss Rachel Jordan. M in Anderson county in Sept.,

1831. R 10/12.

Erasmus Boyle Owsley, of Garrard county, to Miss Caroline E. Talbott, daughter of Presley Talbott, of Jessamine county. M Oct. 11, 1831. R 10/19.

Capt. J. Rogers, of the U. S. Army, to Miss Josephine Preston, daughter of the late Major William Preston. M at Louisville in Oct., 1831. R 11/2.

1831

Capt. John Neet, of Lexington, to Miss Mary Ellen Bohannon, daughter of G. Bohannon. M in Woodford county in Oct., 1831. R 11/2.

R. W. Scott to Miss Elizabeth Brown, daughter of the late Dr. Preston Brown. M in Frankfort in Oct., 1831. R 11/2.

John Grimes to Miss Elizabeth Clark. M in Mercer county in Nov., 1831. R 11/16.

A. L. Magenis, of St. Louis, to Miss Mary MacRea, daughter of Col. MacRea, of the U. S. Army. M in New York in Oct., 1831. R 11/16.

Gabriel S. Slaughter, of Mercer county, to Miss Eliza Drake, daughter of the late Col. A. S. Drake. M in Lexington in Nov., 1831. R 11/28.

George A. Zeumar, of Louisville, to Miss Ann P. Satterwhite, daughter of the late Mann Satterwhite. M in Fayette county in Nov., 1831. R 11/28.

Dr. Benjamin P. Drake to Miss Martha Ann Vance. M in Fayette county in Nov., 1831. R 11/28.

Joseph Charless, Jr., to Miss Charlotte T. Blow, daughter of John Blow. M in St. Louis in Nov., 1831. R 10/28.

Edward Mitchell, of Springfield, Ill., to Miss Eleanor Essex. M in St. Louis in Nov., 1831. R. 10/28.

Hezekiah H. Eaton, Professor at Transylvania University, to Miss Mary R. Harper, daughter of the late James Harper. M Nov. 30, 1831. R 12/7.

Enoch Clarke, of Lexington, to Miss Judith T. Duerson. M in Fayette county in Nov., 1831. R 12/7.

Green Johnson to Miss Jane Thomas. M in Madison county in Nov., 1831. R 12/7.

J. W. Piatt to Miss Harriet Lanman, daughter of the Hon. James Lanman, of Norwich, Conn. M in Cincinnati in Nov., 1831. R 12/7.

Capt. William N. Wickliffe, of the U. S. Army, to Miss Ann, daughter of the late Joseph Hertzog, of Philadelphia. M at Cantonment, Leavenworth, Nov. 14, 1831. R. 12/7.

George James Trotter, editor of the *Kentucky Gazette,* to Miss Mary Ann Hall, daughter of the Rev. N. H. Hall, of Fayette county. M Tuesday Dec. 6, 1831. R 12/21.

William S. Ellis, of Paris, to Miss Frances Graves. M in Fayette county in Dec., 1831. R 12/21.

Samuel Carrington, of Mount Sterling, to Miss Martha Ann Graves. M in Fayette county in Dec., 1831. R 12/21.

Charles Ingersoll to Miss Susan Catherine Brown, daughter of the late Dr.

Samuel Brown. M in Philadelphia in Nov., 1831. R 12/21.

———— Dawson to Miss Mary Jane Bell. M in Lexington in Dec., 1831. R 12/28.

1832

Rev. Samuel D. Blythe, of Hillsborough, O., to Miss Mary Ann Thompson. M in Cincinnati, in Dec., 1831. R. 12/28.

Lieut. Alfred Beckley, of the U. S. Army, to Miss Amelia Neville Craig, daughter of Neville B. Craig. M at Pittsburgh, in Dec., 1831. R 12/28.

Richard Higgins, Jr., to Miss Sarah M. Shelby, daughter of Major Thomas H. Shelby, all of Fayette county. M Jan. 19, 1832. OR 1/20.

Dr. Thomas P. Satterwhite to Miss Mary C. Breckinridge, daughter of the late James Cabell Breckinridge. M Jan. 17, 1832. OR 1/20.

William M. Davis, of Ohio county, to Miss Arabella Scott, daughter of the late Dr. Scott. M in Frankfort in Jan., 1832. R 1/18.

Cabell H. Fenwick, of Lawrenceburg, to Miss Mary Todd, daughter of Judge Samuel Todd. M in Frankfort in Jan., 1832. R 1/18.

William D. Coryell, of Mason county, to Miss Sarah Ann Bryan, daughter of Thomas Bryan. M in Jan., 1832. R 1/18.

John Barton, of Bourbon county, to miss Mary E. Moore, daughter of the late Major Pete Moore, of Fayette county. M in Jan., 1832. OR 1/27.

George Ament to Miss Caroline Armstrong, both of Bourbon county. M Jan. 19, 1832. OR 1/27.

John B. Slaughter to Miss Mary Edwards. M in Russellville in Jan., 1832. OR 1/27.

John Young to Miss Lucinda Burch, daughter of Henry Burch. M in Nicholasville in Jan., 1832. OR 2/3.

Elliot West, Jr., to Miss Nancy Reynolds, daughter of Thomas Reynolds. M in Jessamine county in Jan., 1832. OR 2/3.

James F. Conover to Miss Julia A. E. Sellman, daughter of the late Dr. Sellman, all of Cincinnati. M in Jan., 1832. OR 2/3.

Ephraim Robbins, of Cincinnati, to Miss Jane Hussey, daughter of Asahel Hussey, of Baltimore. M in Zanesville, O., in Jan., 1832. OR 2/3.

Henry Thompson to Miss Elizabeth Pritchard. M in Louisville in Jan., 1832. R 2/1.

Dr. Jordan Pennington, of Princeton, Ia., to Miss Elizabeth A. Snether. M in Louisville, Ky., in Jan. 1832. R 2/1.

Richard F. Barrett to Miss ———— Buckner, daughter of Judge ———— Buckner. M Jan. 31, 1832. R 2/1.

Capt. Joseph Robinson to Miss Margaret P. Innes, daughter of the late Hugh Innes, of Franklin county. M Feb. 8, 1832. O 2/24.

Thomas Grady to Miss Julian Myers, both of Fayette county. M Feb. 14, 1832. O 2/24.

Benjamin Robinson to Miss Somerville Withers, daughter of Mr. M. K. Withers, of Fayette county. M Feb. 16, 1832. O 2/24.

Dr. Appleton Allan to Miss Sarah J. Brown. M in Scott county Feb. 16,

1832. O 2/24.

Charles Hamilton to Miss Martha W. Glenn. M in Scott county, Feb. 16, 1832. O 2/24.

N. W. Edwards to Miss Elizabeth Todd, daughter of Robert S. Todd. M in Lexington in March, 1832. O 3/2.

Dr. Francis A. Williamson, of La., to Miss Ann Eliza Gatewood, daughter of the late Robert A. Gatewood. M in Lexington, Ky., in Mar., 1832. O 3/30.

Edwin Hawes to Miss Cary Ann Trotter, daughter of Gabriel Trotter. M in Winchester Mar. 27, 1832. O 3/30.

Benjamin Hawes to Miss Mary Ann Taylor, daughter of Samuel M. Taylor, of Winchester. M Mar. 28, 1832. O 3/20.

Iram Nye, merchant of Williamstown, Ky., to Miss Mary Eleanor Fish, of Scott county. M Mar. 29, 1832. With the announcement of this wedding the editors of the *Lexington Observer* printed this poem: O 4/6.

> This little *Fish* in love's pure lake
> Had heard her lover sigh,
> His proffered hand she free did take,
> To be forever *Nye*.
>
> In joy the little *Fish* drew *Nye*
> Into the lake of love,
> And vow'd with him to live and die,
> And ever constant prove.
>
> Now all ye anglers that doth sigh
> And toil for *Fish* in vain,
> Go learn the ways of Iram Nye
> And you can *Fish* obtain.

Alfred Warner, of Lexington, to Miss Martha Jane Shackleford, daughter of the late Benjamin Shackleford, of Richmond. M May 1, 1832. O 5/10.

Peterson Bain, of Fayette county, to Miss Mary Theobold, daughter of Thomas S. Theobold, of Georgetown. M May 1, 1832. O 5/17.

Joseph Ford to Miss Sarah Eastham, daughter of William Eastham. M in Georgetown May 10, 1832. O 5/17.

John H. Cooper, of Fayette county, to Miss Susan Wallace, of Scott county. M in Scott county May 10, 1832. O 5/17.

Levi Barkley, of Marion county, Mo., to Miss Elizabeth Grimes, of Fayette county, Ky., May 10, 1832. O 5/17.

Charles McDougle to Miss Harriet Fisher. M in Leesburg, Harrison county, May 20, 1832. O 5/24.

John B. L. Agnes, to Miss Sarah Ann Skidmore, daughter of the late Paul Skidmore, all of Lexington. M May 30, 1832. O 6/7.

Percival Gouch to Miss Julia O. Megowan, both of Lexington. M June 11, 1832. O 6/21.

Stephen T. Twyman, of Frankfort, to Miss Julian Greenwell, of Scott county. M June 19, 1832. O 6/28.

William Brown, Jr., of Georgetown, to Miss Amanda L. Tarlton, daughter of Jeremiah Tarlton. M in Scott county June 26, 1832. O 7/5.

Howard M. Henderson, of N. Hampshire, to Miss Jane Elizabeth Moore, daughter of A. Moore, of Cynthiana. M July 1, 1832. O 7/5.

Charles D. Bilbro, of Ga., to Miss Julian Hudson, of Lexington, Kentucky. M July 25, 1832. O 8/2.

Richard H. Menefee to Miss Sarah B., daughter of the late M. H. Jouitt. M Tuesday Aug. 14, 1832. O 8/16.

Richard H. Stanhope to Miss Ellen Cooper, both of Fayette county. M Aug. 15, 1932. O 9/13.

Abraham Liter to Miss Elizabeth Liter, both of Bourbon county. M Sept. 6, 1832. 9/13.

Thomas Smith, formerly of New York, to Miss Mariah, daughter of John Moffett, of Piqua, Miami county, O. M at the latter place Aug. 30, 1832. O 9/20.

Arthur H. Wallace, of New Orleans, to Miss Letitia P. Hart, M at "Spring Hill", the residence of Nathaniel Hart, in Woodford county, in October, 1832. O 10/11.

Dr. Thomas L. Smith, of Lexington, to Miss Mary Russell, of Fayette county. M Oct. 11, 1832. O 10/18.

George King to Miss Sarah Elvira Hallack, both of Bourbon county. M Sept. 27, 1832. O 10/18.

George Porter to Mrs. Sarah Estes, of Bourbon county. M Oct. 5, 1832. O 10/18.

Henry Clay, Jr., son of the Hon. H. Clay, of Ashland, to Miss Maria Julia, daughter of the late Thomas Prather, of Louisville. M in Louisville Oct. 10, 1832. O 10/18.

Henry H. Timberlake to Miss Mary S. Brand, both of Lexington. M Oct. 17, 1832. O 10/25.

A. M. Rigg, of Owen county, to Miss Catherine L. A. Cochran, daughter of Dr. William Cochran, of Lexington. M Oct. 18, 1832. O 10/25.

Richard Brown to Miss Amy Johnson, both of Lexington. M Oct. 17, 1832. O 10/25.

Adrew K. Miller to Miss Elizabeth B. Holloway, of Lexington. M in Madison county Oct. 18, 1832. O 10/25.

O. H. P. Breckinridge to Miss Nancy Ellis, daughter of Capt. Robert Ellis, all of Bourbon county. M Nov. 1, 1832. O 11/15.

John B. Payne, M. D., of Clarke county, to Miss Elizabeth T. Montgomery, daughter of William Montgomery, of Lexington. M Nov. 15, 1832. O 11/22.

Thomas W. Scott, a white man, to Miss Adeline J. Johnson, a mulatto girl, reputed to be the daughter of the Hon. Richard M. Johnson, Representative in Congress. M Nov. 8, 1832, in Scott county. A few days after this marriage Thomas W. Scott was presented by his wife's father a fine tract of land known as the "Blue Spring Farm." Daniel Pence married Imogene, Colonel Johnson's eldest daughter in 1829 or 1830. O 11/29.

Daniel C. Virden to Miss Artimasa Barnett, both of Lexington. M Nov. 29,

1832. O 12/6.

John T. Campbell to Miss Henrietta Conover, both of Lexington. M Dec. 2, 1832. O 12/6.

Francis Jenkins to Miss Emily A. Barbee. M Nov. 20, 1832. O 12/6.

James Duvall to Miss Patsy Jane Gaugh, both of Lexington. M Dec. 6, 1832. O 12/13.

N. Paschall, of St. Louis, to Mrs. M. Elza Edgar, of Kaskaskia. M Nov. 27, 1832. O 12/13.

Nelson Boon to Miss Phebe Morgan, of Eaton, Ohio. M Nov. 22, 1832. O 12/13.

Francis Gallaher, of Springfield, to Miss Sarah Madden, of Xenia, Ohio. M Dec. 3, 1832. O 12/13.

Frazer D. Herndon to Miss Mary, daughter of Francis Preston, all of Fayette county. M Dec. 11, 1832. O 12/20.

William G. Rice, of Garrard county, to Miss Mary Gurley, daughter of Rev. E. Gillette, D. D., of Hallowell, Me. M at Basin Spring, Clarke county, Dec. 12, 1832. O 12/20.

Major Richard N. Parker to Miss Eliza Rice, both of Fayette county. M Dec. 20, 1832. O 12/27.

Conquest W. Owins, of Washington, Mason county, to Miss Eliza Herndon, of Fayette county. M Dec. 16, 1832. O 12/27.

James M. Holloway to Miss Sarah V. Satterwhite, both of Lexington. M Jan. 2, 1833. OR 1/3.

Walter Wheatly to Miss Catharine H. Boyer. M Jan. 8, 1833. OR 1/17.

Dr. Churchill J. Blackburn, of Scott county, to Miss Sarah, daughter of Oliver Keen, of Lexington. M Jan. 15, 1833. OR 1/24.

Charles Robertson to Miss Priscilla Fleming. M Jan. 16, 1833. OR 1/24.

Elijah O'Bannon to Miss Tabitha Ann Browning. M in Harrison county Jan. 29, 1833. OR 2/7.

Remus Payne, of Fayette county, to Miss Mary S., daughter of John C. Talbott, of Scott county. M Jan. 29, 1833. OR 2/7.

Elisha Warfield, Jr., of Lexington, Ky., to Miss Catharine Ann Ware, of Philadelphia. M in Cincinnati, O., Jan. 28, 1833. OR 2/7.

George W. Landeman to Miss Susan Hostetter, both of Lexington. M Feb. 13, 1833. OR 2/21.

Cassius M. Clay, of Madison county, to Miss Mary Jane Warfield, daughter of Dr. Elisha Warfield, of Fayette county. M Tuesday evening Feb. 26, 1833. OR 2/28.

Brooks B. Talbott to Miss Harriet, daughter of James Hildreth, all of Bourbon county. M Feb. 21, 1833. OR 2/28.

Dr. Edward B. Church to Miss Maria Innes Bodley, daughter of Gen. Thomas Bodley, all of Lexington. M Mar. 8, 1833. OR 3/14.

James Price, of Clarke county, to Miss Charlotte Hart, recently of Georgetown, Ky., and formerly of Marietta, Ohio. M at Colbyville Feb. 25, 1833. OR 3/14.

Theophilus McGlone to Miss Sarah Potter. M in Lexington Mar. 13, 1833. OR 3/14.

Landridge Arnett to Miss Mary Ann White, both of Lexington (or Fayette county). M Mar. 12, 1833. OR 3/21.

Julius L. Dickerson to Miss Louisa J. White, both of Bourbon county. M Mar. 13, 1833. OR 3/21.

Josiah Innes to Miss Elizabeth Stillfield, both of Lexington. M Mar. 19, 1833. OR 3/21.

Dr. Elisha B. Stedman, of Pittsborough, N. C., to Miss Juliann St. Clair Chipley, daughter of the Rev. S. Chipley. M Mar. 20, 1833. OR 3/28.

John Wilson, of Lexington, to Miss Eliza Hull, daughter of Jacob Hull. M in Fayette county Mar. 28, 1833. OR 4/3.

John S. Van De Graaff, of Scott county, to Miss Eliza Jane Brooks, daughter of James A. Brooks. M in Lexington Apr. 3, 1833. OR 4/10.

Dr. Theodore S. Bell, of Louisville, to Miss Susanna F. Hewett, daughter of John M. Hewett. M Apr. 3, 1833. OR 4/10.

Thomas H. Buchannan to Miss Mary, daughter of Jacob Liter, of Bourbon county. M Mar. 28, 1833. OR 4/10.

George Hart to Miss Juliann Butler, both of Fayette county. M Apr. 1, 1833. OR 4/25.

James Cryer, of Tenn., to Miss George Ann Cooper, daughter of Spencer Cooper of Fayette county, Ky. M Apr. 17, 1833. OR 4/25.

Abner Lewis, of Lexington, to Miss Nancy Brown. M in Fayette county May 9, 1833. OR 5/16.

John C. Orrick to Miss Elizabeth A. Graves, both of Lexington. M May 19, 1833. OR 5/23.

James Cowan, of Lexington, to Miss Ann H. Neiss, of Frankfort. M in Frankfort May 16, 1833. OR 5/23.

Rev. George Crawford, of Washington, Va., to Miss Elizabeth Rowe McPheeters, daughter of Charles McPheeters. M in Fayette county, Ky., May 21, 1833. OR 6/6.

Richard Allen to Miss Helen J. Foster, of Natchez, Miss. M in Fayette county, Ky., May 28, 1833. OR 6/6.

George Buckhart, aged about 100 years, to Miss Elizabeth Graybill, aged 60 years. M in Harlan county May 13, 1833. OR 6/6.

Daniel Mayes to Mrs. Elizabeth L. Humphreys, both of Lexington. M May 29, 1833. OR 6/6.

David Murray, publisher of the *Georgetown Sentinel,* to Miss ———— Robinson, of Lexington. M in Lexington July 5, 1833. OR 7/18.

Henry W. Wilkinson to Miss Nancy Cropper. M in Lexington July 18, 1833. OR 7/25.

David Landeman to Miss Mary Ann Hutchison. M July 18, 1833. OR 7/25.

Theodore Taylor to Miss Ann Chalk. M in Georgetown July 26, 1833. OR 8/1.

Rev. A. Smeades to Miss S. Lyell, daughter of Rev. Doct. Lyell. M in New York City July 18, 1833. OR 8/7.

William Wilson to Miss Susan Clarke, both of Lexington. M July 28, 1833, at the First Presbyterian Church in Lexington. OR 8/7.

Samuel A. King to Miss Nancy Miller, both of Hendricks county, Ind. M July 25, 1833. OR 8/7.

George W. Johnson, of Georgetown, to Miss Ann Eliza, daughter of Capt. Willa Viley, of Scott county. M Aug. 20, 1833. OR 8/29.

George W. Dozier to Miss Mary W. Henry, daughter of John Henry. M. Aug. 27, 1833. OR 8/29.

Rev. John Taylor, of Franklin county, aged about 80 years, to Miss ——— Nash, aged about 40 years. M Aug. 16, 1833. OR 8/29.

Dr. J. W. S. Mitchell to Miss H. A. Withers, daughter of Peter Withers. M in Nicholasville Aug. 28, 1833. OR 9/5.

John Herndon, of Scott county, to Mrs. ——— Prewitt, daughter of Mr. ——— Fox, of Woodford county. M in Woodford county, Sept. 5, 1833. OR 9/15.

William Fry to Miss Ann Ransdell, daughter of Presley Ransdell, all of Fayette county. M Sept. 5, 1833. OR 9/15.

Dr. J. C. Jordan, of Demopolis, Ala., to Miss Mary, daughter of John King, of Lexington, Ky. M Friday Sept. 13, 1833. OR 9/19.

Irad Abdill, of Paris, to Miss Rebecca Watson, of Fayette county. M Sept. 5, 1833. OR 9/19.

John Liter to Miss Joanna Harrison, both of Lexington. M Sept. 22, 1833. OR 9/26.

Alexander R. Hann, of Lancaster, Ky., to Miss Leonora F. Macurdy, daughter of Allen F. Macurdy, of Frankfort. M in Frankfort Sept. 19, 1833. OR 9/26.

Albert G. Branham to Miss Jane Major, daughter of James Major. M in Franklin county Sept. 19, 1833. OR 9/26.

Capt. James Daniel, of Grant county, to Mrs. Rachel Venable, of Fayette county. M in latter place Sept. 28, 1833. OR 10/2.

Valentine Linginfelter, Jr., to Miss Mary Kohlhass, daughter of Henry Kohlhass. M in Winchester Sept. 26, 1833. OR 10/2.

Samuel Garrison to Miss Catharine Ann Johnson. M Oct. 3, 1833. Or 10/10

Arthur Berryman to Miss Eliza Jane Hobbs. M Oct. 3, 1833. OR 10/10.

William E. Walker, of Madison county, to Miss Sarah F. Bates, daughter of Col. John Bates. M in Manchester, Oct. 3, 1833. OR 10/10.

Charles R. Thompson to Miss Julia R. Drake, both of Lexington. M Oct. 10, 1833. OR 10/17.

Jacob Lyrick to Miss Mary S. Barton, both of Fayette county. M Sept. 27, 1833. OR 10/17.

Col. James Ford, of Shelby county, to Miss Jane C. Elliott, of Fayette county. M Oct. 15, 1833. OR 10/24.

J. L. Moore to Miss Jane Barker. M Oct. 22, 1833. OR 10/24.

Elisha Bridges to Miss Mary Jane Reed, both of Lexington. M Oct. 22, 1833. OR 10/24.

L. H. Reynolds, of Quincy, Ill., to Miss Gertrude V. L., daughter of Major Walter Preston. M in Clarke county, Ky., Oct. 15, 1833. OR 10/24.

Thomas E. Boswell to Miss Harriet Richards Campfield. M in Lexington Oct. 30, 1833. OR 10/31.

Wallace Keene to Miss Francis Ely. M in Georgetown Nov. 12, 1833. OR 11/14.

Alexander Moore to Miss Mary Anderson. M in Lexington Nov. 12, 1832. OR 11/14.

Robert B. J. Twyman to Miss Margaret C. Elder, of Lexington. M in Fayette county Nov. 21, 1833. Or 11/28.

Col. Jesse Bayles to Miss Rebecca McNitt, daughter of Robert McNitt, all of Lexington. M Monday Dec. 23, 1833. OR 12/26.

1834

John Argabright, of Bourbon county, to Miss Elizabeth Hitticks, eldest daughter of Capt. James Hitticks, of Fayette county. M Jan. 29, 1834. OR 2/6.

Henry G. Poston, of Winchester, to Miss Ann Winn, daughter of Philip B. Winn, of Clarke county. M Jan. 28, 1834. OR 2/6.

Ninian E. Gray, of Elkton, Ky. to Harriet E., daughter of the late Joseph E. Howell, of Philadelphia. M in Christ Church, Lexington, Ky., Feb. 3, 1834. OR 2/13.

Jeptha D. Bradley, of Lexington, to Miss Ann Eliza, daughter of William Suggett, of Scott county. M Feb. 6, 1934. OR 2/13.

Samuel Bell, of Louisville, to Miss C. M. Hedington, daughter of Mrs. Nancy Berry. M in Louisville Feb. 4, 1834. OR 2/20.

Hugh Campbell to Miss Catharine Fry, both of Bourbon county. M Feb. 18, 1834. OR 2/20.

James Johnson, of Indianapolis, to Miss Ann Eliza, eldest daughter of Col. Benjamin Taylor, of Fayette county. M Feb. 14, 1834. OR 2/20.

Daniel Morris, of Scott county, to Miss Susan Logan, daughter of James Logan, of Fayette county. M Feb. 21, 1834. OR 2/28.

Samuel Warner to Miss Sarah Ann Smith, both of Fayette county. M Feb. 27, 1834. OR 3/6.

Joseph C. Lemon, of Louisville, to Miss Zarilda Jane Robards, daughter of William Robards, of Jessamine county. M Feb. 26, 1834. OR 3/6.

Hiram Stevenson to Miss Emily West, daughter of Capt. Lynn West. M in Georgetown, Feb, 27, 1834. OR 3/6.

Clayton Curle, of Richmond, to Mrs. Sophia H. Boggs, daughter of John Hunt, of Fayette county. M Feb. 27, 1834. OR 3/6.

John S. Richardson, M. D., of Blaiden county, N. C., to Miss Eliza, daughter of Rev. S. Chipley, of Lexington, Ky. M Mar. 16, 1834. OR 3/20.

Pendleton Pope to Miss Nancy Johnson, daughter of Col. James Johnson, dec'd. M in Scott county Mar. 20, 1934. OR 3/27.

Thomas Gibbons, Jr., to Mrs. Eliza Page, both of Lexington. M Mar. 26, 1834. OR 3/27.

Dr. Tandy W. Walker, of Morgan county, Ala., to Miss Eliza R. Patterson, daughter of Samuel Patterson, of Fayette county, Ky. M Mar. 20, 1834. OR 3/27.

Charles Emmons to Miss Elizabeth C. Richards. M in Georgetown, Mr. 27, 1834. OR 4/10.

Dr. B. Ellis to Miss Elizabeth B. Collier, both of Bourbon county. M Mar. 29, 1834. OR 4/10.

Benjamin W. Finnell to Miss Eliza C. Wall, daughter of Capt. Garrett Wall. M in Scott county Thursday Apr. 3, 1834. OR 4/10.

Charles McDowell, of Fayette county, to Ann Catharina Redd, of Lexington. M Apr. 1, 1834. OR 4/10.

Dr. W. W. Higgins, formerly of Fayette county, to Miss Jane, daughter of Benjamin Taylor, of Fayette county. M Apr. 15, 1834. OR 4/24.

George Snyder, of Paris, Ky., to Miss Sarah D. Laughlin, daughter of John Laughlin, of Clarke county. M in Clarke county Apr. 22, 1834. OR 5/1.

Richard Higgins, of Lexington, to Mrs. Nancy Young, relict of the Hon. Richard Young, of Jessamine county, and daughter of Walter Carr, Sr., of Fayette county. M in Jessamine county on Apr. 28, 1834. OR 5/1.

Thomas H. Davis, of Richmond, Ky., to Miss Ann Maria Carr, daughter of Charles Carr, of Fayette county. M Apr. 22, 1934. OR 5/1.

Alexander Coyle to Miss Nancy Wallace, both of Fayette county. M May 14, 1834. OR 5/15

John P. Brown, of Winchester, to Miss Lavina Easton. M in Clarke county May 1, 1834. OR 5/15.

Hudson Lewis to Miss Elizabeth Masstin, both of Clarke county. M May 8, 1834. OR 5/15.

William Henry to Miss Emily Sharp. M in Lexington, May 8, 1834. OR 5/15.

John Candy to Miss Celeste F. Robert. M in Lexington May 14, 1834. OR 5/15.

William M. Todd, of the *Western Luminary,* to Miss Mary Ann Farrar, daughter of A. Farrar, of Jessamine county. M May 15, 1834. OR 5/22.

Joseph Carter, of Fayette county, to Miss Elizabeth Timberlake, of Jefferson county. M May 15, 1834. OR 5/22.

Mrs. Isabella, consort of Dr. A. J. Patterson, of Fayette county. She died Friday May 3, 1834, aged 16 years and 6 months. She died at the residence of James Patterson. OR 5/22.

Jordan Carter to Miss Nancy Hackney, both of Lexington. M May 28, 1834. OR 6/5.

B. J. Bontwell to Miss Mary Fisher. M in Lexington May 22, 1834. OR 6/5.

John Morton, of Fayette county, to Miss Mary M. Cook, of Henry county.

M in latter place May 29, 1834. OR 6/5.

Major John Brough to Miss Ann C. Richey, daughter of William Richey. M in Washington, Ky., May 29, 1834. OR 6/5.

Robert S. Finley, of Cincinnati, to Miss Julia W. Robbins, daughter of Hon. Judge ———— Robbins. M in Montgomery county May 29, 1834. OR 6/5.

Edward B. Bartlett to Miss Ann T. Sanders, daughter of the late Col. R. Sanders, of Scott county, both of Grant county. M at the residence of Griffin P. Theobold, May 31, 1834. OR 6/11.

Samuel Ewalt, of Bourbon county, to Miss Eliza P. Smith, of Harrison county. M in Lexington June 7, 1834. OR 6/11.

George Carlisle, of Woodford county, to Miss Mary, daughter of Robert Cunningham, of Clarke county. M June 17, 1834. OR 6/25.

Elisha B. Craven to Miss Armilda, daughter of William Dowden, all of Lexington. M June 19, 1834. OR 6/25.

Bird Taylor to Miss Paulina Hukil. M in June, 1834. OR 6/25.

Samuel Liter to Miss Lucinda Padgett. M June 19, 1834. OR 6/25.

Benjamin R. Wilson to Miss Agnes W. Hailey. M June 19, 1834. OR 6/25.

Elijah McDonald to Miss Susan Vance. M June 19, 1834. OR 6/25.

Rev. Minor M. Cosby, of the Kentucky Conference, to Miss Louisa A. Watkins, daughter of Shasten Watkins, dec'd., of Clarke county. M June 25, 1834. OR 7/2.

Thornton J. Wills to Miss Maria F. Watkins, daughter of Shasten Watkins, dec'd. M in Clarke county June 25, 1834. OR 7/2.

James Allen, of Winchester, to Miss Martha G. Bryan, of Clarke county. M June 26, 1834. OR 7/2.

Thomas Bryan, of Clarke county, to Miss Evaline Harris, of Montgomery county. M June 24, 1834. OR 7/2.

Col. Absolam Fowler, of Arkansas, to Miss Elvira D. Boswell, of Harrison county. She was a grand daughter of Gen. Joseph Desha. M Thursday June 26, 1834. OR 7/9.

Henry Nicholas to Miss Sarah F. Smith, daughter of the Widow Smith, both of Harrison county. M July 1, 1834. OR 7/23.

Robert Calendar to Miss Sarah Hailey. M July 10, 1834. OR 7/23.

George Winter to Mrs. Belinda Hutchcraft, daughter of Capt. Robert Cunningham. M in Scott county July 15, 1834. OR 7/23.

Ambrose Haily to Miss Malinda Sidener, daughter of George P. Sidener, Sr., of Fayette county. M July 31, 1834. OR 8/6.

Archibald Logan, of Lexington, to Mrs. Eleanor Robb, of Fayette county. M Aug. 5, 1834. OR 8/13.

Thomas Bryan to Miss Emaline Baxter. M at Capt. Keizer's Hotel, in Lexington, July 23, 1834. OR 8/13.

Thomas Maddux, Jr., of Woodford county to Miss Matilda B. Grooms, daughter of Elijah H. Grooms, of Lexington. M Aug. 7, 1834. OR 8/13.

Thomas Hart Noble to Miss Rosamond Clarke Johnson, daughter of Dr. Leroy C. Johnson. M in Lexington Aug. 14, 1834. OR 8/20.

James Krusor to Miss Margaret Scrugham, daughter of Col. Joseph, Scrugham, of Lexington. M Aug. 14, 1834. OR 8/20.

Younger R. Pitts to Miss Eleen Hawkins, daughter of Elijah Hawkins. M in Scott county Aug. 12, 1834. OR 8/20.

Rev. John F. Coons, editor of the *Western Luminary,* to Miss Eliza P. Bain. M in Fayette county Aug. 19, 1834. OR 8/27.

Major John McKinney, Jr., of Versailles, to Mrs. Susan H. Shannon, of Lexington. M Sept. 16, 1834. OR 9/17.

Thomas H. Hanley, of Baton Rouge, La., to Miss Jane L. Bain, of Lexington, Ky. M Sept. 2, 1834. OR 9/24.

Alfred Z. Boyer to Miss Zerelda McCoy, both of Lexington. M in Christ's Church, Sept. 24, 1834. OR 10/1.

Dr. Hudson Rutherford, of Jessamine county, to Miss Eleanor Caroline, of Lexington. M in Christ's Church, Lexington, Oct. 8, 1834. OR 10/8.

James T. Johnson, of Georgetown, to Miss Amanda Wood, daughter of William Wood. M in Harrison county Oct. 2, 1834. OR 10/8.

Davis Harlan, of Mercer county, to Miss Martha C., daughter of Henry Prewitt, of Fayette county. M Oct. 8, 1834. OR 10/15.

George C. Dunlap to Miss Martha Ann Crockett, both of Woodford county. M Oct. 22, 1834. OR 10/29.

Reuben Herndon, of Va., to Miss Mary Eliza, daughter of Beverly A. Hicks, of Fayette county, Ky. M Oct. 28, 1834. OR 11/6.

William Grimes, of Bourbon county, to Miss Leannah Grimes, of Lexington. M Nov. 4, 1834. OR 11/5.

William F. Kay to Mrs. Mary B. Kay, both of Fayette county. M Nov. 2, 1834. OR 11/5.

Minos Hearne, of Lexington, to Mrs. ———— Yancy, of Jessamine county. M Nov. 6, 1834. OR 11/12.

Rev. Basil Hunt, of Fleming county, to Mrs. Sarah, F. Wilson, of Fayette county. M Nov. 6, 1834. OR 11/12.

Dr. Charles E. Williams, of Mt. Sterling, to Miss Louann B., daughter of Col. Robert Morrow, of Bath county. M in Bath county Oct. 15, 1834. OR 11/19.

Caleb Williams, of Lexington, to Miss Nancy Rucker, daughter of Isaac Rucker, of Jessamine county. M Nov. 12, 1834. OR 11/19.

Alexander M. Preston to Miss Elizabeth Taylor. M in Winchester, Ky., Nov. 11, 1834. OR 11/19.

George W. Stone to Miss Mary Davis. M in Lexington Nov. 23, 1834. OR 11/26.

Amerose Webster to Miss America Ann Hukle. M in Fayette county Nov. 23, 1834. OR 11/26.

Alexander McKinney to Miss Charlotte M. Lockwood, daughter of John Lockwood. M in Lexington, Nov. 25, 1834. OR 12/3.

John S. Hilton to Miss Isabella Thompson. M in Fayette county, Nov. 26,

1834. OR 12/3.

James Wilson to Miss Georgianna Dunn, daughter of Josephus Dunn. M in Lexington, Nov. 30, 1834. OR 12/3.

Mark Honiker to Miss Cassander Crawley. M in Fayette county, Dec. 2, 1834. OR 12/3.

Lewis Buffington to Miss Mary Shroyer, daughter of John Shroyer, dec'd. M in Georgetown, Nov. 20, 1834. OR 12/3.

Capt. Sidney S. Grimes, of Clarke county, to Mrs. Lydia A. McCann, daughter of John Gess, of Fayette county. M Nov. 20, 1834. OR 12/3.

William N. Gist, of Fayette county, to Miss Mary Jane Brinker, daughter of Major James Brinker, of Newcastle, Ky. M in Newcastle, Nov. 26, 1834. OR 12/3.

Benjamin Shackleford, merchant of Louisville, to Miss Nancy W., daughter of the late Judge ———— Trimble, of near Paris. M Dec. 3, 1834. OR 12/10.

William Duvall to Miss Matilda Price, daughter of William B. Price, all of Fayette county. M Dec. 11, 1834. OR 12/17.

1835

Samuel Elgin, of Georgetown, to Miss America Gaines, daughter of Oliver W. Gaines. M in Scott county Dec. 9, 1834. OR 12/17.

Lewis Chisman, of Jessamine county, to Miss Hester Lyle, daughter of John Lyle, of Fayette county. M Dec. 3, 1834. OR 12/24.

J. R. Sloan to Miss E. S. Morton, daughter of G. W. Morton, all of Fayette county. M Dec. 23, 1834. OR 12/24.

Alfred Willett to Miss Elizabeth Kimbrough, both of Fayette county. M in Bourbon county Dec. 4, 1834. OR 12/24.

Thos. Starker to Miss Julia Ann Kendall, both of Fayette county. M Dec. 4, 1834. OR 12/24.

Alexander McNirney to Miss Lucy Goss, both of Fayette county. M Dec. 23, 1834. OR 12/24.

Capt. Newbold Crockett, of Scott county, to Miss Malinda E. Bridges, of Louisville. M Dec. 22, 1834. OR 12/31.

George Buchanan, of Louisville, to Miss Mary Catherine, eldest daughter of Edward Barry, of Lexington. M Dec. 27, 1834. OR 12/31.

Dr. John H. Thayer, of Harrodsburg, to Miss Marian W., daughter of the Hon. J. L. Bridges, of Harrodsburg. M in Dec., 1834. OR 1/7/1835.

Henry Hart, of Lexington, to Miss Elizabeth Brent, youngest daughter of Hugh Brent, of Paris. M Jan. 7, 1835. OR 1/12.

William Walden, of Lexington, to Mrs. Margaret Haydon, of Jessamine county, daughter of Peter Higbee, of Lexington. M. Dec. 26, 1834. OR 1/12/1835.

William Fothergill to Miss Catharine Robinson, of Lexington. M Jan. 15, 1835. OR 1/21.

Edwin Cahill to Miss Margaret Adams, of Lexington. M in Jan., 1835. OR 1/21.

Ezekiel McClain to Miss Elizabeth Peal, of Bourbon county. M in Jan., 1835. OR 1/21.

Joseph F. Taylor, of Fayette county, to Miss Louisa Eales, of Bourbon county. M Jan. 13, 1835. OR 1/21.

Hervey Lamme to Miss Mary Steele, daughter of the late Col. William Steele. M in Woodford county Jan. 21, 1835. OR 2/4.

John Green, of Lincoln county, to Mrs. Mary Paxton. M in Frankfort Jan. 28, 1835. OR 2/11.

John Smith to Miss Margaret Steffee, both of Georgetown. M Feb. 21, 1835. OR /25.

Creath Shropshire, of Bourbon county, to Mrs. Louisa Ann Thompson, of Scott county. M Feb. 21, 1835. OR 2/25.

John W. Deering to Miss Ann Dimick, both of Scott county. M Feb. 19, 1835. OR 2/25.

George Moore to Miss Jane Elizabeth Boner, daughter of William Boner, both of Fayette county. M Feb. 17, 1835. OR 2/25.

James Cogwill to Miss Margaret A. Brooks, both of Lexington. M Feb. 22, 1835. OR 2/25.

William Copes to Miss Mary J. Hall. M in Fayette county, Mar. 8, 1835. OR 3/11.

Richard Perkins to Miss Rachel Brown, both of Fayette county. M Mar. 8, 1835. OR 3/11.

Dr. James T. Stephenson, of Woodford county, to Miss Nancy Collier, of Bourbon county. M Apr. 2, 1835. OR 4/8.

Asa Farrar, Jr., of Lexington, to Miss Amanda Parker, of Fayette county. M Apr. 1, 1835. OR 4/8.

William Brown, Jr., of Georgetown, to Miss Sarah Ann Ferguson, of Versailles. M at latter place, Mar. 18, 1835. OR 4/8.

Lyne Starling, Jr., of Columbus, Ohio, to Miss Maria A. Hensley, daughter of Benjamin Hensley. M at Frankfort, Ky., Mar. 28, 1835. OR 4/8.

Dr. Charles H. Spilman, of Manchester, Miss., to Miss Mary D. Skillman, daughter of A. T. Skillman, of Lexington, Ky. M in latter place Apr. 9, 1835. OR 4/15.

William D. Skillman, of Lexington, to Miss Elvira Taylor, of Frankfort. M latter place Apr. 9, 1835. OR 4/15.

Richard Harcourt, of Harrison county, to Mrs. Mary Elizabeth Royle, daughter of John Bryan, of Lexington. M in latter place Apr. 14, 1835. OR 4/15.

George W. Norton to Miss Elizabeth Taylor, both of Lexington. M Apr. 14, 1835. OR 4/15.

Charles A. Mullins to Miss Mary Ann Shrock, daughter of John Shrock. M. Apr. 14, 1835. OR 4/15.

James H. Gough to Miss Cordelia C. Jenkins, both of Scott county. M Apr. 24, 1835. OR 4/29.

Francis Bucholts to Miss ———— Thwaites, both of Lexington. M Apr. 28,

1835. OR 5/6.

Thomas Hunt to Miss Mary Tilford, daughter of Major John Tilford. **M in** Lexington, Apr. 28, 1835. OR 5/6.

Dr. Nathaniel L. Turner to Miss Ann Bradford, daughter of Daniel Bradford. M Apr. 30, 1835. OR 5/6.

William R. Logan to Miss Sarah Caldwell, both of Fayette county. M May 5, 1835. OR 5/13.

Robert Campbell, of Richmond, Ky., to Miss Mary C. Jones, daughter of John Jones, of Lexington, Ky. M May 12, 1835. OR 5/20.

James M. Elliott to Miss Rosanna Burns, both of Fayette county. M May 14, 1835. OR 5/20.

William E. [E]stil to Mrs. Sally Ann Bevins. M May 21, 1835. OR 5/27.

Garrard Long, of Mo., to Miss Frances Elizabeth Peyton, daughter of **Mr.** V. Peyton, of Bourbon county, Ky. M May 12, 1835. OR 5/27.

William A. Verbrycke to Miss Mary B. Young, both of Lexington. M May 26, 1835. OR 6/3.

John C. Ruds to Miss Jane Theressa Wilson. M May 27, 1835. OR 6/3.

William P. Warfield to Maria Elizabeth, daughter of John T. Griffith. **M at** Woodburne, May 11, 1835. OR 6/3.

John S. Hart to Miss Anna Maria H. Allee, both of Lexington. M May 21, 1835. OR 6/3.

James P. Reiley to Miss Nancy Sharp, both of Lexington. M June 2, 1835. OR 6/10.

B. W. Todd, merchant of Lexington, to Miss Sarah Ann Thomas, of Fayette county. M June 2, 1835.

George Farrow to Miss Delila Arnett, both of Jessamine county. M June 11, 1835. OR 6/17.

Jacob Tevebough, of Bourbon county, to Miss Lucinda Howell, of Fayette county. M June 18, 1835. OR 6/24.

Benjamin W. Higbee, of Lexington, to Miss Rebecca A. Offutt, daughter of Warren Offutt, of Woodford county. M June 21, 1835. OR 6/24.

James M. Barlow to Miss Elizabeth Barlow, daughter of Thomas Barlow. M in Lexington June 24, 1835. OR 7/1.

Samuel B. Hall to Miss Mary Ann Fitch, daughter of Capt. Samuel **Fitch.** M in Lexington July 2, 1835. OR 7/8.

Capt. William Thompson to Mrs. Sarah Moore, both of Lexington. **M in** Cynthiana, June 17, 1835. OR 7/8.

Minor O'Bannon, of Shelbyville, to Miss Jane P. Richardson, daughter of John C. Richardson. M in Fayette county July 8, 1835. OR 7/15.

Robert Sharp to Miss Matilda Dowden, daughter of ———— Dowden, of Lexington. M there July 16, 1835. OR 7/22.

Thomas McGhagheger to Miss Sarah Lewis, both of Georgetown. **M July 18,** 1835. OR 7/22.

Hiett Vance to Miss Emily Cox, both of Fayette county. M July 17, 1835. OR 7/22.

James Meteer to Miss Elizabeth Hill, both of Bath county. M July 16, 1835. OR 7/22.

Philipp Small to Miss Eliza George, of Fayette county. M in Bath county July 9, 1835. OR 7/22.

James J. Fleming to Miss Mildred Robinson, daughter of Charles Robinson, of Fayette county. M July 14, 1835. OR 7/29.

George W. Caplinger, of Louisville, to Miss Mary Melvina Crawford, daughter of James B. Crawford, of Georgetown. M July 16, 1835. OR 7/29.

William Bell, of Fayette county, to Miss Nancy D. Brown, daughter of William Brown, of Georgetown. M July 21, 1835. OR 7/29.

Rev. Jared R. Avery, of Groton, Conn., to Mrs. Sarah A. Agnew, of Lexington, Ky. M in Lexington July 23, 1835. OR 8/5.

Dr. B. W. Sinclair to Miss Elizabeth Burbridge, daughter of Thomas Burbridge, of Scott county. M July 30, 1835. OR 8/5.

Thomas M. Peck, of Richmond, Ky., to Miss Augusta D. Jones, daughter of John Jones, of Lexington, Ky. M Aug. 18, 1835, in the latter city. OR 8/19.

Alexander McKenzie, of Danville, to Mrs. Nancy Smith, of Lexington. M latter place Aug. 17, 1835. OR 8/19.

Lloyd P. Hallack, lately of Kentucky, to Miss Mary R. Stone, daughter of Elder Barton W. Stone, formerly of Scott county, Ky. M at Jacksonville, Ill., July 30, 1835. OR 8/9.

George D. Prentice to Miss Harriet Benham, daughter of Joseph S. Benham, all of Louisville. M Aug. 18, 1835. OR 8/26.

Alexander Duvall, of Louisville, to Miss Anne Elizabeth Elliott, of Lexington. Mr. Duvall was formerly of Annapolis, Md. They were married in Lexington, Ky., Monday Aug. 24, 1835. OR 8/26.

Dr. J. C. Wilson, of Clay county, to Miss Prudence Barry Kinkead, daughter of John Kinkead. M in Woodford county Sept. 1, 1835. OR 9/9.

Samuel A. Young, of Lexington, to Miss Mary A. Morgan, daughter of Major John Morgan, of Fayette county. M Sept. 1, 1835. OR 9/9.

Givinn R. Tompkins to Miss Mary Anderson Dunn, eldest daughter of Walter Dunn, of Fayette county. M Sept. 8, 1835. KG 9/12.

Garland B. Hale to Miss Emily, only daughter of John McCracken, all of Lexington. M Sept. 17, 1835. KG 9/19.

William Voorheis, of La., to Miss Mary Howard Hart, daughter of Nathaniel Hart, of Woodford county. M in Mercer county Sept. 11, 1835. OR 9/23.

Thomas Gear to Miss Matilda Patterson. M in Lexington in Sept., 1835. KG 9/19.

William Coyle to Miss Eliza Hurst, daughter of James Hurst, of Fayette county. M Sept. 24, 1835. OR 9/30.

Thomas J. Wilby, of New York, to Miss Mary M. Coppuck, of Baltimare. M in Christ Church, Lexington, Ky., Sept. 27, 1835. OR 9/30.

Dr. R. C. Holland to Miss Elizabeth F. Carlisle, daughter of the Rev. T. W. Coit, President of Transylvania University. M in Christ Church, Lexington, Sept. 28, 1835. OR 9/30.

George Vanpelt, of Lexington, to Miss Janet R. Coppuck, of Baltimore. M in Louisville, Sept. 24, 1835. OR 9/30.

———— Preston to Miss Edmonia Hawkins, daughter of Littleberry Hawkins, formerly of Lexington. M in Louisville Sept. 25, 1835. OR 9/30.

Samuel Sidenor to Miss Elizabeth H. Miller, daughter of Thomas D. Miller. M in Fayette county Sept. 24, 1835. OR 9/30.

George W. Ward, of Princeton, Miss., to Miss Sarah Miller, of Scott county, Ky. M Sept. 29, 1835. OR 10/7.

James Nutter to Miss Eliza M. Atkins. M Sept. 29, 1835. OR 10/7.

Samuel T. Brooking, of Woodford county, to Miss Eunice Branham, of Scott county. M Sept. 23, 1835. OR 10/7.

Samuel Moore to Miss Mary W. Davis, both of Scott county. M Sept. 22, 1835. OR 10/7.

Major William B. Kinkead, of Paris, to Miss Elizabeth Wickliffe, d. of Hon. Chas. A. Wickliffe, of Bardstown. M Sept. 22, 1835. OR 10/7.

Samuel McMeeken to Miss Hannah Hilton. M Sept. 29, 1835. OR 10/7.

Dr. Robert Peter to Miss Frances, daughter of Major William S. Dallam, of Lexington. M Oct. 6, 1835. OR 10/14.

James Jackson to Miss Rebecca, daughter Col. Joseph Scrugham, of Lexington. M Oct. 8, 1835. OR 10/14.

Benjamin Porter to Miss Rozanna Ardery. M in Bourbon county Oct. 1, 1835. OR 10/14.

James T. Holmes to Miss Jane Vance, of Fayette county. M Oct. 6, 1835. OR 10/14.

J. O. Cochran, of Lexington, Ky., to Miss Mary A. C. Winston, daughter of Gen. Horatio G. Winston. M in Louisa county, Va., Oct. 7, 1835. OR 10/21.

Waller Bullock to Miss Maria L. Todd, both of Fayette county. M Oct. 20, 1835. OR 10/28.

George Morgan to Miss Rebecca Dennis, both of Lexington. M Oct. 24, 1835. OR 10/28.

Benjamin Kerr to Miss Zeralda Ann Barr. M in Winchester, Oct. 27, 1835. OR 11/4.

William F. Applegate to Miss Catharine M. Clarke, daughter of the Hon. C. L. Clarke, dec'd. M in Georgetown, Oct. 27, 1835. OR 11/4.

Dr. George D. Fisher, of Haynesville, Ala., to Miss Louretta Grimes, daughter of Benjamin Grimes, of Lexington, Ky. M Oct. 22, 1835. OR 11/4.

Hon. John Bell, member of Congress, to Mrs. Jane Yeatman. M at Nashville, Tenn., Oct. 25, 1835. OR 11/4.

Rev. T. Fanning, of Nashville, Tenn., to Miss Sarah Ann Shreve, daughter of Judge W. Shreve, of Nicholasville, Ky. M in latter place Nov. 5, 1835. OR 11/11.

Lewis Payne to Miss Sally Ann Payne, daughter of Nathan Payne. M in Fayette county Nov. 3, 1935. OR 11/11.

Reuben Leusly to Miss Lucinda Sidener, daughter of George P. Sidener, Sr., all of Fayette county. M Nov. 4, 1835. OR 11/11.

Oliver Griffith, of Illinois, to Miss Sarah Scott, of Fayette county, Ky. M Nov. 12, 1835. OR 11/18.

George W. Newcomer, of Louisville, to Miss Ann B. Miles, daughter of Dr. J. I. Miles, of Paris. M Nov. 12, 1835. OR 11/25.

Daniel Waltz to Miss Henrietta Edge, both of Fayette county. M Nov. 5, 1835. OR 11/25.

Dr. Oliver Howe to Mrs. Mary Ragan, both of Lexington. M Nov. 20, 1835. OR 11/25.

Francis G. Brown to Miss Frances J., daughter of Loyd K. Goodwin, of Fayette county. M Nov. 5, 1835. OR 11/25.

William H. Moody to Miss Eveline, daughter of James Sullivan, of Georgetown. M Nov. 12, 1835. OR 11/25.

Caleb Morris to Mrs. Louisa King, daughter of the late James Hutchison, all of Bourbon county. M. Nov. 15, 1835. OR 11/25.

Eldred S. Dudley, of Fayette county, to Miss Mary Ann, daughter of Col. Henry Clay, of Bourbon county. M Nov. 19, 1835. OR 11/25.

Thomas Burke Stevenson, of Frankfort, to Miss Sarah, daughter of Dr. Ennis Combs, of Montgomery county. M in the latter place, Nov. 25, 1835. OR 12/2.

James M. Stifler to Miss Susan Manssin. M in Lexington Nov. 26, 1835. OR 12/2.

James G. Mathers to Miss Mary E. Johnson, daughter of Dr. Leroy Johnson, of Lexington. M Nov. 29, 1835. OR 12/2.

Dr. Luke P. Blackburn, of Versailles, to Miss Davidella, daughter of the late Dr. Joseph Boswell, of Lexington. M Nov. 24, 1835. OR 12/2.

Thomas Van Swearengen, of Virginia, to Miss Elmira Warner, daughter of the late Elijah Warner, of Lexington, Ky. M in Aberdeen, Ohio, Nov. 30, 1835. OR 12/9.

David L. Zimmerman, of Lexington, to Miss Nancy H. Rainey, of Fayette county. M Dec. 3, 1835. OR 12/9.

Robert T. Bowman, of Fayette county, to Miss Elizabeth E. Dickerson, daughter of Elisha Dickerson. M in Winchester Dec. 1, 1835. OR 12/9.

Thomas Huggins to Mrs. Catharine Pilkington, both, of Lexington. M in Christ's Church, Dec. 2, 1835. OR 12/16.

James Cromey, of Louisville, to Miss Priscilla Sayre, of Lexington. M Dec. 8, 1835. OR 12/16.

Mason Brown, of Frankfort, to Miss Mary Yoder, of Spencer county. M latter place Dec. 8, 1835. OR 12/23.

Elijah Kirtley, of Bourbon county, to Miss Minerva Jamison, daughter of James Jamison, of Harrison county. M Dec. 8, 1835. OR 12/23.

Elijah Ennis to Miss Theodocia Dowden. M in Lexington, Dec. 23, 1835.

1836

James McCutchen, of Miss., to Miss Susan P. Mosby, daughter of Dr. ———— Mosby, late of Virginia. M in Oldham county, Ky., Dec. 22, 1835.

OR 1/6/1836

Smallwood C. Hammond, of Cincinnati, to Miss Elizabeth B. Moorehead, of Zanesville, Ohio. M Jan. 2, 1836. OR 1/13.

James S. Jacoby, of Georgetown, to Miss Mary Headdington, of Lexington. M Jan. 14, 1836. OR 1/20.

Rev. Luther Halsey Van Doren, of Lexington, Ky., to Miss Susan, daughter of Jonathan Wynkoop, of Bucks county, Pa. M. Dec. 29, 1836. OR 1/20/1836.

John L. Winter to Miss Jane H. White, both of Lexington. M Jan. 19, 1836. OR 1/20.

Richard C. Richards to Mrs. Eliza Craig, both formerly of Philadelphia. M Jan. 8, 1836. OR 1/27

Jacob Hull, of Lexington, to Miss Mary Ann Williams, of Franklin county. M Feb. 11, 1836. OR 2/17.

George P. Sidener, Sr., to Mrs. Polly Ann Bradley, both of Fayette county. M Feb. 10, 1836. OR 2/17.

John Corlis, Sr., to Miss Emeline Bishop. M in Bourbon county Feb. 14, 1836. OR 2/17.

George Liter to Miss Polly Ann Bryant, both of Bourbon county. M Feb. 11, M there Mar. 6, 1836. OR 3/9.

Asa Anderson, to Miss Martha Allen. M Friday evening, Feb. 12, 1836. On Saturday morning (Feb. 13) hung himself to an apple tree in his father's orchard, and was found dead. M and died in Madison county. OR 2/24.

Joseph T. Sutton, of Lexington, to Miss Nancy Jane Edwards, of Fayette county. M Feb. 25, 1836. OR 3/2.

James Ferguson to Miss Martha Ann Vaughan, both of Fayette county. M Feb. 25, 1836. OR 3/2.

Cabell Roy to Miss Malinda McClain, daughter of Elijah McClain, all of Fayette county. M Feb. 25, 1836. OR 3/2.

Orville H. Browning, of Quincy, Ill., to Miss Eliza H. Caldwell, daughter of Major Robert Caldwell, of Madison county, Ky. M Feb. 25, 1836. OR 3/2.

George Roberts, of Hardin county, to Miss Catharine Watson, of Frankfort. M there Mar. 6, 1836. OR 3/9.

Job Stevenson, of Georgetown, to Mrs. Susan Hunnicut, of Woodford county. M Mar. 7, 1836. OR 3/9.

William M. Bain to Miss Julia L. C. Edwards, both of Lexington. M Mar. 1, 1836. OR 3/9.

Henry Grant to Miss Margaret Alexander. M in Winchester, Mar. 3, 1836. OR 3/9.

Edward Payne, of Fayette county, to Mrs. Mariah Cassell, daughter of Peter Higbee, of Lexington. M Mar. 15, 1836. OR 3/23.

Coleman R. Ammermon to Miss Cynthiann Wilson. M in Harrison county Mar. 8, 1836. OR 3/23

W. Cross to Miss Sophia Ann Shropshire, daughter of Col. B. N. Shropshire. M in Bourbon county Mar. 10, 1836. OR 3/23.

James Kerrick to Miss Elizabeth Robinson, both of Lexington. M Mar. 10,

1836. OR 3/23.

Jacob Parker to Miss Nancy Geers. M Mar. 13, 1836. OR 3/23.

Thomas W. Stevens to Miss Paulina Wharton, daughter of William Wharton. M in Woodford county, Mar. 7, 1836. OR 3/23.

John Powell, of Indiana, to Mrs. Cynthia W. Owens, of Summersville, Ala., daughter of Mr. ———— McEldery, formerly of Scott county, Ky. M in March, 1836. OR 3/23.

Richard L. Taylor to Miss Nancy McMurtry, daughter of David McMurtry, all of Fayette county. M Mar. 24, 1836. OR 3/30.

J. Franklin Tanner, Printer, to Miss Susan Yates, both of Maysville. M in Aberdeen, Ohio, Mar. 24, 1836. OR 4/6.

Robert King to Miss Angelina Headington, daughter of N. Headington. M in Lexington, Apr. 14, 1836. OR 4/20.

James M. Cook to Miss Harriett Grant. M in Winchester, Apr. 11, 1836. OR 4/20.

Benjamin Turner, of Winchester, to Miss Nancy Ragland, of Clarke county. M Apr. 14, 1836. OR 4/20.

James Virden, of Versailles, to Miss Mary Wood, daughter of Mrs. Ann G. Wood. M in Woodford county Apr. 24, 1836. OR 5/4.

John C. Richardson, of Lexington, to Miss Adelaide Wade, of Jefferson county, Miss. M at Oak Hill, Apr. 14, 1836. OR 5/11.

William R. Bradford, of Lexington, to Miss Agnes, daughter of Daniel Bradford, merchant, of Georgetown, Ky. M Tuesday May 17, 1836. KG 5/23.

Thomas J. Harris to Mrs. Ann M. Laudeman, both of Lexington. M May 24, 1836. OR 6/1.

James M. Coons, of Lexington, to Miss Sarah D. Johnson, daughter of John Johnson, of Fayette county. M May 26, 1836. OR 6/1.

James Johnson, of Georgetown, to Miss Paulina Beach, daughter of James Beach, of Fayette county. M May 29, 1836. OR 6/1.

Dr. Samuel C. Trotter, of Lexington, to Miss Mary E., daughter of Louis Virmont, of Millersburg. M in Aberdeen, Ohio, May 31, 1836. KG 6/2.

Lewis D. Rucker, of Georgetown, to Miss Hannah Kruzor, of Lexington. M June 1, 1836. OR 6/8.

William Greenleaf, of Lexington, to Miss Lucinda Stephens, of Jessamine county. M June 2, 1836. OR 6/8.

George W. Coffey to Miss Mary Kerrick, both of Lexington. M June 2, 1836. OR 6/8

Marcus Downing to Miss Ann Eliza Allen, daughter of Major John Allen, all of Fayette county. M May 31, 1836. OR 6/8.

John M. Hewett, Sr., of Lexington, to Mrs. Ann Cullum, late of Mobile, Ala. M June 3, 1836. OR 6/8.

William Gosney to Miss Margaret Carter, both of Fayette county. M June 1, 1836. OR 6/8.

Dr. George B. Harrison, of Athens, to Mrs. Eliza Winn, of Fayette county. M June 2, 1836. OR 6/8.

John F. Bodley, of Vicksburg, Miss., to Miss Sarah Reading, of Lexington, Ky. M June 11, 1836. OR 6/22.

George T. Fishback, of Clarke county, to Miss Louisa H. Patton. M in Woodford county in June, 1836. (In another notice Miss Patton was listed as Lovisa H.) OR 6/22.

James S. Allen, of Winchester, to Miss Mary Ann Smith, youngest daughter of Benjamin Smith, Sr. M in Madison county, June 15, 1836. OR 6/22.

George W. Trice to Miss Mary Penny, both of Spottsylvania county, Va M in Woodford county, Ky., June 22, 1836. KG 6/30.

James Krusor to Miss Susan Clay. M in Lexington June 26, 1836. OR 7/6.

Thomas E. Ritter to Miss Catharine Hill. M in Bourbon county June 28, 1836. OR 7/13.

Ezra N. Offutt to Miss Elizabeth A. Lemon, daughter of the late Joseph I. Lemon. M in Scott county July 4, 1836. OR 7/13.

Leonard N. Finnell, printer, to Miss Rebecca Merritt, both of Lexington. M June 9, 1836.

Major Joseph Callahan to Miss Polly Ann Huffman, daughter of Henry Huffman. M July 12, 1836. OR 7/20.

Richard M. Johnson, Jr., of Scott county, to Miss Eliza M. Johnson, of Georgetown. M Aug. 9, 1836. KG 8/11.

Dr. B. F. Hall, editor of the *Gospel Advocate*, of Lexington, to Mrs. Susan Ball, of Woodford county. M latter place July 19, 1836. OR 7/20.

A. G. Garth to Miss M. A. Lemon, daughter of Joseph I. Lemon, dec'd. M in Scott county, July 14, 1836. OR 7/27.

Reuben Power, of Aberdeen, Ohio, to Miss Rachel Leusley, of Fayette county, Ky. M July 28, 1836. OR 8/10.

Edward B. Wood to Mrs. Ophelia McCracken, both of Versailles. M Aug. 1, 1836. OR 8/10.

John F. Grady to Miss Elizabeth Sidener, daughter of George P. Sidener, Sr., of Fayette county. M Aug. 28. 1836. OR 8/31.

Major John C. Mullay, late of Kentucky, to Miss Catharine D., daughter of John Kenney, of Greene county, Tenn. M in latter place, Aug. 10, 1836. KG 8/29.

W. S. D. Megowan, of Lexington, to Miss Sarah A. H. Price, of Bowling Green. M in Aberdeen, Ohio, Sept. 4, 1836. OR 9/7.

John G. Morrison, of Lexington, to Miss Nancy B., daughter of Gen. William Johnson, of Scott county. M Aug. 30, 1836. OR 9/7.

John G. Praigg, of Louisville, to Miss Abrabella S. Tod, daughter of William Tod, dec'd. M in Lexington Sept. 6, 1836. OR 9/7.

Dr. John R. Smith, of Paris, to Miss Sarah Jane Warfield, daughter of Benjamin Warfield, of Fayette county. M Sept. 1, 1836. OR 9/7.

Gen. James Garrard to Mrs. Mary Williams, widow of the late Gen. Roger Williams, all of Bourbon county. M Sept. 1, 1836. OR 9/14.

Leland J. Bradley, of Lexington, Ky., to Miss Mary Elizabeth, daughter of

Major N. Perkins. M in Franklin, Tenn., Sept. 8, 1836. OR 9/21.

James M. Holloway, merchant of Lexington, to Miss Lucy C. Scott, daughter of Dr. Joseph Scott, of Fayette county. M Sept. 22, 1836. OR 9/28.

James King to Miss Lucretia J. Graves, both of Lexington. M Sept. 27, 1836. OR 9/28.

1836

Samuel Shy, of Lexington, to Miss Marietta Shy, of Louisville. M Sept. 27, 1836. OR 10/5.

Thomas S. Logwood to Miss Susan Randall, daughter of Bryce Randall. M in Lexington, Sept. 29, 1836. OR 10/5.

Martin D. Flint, of Lexington, to Miss Margaret Ann Richardson. M in Fayette county, Sept. 29, 1836. OR 10/5.

John Kyle to Miss Sarah Ann Gilliam. M in Lexington, Sept. 29, 1836. OR 10/5.

Dr. J. T. Nolan, of Miss., to Miss Garnett Frazer, of Lexington, Ky. M Sept. 22, 1836. OR 10/5.

John Fisher to Mrs. Ellen Herring. M in Lexington, Oct. 3, 1836. OR 10/5.

Isiah King to Miss Catharine Young, both of Lexington. M Oct. 5, 1836. OR 10/12.

John B. Huston to Miss Mary J. Allan, daughter of the Hon. Chilton Allan. M in Winchester in Oct., 1836. OR 10/12.

Joseph Sellers to Miss Sarah Garrett. M in Woodford county, Oct. 10, 1836. OR 10/12.

John C. Venable, of Shelby county, to Miss Margaret J. Glass, daughter of David Glass, of Fayette county. M Oct. 4, 1836. OR 10/12.

Dr. Charles E. Pinckner to Miss Ellen Elder, daughter of Mr. W. Elder. M in Lexington, Oct. 18, 1836. (This might also be Dr. Charles F. Pickner.) OR 10/26.

J. S. Sherrod, of Scott county, to Miss Emeline Ewing, daughter of Mr. P. B. Ewing, of Fayette county. M Oct. 18, 1836. OR 10/26.

Thomas Bradley, of Lexington, to Miss Isabella Beard. daughter of Col. Henry Beard, of Fayette county. M Oct. 18, 1836. OR 10/26.

Dr. William A. Smith to Miss Juliann B. Coulter, daughter of Joseph Coulter, of Scott county. M Oct. 25, 1836. OR 11/2.

Thomas Ross, of Lexington, to Miss Ann Mariah, daughter of J. W. Webber, of Jessamine county. M Oct. 27, 1836. OR 11/2.

N. G. Fitch to Miss Ellen B. Lamme, daughter of Jesse Lamme, of Fayette county. M Oct. 13, 1836. OR 11/9.

J. J. Hunter to Miss Margaret A. Bruce, daughter of John Bruce, decd., all of Lexington. M Nov. 3, 1836. OR 11/9.

George W. Laudeman to Miss Sarah Hostetter, both of Lexington. M Nov. 1, 1836. OR 11/9.

John H. Jones, Jr., to Miss Mary Ann Hall. M in Bourbon county, Nov. 3, 1836. OR 11/16.

John George to Miss Rebecca B. Barnett. M in Lexington on Nov. 10, 1836. OR 11/16.

John H. Jones to Miss Mildred R. Mitchell. M in Bourbon county Nov. 13, 1836. OR 11/16.

Philip E. Yeiser to Miss Mary Ann Pinckard. M in Lexington Nov. 15, 1836. OR 11/16.

John D. Treadway, of Lexington, to Miss Polly M. Wilson, of Montgomery county. M Oct. 2, 1836. OR 11/16.

Silas P. Kenney, of Lexington, to Miss Lucinda Clark. M in Bourbon county Nov. 15, 1836. OR 11/23.

Preston West to Miss Elvira S. Crawford, daughter of James Crawford. M in Georgetown, Nov. 22, 1836. OR 11/30.

Albert Bohannon to Miss Henrietta C., daughter of James C. Long, of Woodford county. M Nov. 17, 1836. OR 11/30.

Samuel Clay, of Bourbon county, to Miss Nancy, daughter of Col. Thomas Wornall, of Clarke county. M Nov. 22, 1836. OR 11/30.

Allen H. Clark to Miss Elizabeth Fleming. M Nov. 22, 1836. OR 12/7.

W. H. H. Wright to Miss Sarah Ann Halley, daughter of James Halley, of Clarke county. M Dec. 1, 1836. OR 12/21.

David Laudeman, of Lexington, to Miss Sarah A. Shaddinger, daughter of David Shaddinger, of Cincinnati. M in latter place, Dec. 19, 1836. OR 12/28.

1837

Thomas Anderson to Miss Harriet Potter, both of Lexington. M Dec. 27, 1836. KG 1/5/1837.

Robert H. Russell, of Port William, to Miss Elizabeth R., daughter of Col. Charles S. Todd, of Shelby county. M Jan. 11, 1837. KG 1/19.

James R. Wallace to Miss Mary Jane McLain. M in Fayette county, Jan. 24, 1837. KG 2/2.

Charles Barnett, of Fayette county, to Miss Ann Crim, of Clarke county. M Jan. 12, 1837. KG 2/2.

William J. White to Miss Catharine Grimes, both of Bourbon county. M Jan. 24, 1837. KG 2/2.

James Thorn, of Georgetown, to Miss Susan, daughter of Mr. ———— McClintock, of near Millersburg. M Feb. 9, 1837. KG 2/16.

Thomas W. Powell to Miss Martha M. Darnes, both of Lexington. M Mar. 2, 1837. KG 3/9.

Robert Latham, M.D., of Hopkinsville, Ky., to Miss Sarah Anne, only daughter of Abraham Bowman, of Fayette county. M Mar. 9, 1837. KG 3/16.

Theodore Satterwhite, of Louisville, to Miss Eliza Ann Taylor, daughter of Stark Taylor, of Fayette county. M Mar. 16, 1837. KG 3/23.

Thomas G. Bush, of Clarke county, to Miss Susan Bryan, daughter of William Bryan, of Fayette county. M Mar. 9, 1837. KG 3/30.

Montgomery Meglone to Miss Maria Sharpe, both of Lexington. M Mar. 29, 1837. KG 4/6.

James Tomlinson, of Mo., to Miss Louisa Hurst, of Lexington, Ky. M at St. John's Chapel, Apr. 30, 1837. KG 5/4.

D. W. Dickinson, of Harrison county, to Miss Martha Washington, daughter of Henry D. Elbert, of Scott county. M May 18, 1837. KG 5/25.

Frederick Marsh to Miss Sarah Dedrick, both of Lexington. M May 11, 1837. KG 6/1.

Dr. Z. C. Offutt to Miss Mary Elizabeth, daughter of Benjamin B. Ford, of Georgetown. M May 30, 1837. KG 6/1.

Ira Evans to Miss Eliza Devore, both of Fayette county. M June 1, 1837. KG 6/8.

William R. Chew, of Lexington, to Miss Helen M. Ware. M in Hopkinsville, May 24, 1837. KG 6/8.

Henry B. Ingels to Miss Elizabeth L., daughter of Joseph Bruen, all of Lexington. M July 5, 1837. KG 7/13.

Thomas J. Arnold, of Vicksburg, Va., to Miss Eliza, daughter of the late Judge Robert Trimble. M near Paris, Ky., July 5, 1837. KG 7/13.

Joshua Smith to Miss Nancy Ann Merchant, both of Lexington. M in St. John's Chapel, July 9, 1837. KG 7/13.

Col. Ambrose Dudley to Miss Clarissa Cuny, daughter of Hon. William Miller, all of Cincinnati. M Thursday, July 6, 1837. KG 7/13.

Azariah M. Merrell to Miss Susan Ann Turner, both of Lexington. M July 16, 1837. KG 7/20.

Richard Downing, of Lexington, to Miss Martha Wilkinson, of Miss. M in Aberdeen, Ohio, July 23, 1837. KG 8/3.

Dr. Joseph Weisiger to Mrs. Isabella Clay. M at Crab Orchard, July 13, 1837. KG 8/3.

Isaac Cook to Miss Elvira Carty, both of Lexington, M Aug. 3, 1837. KG 8/10.

Vance W. Taylor to Miss America B. Christy, both of Mercer county. M Aug. 3, 1837. KG 8/10.

Dr. Woodson Dickerson, of Nicholasville, to Miss Eliza Jane, daughter of Dr. B. W. Rhoton, of Versailles. M Aug. 3, 1837. KG 8/10.

David T. Laird, of Lawrenceburgh, Ind., to Miss Clarrissa P. Haydon, of Lexington, Ky. M in Boone county, Ky., Aug. 8, 1837. KG 8/17.

Dr. R. B. Berry, of Fayette county, to Miss Mary Markham. M in Versailles, Aug. 22, 1837. KG 8/31.

Adam Lydick to Miss Ann Holland. M Aug. 31, 1837. KG 9/7.

Lewis S. Eads, son of Rev. M. L. Eads, of Harrison county, to Miss Mary F. Burch, daughter of James Burch, of Pendleton county. M Sept. 14, 1837. KG 9/21.

Dr. Joseph Early to Miss Adeline, daughter of James Rogers, of Fayette county. M Sept. 14, 1837. KG 9/21.

Benjamin Warfield to Miss Nancy Barr. M in Fayette county, Sept. 19, 1837. KG 9/28.

William Henry to Miss Hannah H. Fitch, daughter of Capt. Samuel Fitch.

M in Lexington, Sept. 20, 1837. KG 9/28.

Dr. Joseph Martin, of Louisville, to Miss Martha I. Hammett, of Virginia. M in Lexington, Ky., Sept. 21, 1837. KG 9/28.

William Davis to Miss Ann W. Cozart, both of Mercer county. M Sept. 14, 1837. KG 9/28.

Charles Joseph Cabell, of Miss., to Susan B. Allin, daughter of Thomas Allin, clerk of the Mercer county Court. M Sept. 15, 1837. KG 9/28.

Benjamin F. Crutchfield, of Lexington, to Miss Susan Winn, of Louisville. M Sept. 24, 1837. KG 10/5.

Thomas H. Clay to Miss Mary Mentelle, daughter of William Mentelle, all of Fayette county. M Thursday, Oct. 5, 1837. KG 10/12.

Edward Russell to Miss Elizabeth A. Boswell, both of Lexington. M Oct. 12, 1837. KG 10/19.

Mason Major to Miss Emily Carroll, both of Jessamine county. M Oct. 15, 1837. KG 10/19.

William Bain to Miss Ann Mansell, both of Lexington. M Oct. 16, 1837. KG 10/19.

James Collier, of Harrodsburg, to Miss Rebecca Coyle, of Lexington, daughter of Cornelius Coyle, decd. M Oct. 16, 1837. KG 10/19.

B. J. Knott, editor of the *Frankfort Argus,* to Miss Susan E., daughter of the late Ambrose Quarles. M in Franklin county, Oct. 11, 1837. KG 10/19.

Granville Hulett to Miss Catharine Angel, both of Fayette county. M Oct. 19, 1837. KG 10/26.

Jacob Hardisty to Miss Dianna M. Matthews, both of Fayette county. M Oct. 19, 1837. KG 11/9.

Wyatt K. Higgins, of Lexington, to Miss Pricilla Wilmott, of the same city. M Nov. 7, 1837. KG 11/9.

John Corbin to Miss Sarah Ashurst, both of Bourbon county. M Oct. 24, 1837. KG 11/9.

William B. Thompson to Miss Sarah Franklin, both of Fayette county. M Oct. 26, 1837. KG 11/9.

George Elliott, of Paris, to Miss Sarah Simpson, of Lexington. M Oct. 30, 1837. KG 11/9.

Thomas J. Barr to Miss Eleanora Wood, both of Fayette county. M Nov. 9, 1837. KG 11/16.

William Smedes, of Vicksburg, Miss., to Miss Anna Maria Marshall, daughter of the Hon. Thomas A. Marshall. M in Lexington, Ky., Nov. 9, 1837. KG 11/23.

Capt. James Trotter, of Nicholasville, to Miss ———— Wright, of Jessamine county. M Nov. 30, 1837. KG 12/7.

Washington Howell, of Fayette county, to Miss Louisa Reid, of Bourbon county. M Nov. 30, 1837. KG 12/7.

John P. True to Miss Mary Ann Showalter. M Nov. 20, 1837. KG 12/7.

John R. Nutter, of Bourbon county, Ky., to Mary Jane Nutter, of Fayette county, Ky. M Nov. 29, 1837, in New Albany, Ind. KG 12/7.

Charles G. Barker to Miss Eleanor Sutton. M in Dec., 1837. KG 12/21.

Milton Kidwell to Miss Martha Hulett. M in Dec., 1837. KG 12/21.

D. Clark to Miss Melinda Young. M in Dec., 1837. KG 12/21.

Walter Carr Young, of Jessamine county, to Miss Henrietta Sophia, daughter of John Peck, of Lexington. M Dec. 19, 1837. KG 12/21.

James Sculley, formerly of Cincinnati, to Miss Elizabeth Steele, of Lexington, Ky. M Dec. 24, 1837. KG 12/28.

1838

J. Howard Sheffer, of Philadelphia, to Julia A., daughter of Jacob Hughes, of Fayette county, Ky. M Jan. 9, 1838. KG 1/18.

Dr. David N. Sharp, of Shelbyville, to Miss Paulina W., daughter of Samuel Glass, Sr., decd., of Scott county. M at the Fayette county residence of Major A. Robinson, Jan. 11, 1838. KG 1/8.

Newton Berry to Miss Catharine Stone, both of Fayette county. M Jan. 17, 1838. KG 1/25.

Charles Dennis to Miss America Webster. M Jan. 18, 1838. KG 1/25.

Thompson M. Parrish, of Lake Providence, La., to Miss Mary P., daughter of Edward Blackburn. of Woodford county, Ky. M Jan. 18, 1838. KG 1/25.

Charles Howard to Miss Ann M. Prewitt, of Jessamine county. M Jan. 26, 1838. KG 2/1.

Col. W. Bryan to Mrs. Eliza Crutchfield, both of Fayette county. M Jan. 30, 1838. KG 2/1.

George Metcalf to Miss Nancy Bean. M Feb. 3, 1838. KG 2/8.

W. P. Holloway, of Lexington, to Miss Martha R., daughter of W. B. Booker. M at Springfield. Ky., Jan. 31, 1838. KG 2/8.

W. A. Ellis, of Port Gibson, Miss., to Miss Martha Beverley, daughter of Beverley A. Hicks, of Fayette county, Ky. M at Lafayette Seminary, Feb. 20, 1838. KG 3/1.

Hiram Shaw to Miss Nancy Marsh, both of Lexington. M Mar. 7, 1838. KG 3/15.

Dr. George B. Harrison, of Athens, to Miss Catharine Robinson, daughter of Charles Robinson, of Fayette county. M Mar. 6, 1838. KG 3/15.

Robert H. Cochran, of Ky., to Miss Mary Ann, daughter of Col. Richardson Allen, of Palmyra, Mo. M at latter place, Jan. 16, 1838. KG 3/15.

Warren Viley to Miss Catharine Jane, daughter of Major William H. Martin. M in Scott county, Feb. 27, 1838. KG 3/22.

Benjamin A. Jesse, of Lexington, Ky., to Miss Mary E., daughter of Samuel Jesse, decd., of Shelby county, Ky. M at New Albany, Ind., Mar. 21, 1838. KG 4/5.

James Smith to Miss Susan Runyan, daughter of John Runyan, of Fayette county. M Apr. 10, 1938. KG 4/12.

Samuel P. Winter, of Lexington, Ky., to Miss Josephine, daughter of Zadock Martin, of Martinsville, Falls of Platt River, Upper Mo. M at latter place, Mar. 25, 1838. KG 4/26.

Henry Rogers, of Fayette county, to Mrs. Elizabeth Marsh, of Lexington. M Apr. 24, 1838. KG 4/26.

Samuel C. Bean to Miss Harriet Ann, daughter of Lewis C. Bakes, all of Fayette county. M Apr. 12, 1838. KG 4/26.

Samuel Busby to Miss Lucretia C. Patterson, of Lexington. M at Aberdeen, Ohio, May 7, 1838. KG 5/17.

Philip Manuel to Miss Rebecca Wheeler, both of Fayette county. M May 10, 1838. KG 5/17.

Hon. Thomas M. Hickey to Mrs. Catharine A. Barry, both of Lexington. M at St. Peter's Church, Lexington, Sunday, May 20, 1838. KG 5/24.

John Mitchum to Mrs. Julia Ann Purnell, both of Woodford county. M May 22, 1838. KG 5/24.

Alvin Stephens to Miss Sally Simpson, of Fayette county. M May 28, 1838. KG 5/31.

Arthur Rees to Miss Lavinia Gibbons, both of Lexington. M in Aberdeen, Ohio, May 20, 1838. KG 6/7.

William Creighton, of Centreville, to Miss Sarah E. Frakes, daughter of Joseph Frakes, of Montogmery county. M in Clarke county, June 14, 1838. KG 6/21.

Herbert McConathy to Miss Elizabeth Philips, both of Lexington. M June 26, 1838. KG 6/28.

Mrs. Elizabeth Meredith, relict of Samuel Meredith, of Fayette county, and only sister of the late Gen. Robert and John Breckenridge, of Kentucky and Gen. James Breckenridge, of Virginia. She died July 3, 1838, aged 72 years. KG 7/5.

Thomas B. Warfield, of Leixngton, to Miss Alice, daughter of T. D. Carneal, of Cincinnati. M July 17, 1838. KG 7/26.

Joseph Hufford, of Scott county, to Miss Elizabeth Armstrong, of Fayette county. M Aug. 2, 1838. KG 8/9.

Aaron T. White to Miss Sarah Battaile, of Bath county. M July 21, 1838. KG 8/9.

John Barclay, of Danville, to Miss Sarah, daughter of the Hon. John Green. M in Lincoln county, Aug. 7, 1838. KG 8/16.

H. W. Hollingsworth, editor of the *Whig Banner*, to Miss Charlotte Clarke, daughter of the late Carey L. Clarke. M in Georgetown, Aug. 7, 1838. KG 8/16.

Jesse Bayles, of Lexington, to Miss Mary Jane Head, daughter of Thompson Head, of Harrodsburg. M in latter place, Sept. 3, 1838. KG 9/8.

George Hutchison to Miss Rosanna Pogue. M in Jessamine county, Sept. 11, 1838. OR 9/26.

Alexander Blair, of Nicholas county, to Mrs. Ann Young, of Jessamine county. M Sept. 20, 1838. OR 9/26.

S. Woodson, of Jessamine county, to Miss Margaret Ashby, daughter of Dr. M. Q. Ashby. M in Richmond, Ky., Sept. 11, 1838. OR 9/26.

William G. McCrosky, of Leesburg, to Miss Sarah A., daughter of Samuel Chambers. M Sept. 23, 1838. OR 9/26.

James Davis to Miss Mary Petty, both of Lexington. M Sept. 25, 1838. OR 9/29.

P. W. Gaugh to Miss Mary Schooly, daughter of J. Schooly, both of Lexington. M Oct. 10, 1838. KG 10/11.

Asa McDonald, of Fleming county, to Miss Elizabeth Willgus, of Lexington. M Oct. 4, 1838. KG 10/11.

James G. McKinney, mayor of Lexington, to Mrs. Eliza A. Payne, of Fayette county. M Monday evening, Oct. 15, 1838. KG 10/18.

John E. Patton, to Miss Margaret Ann Wallace, both of Jessamine county. M October 26, 1838. KG 11/1.

Harvey Maguire, of Lexington, Ky., to Miss Mary Ann Thorne. M in Harrodsburg Friday, October 19, 1838. OR 11/3.

B. F. Rogers to Miss Mary A. Coons, both of Fayette county. M Thursday, November 1, 1838. OR 10/14.

Col. Wade Hampton, Jr., of Columbia, S. C., to Miss Margaret Preston, daughter of late Gen. Francis Preston. M at Abington, Va., October 16, 1838. OR 10/14.

Dr. Lewis Perrine, of Cynthiana, to Miss Elizabeth Ann Hinde, daughter of Dr. John W. Hinde. M in Clarke county November 7, 1838. OR 11/17.

Henry Chapize, of Bardstown, to Miss Lucy B. Hord, of Jessamine county. M Tuesday, November 20, 1838. OR 11/28.

William S. Scott to Miss Lucy A. Metcalf, both of Nicholasville. M Wednesday, November 21, 1838. OR 11/28.

Hon. Ogden Hoffman to Virginia E. Southard, daughter of Hon. Samuel L. Southard. M in New York Thursday, November 22, 1838. OR 11/28

Peter Ciscoe to Miss Clarissa Winn. M in Lexington, Ky., Tuesday, November 27, 1838. OR 11/28.

J. W. Cochran, of Lexington, Ky., to Miss Theodosia S. Payne, daughter of Nathan Payne, of Fayette county. M Thursday, October 25, 1838. KG 11/1.

Joseph Scrugham, Lexington, Ky., to Miss Panthe Ewing, daughter of James Ewing, of Fayette county. M Thursday, October 25, 1838. KG 11/1.

Curran Pope to Miss Matilda P. Jacob, daughter of John Jacob, all of Louisville, Ky. M October 23, 1838. KG 11/1.

John Lafon, of Jessamine county, to Mrs. Mary Ann Jones, of Mercer county. M November 13, 1838. OR 12/1.

Robert Gilky, of Montgomery county, to Miss Elizabeth Stratton, of Clarke county. M Tuesday November 13, 1838. OR 12/1.

Willard F. Taft, of Lexington, Ky., to Miss Verlinda A. Grimes, of Bourbon county. M December 10, 1838. OR 12/12.

Desso Duidwit to Miss Joanna Miller, daughter of Isaac R. Miller, all of Lexington, Ky. M December 11, 1838. OR 12/12.

Cosby Vaughn to Miss Louisa M. Grooms, daughter of Mr. E. Grooms, of Lexington, Ky. M December 9, 1838. OR 12/12.

J. A. Willis to Miss Catherine Miller. M Thursday December 13, 1838. OR 12/19.

William D. Jones to Miss Mary Ann Wheelock, both of Lexington. M Sunday, December 16, 1838. OR 12/19.

Philip B. Pendleton, of Virginia, to Miss Rebecca Wood, of Lexington, Ky. M Wednesday, December 19, 1838. OR 12/22.

George W. Smith, of Bourbon county, to Miss Martha Ann Hall, of Fayette county. M Tuesday, December 20, 1838. OR 12/22.

Alexander Hutchison, of Woodford county, to Miss Rebecca Dawson, of Bourbon county. M Thursday, December 20, 1838. OR 12/22.

Samuel G. Oldham to Miss Martha Brown, both of Fayette county. M December 20, 1838. OR 12/22.

Major Abraham Van Buren, eldest son of the President of the United States, to Miss Sarah Angelica Singleton, youngest daughter of Richard Singleton, of South Carolina. M Tuesday, November 27, 1838. OR 12/26.

Benjamin Daley to Miss Sally Ann Ennis, both of Fayette county. M December 20, 1838. OR 12/26.

John Masters to Miss Elizabeth M. Hendrick. M in Jessamine county, December 18, 1838. OR 12/26.

John C. D. Pogue, of Fayette county, to Miss Sarah Jane Campbell, daughter of Thomas P. Campbell, of Henry county, Ky. M Thursday, December 20, 1838. OR 12/26.

Thomas C. Clemson, of Philadelphia, Pa., to Miss Anna Calhoun, daughter of Hon. John C. Calhoun. M at Fort Hill, S. C., November 12, 1838. OR 12/29.

Oliver Frazer, of Lexington, to Miss Martha Mitchell, daughter of late Dr. Alexander Mitchell, of Frankfort. M Tuesday, December 25, 1838. OR 12/29.

Joseph Appleton to Miss Elizabeth Drake, both of Fayette county. M December 28, 1838. OR 1/9/1839.

1839

Benjamin G. Gibbons to Miss George Ann Shears, both of Lexington, Ky. M January 6, 1839. OR 1/9.

Daniel Duvall to Miss Mary Ann Hayes, daughter of David Hayes, all of Clark county. M January 3, 1839. OR 1/9.

West H. Humphreys, of Somerville, to Miss Amanda Pillow of Nashville. M in latter place January 1, 1839. OR 1/9.

John W. Craig, of Versailles, to Miss Laura, daughter of late Dr. Joseph Boswell, of Lexington, Ky. M in Versailles, January 10, 1839. OR 1/12.

Judge Wilkinson, of Mississippi, to Miss Eliza Crozier, of Bardstown, Ky. M latter place Thursday, January 10, 1839.

James S. Clark, of Vicksburg, Miss., to Miss Margaret B. Sproule, of Frankfort, Ky. M in Lexington, Ky., at residence of R. S. Todd, January 15, 1839. OR 1/16.

John M. Hewett to Miss Ruth Potter. M in Louisville, Ky., Thursday, January 10, 1839. OR 1/16.

C. Martin, formerly of Baltimore, to Mrs. Sarah McConnell, formerly of

Lexington, Ky. M at Milton, Ky., December 23, 1839. OR 1/19.

William J. Hickey, of Lexington, to Miss Nancy Tudor, of Madison county. M in Lexington Thursday, January 17, 1839. OR 1/19.

William Brockman to Miss Martha Edwards, both of Fayette county. M Thursday, January 17, 1839. OR 1/19.

Leander W. Macey, of Frankfort, to Miss Sophia J. White, of Lexington. M Thursday, January 17, 1839. OR 1/19.

Whitfield Collins, of Harrison county, to Miss Nancy A. Clark, of Lexington. M Thursday, January 17, 1839. OR 1/19.

Augustus Steinman, formerly of Lancaster, Ohio, to Miss Mary Kenly, formerly of Baltimore, Md. M Thursday, January 24, 1839. OR 1/26.

John T. Washington, of Cincinnati, to Miss Adelia J., daughter of Thomas Tibbatts, of Lexington, Ky. M Sunday, January 20, 1839. OR 1/26.

Allen Dodd, of Mississippi, to Miss Mary C. McKee, of Lancaster, Ky. M Thursday, January 10, 1839. OR 1/26

William McConnell, of Arkansas, to Mrs. Adeline Vaughn, of Lexington, Ky. M Thursday, January 24, 1839. OR 1/26

James H. Davis, of Albemarle, Va., to Miss Mary Jane Hawkins, of Winchester, Ky. M Houston, Texas, January 10, 1839. OR 2/5.

Lewis Rogers, M. D., to Miss Mary E., daughter of Charles M. Thurston. M Louisville, Ky., Thursday, January 31, 1839. OR 2/5.

Robert Dougherty to Miss Harriet Ann Herriott, daughter of John Herriott, all of Scott county. M January 22, 1839. OR 2/5.

Harvey Scott to Miss Jane Trimble, both of Fayette county. M January 17, 1839. OR 2/5.

Stother Bowman to Mrs. Elizabeth Rainey. M in Saundersville January 31, 1839. OR 2/6.

Edwin C. Hickman to Miss Amanda Best, daughter of late Dr. Robert Best of Lexington. M in Cincinnati Feb., 1839. OR 2/9.

Dr. James B. Campbell, of Ark., to Miss Mary E. Smith, daughter of Clement Smith, of Lexington, Ky. M Thursday, Feb. 7, 1839. OR 2/9.

J. Madison Jennings, M. D., formerly of Miss., to Miss Jane Ellen O'Neal, of Jessamine county. M latter place Feb. 10, 1839. OR 2/16.

E. R. Spencer to Miss Amelia A. Adams, both of Lexington. M Thursday, January 14, 1839. OR 2/16.

Samuel Bell, of Locust Grove, Fayette county, to Miss Emma A. C. Flynt, of Lexington. M Thursday, Feb. 14, 1839. OR 2/16.

Harvey Howell to Miss Frances S. Pittman. M in Lexington Thursday, Feb. 14, 1839. OR 2/16.

Marshall Headly, of Fayette county, to Miss Margaret, daughter of Aaron Farra, of Jessamine county. M Thursday, Feb. 21, 1839. OR 2/27.

George W. Dodd to Mrs. Sally Jenkins, both of Sandersville. M Feb. 24, 1839. OR 2/27.

John W. Boyle, of Ill., to Miss Tabitha Lamme, of Fayette county, Ky. M Tuesday, Feb. 26, 1839. OR 3/2.

James Berry to Mrs. Phebe Jackson, both of Crab Orchard. M Feb. 28, 1839. OR 3/6.

Charles Quin, late of county of Tyrone, Ireland, to Miss Dolly Madisonia, daughter of late Judge Todd, of Frankfort, Ky. M Wed. Feb. 20th, 1839, at residence of William T. Washington, in Jefferson county, Va. OR 3/9.

John Artt, Jefferson county, to Miss Armilda McConnell, daughter of Mrs. Sarah McConnell, of Woodford county. M Feb. 20, 1839. OR 3/9.

Hon. Joseph R. Underwood, member of Congress from Ky., to Miss Elizabeth, daughter of Col. John Cox, Mayor of Georgetown, D. C. M Feb. 27, 1839. OR 3/13.

Nathaniel Barbee, Scott county, to Mrs. Sally Ann Buckner, of Clark county. M March 5, 1839. OR 3/13.

J. M. Neal. of Fayette county, to Mrs. Mary Ann Neal, of Woodford county. M Thursday, March 14, 1839. OR 3/16.

William Moore to Miss Mary Simpson, both of Fayette count.y M Thursday, March 14, 1839. OR 3/16.

Nathaniel P. Long, of Lexington, to Miss Nancy Prentiss, of Boone county. M Feb. 28, 1839. OR 3/16.

Rev. H. B. Bascom, D. D., Prof. of Moral Science and Belle Lettres, Augusta College, Ky., to Miss Eliza Van Antwerp, daughter of late Thomas Van Antwerp, of New York. M latter place Thursday, March 14, 1839. OR 3/20.

William R. Hervey to Miss Eveline Butler, of Lexington. M in Aberdeen, Ohio, Friday, March 22, 1839. OR 3/20.

Edward Allen to Miss Mary, daughter of late David Bryan, all of Fayette county. M at New Albany, Ind., Thursday, March 21, 1839. OR 3/20.

James F. Robinson, of Georgetown, to Miss Willina S. Herndon, of Scott county. M latter place March 21, 1839. OR 3/27.

Albert Talbot, to Mrs. Elizabeth ·Talbot, daughter of Judge Owsley. M at Lancaster, Ky., Feb. 24, 1839. OR 3/27.

B. W. Twyman to Miss Mary E. Craig, daughter of J. W. Craig, of Versailles. M Wed., March 25, 1839. OR 3/27.

Williamson P. Fisher, of Louisville, to Miss Margaret Jane, daughter of the Rev. W. H. Rainey, of Harrison county. M Tuesday, April 2, 1839. OR 4/6.

William B. Risk to Miss Isabelle Eleanor Herriott, daughter of John Herriott, all of Scott county. M Apr. 2, 1839. OR 4/10.

Thomas McIlroy, of Lexington, to Miss Corrilla Davis, of Fayette county. M Apr. 7, 1839. OR 4/10.

Theodore Kohlhass to Miss Arabella C., daughter of James W. Keeth. M in Winchester, Ky., Wed., Apr. 3, 1839. OR 4/10.

Robert N. Long, formerly of Chillicothe, Ohio, to Miss Alsey Ann Taylor, daughter of Col. C. H. Taylor, of Colbyville, Clark county, Ky. M Apr. 11, 1839. OR 4/17.

George Washington Brand, of Lexington, to Miss Nancy Abercrombie, daughter of John T. Griffih, of Natchez, Miss. M at Lexington, residence of

Daniel Vertner, Tuesday, Apr. 16, 1839. OR 4/20.

Cary A. Lee, of Mo., to Miss Elizabeth M. Woodson, of Jessamine county, Ky. M Wed., Apr. 17, 1839. OR 4/20.

Joel W. Twyman to Miss Ellen V. Carter, both of Woodford county. M Wednesday, April 17, 1839. OR 4/20.

James Weir of Greenville, Ky., to Miss Jane A. Short, of Louisville. M April 23, 1839, in latter city. OR 4/27.

William Ernest, formerly of Lexington, to Miss Lydia Ann Bush, daughter of P. Bush, all of Covington. M Apr. 23, 1839. OR 5/1.

Dr. R. A. Gibney, of Bourbon county, to Miss Pamelia Pendleton, daughter of General E. Pendleton, of Clark county. M Apr. 30, 1839. OR 5/4.

Isaac C. Miller, of Cincinnati, to Miss Elizabeth J. Barr, youngest daughter of Mrs. Martha A. Barr. M in Fayette county, Apr. 30, 1839. OR 5/4.

Joseph Holt, of Vicksburg, Miss., to Miss Louisa Harrison, daughter of Dr. Burr Harrison, of Bardstown, Ky. M Apr. 24, 1839. OR 5/4.

Major General E. P. Gaines, of the U. S. Army, to Mrs. Myra Clark Whitney, only daughter of late Daniel Clark. M Wed., Apr. 17, 1839, at residence of Louis Bringier, Surveyor General of the state of La. OR 5/8.

Rev. Edward F. Berkley, Minister of Christ Church, Lexington, Ky., to Miss Sarah Ann S. Maury, only daughter of late Francis F. Maury, of Bath county M Thursday, May 2, 1839 at residence of Col. M. Maury, near Owingsville, Bath county, Ky. OR 5/8.

Walter Sharp to Miss Charlotte Ford, daughter of Benjamin Ford, all of Lexington. M in Aberdeen, Ohio, Fri., May 3, 1839. OR 5/8.

Toliver H. Fitzgerald of Lexington to Miss Nancy E. Rawlins of Scott county. M May 9, 1839. OR 5/11.

H. J. Higgins,of Randolph, Ill., to Miss Susan, daughter of Benjamin Tyler, of Fayette county. M Thurs., May 9, 1839. OR 5/11.

Rev. Joseph Leake, to Miss Mary Clarke, daughter of Enoch Clarke, all of Lexington. M Thursday, May 9, 1839. OR 5/11.

O. H. P. Stone, M. D., formerly of Fayette county, Ky., to Miss Mary, daughter of Elder L. Vancamp, formerly of Mason county, Ky. M in LaFayette Co., Mo., Thursday, April 25, 1839. OR 5/15.

Thomas E. Ingles to Miss Agness, daughter of Hiram M. Bledsoe, all of Bourbon county. M at Aberdeen, Ohio, May 11, 1839. OR 5/15.

Elihu Smith to Mrs. Sarah Watson, daughter of George Sidener, Sr., of Fayette county. M Thursday, May 9, 1839. OR 5/18.

John Crow to Mrs. Margaret Pitchford, both of Jessamine county. M May 19, 1839. OR 5/22.

John W. Prewitt, of Frankfort, to Miss Amaryllis A. A. Conover, of Lexington. M May 28, 1839. KG 5/30.

Rev. Edward Winthrop, Prof. of Sacred Literature in the Theological Seminary of Ky., to Miss Elizabeth Andras, daughter of late John Andras, of Bath, England. M in Lexington, Ky., Thursday, June 6, 1839. OR 6/8.

James K. Thompson, of Fayette county, to Miss Susan Ford, daughter of

James Ford, of Bourbon county. M Tues., June 4, 1839. OR 6/8.

James H. Massey to Miss Ann E. Rainey, daughter of James Rainey, all of Miss. M in Mount Sterling, Ky., Thursday, May 30, 1839. KG 6/9.

A. O. Newton, of Lexington, Ky., to Miss Julia Hurlock, daughter of J. Hurlock, of Bloomfield, Del. M latter place Sunday, May 26, 1839. KG 6/9.

Jacob A. Ingram to Miss Leah Helm, daughter of Andrew Helm, decd. M Thursday, May 30, 1839. KG 6/9.

William M. Drake to Miss Mary A. Hampton, both of Lexington. M Tuesday, June 11, 1839. OR 6/15.

C. G. Richardson, of Mount Sterling, to Miss Martha Simpson, of Lexington. M Thursday, June 13, 1839. OR 6/15.

William H. Moore to Miss Elizabeth Ann Ford, both of Fayette county. M May 21, 1839. OR 6/15.

E. A. Hathaway, of Mount Sterling, to Miss Phebe Ann Crawford, daughter of Mr. E. D. Crawford, of Flemingsburg. M latter place June 11, 1839. OR 6/15.

David Porter Keetly, of Nicholasville, to Miss Ann Eliza Cogshell, daughter of John Cogshell, of Lexington. M Tuesday, June 11, 1839. OR 6/15.

Cosby Price, of Fayette county, to Miss Mary Jane Duvall, daughter of George Duvall, of Woodford county. M Tuesday, June 11, 1839. OR 6/15.

George R. Trotter, of Lexington, Ky., to Miss Amanda Galloway, daughter of Major James Galloway, of Xenia, Green Co., Ohio. M latter place June 12, 1839. OR 6/19.

William Daniel Cummins to Miss Harriet Robertson, both of Lexington. M June 20, 1839. OR 6/22.

———— Cook, of Mercer county, to Miss Henrietta, daughter of Lewis Singleton, of Jessamine county. M Tuesday, June 18, 1839. OR 6/29.

Samuel Clear to Miss Elizabeth Francis, both of Lexington. M June 23, 1839. OR 6/29.

Elijah Whitt to Miss Rebecca Ellis. M June 20, 1839. KG 6/27.

John B. Mussey to Miss Susanna S. Hart, of Lexington. M June 26, 1839. OR 7/3.

Persickless Scott, late of Fredricksburg, Va., to Miss Mary Ann, daughter of James Hamilton, of Lexington, Ky. M Tuesday, July 8, 1839. OR 7/10.

William W. Zimmerman, formerly of Lexington, Ky., to Miss Amanthus Tidwell. M in Morgan county, Ill., June 17, 1839. OR 7/13.

Hon. Thomas P. Moore, to Miss Harriet M. Lake, of La. M in Harrodsburg, Ky., July 25, 1839. OR 8/7.

Thomas H. Stewart, of Miss., to Miss Emily M. Sanders, daughter of Mrs. Louisa Sanders. M Aug. 8, 1839. OR 8/17.

Derrick Jeffries to Miss Nancy Petterson, both of Lexington. M Aug. 11, 1839. KG 8/15.

Albert G. Stephenson to Miss Jane Sawkins, of Washington City. M at Lancaster, Ky., July 16, 1839. KG 8/15.

Charles M. Randall, of New Orleans, to Miss Mary E. Davis, daughter of

James E. Davis, of Lexington, Ky. M Aug. 13, 1839. OR 8/17.

Edward Troye to Miss Cornelia A. Van De Graff, daughter of Mrs. Jane Van De Graff, of Scott county. M July 16, 1839. OR 7/20.

M. D. Browning, of Burlington, Iowa Territory, to Miss Ann M., eldest daughter of the Hon. H. O. Brown. M in Cynthiana, Ky., July 16, 1839. OR 7/20.

William Brown, of Richmond, Ky., to Miss Mary Ann Smith, of Fayette county. M July 22, 1839. OR 7/24.

Dr. J. K. Burch, second son of Rev. James K. Burch, of Georgetown, Ky., to Miss Maria, youngest daughter of the late John Drummond, counsellor at law, of Allva North Britton. M July 19, 1839. OR 7/24.

Payton Johnson to Miss Paulina M. Johnson. M at Saundersville, July 31, 1839. OR 8/7.

Henry Rowland to Mrs. Mary Ann Bourne. M at Nicholasville, Aug. 28, 1839. OR 9/11.

Samuel Maddox to Miss Sarah A. Keene, both of Scott county. M Sept. 3, 1839. KG 9/12.

George B. Twyman to Mrs. Lucy Ann Yates, both of Fayette county. M Aug. 22, 1839. KG 8/29.

T. R. Brown to Mrs. Permilia Mann, both of Lexington. M July 4, 1839. KG 9/5.

Thomas Suggard to Mrs. Sarah Thornton. M Sept. 13, 1839. KG 9/19.

Moreau Brown, of Nicholasville, to Miss Eudora Blackwood, of Charleston, South Carolina. M in former place, Sept. 18, 1839. KG 9/26.

E. T. Currens to Miss Mary H. Barr. M at Winchester, Sept. 17, 1839. KG 9/26.

Gray Briggs, of Yazoo county, Miss., to Miss Sarah A. McConnell, of Fayette county, Ky. M Oct. 9, 1839. OR 10/12.

John McMeekin to Margaret Ann Graves, daughter of William Graves, of Scott county. M Sept. 12, 1839. OR 10/16.

Charles Crow to Miss Mary Jane Pilkington, both of Lexington. M Oct. 17, 1839. OR 10/19

Dr. J. B. Coons, of Mo., to Miss Margaret Elgin, daughter of Mr. H. S. Elgin, of Fayette county, Ky. M Oct. 22, 1839. OR 10/23.

Jacob Blain, of Lexington, to Miss Mary Jane Bakes, daughter of Lewis C. Bakes, of Fayette county. M Oct. 31, 1839. OR 11/2.

William R. Estill, of Madison county, to Miss Amanda D. Fry, of Fayette county. M Oct. 30, 1839. OR 11/6.

James McDonald to Miss Mary Shaw, both of Lexington. M Oct. 30, 1839. OR 11/6.

John Trimble to Miss Margaret Ann Curry, both of Clarke county. M Oct. 30, 1839. OR 11/6.

William Daviess to Miss M. W. R. Thompson, daughter of the late J. B. Thompson, all of Shawnee Springs, near Harrodsburg. M Oct. 25, 1839.

OR 11/6.

Henry Hampton, of Lexington, to Miss Margaret A., daughter of William Dishman, of Fayette county. M Nov. 5, 1839. R 11/13.

T. L. Budd to Miss Eliza Jane, eldest daughter of the Rev. John N. Moffitt, of Nashville. M in latter place, Nov. 9, 1839. OR 11/20.

Elisha Warfield Brown to Miss Mary Ann Brent, daughter of Robert Brent, late of Fauquier county, Va. M at Boonville, Mo., Oct. 24, 1839.

Capt. Henry Savary to Miss Ellen Taylor, both of Clarke county. M Nov. 20, 1839. OR 11/27.

Joseph H. Holt, Jr., of Columbia, Ark., to Miss Ellen O. Garrard, daughter of the late Capt. William Garrard, of Bourbon county, Ky. M Nov. 21, 1839. OR 11/27.

John C. Young, D. D., President of Centre College, to Miss Cornelia A. Crittenden, second daughter of the Hon. John J. Crittenden. M in Frankfort, Nov. 20, 1839. OR 11/30.

Alexander P. Churchill, to Miss Mary McKinley, daughter of the Hon. John McKinley, all of Jefferson county. M Nov. 19, 1839. OR 11/30.

Rev. J. M. Frost, of Mt. Vernon, Woodford county, to Mrs. Margaret A. Garth, of Scott county. M Dec. 5, 1839. OR 12/7.

David H. Coulter, of Scott county, to Miss Julia Poindexter, daughter of William Poindetxer, of Lexington. M Dec. 3, 1839. OR 12/7.

William Long, of Shelby county, to Miss Julian Daugherty, daughter of Thomas Daugherty, decd., of Scott county. M Dec. 3, 1839. OR 12/7.

Dr. G. T. Martin, late of Clarke county, to Miss Mary Ellen Mott, of Leesburg. M Nov. 28, 1839. OR 12/11.

Francis J. Keen, of Ark., to Miss Elizabeth, daughter of Mr. A. LeGrand, of Lexington, Ky. M Dec. 11, 1839. OR 12/18.

Samuel S. Graves to Miss Mary Shackleford, both of Fayette county. M Dec. 12, 1839. OR 12/21.

1840

James D. Drake to Miss Mary D. Hoagland, both of Lexington. M Dec. 7, 1839. OR 12/28.

Hon. George W. Cutter, member of the House of Representatives of the Indiana Legislature, to the celebrated actress, Mrs. A. Drake. M Jan. 23, 1840. OR 2/5.

Samuel Downing, of Fayette county, to Miss Amanda, daughter of Sabert Offutt, of Scott county. M Apr. 14, 1840. OR 4/18.

Rev. Robert C. Grundy to Miss Sarah Ann January, daughter of Andrew January, all of Maysville. M Apr. 23, 1840. OR 4/25.

Robert M. Hathaway to Miss Martha J. Frisby, of Scott county. M in Scott county, Apr. 7, 1840. OR 4/15.

James H. Henderson, of Lexington, to Miss Margaret P. Risk, of Scott county. M Feb. 4, 1840. OR 2/12.

Frederick William De Kautzow, of Stockholm, Sweden, to Miss Eloise, daughter of the late Mr. T. Bullitt. M in Louisville, Ky., Mar. 19, 1840. OR 4/1.

Dr. James M. Kelly, of Ala., to Miss Theresa Armstrong, of Lexington, Ky. M Mar. 4, 1840. OR 4/1.

Milton Kirtly, of Boone county, to Miss Frances Carroll, of Scott county. M Jan. 9, 1840. OR 1/22.

Capt. Robert R. Logan, of Shelby county, to Miss Sarah Margaret Risk, of Woodford county. M Jan. 14, 1840. OR 1/22.

George S. Shanklin to Miss Martha West, daughter of T. E. West. M in Jessamine county, Feb. 20, 1840. OR 2/26.

William J. Smart, of Bourbon county, to Miss Mary Ann McMeekin. M Jan. 14, 1840. OR 2/5.

Thomas B. Smith to Miss Martha A. Lightfoot, both of Bath county. M at Owingsville, Jan. 28, 1840. OR 5/12.

William Sodowsky to Miss Ann Eliza, daughter of S. C. George, both of Jessamine county. M Apr. 5, 1840. OR 4/8.

J. E. Spilman to Miss Mary B., eldest daughter of Major John Menifee, all of Jessamine county. M Feb. 13, 1840. OR 2/22.

Samuel Steel to Mrs. Mary Beech, both of Lexington. M Apr. 14, 1840. OR 4/25.

Harrison Taylor, of Mason county, to Miss Charlotte J. Duke, of Scott county. M Jan. 14, 1840. OR 1/22.

John Waller Wood, of Georgetown, Ky., formerly of Albermarle county, Va., to Miss Margaret, second daughter of Major James Catling. M at White Cottage, Holmes county, Miss., Feb. 24, 1840. OR 4/25.

Samuel A. Young, of Lexington, to Miss Frances, daughter of Frederick B. Nichols, of Clarke county. M in Aberdeen, Ohio, Apr. 19, 1840. OR 4/22.

Cypian Clay to Miss Lydia Tudor. M in Lexington, Jan. 1, 1840. OR 1/4.

Joseph Hulett, of Lexington, to Miss Sarah Daley, daughter of Capt. J. Daley, of Fayette county. M Mar. 18, 1840. KG 3/18.

Richard Perkins to Miss Elizabeth Eads. M Dec. 29, 1839. KG 1/2/1840.

Levi Kebler to Miss Virginia C. Hundley. M Dec. 31, 1839. KG 1/2/1840.

James D. Drake to Miss Mary D. Hoagland, both of Lexington. M Jan. 7, 1840. KG 1/2.

Beriah Magoffin, of Harrodsburg, to Miss Anna Nelson, eldest daughter of Isaac Shelby, of Arcadia, Lincoln county. M Apr. 21, 1840. OR 5/13.

James White to Miss Martha M. Campbell. M in Woodford county, Apr. 28, 1840. OR 5/16.

Rodney M. Hinde to Miss Catharine Scholl, both of Clarke county. M May 8, 1840. OR 5/20.

Robert C. Clark, of Richmond, Ky., to Miss Eliza C. Moore, daughter of Capt. Charles C. Moore, of Fayette county. M May 19, 1840. OR 5/23.

William Beach to Miss Eliza G. Broadwell, daughter of Jacob G. Broadwell. M in Lexington, May 19, 1840. OR 5/23.

William Secrest to Miss Jane Vaughn, both of Fayette county. M May 21, 1840. OR 5/23.

Upton L. Hagar to Miss Malvina Chapman, of Woodford county. M Apr. 12, 1840. OR 5/23.

John P. Campbell to Miss Mary Ann, daughter of Gen. Thomas Metcalfe. M at Forest Retreat, May 14, 1840. OR 5/23.

Caleb W. Taylor to Miss Mary E. Morton, both of Eutaw, Ala. M May 6, 1840. OR 5/27

Gen. Samuel Houston, of Texas, to Miss Margaret Lea. M in Marion, Ala., May 8, 1840. OR 5/27.

Henry Ruckel, of Lexington, to Mrs. Catharine Ann Graham, late of Mobile, Ala. M June 4, 1840. OR 6/6.

William H. McCardle, Sr., editor of the *Vicksburg Whig,* to Miss Emily Caroline Byrnes, only daughter of the late Robert Ralston Byrnes. M at Cold Springs, Miss., May 28, 1840. OR 6/6.

Richard H. Coke, of Springfield, Ky., to Miss Mary E., daughter of James Guthrie, of Louisville. M June 2, 1840. OR 6/10.

William Campbell, editor of the *Western Visitor,* to Miss Charlotte Woodyard, both of Cynthiana. M June 8, 1840. OR 6/13.

Henry B. Brown to Miss Mary A., eldest daughter of Col. S. G. Tillett, all of Lancaster, Ky. M June 11, 1840. OR 6/20.

Francis K. Hunt, of Lexington, to Miss Julia, daughter of Dr. E. Warfield, of Fayette county. M June 23, 1840. OR 6/27.

Lafayette Maltby, of Brazoria, Texas, to Miss Frances J., daughter of Martin P. Marshall, of Fleming county, Ky. M June 25, 1840. OR 7/4.

B. Howard Preston, of Clarke county, to Miss O. Jane Blair. M in Fayette county, July 1, 1840. OR 7/4.

Henry C. Offutt, of Shelby county, to Mrs. Mary S. Glass, of Fayette county. M July 1, 1840. OR 7/11.

Nicholas Brian to Miss Julia Ann Payne, of Woodford county. M July 16, 1840. OR 7/22.

William Dewson to Mrs. Catharine Bristow, both of Lexington. M July 22, 1840. OR 7/25.

Dr. Thomas B. Pinckard, of Lexington, to Miss Lucy Ann, daughter of John Lyle, of Fayette county. M July 22, 1840. OR 7/25.

John Stone to Miss Eliza Waller. M in Lexington, July 27, 1840. OR 7/29.

W. R. Beatty, formerly of Mason county, to Miss Ann W. Boyce. M in Greenup county, July 15, 1840. OR 8/1.

Richard F. Richmond to Mrs. Edmonia Barton. M in Frankfort, July 29, 1840. OR 8/1.

Capt. Harrison W. Davis, of Texas, to Miss Jane Moore, of Fayette county, Ky. M July 14, 1840. OR 8/1.

Derrick Warner, of Lexington, to Miss Martha B. Price, of Harrodsburg. M in latter place, Aug. 12, 1840. OR 8/19.

Charles B. Richardson to Miss Sarah E., daughter of Mr. D. Bosworth, of

Fayette county, Ky. M at Holley Place, Lake Providence, La., July 23, 1840. OR 8/19.

Hon. North Parker, of Ill., to Mrs. Margaret Walden, of Lexington. Ky. M Aug. 17, 1840. OR 8/22.

John J. Cowden, of Rodney, Miss., to Miss Eleanor, eldest daughter of Capt. Simon Bradford, of Nashville, Tenn. M in latter place, Aug. 13, 1840. OR 8/22.

Joseph W. Harper to Miss Elizabeth Jane Harper, daughter of Capt. William Harper, all of Woodford county. M July 21, 1840. OR 8/22.

W. D. Crockett to Miss Mary Ann, daughter of Thomas C. Graves, all of Fayette county. M Aug. 18, 1840. OR 8/26.

Dr. H. Claggett, of Lexington, to Miss Elizabeth B., daughter of Dudley Shipp, of Fayette county. M Oct. 15, 1840. KG 10/22.

J. W. Davidson, of Logan county, to Miss M. C. Keene, daughter of Greenup Keene. M in Frankfort, June 14, 1841. *Commonwealth* 1/19.

1841–43

George W. Craddock, of Hart county, to Miss Harriet W. Theobalds, of Frankfort. M Jan. 14, 1841. *Commonwealth* 1/19.

Osborn Belt to Mrs. Francis McCracken, both of Frankfort. **M Jan. 14, 1841.** *Commonwealth* 1/19.

Matthew I. Patterson, of Scott county, to Miss Mary Ann, daughter of Gen. Joseph Patterson, of near Cynthiana. M Aug. 24, 1841. *Western Visitor* 9/9.

John W. Finnell, junior editor of the *Lexington Intelligencer,* to Miss Elizabeth C. Wall, daughter of Capt. (Major) William K. Wall, of Cynthiana. M Sept. 7, 1841. *Western Visitor* 9/9.

Jacob Burrier, of Jessamine county, to Miss Eliza McCrosky, of Fayette county. M Sept. 15, 1842. *Lexington Intelligencer* 10/14.

William C. Petit, of Arkansas, to Miss Eliza Bullock, of Shelbyville, Ky. M Sept. 20, 1842. I 10/14.

Paul T. Maccoun, of Paris, to Miss Catharine Potts, of Millersburg. M Sept. 29, 1842. I 10/14.

Isaac C. Vanmetre, of Fayette county, to Miss Frances H. Hull, of Clarke county. M at the Clarke county residence of I. Vanmetre, Oct. 4, 1842. I 10/14.

W. C. Lyle, editor of the *Paris Citizen,* to Miss Sarah Ellen Bell. Married at the Fayette county residence of Robert C. Boggs, Oct. 11, 1842. I 10/14.

Col. Alexander R. McKee, of Lancaster, Ky., to Miss Martinette Hardin, daughter of the late Gen. Martin D. Hardin. M at Jacksonville, Ill., in Oct., 1842. I 11/14.

Hyram Sanford to Miss Eleanor E. Young. M near Paris, Ill., May 25, 1843. *Protestant & Herald* 6/29.

James McCown, of New Albany, Ind., to Miss Amanda J. Troxwell, of Madison, Ia. M June 11, 1843. *Protestant & Herald* 6/29.

Thomas King, of Trimble county, Ky., to Miss Clementine King, of Madison, Ia. M June 11, 1843. *Protestant & Herald* 6/29.

Rev. Joseph Platt, of Paris, Ill., to Miss Elizabeth C. Fullinwider, of Montgomery county, Ia. M near Waveland June 13, 1843. *Protestant & Herald* 6/29.

Daniel White, of Clay county, Ky., to Miss Mildred D., second daughter of Gen. Daniel Morgan, of Fleming county, Ky. M June 20, 1843. *Protestant & Herald* 6/29.

John F. Kimball to Miss Maria M. Hankins, eldest daughter of Col. Hankins, of Connersville, Ind. M Apr. 18, 1844. OR 5/8.

Evan Shelby, of Fayette county, to Miss Amanda, daughter of Joseph Bruen, of Lexington. M May 23, 1844. OR 5/25.

1844

Charles F. Rogers, of Fayette county, to Miss Margaret A. Ford, of Paris. M May 21, 1844. OR 5/25.

John P. Sullivan, of Todd county, to Miss Sarah B., daughter of Fielding Bush, of Clarke county. M May 23, 1844. OR 5/29.

Joseph Beard, of Lexington, Ky., to Miss Julia Boswell, daughter of the late Bushrod Boswell. M in Platteville, Wisconsin, May 9, 1844. OR 6/1.

Robert E. Woodson to Miss Rosanna Barnett, both of Jessamine county. M June 4, 1844. OR 6/12.

Robert A. Hayes to Miss Mary Ann, daughter of Joseph Bowman, all of Fayette county. M June 11, 1844. OR 6/12.

William Cornwall, of Louisville, to Miss Mary P. Baldwin, of Lexington. M June 12, 1844. OR 6/15.

William Marrs to Miss Rebecca Jane Farra, late of Jessamine county. M June 16, 1844. OR 6/19.

Glendy Burke, of New Orleans, to Miss Sallie Carneal, daughter of T. D. Carneal. M in Cincinnati, O., June 11, 1844. OR 6/19.

John B. Tilford to Miss Catharine H. Curd, both of Lexington. M June 20, 1844. OR 6/26.

John B. Alexander, M. D., of Shelby county, to Miss Mary Elizabeth, daughter of John C. Richardson, of Miss. M at Oakland College, Miss., June 20, 1844. OR 7/6.

Thomas B. Dyer to Miss Cornelia C. Carr, daughter of the Hon. William C. Carr, all of St. Louis. M June 26, 1844. OR 7/6.

Dr. A. A. Riley, of Mo., to Miss Jessamine Young, daughter of Dr. A. Young, of Jessamine county, Ky. M July 1, 1844. OR 7/6.

Emelius K. Sayre, of Lexington, Ky., to Elizabeth S., daughter of the late Elijah Pierson, of New York. M at the Presbyterian Church at Madison, Morris county, N. J., June 30, 1844. OR 7/13.

St. Sterling E. Broadwell, of Cynthiana, Ky., to Miss Drusilla C. Ball, of Lexington. M July 11, 1844. OR 7/17.

David D. Johnson, of Versailles, to Miss Mary Jane, daughter of William Vanpelt, of Lexington. M July 25, 1844. OR 7/27.

Samuel H. Moseley to Miss Mary Ann Singleton, daughter of Mason Singleton, all of Jessamine county. M July 25, 1844. OR 7/31.

Archibald Bonds to Miss Martha Edger, both of Harrison county. M July 28, 1844. OR 8/7.

James Clark, of Fayette county, to Miss Lydia Evans, of Jessamine county. M July 23, 1844. OR 8/7.

William Elden, merchant of Lexington, Ky., to Miss Jerusha M. Morrell, daughter of Abram Morrell, of Albany, N. Y. M at Portsmouth, Ohio, Aug. 1, 1844. OR 8/7.

Dr. William G. Rodes, formerly of Lexington, Ky., to Mrs. Mary E. Roper, of Jackson. M July 30, 1844. (Notice from the *Huntsville* (Ala.) *Advocate* OR 8/17.

Walter A. Buck to Miss Cassandra Hale. M in Franklin county, Aug. 1, 1844. OR 8/17.

James M. Kidd to Miss Margaret J. Bell, both of Lexington. M Aug. 15, 1844. OR 8/24.

Henry E. Lawrence, of New Orleans, to Miss Frances C. Brashear, daughter of Dr. Walter Brashear, of La. M at the (Lexington, Ky.) residence of Benjamin Warfield, Aug. 20, 1844. OR 8/24.

Willis Green, M. D., to Louisa H. (Smith), eldest daughter of the Bishop of St. Paul's Church, Louisville. M Aug. 15, 1844. OR 8/24.

Jay Cooke, of Philadelphia, to Miss E. De Allen, daughter of the late Richard Allen, of Baltimore. M Aug. 22, 1844. OR 8/24.

J. G. Forman, of Cincinnati, to Miss Sarah Elizabeth Carpenter, of Peeksville, Westchester county, N. Y. M at latter place, Aug. 20, 1844. OR 9/4.

James T. Hart, of Fayette county, to Miss Nancy E. Karrick, of Winchester. M at Aberdeen, O., Aug. 29, 1844. OR 9/4.

F. Uttinger, of Jessamine county, to Miss Elizabeth Crim, of Fayette county. M Sept. 3, 1844. OR 9/4.

Robert C. Clark, of Winchester, Ky., to Miss Sarah Wilcox, of Richfield, Ohio. M in former place. Aug. 26, 1844. OR 9/7.

Rev. Drummond Welburn, of the Kentucky Annual Conference, to Miss Mary E. Schwing, daughter of John G. Schwing, of Louisville. M Sept. 4, 1844. OR 9/11.

Addison White, of Abingdon, Va., to Miss Sarah L. Irvine, eldest daughter of Col. David Irvine. M at Irvinton, Sept. 4, 1844. OR 9/11.

Col. B. J. Boswell, of Harrison county, to Miss Susan W. Smith, of Bourbon county. M Sept. 12, 1844. OR 9/14.

George W. Wheatly to Miss Sophrona Deweese, both of Harrodsburg. M Sept. 12, 1844. OR 9/14.

Dr. Thomas B. Pinckard to Mrs. Mary R. Eaton, daughter of the late James Harper, both of Lexintgon. M Sept. 17, 1844. OR 9/21.

James Bennett, of Woodford county, to Miss Martha Merrell, of Lexington. M Sept. 17, 1844. OR 9/21.

S. S. Wilson to Miss Nancy Thompson, of Fayette county. M Sept. 19, 1844. OR 9/21.

J. Milton McCann, of Fernside, in Fayette county, to Miss Joanna P. Smith, daughter of Abram Smith. M at Smithland, in Mercer county, Oct. 2, 1844. OR 10/9.

Capt. George H. Bowman, of Fayette county, to Mrs. Ann J. Guyton, of Miss. M Sept. 24, 1844. OR 10/9.

Belfield Cave, of Boone county, to Miss Susan Mitchum, of Woodford county. M in October, 1844. OR 10/9.

Samuel C. Pilkington, of Lexington, to Miss Mary L. McDowell, daughter of Col. John L. McDowell, of Fayette county. M Oct. 10, 1844. OR 10/16.

Dr. James L. Lane to Miss Mary W. Montgomery. M Oct. 8, 1844. OR 10/16.

John Gorham to Miss Mary J. Vance. M in Fayette county, Oct. 9, 1844. OR 10/16.

Robert Rodes Stone to Miss Elizabeth Walker, daughter of James Walker, all of Richmond, Ky. M Oct. 2, 1844. OR 10/16.

Joseph C. Price, of Nicholasville, to Miss Susan M. Thompson, daughter of William L. Thompson, of Jefferson county. M Oct. 3, 1844. OR 10/16.

William P. Davis, of Lexington, to Miss Elizabeth P. Todd, daughter of William Todd, of Fayette county. M Oct. 15, 1844. OR 10/19.

J. J. Dudley to Miss Eliza G. Peck, daughter of John Peck, both of Lexington. M Oct. 16, 1844. OR 10/19.

Charles Gallagher, of Louisville, to Miss Winny, daughter of M. T. Scott, of Lexington. M Oct. 15, 1844. OR 10/23.

William L. Vance, of Memphis, Tenn., to Miss Letitia H. Thompson, youngest daughter of Col. George C. Thompson. M at ''Shawnee Springs,'' Oct. 16, 1844. OR 10/23.

Charles A. Allguir, of Georgetown, to Miss Mary F. Sharpe, of Lexington. M Oct. 23, 1844. OR 10/23.

Abram Bowman, Jr., to Miss Mary G., daughter of George H. Bowman, all of Fayette county. M Oct. 22, 1844. OR 10/26.

Robert A. Wood, of Woodford county, to Miss Sarah A. Keas, daughter of James Keas, of Clarke county. M Oct. 15, 1844. OR 10/26.

David T. Adams, of Woodford county, to Miss Betsey Johnson, daughter of Joel Johnson, of Woodford county. M Oct. 22, 1844. OR 10/26.

Thomas D. Tilford, of Danville, to Miss Ann Eliza, daughter of Thomas S. Page, of Frankfort. M Oct. 22, 1844. OR 10/26.

David Merriwether to Miss Mary Ann Watson, both of Frankfort. M Oct. 22, 1844. OR 10/26.

Robert H. Crittenden to Miss Adeline Theobald. M in Frankfort, Oct. 17, 1844. OR 10/26.

William Matthews Merrick, of Frederick City, Maryland, to Miss Mary B. Wickliffe, daughter of the Hon. Charles A. Wickliffe, of Kentucky. M in Washington City, Oct. 22, 1844. OR 10/30.

W. H. Haldeman, editor of the *Louisville Morning Courier,* to Miss Elizabeth, daughter of W. M. Metgalf, of Cincinnati. M in latter place, Oct. 30, 1844. OR 11/16.

A. K. Bishop, A. M., professor of Languages in Independence Academy, to Mrs. Mary Smith, formerly of Kentucky. M former place, Oct. 8, 1844. OR 11/6.

Daniel C. Wickliffe, editor of the (Lexington) *Observer and Reporter,* to Miss Virginia W., daughter of the late Rev. Spencer Cooper. M Nov. 7, 1844. OR 11/9.

Charles S. Bodley to Miss Frances P. Curd, second daughter of the late Richard A. Curd. M in Lexington, Nov. 7, 1844. OR 11/16.

Henry Buford, of Scott county, to Miss Betsey H., daughter of James K. Marshall, of Bourbon county. M in latter place, Nov. 14, 1844. OR 11/27.

William R. Snyder, of Philadelphia, to Miss Eliza McCarton, of Fayette county, Ky. M Nov. 27, 1844. OR 11/30.

John McCauley to Miss Mary M., daughter of James Coleman, all of Fayette county. M Nov. 26, 1844. OR 12/4.

B. B. Sayre to Miss Ruth, daughter of Dr. Samuel Theobold, formerly of Lexington, Ky. M in South Frankfort, Dec. 5, 1844. OR 12/7.

William Darnaby to Miss M. Downing, daughter of Joseph Downing. M Nov. 28, 1844. OR 12/7.

Patrick Doyle to Miss Mary A. Hawn, all of Lexington. M Dec. 5, 1844. OR 12/7.

Pierce G. Grace to Miss Ann E., daughter of Capt. Andrew Harper, all of St. Louis. M Dec. 5, 1844. OR 12/7.

John E. Owsley, of Lincoln county, to Miss Mary, daughter of Hon. Bryan Y. Owsley. M in Jamestown, Nov. 25, 1844. OR 12/18.

John Kincaid to Miss Martha Susan, daughter of Henry Owsley, all of Owsley county. M Nov. 28, 1844. OR 12/18.

Rev. J. L. Kemp, of Transylvania University, to Miss Mary A., daughter of the late Thomas Van Antwerp, of New York City. M in Lexington, Ky., Dec. 19, 1844. OR 12/21.

James Elliott to Miss Julia, daughter of Abner Legrand. M Dec. 18, 1844. OR 12/21.

1845

Alexander Moreland to Miss Elizabeth J. Hawkins, of Fayette county. M Dec. 14, 1844. OR 12/25.

Robert McClanahan to Miss Mary McClelland, both of Fayette county. M Dec. 18, 1844. OR 12/25.

Atterson Bernaugh to Miss Nancy Jane Stafford, of Jessamine county. M Dec. 19, 1844. OR 12/25.

Dr. William W. Henderson, of Crittenden, Ky., to Miss Susan H. Parrish, daughter of Edward H. Parrish, of Bourbon county. M Dec. 19, 1844. OR 12/25.

Sanford Hicks, of Shelby county, to Miss Margaret Payne, of Fayette county. M Dec. 19, 1844. OR 12/28.

Samuel Hendrix to Miss Elizabeth Lyon, both of Jessamine county. M in

Aberdeen, Ohio, Dec. 26, 1844. OR 1/4/1845.

Thompson T. Taylor to Miss Elizina Jane Purdom, both of Garrard county. M in Aberdeen, Ohio, Dec. 29, 1844. OR 1/4/1845.

John F. Otwell, of Scott county, to Miss Mary H. Taylor, daughter of Stark Taylor, of Fayette county. M Dec. 19, 1844. OR 1/4/1845.

James P. Ford to Miss Elizabeth Harper, both of Woodford county. She was a daughter of Thomas Harper, of Mills Point. M in Jan., 1845. OR 1/11.

Morgan Vance, of Tenn., to Miss Susan P. Thompson, daughter of Col. George C. Thompson, of Shawnee Spring, Mercer county. M Jan. 8, 1845. OR 1/15.

Edmund P. Armstrong to Miss Elizabeth R. George, daughter of S. C. George, all of Jessamine county. M Jan. 16, 1845. OR 1/18.

J. W. Goecker to Miss Margaret Jarvis, both of Lexington. M Jan. 23, 1845. OR 1/25.

Capt. Charles S. Gatewood to Mrs. Maria Grant, daughter of Gen. Samuel L. Williams, all of Montgomery county. M Jan. 9, 1845. OR 1/25.

James O. Pettit to Miss Many Ann Frances Blackwell, both of Clarke county. M Jan. 25, 1845. OR 1/29.

Dr. Charles T. Overton, of Lexington, to Miss Mary Ellen Leonard, of Frankfort. M latter place, Jan. 30, 1845. OR 2/5.

George W. Noble to Mrs. Margaret L. Moore, both of Louisville. M Feb. 5, 1845. OR 2/12.

Joseph W. Anderson, of Scott county, to Miss Theresa E. Montgomery, daughter of James Montgomery, decd., of Washington, Ky. M Feb. 9, 1845. OR 2/15.

Marshall M. Matthews, of North Middletown, Ky., to Miss Harriet A. Cox, daughter of John Cox, of Hardin county. M Jan. 26, 1845. OR 2/15.

1845

George F. Holmes to Miss Lavalette Floyd, youngest daughter of the late Governor Floyd, of Va. M Feb. 3, 1845. OR 2/19.

Walter Nichols, of Lincoln county, to Miss Martha A. Dunlap, of Fayette county. M Jan. 16, 1845. OR 2/15.

Richard Apperson, of Mt. Sterling, to Miss Harriet S., daughter of Dr. Rogers, of Louisville. M latter place, Feb. 18, 1845. OR 2/22.

James A. Harper to Miss Mary E. Bishop, both of Lexington. M Mar. 4, 1845. OR 3/8.

G. F. Cowgill to Miss Julian E. Grooms, both of Fayette county. M Feb. 19, 1845. OR 3/8.

George W. Vaughn to Miss Georgeann Scantling, both of Fayette county. M Feb. 19, 1845. OR 3/8.

John I. Jacob, Jr., of Jefferson county, to Miss Evelyn, only daughter of Darwin Johnson, of Fayette county. M Mar. 11, 1845. OR 3/12.

George W. Dunlap, of Louisville, Ky., to Miss Mary Jane Carr, of Charleston, Iowa. M latter place, Mar. 23, 1845. OR 3/29.

William W. Alexander, of Paris, Ky., to Miss Jane Stamps, of Miss. M near

Woodville, Miss., Feb. 27, 1845. OR 3/29.

Charles S. Boswell to Miss Florida P., daughter of the Rev. N. H. Hall, of Fayette county. M Apr. 1, 1845. OR 4/9.

August Bailey to Miss Frances Weaver, both of Lexington. M Mar. 25, 1845. OR 4/5.

Henry Y. Elbert, of Benton county, Mo., to Miss Hester Hutchinson, of Fayette county. M Apr. 1, 1845. OR 4/9.

Lawrence B. Robinson, of Georgetown, to Miss Elizabeth H. Payne, daughter of the late Col. James B. Payne, of Fayette county. M Apr. 3, 1845. OR 4/9.

Dr. James P. Henry, of Cynthiana, to Miss Ellen C. Smith, of Clarke county. M Apr. 2, 1845. OR 4/9.

J. R. Estill, late of Ky., to Miss Mary A., second daughter of Talton Turner. M in Howard county, Mo., Mar. 20, 1845. OR 4/9.

Nathaniel P. Porter, Jr., to Miss Hannah M., daughter of George T. Chrisman, of Jessamine county. M latter place, Apr. 3, 1845. OR 4/21.

Col. John L. Howard to Miss Jane Cordelia Lincoln, both of Fayette county. M in Aberdeen, Ohio, Apr. 13, 1845. OR 4/19.

J. S. Spilman, of Nicholasville, to Miss Eliza S., daughter of the late Hancock Taylor, of Jefferson county. M Apr. 10, 1845. OR 4/19.

James Mitchell Lawrence, of Lexington, to Miss Margaret Lawrence, of Bourbon county. M Apr. 16, 1845. OR 4/26.

Henry C. Morton, of Louisville, to Miss Prudence Blackburn, daughter of Dr. Churchill J. Blackburn. M in Woodford county, Apr. 15, 1845. OR 4/26.

Wyatt Embry, of Madison county, to Miss Celia Outten, of Fayette county. M Apr. 17, 1845. OR 4/30.

E. S. Hastings to Miss Ellen Megowan, both of Lexington. M Apr. 29, 1845. OR 5/3.

James J. Crump, of Tenn., to Miss Margaret P. Carson, of Lexington, Ky. M Apr. 28, 1845. OR 5/3.

Charles C. Norton to Miss Virginia Bell, daughter of William C. Bell, of Lexington. M Apr. 30, 1845. OR 5/7.

H. J. Van Emburgh, late of New York, to Miss Adne Bosworth, daughter of David Bosworth, of Fayette county, Ky. M May 6, 1845. OR 5/7.

John Williams, of Harrison county, to Miss Maria Webber, of Jessamine county. M May 8, 1845. OR 5/10.

Perry W. Gaugh to Miss Mary J. Clugston, daughter of John Clugston, all of Fayette county. M May 15, 1845. OR 5/17.

Henry W. D. Kyle, of Baltimore, to Miss Anna C. Castleman, daughter of David Castleman, of Fayette county, Ky. M May 13, 1845. OR 5/17.

O. B. Dorsey, of Sharpsburg, to Miss Virginia Stockton, of Mt. Sterling. M May 13, 1845. OR 5/17.

Dr. William Y. Gadberry, of Benton, Miss., to Miss Helen B. Price, daughter of the late Daniel Price, of Woodford county, Ky. M May 15, 1845. OR 5/17.

Ephraim Sodowsky to Miss Hester Collins. M in Jessamine county, May 12, 1845. OR 5/17.

Dr. G. P. Robinson, of Fayette county, to Miss Ann M. Turner, of Jefferson county. M in Louisville, May 6, 1845. OR 5/21.

James W. Dawson to Miss Maria L. Vanpelt, daughter of William Vanpelt, all of Lexington. M May 22, 1845. OR 5/24.

Hon. William Allen to Mrs. Effie Coons, daughter of the late Gov. McArthur. M in Chillicothe, Ohio, May 16, 1845. OR 5/24.

Dr. Joseph W. Putnam to Miss Eloise I. Sanders, daughter of Durham Sanders, of Greene county, Ky. M May 14, 1845. OR 5/28.

John C. King, of Lexington, to Miss Ann E. Thomasson, daughter of Capt. Richard Thomasson, of Scott county. M in latter place, June 5, 1845. OR 6/7.

George W. Pickle to Miss Araminta D. Rogers, eldest daughter of Thomas Rogers, both of Lexington. M June 8, 1845. OR 6/11.

Dr. Joseph Duncan, of Winchester, Ky., to Miss Mary Ellen, daughter of Isaac N. Renton, of Zanesville, O. M latter place, May 29, 1845. OR 6/11.

Robert Blain, Jr., to Mrs. Catherine R. Bell, of Fayette county. He was from Stanford. M June 10, 1845. OR 6/14.

Samuel Simpson to Miss Elizabeth Wallace, both of Fayette county. M June 12, 1845. OR 6/18.

Reuben S. Holton, of Frankfort, to Miss Sarah Ann Ready, of Versailles. M June 10, 1845. OR 6/18.

John H. Hunter, of Lexington, to Miss C. A. Campbell, daughter of John Campbell, of Mt. Sterling. M latter place, June 17, 1845. OR 6/21.

B. L. Burbridge, of Clarke county, to Miss Sally Ann Smith, of Montgomery county. M June 12, 1845. OR 6/25.

Thomas Theobald, of Frankfort, to Miss Susan Moffett, of Trimble county, Ky. M June 10, 1845. OR 6/28.

Leonidas M. Logan, of Woodford county, to Miss Elizabeth Martin, of Lexington. M July 8, 1845. OR 7/9.

Henry C. Allan to Miss Elizabeth, daughter of Samuel G. Jackson, of Clarke county. M in Winchester, July 1, 1845. OR 7/9

Capt. Harrison W. Davis, of Texas, to Miss Mary E. Gaunt, of Fayette county. M July 15, 1845. OR 7/23.

James W. Ball to Miss Mary H. Johnson, both of Shelby county. M July 24, 1845. OR 7/30.

Benjamin G. Willis, of Burlington, to Miss Clara Payne, daughter of Gen. John Payne, of Augusta, Ky. M latter place, July 29, 1845. OR 8/13.

George C. Venable to Miss Elizabeth F. Linegar, both of Lexington. M Aug. 14, 1845. OR 8/16.

Andrew J. Briscoe to Miss Mary E., daughter of Robert P. Snell, all of Scott county. M Aug. 24, 1845. OR 8/30.

Francis Bashford, of Lexington, Missouri, to Miss Catherine E. Steele, of Fayette county, Ky. M Sept. 2, 1845. OR 9/6.

John L. Walker, of Paris, to Miss Amanda F. Johnson, of Harrison county. M. Aug. 28, 1845. OR 9/6.

Hon. Garrett Davis to Mrs. Eliza J. Elliott, both of Bourbon county.

M Sept. 10, 1845. OR 9/13.

Albert Allen, late of Bethany College, Va., to Miss Ann Eliza, only daughter of Dr. Ezra Offutt, dec'd. M Sept. 11, 1845, in Fayette county, Ky. OR 9/13.

H. D. Fisk to Miss Maria E. Goss, both of Lexington. M Sept. 15, 1845. OR 9/17.

William L. Grant, of Henderson, Ky., to Miss Laura B., daughter of the late Hon. William W. Southgate, of Covington, Ky. M Sept. 10, 1845. OR 9/17.

Elisha Fitch, of Mt. Sterling, to Miss Amanda J., only daughter of Major John Walker, of Fleming county. M Sept. 16, 1845, in Fleming county. OR 9/20.

Hon. A. V. Brown, Governor Elect of Tenn., to Mrs. Cynthia Saunders, of Davidson county. M Sept. 16, 1845. OR 9/24.

F. Hartze to Miss Frances A. Harris. M in Versailles, Sept. 15, 1845. OR 9/24.

Willie P. Duvall, of Fayette county, to Miss Mary Elizabeth, daughter of John Williams, of Woodford county. M Sept. 23, 1845. OR 10/4.

Isaac Miller to Miss Sally Lewis, daughter of Alpheus Lewis, all of Clarke county. M Sept. 25, 1845. OR 10/4.

John Wesley Vick, of Vicksburg, to Miss Catherine Ann Barbour, daughter of the late Major James Barbour, of Danville. M in Boyle county, Oct. 7, 1845. OR 10/15.

Alfred Cohen, of Fayette county, to Miss Jane Faris, of Madison county. M in latter place, Oct. 9, 1845. OR 10/15.

Elijah Burdsal, of Cincinnati, to Miss Lucy Leathers, of Covington, Ky. M Oct. 9, 1845. OR 11/15.

Samuel W. Chiles to Miss Susan, daughter of the late Dr. William Webb, all of Clarke county. M Oct. 14, 1845. OR 10/18.

Lafayette Armstrong, of Lexington, to Miss Charlotte, daughter of Col. Ambrose Dudley, of Cincinnati. M in latter place, Oct. 15, 1845. OR 10/22.

Howard Matthews to Miss Susan E. Combs, daughter of Dr. Ennis Combs, formerly of Montgomery county, Ky. M at Independence, Mo., in October, 1845. OR 10/25.

Levi Prewett to Miss Mary E. Coleman, both of Fayette county. M Oct. 23, 1845. OR 10/25.

William L. Waller to Miss Ann Delia Johnson, both of Scott county. M Oct. 20, 1845. OR 10/29.

George W. Bradley to Miss Eliza P., daughter of John Woods, all of Mercer county. M Oct. 21, 1845. OR 10/29.

Dr. John D. Grissim, of La., to Miss Hannah A. K., daughter of Capt. C. C. Moore, of Fayette county, Ky. M Oct. 23, 1845. OR 11/1.

Dr. Alfred N. Ross, of Cincinnati, to Miss Louisa I. Dodd, of Lexington, Ky. M Oct. 29, 1845. OR 11/1.

Levi T. Carr, of St. Joseph, Mo., to Miss Eliza Ann, daughter of Emanual Block, of St. Louis. M Oct. 21, 1845. OR 11/1.

Dr. Samuel Griffith, of Louisville, to Miss Emily B. Moffett, of Lexington. M Nov. 4, 1845. OR 11/5.

John Quincy Adams to Miss Harriet Sharp, both of Lexington. M Oct. 30, 1845. OR 11/5.

Benjamin J. Adams to Miss Caroline Scott, only daughter of Major Aris Throckmorton, all of Louisville. M Oct. 29, 1845. OR 11/5.

Col. Daniel Breck, of Ky., to Miss H. E. A. Ramsey, eldest daughter of Dr. J. G. M. Ramsey, of Mecklenburg, Tenn. M in latter named place, Oct. 22, 1845. OR 11/5.

Alexander Breckinridge to Miss Martha Tempy, both of Fayette county. M Nov. 2, 1845. OR 11/5.

James E. Gillispie to Miss Elizabeth D. Vanpelt, both of Lexington. M Nov. 6, 1845. OR 11/8.

John McHenry Robinson to Miss Ellen B., daughter of Col. Thomas Anderson, all of Louisville. M Nov. 5, 1845. OR 11/22.

John Travis to Miss America Jenkins, both of Lexington. M in Georgetown, Nov. 2, 1845. R 11/12.

R. W. Keene, merchant of Georgetown, to Miss Catharine Williams, of Woodford county. M in Versailles, Oct. 29, 1845. OR 11/12.

Francis Webb, of Scott county, to Miss Mary Louisa, second daughter of the Rev. William F. Broaddus. M at "Woodford", Ky., Nov. 11, 1845. OR 11/15.

John R. Smith, of Mercer county, to Miss Ophelia, daughter of John G. Chiles, of Lexington. M in Harrodsburg, Nov. 12, 1845. OR 11/15.

Robert B. Hopkins to Miss Catherine M., eldest daughter of Dr. W. E. Ewing, all of Lexington. M in Louisville, Nov. 6, 1845. OR 11/15.

Junius W. Barbee, of Scott county, to Miss Elizabeth Davis, of Clarke county. M Nov. 4, 1845. OR 11/19.

N. C. Harris, of Woodford county, to Mrs. Sarah A. Curry, of Paris. M Nov. 18, 1845. OR 11/22.

Lewis Dedman, of Fayette county, to Miss Susan Magee, of Jessamine county. M in Aberdeen, Ohio, Nov. 17, 1845. OR 11/22.

W. C. Downey, of Winchester, to Miss Lucy Ann, daughter of Joseph Embry, of Madison county. M Nov. 18, 1845. OR 11/26.

A. S. Mitchell, assistant Secretary of State, to Miss Judith Ann, daughter of Harry I. Bodley, formerly of Lexington. M in Frankfort, Nov. 18, 1845. OR 11/29.

Samuel Magoffin, of Mexico, to Miss Susan H., daughter of Isaac Shelby, of Lexington. M Nov. 25, 1845. OR 11/29.

Elbert Walker to Miss Nancy Shackel, both of Fayette county. M Dec. 4, 1845. OR 12/6.

William Wheatly to Miss Martha A., daughter of Major James Rouse, all of Henderson, Ky. M Nov. 13, 1845.

G. Drummond Hunt, of Lexington, to Mrs. Letitia Parrish, of Fayette county. M Dec. 2, 1845. OR 12/6.

Charles F. Shivel to Miss Lucinda Hutchison, both of Lexington. M Dec. 9, 1845. OR 12/10.

James Taylor, of Fayette county, to Miss Elizabeth Radford, of Shelby county. M Dec. 3, 1845. OR 12/10.

Smith Burton, of Lexington, to Miss Hannah Barker, of Fayette county. M Dec. 10, 1845. OR 12/13.

Independent Gist, of Kentucky, to Miss Elizabeth Porcher, youngest daughter of the late States Gist, of Charleston. M Nov. 12, 1845. OR 12/13.

George A. Armstrong to Miss Elizabeth P. McKinney, both of Boyle county. M Dec. 11, 1845. OR 12/17.

John Nutter to Miss Elizabeth Hukell. M Dec. 15, 1845. OR 12/20.

William G. Talbott to Miss Ellen Sophia, daughter of the late Capt. Thomas P. Hart, of Frankfort. M Dec. 10, 1845. OR 12/20.

John Hughs to Miss Mary Jane, daughter of Dr. Jeptha Dudley, all of Jessamine county. M Dec. 23, 1845. OR 12/24.

William Oots, of Lexington, to Miss Virginia Barbee, of Georgetown. M in former place, Dec. 16, 1845. OR 12/24.

George W. Smith to Miss Mary, daughter of Joshua Cromwell. M in Fayette county, Dec. 23, 1845. OR 12/27.

W. A. Dudley to Miss Mary Hawkins, both of Lexington. M Dec. 23, 1845. OR 12/27.

Joshua Woodrow, of Hillsborough, O., to Miss Margaret T. Stuart, daughter of Rev. Robert Stuart, of Ky. M in former place, Dec. 27, 1845. OR 1/3/1846.

1846

Rev. G. W. Burris to Miss Mary Jane, daughter of John Prather, of Fayette county. M Jan. 1, 1846. OR 1/3.

David F. Oak, of Philadelphia, to Miss Elfrida D. Porter, daughter of Charles C. Porter, of North Middletown, Ky. M in latter place in December, 1845. OR 1/3/1846.

Richard King, of Harrison county, to Miss Ann Maria, daughter of Silas M. King, of Pendleton county. M Dec. 25, 1845. OR 1/7/1846.

William S. Haviland to Miss Mary Elizabeth, daughter of John R. Whitehead, all of Harrison county. M Dec. 30, 1845. OR 1/7/1846.

S. T. Connellee, of Georgetown, to Miss Lucy A., daughter of Thomas Wood, of Lexington. M Jan. 9, 1846. OR 11/10.

Cincinnatus Shryock, of Lexington, to Miss Olivia Shryock, of Woodford county. M Nov. 18, 1845. OR 1/10/1846.

William E. Blackburn, of Lake Providence, La., to Miss Henrietta C. Everett, daughter of S. D. Everett. M Jan. 6, 1846. OR 1/10.

Dr. Henry Morehead, of Keene, Jessamine county, to Mrs. Marcia B. Foster, of Frankfort. M Dec. 23, 1845. OR 1/10/46

John F. Lander to Miss Sally M. Scott, both of Bourbon county. M Dec. 30, 1845. OR 1/14/1846.

William H. Spencer to Miss Rebecca B., daughter of R. E. Brocking, all of Clarke county. M Jan. 13, 1846. OR 1/17.

John McCormick to Miss Mary Jane Argobright, both of Lexington.

M Jan. 15, 1846.   OR 1/17.

Oscar H. Burbridge, of Scott county, to Miss Rebecca Matson, daughter of Col. James Matson, of Bourbon county.   M Jan. 8, 1846.   OR 1/21.

Robert S. Russell, of Fayette county, to Miss Louisa Jane Matson, daughter of Col. James Matson, of Bourbon county.   M Jan. 8, 1846.   OR 1/21.   See above.

M. C. Sorrelle, of Lexington, to Miss Jane Amanda, daughter of the late James Coleman, of Mercer county.   M Jan. 8, 1846.   OR 1/21.

Belverd D. Packer, of Bourbon county, to Miss Sarah H. Sprake, daughter of Thomas Sprake, of Fayette county.   M Jan. 15, 1846.   OR 1/21.

B. Riley, of Versailles, to Miss Jane P. Tanner, of Scott county.   M Jan. 15, 1846.   OR 1/24.

Joseph Hughes, of Boone county, to Miss Amanda, daughter of Rev. William Tucker, of Grant county.   M Jan. 29, 1846.   OR 2/4.

William Bruen, of Grant county, to Miss Mary Cowgill, of Fayette county. M Jan. 22, 1846.   OR 2/4.

John C. Young, of Jessamine county, to Miss Elizabeth, daughter of Mrs. Margaret Drew, of Clay county.   M Jan. 1, 1846.   OR 2/7.

J. F. Houx, of Boonville, Mo., to Miss Frances Ann, daughter of Elisha. Dickerson, of Winchester, Ky.   M Jan. 6, 1846.   OR 2/11.

James W. Cook to Miss Eliza A. Pickett, both of Lexington.   M Feb. 5, 1846.   OR 2/11.

Joshua Smith, of Fayette county, to Mrs. H. M. White, of Franklin county. M Feb. 3, 1846.   OR 2/11.

Caswell Tate, of Clarke county, to Miss Amanda Rabourn, of Madison county.   M Feb. 3, 1846.   OR 2/14.

John Herriott to Miss Ursula Emarine Herriott, both of Scott county. M Nov. 25, 1845.   OR 2/14/1846.

John C. McRoberts to Miss Susan E. Bradley, of Scott county.   M Dec. 31, 1845.   OR 2/14/1846.

Eli O. Smith, to Miss Abagil R. Logan, both of Fayette county.   M Jan. 29, 1846.   OR 2/14.

Joseph W. Hogan to Miss Mary Garrison, both of Jessamine county. M Feb. 9, 1846.   OR 2/14.

Edwin D. Payne, of Bourbon county, to Miss Maria E., daughter of Moses Ryan, of Bath county.   M Jan. 27, 1846.   OR 2/18.

James W. Wright, of Bourbon county, to Miss Harriet, daughter of Lindsey Thomas, of Shelby county.   M in former place, Feb. 11, 1846.   OR 2/18.

John Young, of Jessamine county, to Miss Rosannah Ricketts, of Fayette county.   M Feb. 17, 1846.   OR 2/18.

Charles Poston to Miss Mary Flanagan.   M in Winchester, Ky., Feb. 11, 1846.   OR 2/21.

Joseph Ketram to Miss Abby Combs, both of Jessamine county.   M at Megowan's Hotel, Lexington, Feb. 23, 1846.   OR 2/25.

Joseph James Barbee, Junior Editor of the *Kentucky Tribune,* to Miss Mary

Jane Orkiess. M in Danville, Feb. 18, 1846. OR 2/25.

Rev. George W. Smiley to Miss Sarah Norton, daughter of the late Rev. Spencer Cooper. M Feb. 25, 1846. OR 2/28.

Rev. William W. Pratt, Pastor of the Baptist Church at Lexington, to Miss Mary E. Dillard, daughter of the Rev. R. T. Dillard. M in Fayette county, Mar. 4, 1846. OR 3/11.

John Cornwall to Miss Amelia S. Bucklin, both of Lexington. M Mar. 6, 1846. OR 3/14.

Hiram P. Wilson, of Paris, to Miss H. Clay Gist, daughter of the late Resin H. Gist, of Montgomery county. M in latter place, Mar. 3, 1846. OR 3/14.

James H. Turner, formerly of Lexington, to Miss Rachel Gist, daughter of the late Resin H. Gist, of Montgomery county. M latter place, Mar. 3, 1846. See above. OR 3/14.

R. P. Austin, of Harrison county, to Miss Lucinda Dean, of Lexington. M Mar. 15, 1846. OR 3/18.

Levin Burkley, of Clarke county, to Miss Rachel Stivers, of Fayette county. M Feb. 26, 1846. OR 3/18.

Capt. Lewis Arnold to Miss Elvira, daughter of Boon McDaniel, all of Woodford county. M Feb. 26, 1846. OR 3/18.

Thomas P. Porter, of Versailles, to Miss America McAfee, of Louisville. M Mar. 11, 1846. OR 3/18.

Joseph R. Megowan to Miss Martha J. Martin, both of Lexington. M Mar. 24, 1846. OR 3/25.

Columbus Davis, of Clarke county, to Miss Maria True, of Fayette county. M in Georgetown, Mar. 15, 1846. OR 3/25.

Alexander J. Mitchell, late of the U. S. Navy, to Miss Mary Rebecca, eldest daughter of Gen. Leslie Combs. M Mar. 25, 1846. OR 3/28.

John Parker, of Fayette county, to Miss Sarah Laudeman, of Lexington. M Mar. 26, 1846. OR 3/28.

S. Schoonmaker, formerly of Patterson, N. J., to Miss Sarah, daughter of Leonard Taylor, of Lexington. M Mar. 26, 1846. OR 3/28.

Henry C. Bowman to Miss Sally Bowman, both of Fayette county. M Mar. 31, 1846. OR 4/1.

Oliver H. Perry, of Jessamine county, to Miss Frances Scott, daughter of Mrs. Mary Scott. M Mar. 24, 1846. OR 4/1.

George W. Babcock, of Lexington, to Miss Sabina Ann, oldest daughter of John Lewis, of Jessamine county. M Apr. 5, 1846. OR 4/8.

Robert C. Rice, an Evangelist of the Christian Church, to Miss Ann Eliza Myles, of Shelby county. M Apr. 2, 1846. OR 4/8.

James W. Steele, of Richmond, Ky., to Miss Sarah, daughter of John Hart, Sr., of Fayette county, Ky. M Mar. 31, 1846. OR 4/8.

Dr. F. M. Miller to Miss Caroline, daughter of Tarlton Embry, all of Madison county. M Mar. 31, 1846. OR 4/8.

Tarlton Embry, Jr., of Madison county, to Miss Martha, daughter of John Foster, of Clarke county. M latter place, Apr. 1, 1846. See above. OR 4/8.

Dr. John W. Scott, formerly of Lexington, Ky., to Miss Jane Heyer, daughter of the late C. R. Suydam, all of New York. M there, Mar. 27, 1846. OR 4/11.

Asa Thomasson, of Scott county, to Miss Mary Perry, daughter of James Perry, of Shelby county. M in latter place, Mar. 12, 1846. OR 4/15.

Hon. David Yulee, U. S. Senator from Florida, to Miss Nannie C., daughter of the Hon. Charles A. Wickliffe. M at Wickland, Nelson county, Ky., April 7, 1846. OR 4/15.

James Whitcomb, Governor of Indiana, to Mrs. Martha Ann Hurst, daughter of the late William Renick, of Pickaway, Ohio. M at latter place, Mar. 24, 1846. OR 4/15.

William H. F. Lightfoot, formerly of Lexington, to Miss Nancy W., daughter of John Henderson, of Boyle county. M Apr. 7, 1846. OR 4/15.

Elisha A. Beach, of Lexington, to Miss Elizabeth A. Winters, of Newton, Sussex county, N. J. M Mar. 25, 1846. OR 4/18.

Joseph Vanpelt to Miss Ellen Vanpelt, both of Lexington. M Apr. 19, 1846. OR 4/25.

Benjamin Dunn to Mrs. Rebecca A. Finnell, both of Lexington. M Apr. 22, 1846. OR 4/25.

Caleb Walton to Mrs. Mary E. Broadwell, both of Cynthiana. M Apr. 23, 1846. OR 4/29.

Charles Donnelly to Miss Julia Cecelia Mullay, both of Lexington. M Apr. 28, 1846. OR 5/2.

Samuel R. Welch to Miss Catherine Wilmore, both of Jessamine county. M Apr. 23, 1846. OR 5/2.

James A. Welch to Miss Matilda R. Lusk, both of Jessamine county. M Apr. 23, 1846. OR 5/2.

Henry C. Pindell, of Lexington, to Miss J. Ann Pearce. daughter of the late James Pearce, of Louisville. M in Vicksburg, Miss., Apr. 23, 1846. OR 5/6.

Hugh L. Webb to Miss Jane Foreman, both of Lexington. M May 7, 1846. OR 5/9.

John Robinson, of Fayette county, to Miss Mary Jane McGee, of Covington. M latter place, May 5, 1846. OR 5/13.

George T. Cotton to Miss Maria A., daughter of Richard G. Jackson, all of Woodford county. M May 6, 1846. OR 5/16.

John A. Crittenden, of Louisville, to Miss Virginia A., daughter of Richard G. Jackson, of Woodford county. See above. M May 6, 1846. OR 5/16.

William Campbell to Miss Griselda Aiken, both of Lexington. M May 14, 1846. OR 5/16.

John H. Hufford to Miss Rebecca Moore, both of Scott county. M Apr. 30, 1846. OR 5/16.

Collin Shellon Throckmorton to Miss Malvina Laura, second daughter of Robert J. Ward, all of Louisville. M May 5, 1846. OR 5/16.

M. C. Hanly to Miss C. A. Palmer, daughter of the late James W. Palmer, formerly of Lexington. M at Catholic Church in Lexington, May 11, 1846. OR 5/20.

Willis F. Jones, of Richmond, Ky., to Miss Martha M., daughter of William S. Buford, of Woodford county. M May 12, 1846. OR 5/20.

John Henry Chiles, of Chilesburg, to Miss Nannie E. Rogers, daughter of Henry Rogers, of Fayette county. M May 14, 1846. OR 5/20.

John P. Fulwiler, of Louisville, formerly of Lexington, to Miss Elizabeth, daughter of Gen. William Hardin, of Frankfort. M latter place, May 19, 1846. OR 5/23.

Milton Barlow to Miss Anastasia Thompson, both of Lexington. M May 20, 1846. OR 5/23.

Hiram Sullivan, of Georgetown, to Miss Georgetta Haven, of Cincinnati. M May 20, 1846. OR 5/27.

William H. Loyd to Miss Ann Maria, Mayduell, both of Lexington. M in Louisville, May 27, 1846. OR 6/3.

William Richardson, of Fayette county, to Miss Jane, daughter of Thomas Stamps, of Bourbon county. M May 28, 1846. OR 6/6.

Dr. Samuel T. Ross, of Texas, to Miss Aurelia L. Fitch, daughter of the late Capt. Samuel Fitch, of Lexington, Ky. M June 7, 1846. OR 6/10.

William Brockman to Mrs. Catherine Armstrong, both of Fayette county. M June 11, 1846. OR 6/17.

Dr. William Bell to Miss Mary Miller, both of Winchester, Ky. M in West Union, Ohio, June 15, 1846. OR 6/20.

William Kenney, M. D., to Miss Rosannah, daughter of John Vimont, of Millersburg. M June 13, 1846. OR 6/27.

Lewis H. Vimont to Miss Eliza, daughter of James Kennear, of Millersburg. M May 13, 1846. OR 6/27.

Leo Tibbatts, of Newport, to Miss Estelle Florinde Blancagniel, of Louisville. M June 24, 1846. OR 6/27.

James T. Johnson, of Boonville, Mo., to Miss Harriet S., youngest daughter of the late Judge William Brown, of Harrison county, Ky. M in Island Grove, Sangamon county, Ill., June 11, 1846. OR 6/27.

Dr. J. V. Prather, of the medical Department of the St. Louis University, to Miss Henrietta Maria, daughter of Major William B. Booker, of Springfield, Ky. M June 10, 1846. OR 6/27.

Col. Alfred M. Young, of Madison Parish, La., to Miss Mary E., youngest daughter of Charles Carr, of Fayette county, Kentucky. M July 8, 1846. OR 7/11.

William F. Barrett, of Greensburg, to Miss Maria Elizabeth, daughter of William C. Goodloe. M in Frankfort, July 8, 1846. OR 7/18.

Montgomery Blair, Judge of the Circuit Court of Missouri, to Miss Mary E., eldest daughter of the Hon. Levi Woodburry. M in Portsmouth, N. H., July 6, 1846. OR 7/22.

Simeon N. Drake, of Lexington, to Miss Josephine P. Smith, of Garrard county. M in Aberdeen, Ohio, July 28, 1846. OR 8/1.

Edwin L. Singleton, of Flemingsburg, to Miss Mary E. Stockton, of Mt. Sterling. M latter place, July 22, 1846. OR 8/1.

John M. Viley to Miss Susan A. Long, daughter of James Long, all of Scott county. M July 28, 1846. OR 8/1.

Patrick Dolan to Miss Hannah Gilbert, both of Fayette county. M July 29, 1846. OR 8/1.

John Lackland, merchant of Mt. Sterling, to Miss Elizabeth Daly, daughter of Capt. L. Daly, of Fayette county. M July 28, 1846. OR 8/5.

Asa Eden to Miss Catharine J. Hayden, both of Lexington. M Aug. 2, 1846. OR 8/5.

Andrew Miller to Miss Martha Jane Tankersly, both of Lexington. M Aug. 4, 1846. OR 8/8.

Frederick Bush to Miss Maria McNitt, both of Lexington. M Aug. 6, 1846. OR 8/8.

J. W. Martin to Miss Elizabeth, daughter of Christopher I. Hunt, all of Fayette county. M Aug. 20, 1846. OR 8/22.

R. H. Davis, of Midway, to Miss Susan H. Branham, of Woodford county. M Aug. 18, 1846. OR 8/29.

David Wilson to Miss Mary, daughter of Samuel G. Herndon, of Bath county. M Aug. 25, 1846. OR 8/29.

Hon. Orlando B. Ficklin, of Ill., to Miss Elizabeth H., eldest daughter of the Hon. Walter T. Colquitt. M at Lagrange, Ga., Aug. 29, 1846. OR 9/5.

A. D. Long, of Woodford county, to Miss Mildred D. Bullock, of Clarke county. M Sept. 1, 1846. OR 9/5.

William J. Bradley, of Fayette county, to Miss M. Annie Iddings, of Cincinnati. M in latter place, Sept. 3, 1846. OR 9/9.

William H. Huggins, formerly of Lexington, to Miss Sarah A. Wake, of Nicholasville. M Sept. 8, 1846. OR 9/12.

Henry Hughes, of Jessamine county, to Miss Mildred Kellar, of Louisville. M Sept. 1, 1846. OR 9/12.

George W. Ewing, of Russellville, to Miss Nannie L. Williams, daughter of Gen. Samuel L. Williams, of Montgomery county. M Aug. 28, 1846. OR 9/16.

Thomas Lewis to Miss Margaret Martin, of Fayette county. M Sept. 13, 1846. OR 9/16.

Joshua Marsh to Mrs. Mary Bentley, of Clarke county. M Sept. 13, 1846. OR 9/16.

Dr. John T. Lewis, of Lexington, to Miss Sarah Jane Bosworth, of Fayette County. M Sept. 17, 1846. OR 9/19.

David Duck to Miss Susannah Shiddell, both of Lexington. M Sept. 15, 1846. OR 9/19.

J. Nevien West, of Ga., to Miss Isabella D., daughter of the late Hamilton Athison, of Fayette county, Ky. M Sept. 16, 1846. OR 9/19.

James Hinton to Miss Sarah E., daughter of William Wheat, all of Bourbon county. M Sept. 17, 1846. OR 9/19.

Oliver Barkley, of Clarke county, to Miss Elizabeth Hazelriggs, of Mt. Sterling. M latter place Sept. 8, 1846. OR 9/19.

Thomas J. Mitchell, of Montgomery county, to Miss Emily Gaitskill, of

Clarke county. M Sept. 1, 1846. OR 9/19.

Michael Cummings, of Lexington, to Miss Minerva J. Breckinridge, of Fayette county. M Sept. 10, 1846. OR 9/23.

Dr. Samuel Pouzee, of Fayette county, to Miss Albinas Whitesides, of Clarke county. M Sept. 10, 1846. OR 9/23.

Lieut. John H. Gore, of the U. S. Army, to Miss Lucy A., daughter of the Hon. James T. Morehead. M at Covington in September, 1846. OR 9/26

William Short, of Louisville, to Miss Catherine M. Strader, of New York City. M in former place, Sept. 23, 1846. OR 9/26.

John S. Brannin, of Lake Providence, La., to Miss Laura G., daughter of E. W. Craig, of Lexington, Ky. M Sept. 15, 1846. OR 9/26.

Llewellyn L. Hawkins, formerly of Lexington, Ky., to Miss Mary C., daughter of Dr. D. C. Glasscock, of St. Louis. M in Hannibal, Mo., Sept. 1, 1846. OR 9/26.

John L. Keyes to Mrs. Mary Ann Rogers, of Fayette county. M Sept. 27, 1846. OR 9/30.

Alfred Warner, of Lexington, to Mrs. Harriet L. McLean, of Fayette county. M Sept. 29, 1846. OR 9/30.

George A. Worthen, of Helena, Ark., to Miss Elizabeth B. McMillin, of Lexington, Ky. M near latter place, Sept. 29, 1846. OR 9/30.

Horace B. Boardman to Miss Elizabeth E. Wardle, both of Lexington. M Oct. 1, 1846. OR 10/3.

Stephen Vandierer, of Bracken county, to Miss Nancy McMurtry, of Clarke county. M Sept. 30, 1846. OR 10/3.

Hon. Bryan Y. Owsley, of Jamestown, Russell county, to Mrs. Amelia Anderson, of Garrard county. M in Frankfort, Sept. 30, 1846. OR 10/7.

J. H. McLaughlin to Miss Eliza Ann Neal, both of Lexington. M Oct. 7, 1846, at 5 o'clock a. m. OR 10/10.

James Harlow to Miss Margaret Chevis, daughter of David Chevis, all of Lexington. M Oct. 8, 1846. OR 10/10.

James M. Scott to Miss Esther M. Logan, daughter of James Logan, all of Fayette county. M Oct. 1, 1846. OR 10/14.

George W. Adams to Miss C. R. E. Laudeman, both of Fayette county. M Oct. 1, 1846. OR 10/14.

James Shaver to Miss Mary Ann Wood, of Fayette county. M Sept. 29, 1846. OR 10/14.

Major Daugherty White, of Clay county, to Miss Sarah, daughter of David Watts, of Fayette county. M Oct. 8, 1846. OR 10/14.

Dr. J. F. Warren to Miss Mary Jane Bush, both of Lexington. M Oct. 13, 1846. OR 10/14

Wilson S. Hunt, of Fayette county, to Miss Mary Jane, daughter of Solomon Crumbaugh, of Scott county. M Oct. 6, 1846. OR 10/14.

Elisha N. Warfield to Miss Elizabeth H. Brand, daughter of the late William Brand, all of Lexington. M Oct. 15, 1846. OR 10/17.

John T. Miller, of Lexington, to Miss Mary Sheely, of Jessamine county.

M Oct. 13, 1846. OR 10/17.

William T. French, of Prince William county, Va., to Miss Louisa Clay, daughter of the late Benjamin F. Thomas. M at Mt. Sterling, Ky., Oct. 15, 1846. OR 10/17.

Warren Wheeler to Miss Martha R., daughter of Stark Taylor. M Oct. 15, 1846. OR 10/17.

Richard C. Shackelford, of Hannibal, Mo., to Miss Ann Maria Caroline, daughter of Jefferson Scott, of Bourbon county, Ky. M Oct. 14, 1846. OR 10/17.

Capt. George Moore to Mrs. Nancy Garrard, both of Bourbon county. M Oct. 13, 1846. OR 10/17.

Rev. John B. Ewan to Miss Elizabeth, daughter of Dr. Avery Grimes, of Fleming county. M Oct. 13, 1846. OR 10/21

S. A. Hawkins, of Woodford county, to Miss Elizabeth Clore, of Oldham county. M latter place, Oct. 13, 1846. OR 10/24.

William Hughes, of Louisville, to Miss Letitia C., daughter of George W. Tarlton, of Miss. M Oct. 21, 1846. OR 10/28.

James McClellan to Miss Lucy A., daughter of John Wallace, of Jessamine county. M Oct. 21, 1846. OR 10/28.

Henry Ballard to Mrs. Eliza Jane Greggs. M in Sandersville, Oct. 29, 1846. OR 10/31.

John L. Walker to Miss Sarah Black, both of Woodford county. M Oct. 30, 1846. OR 11/4.

George W. Burch, of Scott county, to Miss Martha Jane, daughter of Jacob Embry, of Fayette county. M Nov. 2, 1846. OR 11/4.

William W. McKenney to Miss Sarah Ferguson, daughter of the late William Ferguson, of Clarke county. M Oct. 22, 1846. OR 11/7.

George B. Kinkead, Secretary of State, to Miss Eliza Pierce, of Louisville. M latter place, Oct. 20, 1846. OR 11/7.

William Thompson, of Scott county, to Miss Matilda Black, of Bourbon county. M Oct. 28, 1846. OR 11/7.

B. B. Groom to Miss Elizabeth Clay, daughter of Harrison Thompson, of Clarke county. M Nov. 5, 1846. OR 11/11.

Major W. M. Irvine to Miss Elizabeth S., daughter of Col. David Irvine, all of Madison county. M Nov. 3, 1846. OR 11/11.

Clayton Anderson to Miss Elvina, daughter of Baylor Jennings, all of Garrard county. M Oct. 29, 1846. OR 11/11.

Henry S. Kemp, of Quincy, Ill., to Miss Caroline V. Laughlin, of Clarke county, Ky. M Nov. 5, 1846. OR 11/14.

Ben Berry, Jr., of Fayette county, to Miss Carmilla F. Catlet, of Morganfield, Union county. M latter place, Nov. 4, 1846. OR 11/14.

William V. Barr to Miss Janetta, daughter of the Rev. J. K. Burch, all of Cincinnati. M Nov. 10, 1846. OR 11/18.

Dr. Richard W. Dunlap, of Danville, to Miss Elizabeth B. Warner, of Russellville. M latter place, Nov. 11, 1846. OR 11/18.

Dr. Lewis T. Frazee, of Maysville, to Miss Matilda J. Burbridge, of Scott county. M latter place, Nov. 12, 1846. OR 11/21

Rev. Dr. W. W. Hall, of Paris, Ky., to Miss Hannah, daughter of Richard Mattack, late of New Jersey. M in Philadelphia, Nov. 2, 1846. OR 11/25.

James Moore to Miss Edward Ann Bosworth, both of Lexington. M Nov. 24, 1846. OR 11/25.

Benjamin N. Webster to Miss Rhoda A. Gilbert, both of Richmond, Ky. M Nov. 17, 1846. OR 11/25.

Joseph A. Logan to Miss Jane S., daughter of William Alexander, of Bourbon county. M Nov. 24, 1846. OR 11/28.

John Breckinridge to Miss Nannie Kerr, both of· Bourbon county. M Nov. 24, 1846. OR 11/28.

James W. Parrish, of Winchester, to Mrs. Sarah F. Robinson, daughter of Mr. E. Berry, of Fayette county. M Nov. 26, 1846. OR 12/2.

Coules G. Meade, of Miss., to Miss Sallie Wolfolk, daughter of Col. Joseph Woolfolk, of Woodford county. M Dec. 1, 1846. OR 12/5.

John M. Tompkins to Miss Martha M. Hendrick, both of Jessamine county. M Nov. 26, 1846. OR 12/5.

David Newman, of Estill county, to Miss Nancy J. Hazelwood, of Jessamine county. M Nov. 26, 1846. OR 12/5.

Ephriam E. Cooper, formerly of Lexington, to Miss Malvina Young, daughter of the late Thomas A. Young. M at the Lexington residence of Richard B. Young. Dec. 1, 1846. OR 12/9.

William M. Biles, formerly of Noomelsdorf, Pa., to Miss Margaret E., daughter of Isaac Huttsell, of Bourbon county, Ky. M Nov. 26, 1846. OR 12/9.

L. B. Taylor, of Mortonsville, Woodford county, to Miss Nannie W., daughter of Evan Shelby, of Lincoln county. M Dec. 3, 1846. OR 12/16.

Robert Hume, of Clark county, to Miss Letitia, daughter of the Rev. D. J. Flournoy, of Arcadia. M Dec. 15, 1846. OR 12/19.

Edward Parmele, of New Orleans, to Miss Helen, daughter of the late Archy Allen, of Louisville, Ky. M in former place, Dec. 16, 1846. OR 12/19.

James H. Shackelford to Miss Melissa Walker, both of Richmond, Ky. M Dec. 15, 1946. OR 12/23.

Col. Joseph Nifong, of Mercer county, to Miss Mary Ann, daughter of David Nuckols, of Barren county. M in latter place, Dec. 19, 1846. OR 12/23.

Thomas E. Broaddus to Miss Emily Bond, formerly of Lexington. M in Franklin county, Dec. 20, 1846. OR 12/26.

Charles T. Butler to Miss Virginia Van Swearingen, formerly of Lexington, youngest daughter of the late Thomas Van Swearingen, all of Jefferson county, Va. M Dec. 9, 1846. OR 12/26.

Franklin Wheat, of Bourbon county, to Miss Mary Ann Camplin, of Clark county. M Dec. 8, 1846. OR 12/26.

Dr. J. T. Hickman to Miss Frances D., daughter of Dr. J. T. Lewis, all of Fayette county. M Dec. 24, 1846. OR 12/30.

James L. Blakemore to Miss Mahala J. Bush, both of Clark county.

M Dec. 24, 1846.   OR 12/30.

James M. White to Miss Mary Ann Taylor.   M Dec. 23, 1846.   OR 12/30.

Thomas Probert to Miss Mary E. Dimond, both of Lexington.   M Dec. 23, 1846.   OR 12/30.

John Sanford, of Sharpsburg, to Miss Margaret, daughter of the late Thomas J. Fletcher, of Bath county.   M at Bethel, Ky., Dec. 20, 1846.   OR 1/6/1847.

Merritt Woods to Miss Elizabeth, daughter of Lewis Collins.   M in Jessamine county, Dec. 24, 1846.   OR 1/13/1847.

William Hedger to Miss Sarah Elizabeth, daughter of Thomas Collins, of Jessamine county.   M latter place Dec. 24, 1846.   OR 1/13/1847.

James B. Haggin, of Shelbyville, to Miss Eliza Jane, eldest daughter of Col. Lewis Sanders, Jr., of Natchez.   M Dec. 27, 1846.   OR 1/16/1847.

R. B. Logan to Miss Elizabeth V. Byrnes, both of Fayette county.   M Dec. 23, 1846.   OR 2/10/1847.

1847

John Hukill to Miss Hannah Lawrence, both of Lexington.   M Jan. 3, 1847.   OR 1/6.

Dr. Joseph S. Halstead, of Lexington, to Miss Maria E. Worley, of Fayette county.   M Jan. 7, 1847.   OR 1/9.

Thomas S. Martin to Miss Mary E., daughter of Capt. Hubbard Taylor, all of Paris.   M Jan. 5, 1847.   OR 1/9.

William G. Royster, of Lexington, to Miss Mary, daughter of Samuel Bryan, of Fayette county.   M Jan. 8, 1847.   OR 1/13.

James Murphy to Mrs. Susan Steele, both of Lexington.   M Jan. 10, 1847.   OR 1/13.

John V. McCall, of Mt. Vernon, Ky., to Miss Priscilla B., daughter of Caleb Parrish, of Clark county.   M Jan. 12, 1847.   OR 1/27.

Samuel H. Henderson, of Fayette county, to Miss Mary P. Bush, of Clark county.   M Jan. 21, 1847.   OR 1/27.

Dr. William Baker, of Ill., to Miss Zerilda B., daughter of William Poindexter, of Lexington, Ky.   M Jan. 21, 1847.   OR 1/23.

Joseph D. Helm, of Woodford county, to Miss Mary Logan, eldest daughter of the late Joseph Logan, of Fayette county.   M in Lexington, Jan. 21, 1847.   OR 1/23.

Charles E. Marshall, Representative from Henry county, to Miss Judith Fry Langhorne, daughter of the late Maurice Langhorne.   M in Mason county, Jan. 17, 1847.   OR 1/23.

J. H. Williams to Anna E., daughter of J. W. Redd, all of Woodford county.   M Jan. 18, 1847.   OR 1/30.

J. B. Frost to Miss Mary Jane Hickey, formerly of Lexington.   M in Madisonville, Hopkins county, Ky., Jan. 12, 1847.   OR 1/30.

Daniel D. Atchison, of Galveston, Texas, formerly of Lexington, Ky., to Miss

Frances A., daughter of Mr. J. R. Alexander, of Woodford county, Ky. M in Paducah, Jan. 26, 1847. OR 2/3.

Addison McPheeters to Miss Susan A. Richardson, daughter of Capt. William H. Richardson, all of Fayette county. M Dec. 2, 1847. OR 2/6.

Isaac S. Todd to Miss Sarah, Daughter of Thomas P. Wilson, all of Shelby county. M Jan. 26, 1847. OR 2/6.

Robert G. McIntire to Miss Martha Hutchinson, both of Lexington. M Feb. 4, 1847. OR 2/6.

Hamlet W. Chiles to Miss Eddie A. Payne, both of Lexington, Ky. M in Aberdeen, O., Jan. 29, 1847. OR 2/10.

Dr. A. J. Burnam, of Richmond, to Miss Sarah J. Clark. M in Lexington, Feb. 9, 1847. OR 2/13.

G. Washington Miller, of Bourbon county, to Miss Susan A., daughter of William Ellis, of Fayette county. M Feb. 11, 1847. OR 2/13.

James B. Waller, of Lexington, to Miss Lucy, daughter of the late Robert Alexander, of Frankfort. M latter place, Feb. 11, 1847. OR 2/17.

Benjamin F. Graves to Miss Lucretia Griffin, both of Fayette county. M Feb. 17, 1847. OR 2/20.

Theodore Riley, of Jessamine county, to Miss Mary C. Ruckel, only daughter of Henry Ruckel, of Lexington. M Feb. 16, 1847. OR 2/20.

C. F. Lilly, of Lexington, to Miss Henrietta Downing, of Scott county. M Feb. 25, 1847. OR 2/27.

Charlton Alexander, of Paris, to Miss Catherine H. Butler, of Montgomery county. M Feb. 18, 1847. OR 2/27.

Samuel L. Bailey to Miss Catherine Allen, both of Fayette county. M Feb. 25, 1847. OR 2/27.

Turner Taylor to Miss Jane Stewart, both of Fayette county. M Feb. 25, 1847. OR 2/27.

James S. Jackson, of Fayette county, to Miss Patsy, daughter of Charles Buford, of Scott county. M Feb. 23, 1847. OR 3/3.

Dr. M. L. Keith, of South Carolina, to Miss Susanna W. Ball, of Lexington, Ky. M Mar. 4, 1847. OR 3/6.

Dr. B. M. Darnaby, of Stamping Ground, to Miss Elizabeth A., daughter of the late Sinett Triplett, of Burtsville, Scott county, Ky. M Mar. 2, 1847. OR 3/6.

John C. Richardson to Miss Mary E., daughter of Isaac Lionberger, both of Boonville, Mo. M. Feb. 16, 1847. OR 3/13.

James A. Morgan, of Madison county, to Miss Rebecca Ann New, of Woodford county. M Mar. 11, 1847. OR 3/17.

Rev. D. R. Campbell, of Georgetown, to Mrs. Maria L. McRery, daughter of Henry Wingate. M in Frankfort, Feb. 9, 1847. OR 3/20.

George W. Throckmorton, of Nicholas county, to Miss Mary Jane Devers, of Scott county. M in Aberdeen, O., in March, 1847. OR 3/24.

Thomas S. Williams, of Woodford county, to Miss Ann Eliza, daughter of Jesse Beauchamp, of Fayette county. M Feb. 25, 1847. OR 3/24.

William C. Jones, of New Orleans, to Miss Eliza P. C. Benton, eldest daughter of the Hon. Thomas H. Benton, of Mo. M in Washington City, March 18, 1847. OR 3/27.

Thomas Cook, of Fayette county, to Miss Susan Garrett, of Scott county. M at Aberdeen, O., Mar. 21, 1847. OR 3/27.

Col. Robert Innes, of Fayette county, to Miss Catherine Conn, of Lexington. M Apri. 14, 1847. OR 4/17.

Marshall H. Adcock, of Richmond, Va., to Miss Eliza Ann Moody, of Lexington, Ky. M Apr. 11, 1847. OR 4/17.

Thomas Powers, of Mo., to Miss Susan Catherine Wallace, of Lexington, Ky. M Mar. 18, 1847. OR 4/17.

W. T. Woodford to Miss Mary A. Hallack, of Paris. M Apr. 14, 1847. OR 4/17.

Rev. E. P. Humphrey to Miss Martha Ann Pope, daughter of the late Alexander Pope, all of Louisville. M Apr. 13, 1847. OR 4/17.

Dr. Isaac Bowman, formerly of Fayette county, Ky., to Miss Eveline Rochel, of the Parish of St. Mary's, La. M in New Orleans, Apr. 6, 1847. OR 4/24.

Samuel O. Berry, of Fayette county, to Mrs. Susan Vickery, of Scott county. M Apr. 15, 1847. OR 4/24.

Dr. B. F. Trimble, of Mo., to Miss Catharine B. Dishman, daughter of the late William Dishman, of Fayette county, Ky. M Apr. 22, 1847. OR 5/1.

John S. Wilson, of Lexington, to Miss Lydia A. Wickliffe, daughter of Nathaniel Wickliffe, of Bardstown. M in latter place, Apr. 20, 1847. OR 5/5.

Dr. Robert C. Palmer, of Washington county, to Miss Harriet S., daughter of Col. Marshall Key, of Mason county. M May 5, 1847. OR 5/8.

John A. Lewis to Miss Martha Jane Bell, both of Lexington. M Apr. 29, 1847. OR 5/12.

Lucian Laws to Miss Margaret Castle, both of Lexington. M May 13, 1847. OR 5/19.

Leo W. Stapleton, of Shelby county, to Miss Sarah Massie, of Clark county. M May 11, 1847. OR 5/22.

William T. Buckner to Miss Lucy Woodford, of Bourbon county. M May 13, 1847. OR 5/22.

Charles F. Coppage to Miss Maria T. Hickman, eldest daughter of James L. Hickman, of Lexington. M May 20, 1847. OR 5/22.

J. Kinley Boswell to Miss Eliza Linegar, both of Lexington. M in Cincinnati, May 24, 1847. OR 5/29.

T. Allen Gunnell, of Saline, Mo., to Miss Marion Wallace, daughter of Gen. David Thompson, of Pettis county, Mo., formerly of Scott county, Ky. M May 4, 1847. OR 5/29.

1847

M. T. Garnett, of Harrodsburg, to Miss Margaret E. Hunt, of Montgomery county. M May 26, 1847. OR 5/29.

James M. Todd, of the *Cincinnati Atlas,* to Miss Allisonia B., daughter of Col. A. H. Renwick, of Frankfort. M latter place, May 18, 1847. OR 5/29.

Dr. Clifton Branham to Miss Mary Ann Thomson, both of Scott county. M May 27, 1847. OR 6/5.

George E. Weigart to Miss Catharine Lankart, both of Lexington. M June 3, 1847. OR 6/5.

Clifton Ross to Miss Sarah J. McDowell, daughter of Capt. John McDowell, all of Fayette county. M June 1, 1847. OR 6/9.

John Finney, of New Orleans, to Miss Jouetta, daughter of Judge J. E. Davis, of Lexington, Ky. M former place, June 1, 1847. OR 6/19.

Isaac H. McKee of St. Louis, to Miss Mary A. Paul, eldest daughter of Hugh Paul, of Woodford county, Ky. M June 16, 1847. OR 6/19.

James F. Robinson, of Paris, to Miss Lucretia Frances Graves of Fayette county. M June 10, 1847. OR 6/19.

Jerome Crandle to Miss Cassandra Martin, daughter of David Martin, all of Fayette county. M June 17, 1847. OR 6/23.

John H. Hunter, of Lexington, to Miss Augusta Sheppard, daughter of Dr. H. H. Sheppard, of Fayette county. M at Aberdeen, Ohio, June 17, 1847. OR 6/23.

George W. Ward, of New Orleans, to Miss Josephine Harris, of Newport, Ky. M latter place, June 15, 1847. OR 6/23.

John B. Coggshell to Miss Mary Ann Wardle, both of Lexington. M June 22, 1847. OR 6/27.

James R. Stevenson to Miss Sarah Caroline Elliott, both of Woodford county. M June 22, 1847. OR 6/27.

Cary Crump to Mrs. Sally Ann McKnight, both of Frankfort. M Apr. 1, 1847. OR 6/27.

Dr. David E. Harrison to Miss Sarah, daughter of George Bowman, of Garrard county. M June 29, 1847. OR 7/3.

L. P. Young to Mrs. Nancy Long, both of Lexington. M June 29, 1847. OR 7/3.

Dr. Solon D. Martin to Miss C. H. Pinkerton, daughter of William Pinkerton, all of Midway. M June 30, 1847. OR 7/7.

Capt. J. H. Thompson to Miss Esther A. Martin, youngest daughter of William H. Martin, all of Scott county. M July 1, 1847. OR 7/7.

David Barrow, of La., to Mrs. Susan A. Rowan, daughter of Col. Joseph H. Woolfolk. M at Oak Hill, Woodford county, June 29, 1847. OR 7/10.

J. F. Jacoby to Miss Mary F. Kenney, both of Bourbon county. M July 6, 1847. OR 7/10.

Dr. Thomas Kilpatrick to Miss Mary Smithers, formerly of Lexington, Ky. M in Nashville, Tenn. June 6, 1847. OR 7/14.

C. H. Barkley, of Lexington, to Miss Elizabeth C. Best, of Clarke county. M July 13, 1847. OR 7/17.

Rev. Robert L. Breck to Miss Martha G., daughter of Col. William Rodes, all of Madison county. M July 20, 1847. OR 7/24.

William H. Worthington to Miss Anna E., daughter of Dr. Tomlinson, of Harrodsburg. M latter place July 14, 1847. OR 7/24.

Cornelius S. Bergin to Miss Mary Ann Ewing, both of Louisville. M July 21, 1847. OR 7/28.

William T. Curry to Miss Bettie F. Butler, of Mercer county. M July 20, 1847. OR 7/28.

Gen. Hugh W. Dunlap, of Madison Parish, La., to Mrs. Susan F. Kerr. M in Fayette county, July 19, 1847. OR 7/28.

Walter C. Ferguson, of Fayette county, to Mrs. Rebecca Devilbiss, of Lewis county, Mo. M July 13, 1847. OR 7/28.

Richard Higgins, Jr., of Crittenden county, Ark., to Miss Elizabeth B. Brand, of Lexington, Ky. M July 28, 1847. OR 7/31.

James Foley to Miss Hannah Wharton, both of Jessamine county. M July 29, 1847. OR 8/4.

Dr. Horace Fletcher, of Jessamine county, to Miss Margaret Wilson, of Nicholasville. M Aug. 2, 1847. OR 8/7.

B. F. Emison to Miss Ellen McDonald, both of Scott county. M Aug. 3, 1847. OR 8/14.

Dr. John R. Hall to Miss Julia M. Snell, both of Scott county. M. Aug. 3, 1847. OR 8/11.

Darius A. Mason, of Paterson, N. J., to Miss Jerusher Beach, of Lexington, Ky. M Aug. 9, 1847. OR 8/14.

Joseph A. Davis, formerly of Lexington, Ky., to Miss Elizabeth E. Harris, of New Orleans. M in latter city, July 26, 1847. OR 8/8.

Dr. Henry C. Bradbury, to Miss Frances E. Shelton, youngest daughter of Col. Medley Shelton, all of Versailles. M in Covington, Aug. 15, 1847. OR 8/21.

Charles M. Stewart to Miss Margaret Kirkpatrick, both of Fayette county. M Aug. 19, 1847, in Saundersville. OR 8/21.

Hugh B. Thompson to Miss Mary Jane Perkins, both of Fayette county. M Aug. 24, 1847. OR 8/28.

W. W. Peyton to Miss M. E. Campbell, daughter of J. R. Campbell, all of Mt. Sterling. M Aug. 17, 1847. OR 8/28.

Charles C. Hazen to Miss Priscilla H. Allender, both of Lexington. M Sept. 8, 1847. OR 9/4.

Hezekiah Culbertson, of Troy, Ohio, to Miss Susan, daughter of Robert Kinkead, of Versailles, Ky. M Sept. 2, 1847. OR 9/8.

John Kissenger to Miss Maria Louisa Castle, both of Lexington. M Sept. 5, 1847. OR 9/11.

Capt. A. J. Pennington to Miss Elizabeth, daughter of Stephen R. Chenoweth all of Louisville. M Sept. 7, 1847. OR 9/11.

T. P. Pierson, of Frankfort, to Miss Martha M. Thomasson, of Scott county. M Sept. 2, 1847. OR 9/11.

William Radcliff, of Shelby county, to Miss Elizabeth Thomasson. M Sept. 2, 1847. OR 9/11.

Elijah Ennis, of Lexington, to Miss Charlotte A., daughter of John S.

Nichols, of Harrison county. M. Sept. 9, 1847. OR 9/11.

Francis P. Blair, Jr., of St. Louis, to Miss Apoline Alexander, daughter of the late Andrew Alexander of Woodford county, Ky. M Sept. 8, 1847. OR 9/11.

Charles C. Parkhill of New Orleans, to Miss Letitia Breckinridge, youngest daughter of the late J. Cabell Breckinridge, of Lexington, Ky. M in Frankfort, Sept. 6, 1847. OR 9/18.

Dr. Lloyd W. Brown, of Boonesville, Mo., to Miss Rebecca P., eldest daughter of Dr. Lloyd Warfield, of Lexington, Ky. M Sept. 16, 1847. OR 9/22.

John Dishman to Miss Jane Atchinson, daughter of the late Alexander Atchison, of Fayette county. M Sept. 16, 1847. OR 9/22.

Philip D. Yeiser to Miss Margaret Craig, both of Danville. M in Sept. 1847. OR 9/22.

J. Preston Bull, of Louisville, to Miss Lucy Linthicune, of Paris, Ky. M in latter place, Sept. 14, 1847. OR 9/22.

John W. Cannon to Miss Mary Ann Sharp, eldest daughter of R. P. Sharp, all of Lexington. M Sept. 22, 1847. OR 8/25.

Churchill H. Blackburn to Miss Frances Jane Hale, both of Woodford county. M Sept. 23, 1847. OR 9/25.

George W. Weissenger, one of the editors of the *Louisville Journal*, to Miss Eliza, daughter of David R. Poignand. M in Spencer county, Sept. 21, 1847. OR 9/25.

P. L. Cable, of Scott county, Ky., to Miss Mary J., daughter of Col. Benjamin Taylor, of Chicot county, Ark. M Sept. 16, 1847. OR 9/25.

Dr. Paul Rankin to Miss Malvina, daughter of the late Rodes Burch, all of Scott county. M Sept. 15, 1847. OR 9/25.

W. W. Hunt, of Mt. Sterling, to Miss E. Kennedy, of Winchester. M Sept. 13, 1847. OR 9/25.

Silas Barkley, of Clarke county, to Miss Ann Lane, daughter of William N. Lane, of Bath county. M Sept. 22, 1847. OR 9/29/1847.

John Marrs to Miss Martha Kennedy, both of Jessamine county. M Sept. 23, 1847. OR 10/2.

Harlow Spencer, of Fayette county, to Miss Martha Ann Aiken, of Woodford county. M Oct. 3, 1847. OR 10/6.

Benjamin C. Glass to Miss Margaret A. Glass, both of Scott county. M Oct. 7, 1847. OR 10/9.

George Stepp, of Fayette county, to Miss Sarah Rose, of Lexington. M Oct. 7, 1847. OR 10/9.

Edward Woolridge, of Hopkinsville, to Miss Bettie, eldest daughter of Henry Moss, of Woodford county. M Sept. 29, 1847. OR 10/9.

H. Howard Gratz to Miss Minerva, daughter of Col. Oliver Anderson, all of Lexington. M Oct. 5, 1847. OR 10/13.

Micajah Merrill to Miss Susan Kirkpatrick, both of Lexington. M Oct. 20, 1847. OR 10/23.

Martin C. Hoagland to Miss Maria Agnes Elliott. M in Lexington Oct. 13, 1847. OR 10/23.

Harlow Spencer, of Fayette county, to Miss M. A. Aiken, of Woodford county. M Oct. 3, 1847. OR 10/23. See above.

Dabney Todd, of Frankfort, to Miss Mary L., daughter of David H. Bosworth, of Fayette county. M Oct. 17, 1847. OR 10/27.

James Curtis, of Mason county, to Miss Drucilla S. Coleman, of Harrison county. M latter place, Oct. 20, 1847. OR 10/27.

Dr. R. C. Hewett to Sidney, eldest daughter of James Anderson, of Louisville. M Oct. 20, 1847. OR 10/27.

E. Barbaroux to Emily F., second daughter of James Anderson, of Louisville. M Oct. 20, 1847. OR 10/27.

Dr. James A. Johnson, of Grant county, to Miss Elizabeth G. Carter, of Fayette county. M Oct. 27, 1847. OR 10/30.

Charles H. Kellogg, of New Orleans, to Miss Margaret, daughter of R. S. Todd, of Lexington, Ky. M Oct. 28, 1847. OR 10/30.

Wesley Covington, of Millersburg, to Miss Margaret Ann Johnson, of Virginia. M in Mt. Sterling, Oct. 19, 1847. OR 10/30.

Samuel P. Barbee, of Danville, to Miss Mary O. Harris, step-daughter of Benjamin Alsop, of Mercer county. M in Danville, Oct. 25, 1847. OR 11/3.

Phillip Willging to Miss Anne Shindlebower, of Fayette county. M Oct. 28, 1847. OR 11/6.

A. G. Tompkins, of Paris, to Miss Laura Hutchcraft, of Bourbon county. M Nov. 4, 1847. OR 11/6.

John A. Monroe to Miss Maria E. Bacon, daughter of the late W. W. Bacon, all of Franklin county. M Oct. 26, 1847. OR 11/6.

Col. Oliver Anderson, of Lexington, to Miss Louisa Price, of Clarke county. M Nov. 2, 1847. OR 11/10.

Dr. James L. Roberts to Miss Margaret Stout, both of Leesburg, Ky. M Oct. 17, 1847. OR 11/10.

Joseph Weisiger, Jr., to Miss Mary Ann Kincaid, both of Danville, M Nov. 3, 1847. OR 11/10.

Marion F. Lee to Miss Ellen S. Blain, both of Lincoln county. M Oct. 26, 1847. OR 11/10

Dr. James M. Bruce to Miss Elizabeth, daughter of the late Stephen P. Norton. M Nov. 9, 1847. OR 11/13.

S. W. Atkinson of Russellville, to Mrs. Maria L. Gatewood, daughter of Gen. Samuel L. Williams, of Montgomery county. M latter place, Oct. 26, 1847. OR 11/13.

Capt. Speed S. Fry, of Danville, to Miss Mildred T. Smith. M in Jefferson county, Nov. 4, 1847. OR 11/13.

Robert M. Allen, of Port Royal, Va., to Miss Mary Elizabeth, daughter of Elder T. M. Allen, formerly of Fayette county, Ky. M in Boone county, Missouri, Oct. 26, 1847. OR 11/17.

Abram Hale, of Lexington, to Miss Martha Ann, eldest daughter of Peter Evans, of Fayete county. M Nov. 11, 1847. OR 11/17.

John B. Wilgus of Lexington, to Miss Lucy T. Cox, of Mt. Sterling.

M Nov. 23, 1847. OR 11/24.

John T. McClelland to Miss Margaret B. Tilford, of Mercer county. M. Nov. 11, 1847. OR 11/24.

James D. Carpenter, of Woodford county, to Miss Frances A. Kidd, of Lexington. M Nov. 18, 1847. OR 11/24.

David J. Merrell to Miss Mary C. Tucker, both of Fayette county. M in Lexington, Dec. 2, 1847. OR 12/4.

James D. Cook to Mrs. Mary Jane Atchinson, both of Fayette county. M Dec. 2, 1847. OR 12/4.

Thomas Conn to Miss Lucy W., eldest daughter of Jacob Swigert. M in Frankfort, Nov. 23, 1847. OR 12/4.

Rev. J. W. Goodman, Pastor of the Frankfort Baptist Church, to Mrs. Eliza Ann Koch, of Shelby county. M Nov. 22, 1847. OR 12/4.

John M. Crane, of Covington, to Miss Mary E., daughter of Preston West, of Charleston, S. C. M in Georgetown, Ky., Nov. 25, 1847. OR 12/4.

Dr. William M. Garrard of Paris, to Miss Matilda Coburn, daughter of the late Dr. Wilson Coburn, of Mason county. M in Maysville, Nov. 25, 1847. OR 12/4.

Hamilton A. Headley to Miss Sally Ann Farra, of Jessamine county. M Nov. 25, 1847. OR 12/4.

Dr. Joseph L. Cartwright, of Princeton, Ky., to Miss Nancy E., daughter of L. K. Goodwin, of Fayette county. M Dec. 2, 1847. OR 12/8.

Roger Jones to Miss Elizabeth, daughter of Mrs. Mildred Poston, all of Clarke county. M Dec. 2, 1847. OR 12/8.

Capt. Theodore Kohlhass, of Winchester, to Miss Ann Wirt, of Lexington. M Dec. 9, 1847. OR 12/15.

Thornton M. Cox, of Mt. Sterling, to Miss Sally Ann, daughter of Samuel G. Jackson, of Lexington. M Dec. 7, 1847. OR 12/15.

Hypolite Hertzog, of Natchitoches, La., to Miss Cecil J. Giron, daughter of Mr. M. Giron, formerly of Lexington. M in Maysville, Ky., Dec. 7, 1847. OR 12/15.

Samuel Hanson, of Winchester, to Mrs. Minerva Whitefield. M at Sweet Lick Springs, Nov. 30, 1847. OR 12/15.

Henry Fox to Miss Margaret Shiddell, both of Lexington. M Dec. 14, 1847. OR 12/18.

1848

William H. Greenup, of Frankfort, to Mrs. Elizabeth Dohoney. M in Woodford county, Dec. 16, 1847. OR 12/18.

Elzy Harney to Miss Mary Ann Elliott, both of Lexington. M Dec. 23, 1847. OR 12/18.

John Childers to Miss Margaret Ross. M at the Fayette county residence of William Ross, Dec. 17, 1847. OR 12/25.

Thomas J. Hunter, of Raymond, Miss., to Miss Martha Dowden, of Lexington, Ky. M in former place Dec. 9, 1847. OR 12/25.

Dr. Thomas W. Foster to Miss Lucy J. McBrayer, both of Jassamine county.

M Dec. 16, 1847. OR 12/29.

John Machir, of St. Louis, to Miss Mary Eliza, eldest daughter of John M. January, of Maysville, Ky. M in Cynthiana, Dec. 28, 1847. OR 1/5/1848.

John S. Boyd to Miss Clementina, third daughter of John M. January, of Maysville. M in Cynthiana, Dec. 28, 1847. See above. OR 1/5/1848.

William R. Elley to Miss Louisa, daughter of Capt. Henry John Johnson, all of Lake Washington, Miss. M Dec. 21, 1847. OR 1/12/1848.

John Hill to Miss Frances A., daughter of Col. Thompson Ware, all of Bourbon county. M Dec. 30, 1847. OR 1/12/1848.

William B. Robinson, formerly of Fayette county, to Miss Clara Anderson, daughter of Alexander Anderson, all of Garrard county. M Jan. 5, 1848. OR 1/12.

J. W. Royster, of Lexington, to Miss Ann A, daughter of the late Leonard I. Fleming, of Woodford county. M Jan. 18, 1848. OR 1/22.

Dr. James J. Hatchitt to Miss E. D. Harlan, daughter of the Hon. James Harlan, of Frankfort. M Jan. 11, 1848. OR 1/22.

Benjamin Arnett, of Jessamine county, to Miss Amanda H. Smith, of Fayette county. M Jan. 20, 1848. OR 1/22.

John Webb to Miss Sarah McCrosky, both of Fayette county. M Jan. 18, 1848. OR 1/26.

Dr. William Johnston, of Ohio, to Miss Rebecca Vanderhoof, late of New York City. M in Lexington, Ky., Jan. 23, 1848. OR 1/26.

David Hubbard, of Savannah, Ga., to Miss Susan E. Smithers, of Lexington, Ky. M in Columbia, Tenn., Jan. 17, 1848. OR 1/26.

Saunders D. Bruce to Miss La Belle, daughter of General Leslie Combs, all of Lexington. M Jan. 27, 1848. OR 1/29.

Samuel Hall to Miss Mary J. Salyers, both of Fayette county. M Jan. 27, 1848. OR 1/29.

William Duke, of Scott county, to Miss Caroline, daughter of John L. Hickman, of Paris. M Jan. 27, 1848. OR 2/2.

Ephraim Hardy, late of New York, to Miss Laverna Jane, daughter of Ezekeal Rose, of Montgomery county, Ky. M Jan. 30, 1848. OR 2/2.

Dr. Samuel H. Chew to Miss Emily, daughter of James P. Highbee (Higbee), of Fayette county. M Feb. 1, 1848. OR 2/5.

Oscar S. Warner, of Lexington, to Miss Mary C. Gardner, of Louisville. M. Jan. 30, 1848. OR 2/5.

James B. Peck, of Lexington, to Miss Jane W. A. Thornton, of Loudon county, Va. M in Lexington, Ky., Feb. 3, 1848. OR 2/9.

Henry Rowland, of Nicholasville, to Miss Amanda Pearce, of New Castle, Ky. M Feb. 2, 1848. OR 2/9.

William W. Allen, of Scott county, to Miss Frances Ann, daughter of William G. Skillman, of Fayette county. M Feb. 8, 1848. OR 2/9.

Col. A. Backwell to Miss Sallie Jane Jones, daughter of the late Thomas Ap. Jones, all of Clarke county. M Feb. 9, 1848. OR 2/16.

Dr. H. O. Clark, of Cincinnati, to Miss Margaret B. Desha, of Danville, Ky.

M latter place, Feb. 17, 1848. OR 2/23.

Owen G. Bullitt, M. D., of Paducah, to Miss Virginia Berry, of Fayette county. M Feb. 23, 1848. OR 2/26.

Capt. W. J. Dunlap, of Fayette county, to Miss Harriet Vandell, of Lexington. M Feb. 24, 1848. OR 2/26.

Robert Gay to Miss Martha Ann Scott, both of Clark county. M Feb. 10, 1848. OR 2/26.

William B. Payne, of Jessamine county, to Miss Hannah E. Allender, daughter of Edward Allender, of Lexington. M Feb. 24, 1848. OR 2/26.

Josiah Ennis to Mrs. Caroline Coolidge, both of Lexington. M Feb. 29, 1848. OR 3/1.

James A. Beasley, of Garrard county, to Miss Mary E., daughter of William Simpson, of Jessamine county. M Feb. 23, 1848. OR 3/1.

Dr. M. J. Drysadle(Drysdale?) to Miss Mary H., daughter of Andrew Hampton, all of Jessamine county. M Feb. 23, 1848. OR 3/1.

Rev. James Lawrence to Miss Kate Allen, of Scott county. M Mar. 1, 1848. OR 3/4.

Dr. James L. Offutt to Miss Sophia, daughter of G. K. Smith, all of Scott county. M Feb. 29, 1848. OR 3/11.

Abraham S. Drake to Miss Sarah C. Elliott, of Clark county. M in Lexington, Mar. 9, 1848. OR 3/15.

John Messick, of Jessamine county, to Miss Maria A. Fitch, youngest daughter of the late Capt. Samuel Fitch. M Mar. 10, 1848. OR 3/18.

Rev. George S. Savage, M. D., of Lexington, to Miss Clara C. Bright, daughter of Dr. J. W. Bright, of Louisville. M in latter place, Mar. 12, 1848. OR 3/22.

John Arthur, of Independence, Mo., to Miss Ann F., eldest daughter of Walter C. Young, of Jessamine county, Ky. M Mar. 22, 1848. OR 3/25.

N. D. Moore, of Harrison county to Miss Annastasia P. Goddard, of Winchester. M Mar. 21, 1848. OR 3/25.

William P. Crenshaw, of Scott county, to Miss Mary, daughter of Jacob Sidener, of Fayette county. M Mar. 2, 1848. OR 3/25.

James Ferguson, formerly of Lexington, to Miss Mary E. Buckner, daughter of Capt. B. F. Buckner, of Texas. M in Shelby county, Ky., Mar. 16, 1848. OR 3/25.

Henry Williams, of Harrison county, to Miss Lucy Hemphill of Jessamine county. M Mar. 21, 1848. OR 3/25.

John A. Carrick to Miss Nancy R. Hurst, daughter of Capt. James Hurst, all of Fayette county. M Mar. 23, 1848. OR 3/25.

Rev. Jackson S. Willis, of Jessamine county, to Miss Mary Jane Long, of Shelby county. M Mar. 23, 1848. OR 4/1.

James Burt to Miss Elizabeth Patterson, both of Fayette county. M Feb. 22, 1848. OR 4/5.

James H. Kimbrough to Miss Helen T. Brock, both of Harrison county. M Mar. 20, 1848. OR 4/5.

James N. Willard, of Lexington, to Miss Mary J. Creighton, of Louisville.

M Mar. 29, 1848. OR 4/8.

Benjamin F. Ford, late of Jacksonville, Ill., to Miss Emily W. Vaughn, of Lexington, Ky. M Apr. 6, 1848. OR 4/12.

John H. Moore, of Cincinnati, to Miss Frances O. Smith, daughter of Thomas P. Smith, of Paris. M in latter place, Apr. 12, 1848. OR 4/15.

Dr. R. P. Letcher to Miss Emily Ingram, both of Henderson, Ky. M Apr. 6, 1848. OR 4/15.

Francis T. Chambers, of Mason county, to Miss Elizabeth L. Febiger, of Cincinnati. M former place, Apr. 13, 1848. OR 4/19.

William E. Bell, of Lexington, to Miss George A., daughter of George W. Clark, of Fayette county. M Apr. 11, 1848. OR 4/22.

John A. Gex, of Gallatin county, Ky., to Miss Henrietta R., daughter of Robert E. Brooking, of Clarke county. M latter place, Apr. 11, 1848. OR 4/22.

Francis Bourn to Mrs. Elizabeth St. Clair, both of Jessamine county. M Apr. 20, 1848. OR 4/26.

John Perry, of Jessamine county, to Miss Elizabeth Gess, of Fayette county. M Apr. 27, 1848. OR 5/6.

Hon. C. H. Smith, Judge of the Probate Court of Cooper county, Mo., to Mrs. Emily E. Black, daughter of the Rev. Nathan H. Hall, of Fayette county, Ky. M May 2, 1848, at Arrow Rock, Saline county, Mo., at the residence of Dr. N. W. Hall. OR 5/24.

Ashurst Nunnelly to Miss Mary Ann Crumbaugh, both of Fayette county. M May 2, 1848. OR 5/6.

William H. Grimes to Mrs. Nancy L. Gaines, of Lexington. M May 2, 1848. OR 5/6.

Reuben T. Taylor, Jr., to Miss Mary E., daughter of John Ryon, Esq., of Clark county. M May 5, 1848. OR 5/10.

Rev. P. W. Gruelle, of Versailles, to Mrs. Kitturah Steele, daughter of Governor Metcalfe. M May 9, 1848, at Forest Retreat, in Nicholas county OR 5/20.

Rev. Thornton A. Mills of Cincinnati, to Miss Sallie, daughter of William A. Mengies, of Richwood, Boone county, Ky. M May 9, 1848. OR 5/17.

A. F. Sheppard, of Georgetown, to Mrs. Juretta W. Roman, of Lexington. M May 9, 1848. OR 5/13.

A. Comingo to Miss Lucy Morton, both of Boyle county. M May 10, 1848. OR 5/17.

William Chrisman to Miss Lucy Anne Lee, daughter of George Lee, all of Boyle county, M May 10, 1848. OR 5/17.

Dr. John B. Burbridge, of Clark county, Ky., to Miss Emmeline O., second daughter of James Buchanan Esq. of Baltimore Md. M at Lexington, Ky., residence of Prof. Annen, May 11, 1848. OR 5/13.

James C. Lemon, of Scott county, to Miss Julia Wells, of Scott county M May 12, 1848, at Covington. OR 5/6.

Thomas B. Baxter, of Lexington, to Miss Mary, daughter of James Kinnear, of the same city. M at Millersburg, May 13, 1848. OR 6/17.

William S. Turner, of Richmond, Ky., to Miss Bettie A. Crittenden, daughter of the late Robert Crittenden, of Ark. M in Franklin county, May 16, 1848. OR 5/27.

Dr. John C. Richardson, of Lexington, to Miss Mary Ann Price, daughter of Willis Price, of Fayette county. M May 17, 1848. OR 5/20.

Dr. D. B. Flournoy, of Lexington, Mo., to Miss Sarah Garth, of Lexington, Ky. M May 17, 1848. OR 5/20.

J. F. Stonestreet, of Clark county, to Miss Amelia McClanahan, daughter of Major W. McClanahan, both of Clark county. M in Richmond, May 18, 1848. OR 5/27.

Thomas J. Nicholson to Miss Lucy B. Mason, both of Montgomery county. M May 30, 1848. OR 6/10.

Edward A. Tilford to Miss Anna L., daughter of Prof. B. W. Dudley, all of Lexington, M June 6, 1848. OR 6/10.

Robert C. McKee to Mrs. Zerelda Boyer, both of Frankfort. M there June 6, 1848. OR 6/10.

William A. McKim to Miss Lucinda, daughter of John Cunningham, of Bourbon county. M June 8, 1848. OR 6/17.

Frederick A. Jones, of Henderson, Ky., to Miss Eliza, daughter of Gen. Zachariah Easton, formerly of Fayette county, then of Henderson. M June 13, 1848. OR 6/24.

John Jay Caughey, of Miss., to Miss Mary H. Moffett, of Lexington, Ky. M June 14, 1848. OR 6/17.

T. O. Shackelford, of Paris, to Miss Phoebe Agnes Whitaker, daughter of Major James S. Whitaker, of Shelbyville. M June 22, 1848. OR 7/1.

William H. Grey, merchant of Harrodsburg, to Miss S. B. Swindells, formerly of Ohio. M in former place, June 27, 1848. OR 7/15.

James Taylor, of Clark county, to Miss S. Margaretta Talliaferro, of Paris. M June 27, 1848. OR 7/1.

W. B. Victor to Mrs. Mary Jane Davis, both of Paris. M June 29, 1848. OR 7/1.

Robert Taylor, of Clark county, to Miss Elizabeth E. Thompson, of Paris. M July 4, 1848. OR 7/12.

Rev. B. T. Blewitt to Miss Avis W. Hedge, of Fayette county. M July 4, 1848, at the Georgetown residence of Dr. S. F. Gano. OR 7/8.

Col. James M. Bullock, of Shelbyville, Ky., to Miss Anna E. Prescott, only daughter of Eustis Prescott, of New Orleans. M at Grace Church, Boston, Mass., July 3, 1848. OR 7/22.

John S. Withrow, merchant of Frankfort, to Miss Catherine, daughter of James McKee, of Woodford county. M latter place, July 5, 1848. OR 7/15.

Francis A. West, of Lexington, to Miss Alvina V. Fish of Crab Orchard. M in Danville, July 12, 1848. OR 7/19.

John B. Cochran to Miss Jane Hamilton, daughter of James Hamilton, all of Lexington. M July 18, 1848. OR 7/22.

William F. Hatch, of Georgetown, Ky., to Miss Rebecca J. Cooper, of Cincinnati. M latter place, July 19, 1848. OR 7/26.

Oliver Davis to Miss Rachel Ann Brown, both of Jessamine county. M July 20, 1848. OR 7/26.

John D. Willis to Mary D. Fish, of Scott county. M July 26, 1848. OR 8/5.

Rev. Joseph Cross, Professor at Transylvania University, to Mrs. Jane T. Hardin, daughter of Christopher Chinn, of Harrodsburg. M in Shelbyville, July 29, 1848. OR 8/5.

Lafayette Marshall, of Danville, to Sarah D. Woods, of Mercer county. M Aug. 1, 1848. OR 8/12.

James H. Lauderman to Miss Martha Montague, both of Fayette county. M Aug. 1, 1848. OR 8/2.

W. T. Adams to Mary Jane Gilbert, daughter of John Gilbert, all of Fayette county. M Aug. 2, 1848. OR 8/5.

Dr. Thomas W. Owings to Mary Agnes Hickman, daughter of the late William Hickman, all of Paris. M Aug. 2, 1848. OR 7/5.

J. A. Armstrong to Miss Elizabeth C. Scott. M Aug. 3, 1848. OR 8/5.

B. A. Chapman to Miss Elvira D. Scott. M Aug. 3, 1848. OR 8/5.

Dr. Burton Randall, of the U. S. Army, to Miss M. V. Taylor, daughter of the late John G. Taylor, of Jefferson county. M Aug. 10, 1848. OR 8/16.

George M. Wilson, of Palmyra, Mo., to Miss Mary E. Trabue of Jessamine county, Ky. M Aug. 15, 1848. OR 8/19.

Isaac N. Shepherd to Miss Sarah Shrewsberry, of Lexington. M Aug. 15, 1848. OR 8/16.

Robert Fairhead to Mary Ann, daughter of William McMeekin, all of Fayette county. M Aug. 16, 1848. OR 8/19.

Martin R. True, of Keene, Jessamine county, to Miss Eliza B. Atchison, of Fayette county. M in Aberdeen, Ohio, Aug. 17, 1848. OR 8/23.

Samuel H. Peak of Miss., to Miss Eliza A. Bridges, daughter of Judge John L. Bridges, of Danville. M Aug. 21, 1848. OR 8/30.

F. W. Wall, of Owensboro, to Miss Sarah S., daughter of Col. Charles S. Todd. M at Stockdale, in Shelby county, Aug. 22, 1848. OR 9/9.

P. B. Morrow, of Versailles, to Miss Rebecca A. Davis. M in Midway, Aug. 22, 1848. OR 8/30.

F. W. Capers, Professor of Ancient Languages and Literature at Transylvania University, to Miss Hannah H. Bascom, both of Lexington. M Aug. 24, 1848. OR 8/26.

Independent Gist to Miss Eliza M. Bell, daughter of the late William C. Bell, all of Lexington. M Aug. 30, 1848. OR 9/6.

Alexander Weigart to Miss Martha A. Linegar, both of Lexington. M Aug. 31, 1848. OR 9/2.

Boswell Beebe, of Little Rock, Ark., to Miss Julia McMillin, recently of Harrison county, Ky. M Sept. 4, 1848. OR 9/30.

Daniel Clinger to Miss Rosa Shiddell, both of Lexington. M Sept. 4, 1848. OR 9/9.

Coleman Dixon to Miss Mary Isabella Ellis, both of Fayette county. M Sept. 4, 1848. OR 9/9.

J. G. Allen, of Fayette county, to Miss Barbary J. Bush, of Clark county. M Sept. 5, 1848. OR 9/13.

George Breckinridge to Miss Elizabeth Ardery, both of Bourbon county. M Sept. 5, 1848. OR 9/9.

William M. Bush to Miss Nancy G. Elkin, both of Clark county. M Sept. 6, 1848. OR 9/13.

John Webb to Miss Margaret D. Haynes, both of Fayette county. M Sept. 7, 1848. OR 9/20.

Nelson McIntosh, of Estill, Ky., to Sarah Hagan, of Sandersville. M latter place, Sept. 7, 1848. OR 9/9.

Robert Scrugham, of Lexington, to Miss Christie Ann Smith, daughter of Jacob Smith, of Mercer county. M latter place, Sept. 12, 1848. OR 9/16.

Henry Herspurger to Miss John Ann, daughter of the late Col. John Moseley, of Jessamine county. M Sept. 12, 1848. OR 9/13.

Samuel F. January, of Cynthiana, to Josephine B. Stephens. M Sept. 13, 1848. OR 9/23.

Marquis Broadwell, of Cynthiana, to Miss Sallie, daughter of Benjamin Finnell, of Scott county. M Sept. 19, 1848. OR 9/30.

Samuel M. Tarlton, of Oldham county, to Miss Leonora, daughter of Leo Tarlton, of Lexington. M Sept. 19, 1848. OR 9/23.

S. Vanmeter, of Fayette county, to Miss Lucy Hockaday, of Winchester. M Sept. 20, 1848. OR 9/23.

C. J. Graves, of Scott county, to Miss Jane C. McFall, of Fayette county. M Sept. 26, 1848. OR 9/30.

David S. Coleman, of Lexington, to Miss Judith Chiles, daughter of the late John C. Chiles, of Indiana. M Sept. 27, 1848. OR 8/30.

Joseph M. Pilkington, of Arkansas, but late of Lexington, Ky., to Miss Mary E. Hanley, daughter of Major John H. Hanley. M in Jessamine county, Oct. 3, 1848. OR 10/7.

Samuel Pryor to Miss Elizabeth C. Talbott, both of Bourbon county. M Oct. 3, 1848. OR 10/7.

E. P. Hord, of Jessamine county, to Miss M. C. Martin, daughter of Dr. S. D. Martin, of Clark county. M Oct. 3, 1848. OR 10/7.

Reuben Cook, of Jessamine county, to Miss Elizabeth Easley, of Fayette county. M Oct. 5, 1848. OR 10/25.

Thomas J. Harrison to Miss Margaret B., second daughter of Isaac R. Miller, of Lexington. M Oct. 12, 1848. OR 10/14.

Larkin Montgomery, of Owen county, to Miss Mary E. Estis. M in Bourbon county, Oct. 18, 1848. OR 11/1.

Hiram Wilhoit, of Woodford county, to Miss Sophia Thornton, of Frankfort. M Oct. 18, 1848. OR 10/28.

James M. Yates, of Jessamine county, to Mrs. Lucy H. Garnett, of Woodford county. M Oct. 18, 1848. OR 10/25.

William D. Sutherland to Miss Eliza H., daughter of Robert E. Martin, of Clark county. M at the Dennison House, Cincinnati, Oct. 18, 1848. OR 10/25.

Logan McKnight, of Louisville, to Miss Lucy, daughter of Martin P. Marshall, of Fleming county. M Oct. 19, 1848. OR 10/25.

Francis M. Brennan to Miss Mary Jane, eldest daughter of Isaac N. Thomdon(Thomson? or Thompson?). M in Harrodsburg, Oct. 20, 1848. OR 11/1.

William Patterson to Miss Mary Ann Runyon, both of Fayette county. M Oct. 22, 1848. OR 10/28.

Dr. P. H. Chambers, of Middleton, Mo., to Miss Margaret E., daughter of Henry Wallace, late of Woodford county, Ky., but now of Lexington, Mo. M latter place, Oct. 24, 1848. OR 11/15.

Elder Thomas P (arker) Dudley to Mrs. Caroline E. Harrison, both of Lexington. M Tuesday Oct. 24, 1848, by Elder William Rash. OR 10/28.

A. D. Hamon to Miss Eliza J. Hardisty, both of Fayette county. M Oct. 25, 1848. OR 11/1.

Hiram Barkley, of Clark county, to Miss Bettie, daughter of Whitaker Campbell, of Garrard county. M Oct. 26, 1848. OR 11/8.

Daniel McAlister, of Louisville, to Mrs. Rebecca Brooks, of Bullitt county. M Oct. 26, 1848. OR 11/1.

Stephen Manship to Miss Jane Catherine Jeter, both of Lexington. M Oct. 26, 1848. OR 10/28.

Henry C. Dunlap, of Fayette county, to Miss Martha E. Boyce, daughter of William Boyce, of Lexington, Mo. M at the Washington, Mason county, Ky., residence of ——————— Oct. 30, 1848, by the Rev. J. H. Condit. OR 11/4.

Dr. William B. Cromwell of Lexington, to Miss Elizabeth A., daughter of the late Benjamin Scott, of Fayette county. M Oct. 31, 1848. OR 11/4.

Jacob S. Foley to Miss Margaret Cravens, both of Fayette county. M Nov. 2, 1848. OR 11/18.

David R. Haggard of Cumberland county, to Miss Jane Mary, daughter of the late Benjamin O. Johnson, of Frankfort. M Nov. 14, 1848. OR 11/18.

John P. Crane to Miss Margaret Self, both of Fayette county. M Nov. 15, 1848. OR 11/18.

James Deering, of New Orleans, to Miss Kate Louisa Morrison, of Maysville. M latter place, Nov. 16, 1848. OR 11/29.

Thomas E. Quisenberry, of Carlisle, to Miss Anne F. Price, of Jessamine county. M Nov. 16, 1848. OR 11/25.

William Murray, of Harrodsburg, to Miss Harriet, daughter of Thomas Q. Roberts, of Louisville. M latter place, Nov. 21, 1848. OR 11/25.

John Roberts to Miss Cordelia A. Stout, both of Frankfort. M Nov. 21, 1848. OR 11/25.

Capt. Ben. Milam to Miss Martha Jane Shockley, of Frankfort. M Nov. 21, 1848. OR 11/25.

John Morgan to Miss Rebecca Bruce, both of Lexington. M Nov. 21, 1848. OR 11/25.

Dr. John A. Lyle, of Paris, to Miss Laura, daughter of the Hon. John Chambers, of Mason county, M Nov. 22, 1848. OR 11/25.

John H. Haun, of Louisville, to Miss Mary H., daughter of Jesse Ellis, of Lexington. M Nov. 22, 1848. OR 11/25.

William Stout to Miss Judith Ann Jameson, both of Woodford county. M in December, 1848. OR 12/27.

L. R. Miller, of Bourbon county, to Miss Amanda F. Scott, daughter of Thomas J. Scott, of Fayette county, M in Aberdeen, Ohio, Dec. 2, 1848. OR 12/16.

T. Bigelow Lawrence, of Boston, Mass., to Miss Sallie, daughter of Robert J. Ward, of Louisville. M Dec. 5, 1848. OR 12/9.

J. L. Wilmot to Miss Sallie, daughter of George Bowman, of Fayette county. M Dec. 7, 1848. OR 12/23.

Charles W. Caps to Nancy J. Elkin, daughter of Enoch Elkin, both of Clark county. M Dec. 7, 1848. OR 12/13.

John A. Garrison to Miss Sarah K. Steele, both of Jessamine county. M there Dec. 8, 1848. OR 12/13.

Dr. W. C. Overstreet, of Munday's Landing, Ky., to Miss Mary A. Seaton, of Harrodsburg. M at Granite, Ill., Dec. 11, 1848. OR 1/3/1849.

Randolph J. Haley to Miss Mary Bunnell both of Fayette county. M Dec. 12, 1848. OR 12/20.

Nathaniel C. Hart to Miss Mary E. Dudley, both of Fayette county. M Dec. 12, 1848. OR 12/16.

1849

David T. Hume to Miss Martha A. Talbott, both of Bourbon county. M Dec. 14, 1848. OR 12/30.

Henry Clay Stone to Miss Eliza C. Foushee, both of Versailles. M Dec. 20, 1848. OR 12/27.

Capt. James C. Stone, of Madison county, to Miss Matilda R., daughter of Samuel Hanson, of Winchester. M Dec. 21, 1848. OR 1/3/1849.

Dr. M. Robinson, of Athens, to Miss E. Wyatt, of Bourbon county. M Dec. 21, 1848. OR 12/30.

William Warfield to Miss Mary Breckenridge, daughter of Rev. Robert J. Breckenridge, D.D. M in Lexington, Dec. 21, 1848, by the Rev. William L. Breckenridge. OR 12/27.

Jerome A. Broadwell, of Cynthiana, to Miss Sarah Baskett, of Henderson county. M Dec. 21, 1848. OR 1/17/1849.

Warwick Tunstall, of St. Louis, Mo., to Mrs. Florida P. Boswell, daughter of the Rev. Nathan H. Hall, D.D. M in Lexington, Ky., Dec. 21, 1848. OR 12/23.

Samuel H. Bradley to Miss Janetta Smith, both of Versailles. M Dec. 27, 1848. OR 1/3/1849.

R. B. Wilson to Miss Martha Jane Alwell, both of Versailles M there Dec. 27, 1848. OR 1/3/1849.

John Bowman to Miss Pamela Headington, both of Lexington. M Dec. 28, 1848. OR 12/24.

Dr. Alexander M. Blanton to Miss Emma M. Swigert, daughter of Jacob Swigert, all of Frankfort. M Dec. 28, 1848. OR 12/30.

Jacob Rathvon to Miss Ellen Carson, both of Lexington. M Dec. 28, 1848. OR 12/30.

Rev. Neal M. Gordon, of Nicholasville, to Miss Catherine M. Smith, daughter of the Rev. Dr. Smith, of Shelby county. M Jan. 1, 1849. OR 1/6.

Charles N. Anderson to Miss Ann Jane Noble, both of Lexington. M Jan. 1, 1849. OR 2/7.

Irvine McClanahan, of Richmond, Ky., to Miss Jane, daughter of the Hon. B. Monroe, of Frankfort. M Jan. 4, 1849. OR 1/10.

Col. Nathaniel G. Woods, of Danville, to Mrs. Sarah Ann Moss, of St. Louis, Mo. M Jan. 7, 1849. OR 1/17.

John Cook to Mrs. Sarah S. Wheelock, both of Lexington. M Jan. 7, 1849. OR 1/10.

V. W. Keen, of Gallatin county, to Miss Maria, daughter of William Pointdexter. M Jan. 8, 1849. OR 1/10.

Dewitt C. Harris, of Houston, Texas, to Miss Saville Fenwick, daughter of the late James Fenwick, of Scott county, Ky. M Jan. 16, 1849. OR 1/20.

H. M. Beauchamp to Miss Lucy M., daughter of Silas Payne, all of Fayette county. M Jan. 16, 1849. OR 1/20.

Joseph Patterson, of Woodford county, to Miss Susan E. Haggin, eldest daughter of Terah T. Haggin. M in South Frankfort, Jan. 23, 1849. OR 1/27.

Daniel Bryan to Miss Sarah Pettit, eldest daughter of Henry Pettit, all of Fayette county. M Jan. 25, 1849. OR 1/31.

Elijah C. Bryan to Miss Lucy, daughter of the late Andrew Kay. M Jan. 30, 1849. OR 1/31.

Capt. E. A. Graves, of Lebanon, to Miss Catherine H., daughter of David Merriwether, of Jefferson county. M Jan. 30, 1849. OR 2/10.

John Thorn, of Boyle county, to Miss Theodosia Vallandingham, of Fayette county. M latter place, Jan. 31, 1849. OR 2/14.

Stephen Donaldson to Miss Elizabeth Corbin, both of Bourbon county. M Jan. 31, 1849. OR 2/24.

William E. Milton, of Lexington, to Miss Louisa, daughter of Col. A. H. Rennick, of Frankfort. M Feb. 6, 1849. OR 2/10.

William G. Ford, of Memphis, Tenn., to Miss Mary A. Sanders, of Lexington. M Feb. 6, 1849. OR 2/7.

W. S. Worsham to Miss Frances Montague. M Feb. 8, 1849. OR 2/10.

J. W. Gilbert, of Richmond, to Miss Isabella, daughter of Joseph F. Miller, of Lexington. M Feb. 8, 1849. OR 2/10.

Thomas P. Dobyns, of Montgomery county, to Miss Julia F. McCann, of

Fayette county. M Feb. 15, 1849. OR 2/24.

Alexander Graham, of Warren county, to Miss Corrilla, daughter of H. B. Innes, of Franklin county. M Feb. 15, 1849. OR 2/24.

William Devlin, of Lexington, to Miss Emily W. M. Rochel, of St. Mary's Parish, La. M latter place, Feb. 20, 1849. OR 3/17.

Samuel F. Brown, of Lexington, to Miss Christiana Potter, of Louisville. M latter place, Feb. 22, 1849. OR 2/28.

John W. Hunt, of Jessamine county, to Miss Minerva P., eldest daughter of Derrick Warner, of Lexington. M Feb. 27, 1849. OR 2/28.

Abram Clay Bryon to Miss Elizabeth Oder, both of Cynthiana. M Mar. 1, 1849. OR 3/10.

Thomas Richardson to Miss Kitty Ann Kibler, both of Fayette county. M Mar. 1, 1849. OR 3/14.

Robert Foster to Mary M. Sinclair, both of Jessamine county. M Mar. 1, 1849. OR 3/14.

Henry M. Sallee to Miss Sallie J., daughter of Benjamin Netherland, all of Jessamine county. M Mar. 4, 1849. OR 3/14.

Henry V. Barringer to Catharine Foreman, both of Lexington. M March 8, 1849. OR 3/10.

Alexander Moore to Miss Margaret Randolph, both of Fayette county. M Mar. 22, 1849. OR 3/28.

James Henderson to Miss Susan Hardesty, both of Bourbon county. M Mar. 22, 1849. OR 3/28.

Ephraim A. Herriott to Miss Elizabeth L. Washington, both of Scott county. M Mar. 22, 1849. OR 3/28.

James W. Lewis to Miss Agnes C. E. Herriott, both of Scott county. M Mar. 22, 1849. OR 3/28.

Dr. James E. Baker, of South Carolina, to Miss Semira M. Bronston, daughter of Thomas M. Bronston, of Madison county, Ky. M Mar. 22, 1849. OR 3/31.

Robert Hamilton to Mrs. Catharine Gibbs, of Charleston, S. C. M in Nicholasville, Ky., Mar. 25, 1849. OR 4/21.

O. Anderson to Miss Caroline Timberlake. M in Paris, Mar. 26, 1849. OR 3/31.

Franklin P. Bedford, of Bourbon county, to Miss Mary C. Hume, of Clark county. M Mar. 29, 1849. OR 4/7.

Samuel Stockwell, Jr., of Flemingsburg, to Miss Charlotte C., second daughter of Jacob Ashton, of Lexington. M Apr. 3, 1849. OR 4/7.

Charles W. Innes, of Fayette county, to Miss Mary Russell, daughter of the late Dr. Robert Russell, of Mo. M at the Harrison county, Ky., residence of her grandfather, Col. T. Ware, April 5, 1849. OR 7/14.

Philip Willging, of Georgetown, to Miss Martha Wainscott, of Richmond, both recently of Lexington. M Apr. 5, 1849. OR 4/21.

John Roy, of Clark county, to Miss Ann Sidener, of Fayette county. M Apr. 10, 1849. OR 7/14.

George W. Ward to Miss Maria Ellen Harney. M at the Paris Hotel, April 10, 1849. OR 7/14.

Joseph R. Cross, of Lexington, to Miss Julia, daughter of George W. Clark, of Fayette county. M Apr. 10, 1849. OR 5/25.

James P. Breckenridge, formerly of Lexington, to Miss Maria, daughter of James Alves, all of Henderson, Ky. M Apr. 10, 1849. OR 5/2.

Edward Wilkerson, of Hardinsburgh, to Miss Caroline, daughter of the late P. B. Ewing, of Shelby county. M in Georgetown, Apr. 11, 1849. OR 4/18.

Gen. Leslie Combs, of Lexington, to Mrs. Mary E Man, of Cumberland, R. I. M in Manville, R. I., Apr. 11, 1849. OR 4/21.

Daniel H. Harrison, of Christian county, to Miss L. Minerva Norwood, daughter of Charles Norwood, of Versailles. M latter place, Apr. 17, 1849. OR 4/25.

John James Key, of Maysville, to Miss Hetty A. Rudd, of Jessamine county. M Apr. 18, 1849. OR 4/25.

Robert Fleming Ratcliff, of Ohio, to Miss Martha Helm, eldest daughter of Samuel Pike, editor of the *Maysville Flag.* M Apr. 29, 1849. OR 5/4.

J. Randolph Bull to Miss Helen Mar, daughter of I. Raphael, all of Louisville. M May 1, 1849. OR 5/9.

William H. Scearce, of Woodford county, to Mary Elizabeth Johnston, daughter of Stephen Johnston, dec'd., of Shelby county. M May 1, 1849. OR 5/12.

Dr. William T. Shortridge, of Fulton, Mo., to Miss Thomasella V. Bartlett, of Lexington. M latter place, May 2, 1849. OR 5/5.

Thomas B. Page, of Lexington, to Miss Harriet Clarke, daughter of Joseph Clarke, of Franklin county. M May 3, 1849. OR 5/9.

Dr. L. E. Bennett, of Covington, to Miss Ellen C., daughter of Col. A. Dudley, of Cincinnati. M May 3, 1849. OR 5/16.

William T. Buckner, of Hopkinsville, to Miss Lucy E. Jackson, of Fayette county. M at the residence of James S. Berryman, May 8, 1849. OR 5/12.

David O. Harris to Miss Mary Hannah McKinney, both of Woodford county. M May 8, 1849. OR 5/12.

George C. Bain, of Lexington, to Miss Catharine, daughter of Lewis Y. Martin, of Fayette county. M May 8, 1849. OR 5/12.

Colby T. Quisenberry to Miss Mary M. Weathers, of Clark county. M May 10, 1849. OR 5/16.

Christopher C. Sayre to Miss Margaret A. Sallee, both of Fayette county. M May 16, 1849. OR 5/23.

1849

John C. Young, of Lexington, to Miss Mary Canon, of Scott county. M May 16, 1849. OR 5/26.

J. S. McGee, of Jessamine county, to Miss Mary E. Clay, daughter of the late Joseph H. Clay, of Bourbon county. M May 17, 1849. OR 5/26.

John Lewis to Mrs. Ellen Scott, both of Lexington. M May 19, 1849.

OR 5/26.

Jesse Woodruff, of Lexington, to Miss Anne H. Anderson, of Cynthiana. M May 22, 1849. OR 5/26.

James Wirt to Miss Martha Tandy, both of Lexington. M May 22, 1849. OR 5/26.

Robert McClelland, of Bourbon county, to Miss Frances A., daughter of Lewis C. Suggett, of Scott county. M May 22, 1849. OR 6/2.

William G. Timberlake, of Paris, to Mrs. Isabella Morton, of Louisville. M May 23, 1849. OR 5/26.

William C. Stamps to Miss Mary Louise Keller, daughter of Jacob Keller, all of Bourbon county. M May 24, 1849. OR 5/26.

Joseph McCann to Miss Maria Louisa, daughter of General James Dudley, all of Fayette county. M May 24, 1849. OR 5/26.

Rev. S. M. Bayliss to Miss Elizabeth, daughter of Eben Milton, of Fayette county. M May 28, 1849. OR 6/2.

Richard H. Hanson to Miss Sarah Eveline, daughter of Charles Talbutt, all of Paris. M May 29, 1849. OR 6/2.

Capt. O. H. P. Beard to Miss Rebecca, daughter of Jesse Ellis, all of Lexington. M in Aberdeen, Ohio, May 29, 1849. OR 5/30.

Edward O. Stevenson, of Circleville, Ohio, to Miss Eliza, daughter of the Rev. D. J. Flournoy, of Scott county. M June 4, 1849. OR 6/16.

William Flanagan to Miss Laura Laughlin, both of Winchester. M June 7, 1849. OR 6/13.

James Lock Ballard to Miss Mary G. Spires, both of Nicholasville. M June 12, 1849. OR 6/16.

Dudley Nunnelley, of Fayette county, to Miss Juretta Hudson, daughter of Col. Spencer Hudson, of Somerset. M June 12, 1849. OR 6/27.

Wesley R. Orear, Post Master at Danville, to Mrs. Amanda F. Greenwood, late Post Mistress of Danville. M June 13, 1849. OR 6/20.

Dr. William B. Paxton, of Scott county, to Miss E. F. Offutt, daughter of Mrs. Ann Offutt, of Fayette county. M June 13, 1849. OR 6/23.

Herbert McConnell to Miss Armelda Ann Scott, both of Lexington. M June 13, 1849. OR 6/16.

James C. Price to Miss Frances Ann, eldest daughter of Leonard Cassell, all of Jessamine county. M July 26, 1849. OR 8/1.

William Keiser to Miss Amanda Steppe, both of Fayette county. M July 25, 1849. OR 8/1.

Jonathan T. Estill to Miss Louisa, daughter of Abner Oldham, all of Madison county. M July 24, 1849. OR 7/28.

John C. Keller to Mary E. Simpson, both of Bourbon county. M June 14, 1849. OR 6/27.

D. J. Lyons, of Louisville, to Miss Virginia, daughter of Joseph Putnam, of Drennon, Ky. M June 20, 1849. OR 6/27.

Robert Michael to Elizabeth Ann Perkins, both of Fayette county. M June

21, 1849.   OR 6/27.

T. C. Coleman, Jr., of Louisville, to Miss Dulciena, daughter of Gen. William Johnson, of Scott county.   M July 31, 1849.   OR 7/11.

W. D. Crockett, of Scott county, to Miss Eliza H. Ware, of Bourbon County. M July 5, 1849.   OR 7/14.

Hector Donnigan to Miss Amanda Atchison, both of Fayette county. M July 5, 1849.   OR 7/11.

Madison M. Moore to Miss Drusilla Owsley.   M in Winchester July 5, 1849.   OR 7/21.

Joshua Nolan to Miss Lucretia Hopper, both of Fayette county.   M July 15, 1849.   OR 7/21.

P. Gatewood Lincoln, of Fayette county, to Miss M. A. W. H. Nelson, of New Orleans.   M July 31, 1849.   OR 8/8.

Mason Brown, of Fayette county, to Mrs. Sarah A. Hicklin, of Bourbon county.   M Aug. 2, 1849.   OR 8/11.

James McGray, of Bourbon county, to Miss Susan, daughter of John Judy, of Clarke county.   M Aug. 9, 1849.   OR 8/15.

William R. Frazer, of Lexington, to Miss Susan Moore, of Maysville. M Aug. 9, 1849.   OR 8/15.

John Atkinson, printer of Lexington, to Miss Mary A. Matthews, youngest daughter of Dr. Samuel Matthews, of Bryant's Station.   M Aug. 9, 1849. OR 8/11.

Samuel Chevis, of Lexington, to Miss Georgeann McMeekin, of Fayette county.   M Aug. 22, 1849.   OR 8/25.

William A. Adams to Miss Mary Jane, daughter of James L. Brown, both of North Middletown, Ky.   M Aug. 26, 1849.   OR 9/1.

Milton Stevenson, of Georgetown, to Miss Nancy Griffith, daughter of Clement Griffith, of Scott county.   M Aug. 28, 1849.   OR 9/1.

Col. John H. Shackelford, of Richmond, Ky., to Miss Ann M. Hickman, of Bourbon county.   M Aug. 29, 1849.   OR 9/1.

Dr. D. F. Todd, of Louisville, to Miss Jane H., daughter of Beverley A. Hicks.   M Aug. 29, 1849.   OR 9/1.

Richmond Arnold to Miss Martha Jane Martin, both of Clarke county. M Aug. 29, 1849.   OR 9/5.

Dr. James B. Riley, of Richmond, Ky., to Miss Emily Bibb, of Jessamine county.   M Aug. 30, 1849.   OR 9/8.

Samuel J. Walker to Miss Martha C., daughter of the late Hon. W.W. Southgate, all of Covington.   M Sept. 4, 1849.   OR 9/8.

Major William R. Davis to Miss Mary A., daughter of Willis Muir, all of Fayette county.   M Sept. 4, 1849.   OR 9/8.

Wesley Spencer to Miss Mary, daughter of L. Taylor, all of Lexington. M Sept. 6, 1849.   OR 9/8.

Dr. L. W. Taylor, Carrollton, Ky., to Miss Mary F. Malin, daughter of Judge Malin, of Florence, Ind.   M Sept. 10, 1849.   OR 9/19.

Marcus E. Browning, of Lexington, to Miss Angeline Rees, daughter of the late Daniel Rees, of Mason county. M in Maysville, Sept. 11, 1849. OR 9/15.

Capt. Leander M. Cox, of Flemingsburg, to Miss Susan R. Gist, daughter of the late Rezin H. Gist, of Montgomery county. M July 19, 1849, by the Rev. John D. Cladbourne, Rector of the Nativity Church, Maysville. OR 7/25.

Major John D. Harris to Miss Nannie J. White, daughter of the late Valentine M. White, all of Madison county. M Sept. 20, 1849. OR 10/6.

Benjamin F. Moore, of Iberville, La., to Miss S.E. Taylor, eldest daughter of Major James Taylor, of Harrodsburg. M Sept. 20, 1849. OR 9/29.

Thomas Elley to Miss Mary Jane Bledsoe, daughter of S. C. Bledsoe. M in Lexington, Sept. 24, 1849. OR 9/26.

Sidney R. Smith, of Lexington, to Miss Bettie B. Dickey, daughter of the late Milus W. Dickey, of Fayette county. M Sept. 25, 1849. OR 9/29.

Benjamin F. Edge to Miss Mary Harney, both of Lexington. M Sept. 25, 1849. OR 9/29.

John Goodwin to Miss Serena Cartwright, of Caldwell county. M in Fayette county, Sept. 26, 1849. OR 9/29.

Talbott M. Bryan, of Lexington, to Miss Sophia Stone, of Fayette county. M at Shelbyville, Oct. 1, 1849. OR 10/6.

Thomas Hawkins, of Jessamine county, to Miss Elizabeth Haydon, of Woodford county. M Oct. 4, 1849. OR 10/6.

R. H. Lindsay, of Paris, to Miss Olivia, daughter of D. P. Bedinger, of Bourbon county. M Oct. 9, 1849. OR 10/13.

James Berry, of Plaquemine, La., to Miss Fanny Berry, daughter of Dr. R. B. Berry, of Woodford county, Ky. M at Versailles, Ky., Oct. 10, 1849. OR 10/24.

Theodore Daviess to Miss Ann Mary, daughter of George Twyman. M at Versailles, Oct. 11, 1849. OR 10/20.

James S. Jacoby to Miss Agnes L., daughter of William M. Kenney, all of Bourbon county. M Oct. 11, 1849. OR 10/20.

Michael Gwartney, of New Orleans, to Miss Julia Ann McChesney, daughter of John McChesney, of Lexington, Ky. M Oct. 16, 1849. OR 10/17.

John P. Smith, of Warren county, to Mrs. Ann B. Hearne, of Bourbon county. M Oct. 18, 1849. OR 10/20.

Walter L. Peters, of Woodford county, to Miss Caroline T. Stockton, both of Mt. Sterling. M Oct. 18, 1849. OR 10/20.

Sol. D. Bayless, Ex-Mayor of Troy, Ohio, to Miss Fannie L. Dillon, of Scotland, Woodford county, Ky. M Oct. 18, 1849. OR 10/20.

Morton Perry, of Jessamine county, to Miss Ellen Cassele, of Woodford county. M Oct. 18, 1849. OR 10/24.

George E. Beatty to Miss Lavinia Brooking, both of Scott county. M Oct. 18, 1849. OR 10/31.

Thomas Boggs to Miss Mary Moxley. M Oct. 21, 1849. OR 10/27.

William Mabon to Miss Mary Lawrence, both of Lexington. M Oct. 23, 1849. OR 10/27.

Guilford O. Talbott, of Danville, to Miss Paulina G. Smith, daughter of Col. John Speed Smith, of Madison county. M Oct. 23, 1849. OR 10/31.

Robert S. Bearding, of Woodford county, to Miss Helen P. Beatty, of Scott county. M Oct. 23, 1849. OR 11/3.

James N. Morrison, of Mason county to Miss Nancy Goddard, youngest daughter of the late Col. William Goddard, of Maysville. M in Flemingsburg, Oct. 25, 1849. OR 11/3.

James S. Gatewood, of Montgomery county, to Miss Mary E. Martin, of Clarke county. M Oct. 25, 1849. OR 11/7.

James P. Gay, of Clarke county, to Miss Mary E. Senseny, of Winchester, Va. M latter place, Oct. 25, 1849. OR 11/10.

S. T. Brooks to Mrs. Phebe Morgan Lamkin, formerly of Nicholasville. M in Palmyra, Mo., Oct. 25, 1849. OR 11/10.

William Satchwell to Miss Mary Downing. M Oct. 26, 1849. OR 10/27.

Robert Grinstead to Miss Urena Martin, both of Fayette county. M Oct. 29, 1849. OR 10/31.

John De Garris, of Lexington, to Miss A. E., daughter of Mr. A. Cannon, of Georgetown. M Oct. 31, 1849. OR 11/10.

Samuel McChesney to Miss Julia Tanner, eldest daghter of William Tanner, editor of the *Yeoman*. M at Frankfort, in October, 1849. OR 10/31.

B. G. Bruce, of Lexington, to Miss Louisa A., daughter of William Chiles, Sr., of Estill Springs. M Nov. 1, 1840. OR 11/10.

Dr. William M. Tomlinson, of Harrodsburg, to Miss Mary Ann Talbott, daughter of A. G. Talbott, of Danville. M Nov. 8, 1849. OR 11/21.

Dr. James H. Taylor, of Clarke county, to Miss Mary Price, daughter of Daniel B. Price, of Nicholasville. M in Lexington, Nov. 8, 1849. OR 11/10.

Smith F. Overstreet, of Mercer county, to Miss Susan Hiette Davis, of Woodford county. M Nov. 8, 1849. OR 11/17.

Capt. William Chiles to Miss Amanda M. Park, daughter of Solomon Park, all of Estill county. M Nov. 8, 1849. OR 11/17.

James H. Bassett, of Louisville, to Miss Georgianna Houston, daughter of Dr. R. R. Houston, of Breckinridge county. M Nov. 13, 1849. OR 11/21.

John Duvall, of Owen county, to Miss Kate Gayle, of Lexington. M Nov. 15, 1849. OR 11/21.

Joseph Thompson to Miss Bettie Ann Harris, both of Jessamine county. M Nov. 20, 1849. OR 11/28.

Robert N. Kersey to Miss Nancy Shrewsbury, both of Lexington. M Nov. 20, 1849. OR 11/24.

Charles E. Smedes, formerly of Lexington, to Miss Martha Love, daughter of Dr. R. H. Brodnax, of Vicksburg, Miss. M Nov. 22, 1949. OR 12/29.

James H. Dean, of Milburn, Ky., to Miss Octavia R., daughter of William Murrain, of Jessamine county. M Nov. 22, 1849. OR 11/24.

William G. Darnaby, of Fayette county, to Miss Mary E., daughter of Burrus Arnett, of Jessamine county. M Nov. 22, 1849. OR 11/28.

Dr. William J. Redman, of Shelbyville, to Miss Mary C. Chisham, of Georgetown. M Nov. 23, 1849. OR 11/28.

Elisha Riggs, Jr., of Washington, D. C., to Miss Mary, daughter of the late George Boswell, of Lexington, Ky. M Nov. 26, 1849, at the St. Stephen's Church, Philadelphia. OR 1/5/1849.

Dr. John W. Gatewood, of the Parish of Assumption, La., formerly of Lexington, Ky., to Miss Mary Ellen Giltner, of Woodford county, Ky. M at the Woodford county residence of Mr. Taylor, Nov. 29, 1849. OR 1/1/1850.

Ben. E. Hall, of Georgetown, to Miss Eleanor E., daughter of Colonel Henry M. Buckner. M Nov. 29, 1849. OR 12/5.

James McBrayer to Miss Emily A., daughter of Thomas M. Bond. M at Frankfort, Nov. 29, 1849. OR 12/8.

John Gunkle, of Lexington, to Miss Araminta Fox, of Cincinnati. Both were deaf and Dumb. M Dec. 13, 1849, in Cincinnati. OR 12/29.

John Hoggins, of Bourbon county, to Mrs. Amanda Longmore, of Kenton county. M Dec. 17, 1849. OR 12/26.

George J. Goodwon, of Fayette county, to Miss Eliza M. Jameson, of Montgomery county. M Dec. 18, 1849. OR 12/26.

Winchester E. Rees, of Maysville, to Miss Anna V., daughter of Capt. John Hutchcraft, of Bourbon county. M Dec. 18, 1849. OR 12/22.

Dr. John A. White, of Madison county, to Miss Mary L. Pepper, of Flemingsburg. M Dec. 19, 1849. OR 12/22.

William P. Wilson, of Lexington, to Caroline E., daughter of Robert Landreth, of Charleston, S. C. M Dec. 20, 1849. OR 12/22.

Jackson Marsh to Miss Arzelia Parker, both of Lexington. M December 24, 1849. OR 12/26.

William Metcalfe to Mrs. E. D. Trimble, both of Lexington. M Dec. 25, 1849. OR 12/29.

1850

Robert W. Megowan to Miss Lucinda Wyatt, both of Lexington. M Dec. 27, 1849. OR 12/29.

Col. Alfred Soward to Mrs. Margaret Gorsuch, both of Mason county. M Dec. 26, 1849. OR 1/2/1850.

Mike S. Allgaier, of Georgetown, to Miss Harriet M. Anderson, of Winchester. M in Aberdeen, Ohio, Dec. 28, 1849. OR 1/2/1850.

James H. Mitchell, of Mt. Sterling, to Miss Mary E. Thomas, daughter of Mrs. Margaret Thomas, of Nelson county. M near Bloomfield, Dec. 25, 1849. OR 1/5/1850.

John Besore, of Lexington, to Miss Lucinda, daughter of Henry Huffman, of Fayette county. M Jan. 3, 1850. OR 1/9.

John Crutcher, of Woodford county, to Miss Mary Jane French, formerly of Mason county. M Jan. 10, 1850, in Lexington. OR 1/12.

John Anderson to Miss Sarah J. Kelly, both of Lexington. M Jan. 14, 1850. OR 1/16.

William H. Matthews, of Jessamine county, to Miss Sarah Ann Porter, of Lewis county. M former place, Jan. 8, 1850. OR 1/16. (Also spelled

William H. Mathews.)

Samuel P. Spalding, of Henderson, Ky., to Miss Margaret E., daughter of Major John H. Hanley, of Jessamine county. M Jan. 17, 1850. OR 1/19.

Ephraim D. Sayre, of Lexington, to Miss Mary, eldest daughter of W. B. Woodruff, of Owensboro. M latter place, Jan. 15, 1850. OR 1/23.

James M. Atkins to Miss Mary E. Reynolds, daughter of Jeremiah Reynolds, all of Lexington. M Jan. 17, 1850. OR 1/23.

Col. Richard S. Ferguson to Mrs. Elizabeth H. Lewis, both of Jessamine county. M Jan. 17, 1850. OR 1/23.

James Monroe to Miss Bettie, daughter of John T. Pendleton, all of Frankfort. M Jan. 22, 1850. OR 1/26.

Milton Cravens to Mrs. Rebecca Cravens, both of Fayette county. M Jan. 21, 1850. OR 1/26.

John C. Vandyke, of Spencer county, to Miss Mary Ann Rice, formerly of Lexington. M Jan. 17, 1850. OR 1/30.

Francis R. Dittoe, of Somerset, Ohio, to Miss Sarah M. Cooper, daughter of Capt. William Cooper, of Fayette county, Ky. M Jan. 24, 1850. OR 2/2.

Mitchell Grimes, of Fleming county, to Miss E. F. Smith, daughter of Enoch Smith, of Montgomery county. M Jan. 22, 1850. OR 2/2.

D. H. Taylor to Miss Sarah B. Jouett, both of Winchester. M Jan. 22, 1850. OR 2/6.

John P. Bush to Miss Mary Redman, both of Clark county. M Jan. 24, 1850. OR 2/6.

James Hall to Miss Nancy A. Huston, daughter of the late John Huston, of Fayette county. M near Paris, Jan. 31, 1850. OR 2/9.

John Boston, of Woodford county, to Miss Sarah Taylor. He was 75 years of age, Miss Taylor 24 years old. She lived in Lexington. They were married Feb. 1, 1850. OR 2/9.

Dudley V. Miller to Miss Christanna, daughter of Nelson Thompson, all of Lexington. M Feb. 7, 1850. OR 2/9.

George Kennedy, of Bourbon county, to Miss Sarah C. Scott, daughter of the late Benjamin Scott, of Fayette county. M Feb. 12, 1850. OR 2/16.

Nelson Carl to Miss Lucinda L. Linegar, both of Lexington. M Jan. 27, 1850. OR 2/20

David McMurtry to Miss Mary Jane Shields, both of Lexington. M Feb. 18, 1850. OR 2/20.

Richard B. Young, of Lexington, to Mrs. Jane E. Jennings, of Woodford county. M Feb. 14, 1850. OR 2/23.

Charles W. Feusheo to Miss Ann M. Harris, both of Versailles. M Feb. 28, 1850. OR 3/16.

Sidney Porwood to Miss Eliza B. Miller, both of Jessamine county. M Feb. 28, 1850. OR 3/6.

George M. Taylor to Miss Thomas Ann Atkinson, both of Winchester. M Mar. 5, 1850. OR 3/6.

Franklin Shannon to Miss Rebecca Harris, both of Lexington. M Mar. 5, 1850. OR 3/9.

Charles F. Payne to Miss Elizabeth Hord, youngest daughter of Francis P. Hord, dec'd., all of Jessamine county. M Mar. 13, 1850. OR 3/16.

William S. Ball, of Woodford county, to Miss Rebecca M., daughter of the late Dr. Webb, of Clark county. M Mar. 12, 1850. OR 3/20.

John Moss, of Jessamine county, to Miss Eleanor Dunn, of Garrard county. M Mar. 14, 1850. OR 3/20.

Samuel S. Boyd, of Louisville, to Miss Elizabeth J. Parker, eldest daughter of Dr. John T. Parker, of Shelby county. M Mar. 13, 1850. OR 3/23.

John Clemerson to Miss Mary J. Bryan, formerly of Fayette county, both now of Shelbyville, Ky. M Mar. 10, 1850. OR 3/23.

William M. Dickey to Miss Elizabeth Peters, youngest daughter of the late James Peters, all of Woodford county. M Mar. 14, 1850. OR 3/23.

Henry A. Griswold to Miss Margaret B. Morton, both of Louisville. M Mar. 12, 1850. OR 3/27.

Charles T. Churchill to Miss Susan C. Payne, daughter of the late James B. Payne, of Fayette county. M at Elizabethtown, Ky., Mar. 21, 1850. OR 3/27.

A. H. Marschalk, of New Orleans, to Miss Isabel Kirkham, of Flemingsburg, Ky. M in Woodville, Miss., Mar. 7, 1850. OR 3/27.

William F. Stanhope to Miss Nancy C. Bowman, daughter of Joseph Bowman, all of Fayette county. M Mar. 20, 1850. OR 3/27.

John B. Powell to Miss Margaret J. Megee, daughter of Seth Megee, of Jessamine county. M Mar. 15, 1850. OR 3/27.

Thomas B. Hart, formerly of Fayette county, Ky., to Miss Aurore, daughter of the late Fernando Gayoso, of the Parish of Nachitochez, La. M in New Orleans, Mar. 16, 1850. OR 3/30.

Prof. James B. Dodd, of Transylvania University, to Miss Eliza J. Ralston, of Quincy, Ill. M latter place, Mar. 7, 1850. OR 3/30.

Charlton Sanders to Miss Isadelpha Duncan, both of Nicholasville. M Mar. 28, 1850. OR 4/3.

A. W. Hamilton, of Mt. Sterling, to Miss Henrietta C. Lindsay, of Bourbon county. M Mar. 28, 1850. OR 4/6.

Levi Arterburne, of Jefferson county, to Miss George Ann Bledsoe, of North Middletown. Both were deaf and dumb. M Mar. 21, 1850. OR 4/6.

James Bean, of Montgomery county, to Miss Ann E. Poyntz, of Scott county. M latter place, in April, 1850. OR 4/13.

Dr. Andrew Hood, of Winchester, to Mrs. Eleanor McAdams, of Lexington. M Apr. 9, 1850. OR 4/13.

James Truman to Miss Phebe Jane Sharp, daughter of Riley P. Sharp, all from Lexington. M Apr. 17, 1850. OR 4/20.

William G. Skillman to Mrs. Catherine Pryer, both of Fayette county. M May 9, 1850. OR 5/11. See also S 5/11.

U. G. Treadway to Miss Eliza Ann Moody, both of Lexington. M May 9, 1850. S 5/11.

George W. Wheatly, of Harrodsburg, to Mrs. Sarah Ann Arnold, of Jessamine county. M May 9, 1850. S 5/15.

William Burton to Miss Polly Turpin, both of Jessamine county. M Mar. 3, 1850. S 5/15.

James S. Roberts to Miss Nancy Ann White, both of Jessamine county. M Apr. 18, 1850. S 5/15.

Eli Crow to Miss Nancy Grow, both of Jessamine county. M May 9, 1850. S 5/15.

Henry F. Turner, of Lexington, to Miss Lucinda Slavens, daughter of Dr. John Slavens, of Harrodsburg. M latter Place, May 8, 1850. S 5/15.

Andrew J. Tribble to Miss Elizabeth T. Halley, daughter of Samuel Halley, all of Madison county. M May 1, 1850. S 5/15.

James P. Tanner, of Pittsburg, to Mrs. Frances E. Tallinghast, of Providence, R.I. M in Lexington, Ky., May 20, 1850. S 5/25.

George Hopps to Miss Charlotte Palmer, both of Lexington. M May 21, 1850. S 5/25.

Thomas Shumate to Miss Susan Dixon. M in Sandersville, Fayette county, May 22, 1850. S 5/25.

Solomon Rice to Mrs. Emeline R. Timberlake, both of Lexington. M June 6, 1850. S 6/8.

Charles O. Faxon to Miss Sarah C. Hickman, daughter of James L. Hickman, formerly of Lexington, Ky. M June 4, 1850, at Clarksville, Tenn. S 6/19.

David Owens, of Jessamine county, to Miss Sarah R. Smith, of Madison county. M May 23, 1850. S 6/22.

James C. Hollis to Miss Mary K. Carson, both of Jessamine county. M June 8, 1850. S 6/22.

James Griffin, of Scott county, to Mrs. Margaret McMurtry, of Lexington. M June 20, 1850. S 6/22.

Daniel Kay, of Fayette county, to Miss Elizabeth Wilson, of Lexington. M June 18, 1850. S 6/26.

James Devers, of Bradfordsville, Madison county, to Miss Cynthia Ann Campbell, of Lexington. M June 18, 1850. S 6/26.

William Shindlebower, of Lexington, to Miss Mary Ann White, of Versailles. M latter place, June 27, 1850. S 6/29.

William N. Robb, of Frankfort, to Miss Letitia P. Dallam, daughter of Mrs. L. Dallam, of Fayette county. M June 20, 1850. S 7/3.

Dr. Lloyd Warfield, of Lexington, to Miss Elmira Burbank, of Bangor, Maine. M in Fayette county, Ky., July 3, 1850. S 7/13.

William Edge to Miss Elizabeth Parker, daughter of the late John Parker, all of Fayette county. M July 23, 1850. S 7/24.

James Thornton, of Woodford county, to Miss Sophia E. Kidd, of Lexington. M. July 30, 1850, in latter place. S 7/31.

Dr. E. F. Naghel to Miss Isabel E. Kensel, both of Lexington. M July 30, 1850. S 7/31.

James W. Griffith to Miss Susan Jane Bennets. M July 31, 1850. S 8/3.

William Shears to Miss Edward Ann Harris, both of Lexington. M Aug. 1, 1850. S 8/3.

E. Q. Naghel to Miss Isabella E. Kensel, both of Lexington. M Aug. 5, 1850. S 8/7.

John A. Price, of Garrard county, to Miss Elizabeth A. Berry, daughter of George Berry, of Fayette county. M Aug. 8, 1850. S 8/14.

Thomas J. Moore to Mrs. Mary Brockway, both of Lexington. M Aug. 12, 1850. S 8/14.

Griffin P. Theobald to Miss Louisa Mentelle, both of Lexington. M at Episcophal Church, Aug. 29, 1850. S 8/31.

Robert B. Shelton, of Versailles, to Miss Nannie E. Curd, daughter of William P. Curd, of Lexington. M latter place, Aug. 29, 1850. S 8/31.

Col. Thomas G. Randall, of Lexington, to Miss Telitha, daughter of John Prather, of Fayette county. M Sept. 10, 1850. S 9/11.

James H. Stivers to Miss Mary Ann Baily, both of Fayette county. M in Aberdeen, Ohio, in September, 1850. S 9/11.

James T. Worthington, of Cincinnati, to Miss Nannie Postlethwaite, eldest daughter of Capt. G. L. Postlethwaite, of Lexington. M Sept. 19, 1850. S 9/21.

Joseph R. Wendover, of St. Louis, to Miss Mary Anne Luyster, daughter of A. R. Luyster. She was the eldest daughter. M in New York City, Sept. 10, 1850. S 9/21.

Dr. Joseph G. Chinn, of Lexington, Mo., to Miss Jurilla W. Shepherd, of Lexington, Ky. M Sept. 23, 1850. S 9/25.

William A. Eades, of Lexington, to Miss Bettie J. Milton, daughter of Thomas Milton, of Nelson county. M latter place, Sept. 17, 1850. S 9/25.

Henry Johnson, Ex-Governor of Louisiana, to Miss Julia, daughter of the late Joel Johnson. M in Lexington, Ky., Oct. 1, 1850. S 10/5.

Ellison Daniel, of Bath county, to Miss Frances P. Elliott. M at the Clark county residence of her grandfather, Joel Hickman, Oct. 3, 1850. S 10/5.

Samuel J. Redd to Miss Cornelia A., daughter of the late Capt. Samuel M. Wallace, all of Lexington. M Oct. 1, 1850. S 10/9.

S. M. Breckinridge, of St. Louis, to Miss Virginia, daughter of David Castleman, of Fayette county, Ky. M Oct. 8, 1850. S 10/12.

B. B. Taylor, editor of the *Kentucky Statesman*, to Miss Lydia, daughter of Col. Henry C. Payne, all of Fayette county. M Oct. 10, 1850. S 10/12.

Edwin E. Shivel, of Lexington, to Miss Mary E., daughter of H. C. Huggins, of Jessamine county. M Oct. 10, 1850. S 10/16.

Patrick H. Reordan, of Lexington, Ky., to Miss Ellen Fitzgerald, of Albany, N.Y. M latter place, Oct. 6, 1850. S 10/19.

S. Stansifer to Miss Lizsie, daughter of N. L. Finnell. M in Franklin county, Oct. 9, 1850. S 10/23.

J. S. Brannin, of New Castle, Ky., to Miss Mary C. Craig, of Lexington. M Oct. 22, 1850. S 10/23.

A. J. Barry to Miss Portia Stribling, formerly of Winchester. M in Lexington, Oct. 29, 1850. S 11/2. (Winchester, Va.)

Samuel Humphreys to Miss Margaret Stribling, formerly of Winchester, Va. (See above.) M in Lexington, Ky., Oct. 29, 1850. S 11/2.

Charles P. Daly, Jr., of Lexington, Ky., U. S. Consul for Nuery, Ireland, and youngest son of Charles Daly, of Colerain, to Miss Annia Caroline, youngest daughter of Robert Huston, Jr., M.D. of Rothsay House. M Oct. 10, 1850, at Bally-Rachane Church, by the Rev. James O'Hara and afterwards at St. Mallacheys, by the Rev. Richard Killen, P.P. S 11/6.

Benjamin P. Hawkins, of Fayette county, to Miss Maria Reed, of Lincoln county. M Oct. 29, 1850. S 11/6.

Thomas W. Reid to Miss Mary Jane White. M Nov. 4, 1850. S 11/6.

J. Warren Grigsby, of Virginia, to Miss Susan Preston Shelby, only daughter of the late Alfred Shelby, of Lincoln county, Ky. M in Lexington, Nov. 5, 1850. S 11/9.

James A. Dunn to Miss Margaret A. Marriott, both of Danville. M Nov. 7, 1850. S 11/13.

T. H. Gilliss to Miss Catherine, daughter of Mr. A. Legrand, all of Lexington. M Nov. 12, 1850. S 11/16.

John C. Cochran, of Lexington, to Miss Ella, daughter of J. Coburn Dewees, of Maysville. M latter place, Nov. 12, 1850. S 11/16.

George W. Cravens to Miss Margaret A., daughter of Matthias Outten, all of Fayette county. M Nov. 14, 1850. S 11/20.

P. Salmon to Miss Davidella S. Wallace, both of Fayette county. M Nov. 21, 1850. S 11/23.

John J. Franklin to Miss E. W. Smither, both of Fayette county. M Nov. 21, 1850. S 11/23.

William B. Houston (or Huston), of Maysville, to Miss Maria E., daughter of the late Thomas W. Hawkins, of Lexington. M Nov. 12, 1850. S 11/23.

Abner C. Harris, formerly of Louisville, to Miss Anna R., daughter of the late Dr. James Jones, of Lexington. M Nov. 14, 1850. S 11/27.

Cornelius Vaughn to Mrs. Emily Fitzpatrick, both of Fayette county. M Nov. 14, 1850. S 11/27.

James H. Lowry to Miss Jane Hill, both of Jessamine county. M Nov. 24, 1850. S 11/30.

James P. Higbee, of Lexington, divorced in December, 1850, by Mrs. Sarah E. Higbee. S 12/18.

Henry Wilkie, of Brownsville, Texas, to Miss Ellen Stafford, of Lexington, Ky. M Dec. 23, 1850. S 12/25.

Joshua Noland to Miss Rosanna McCoy, of Woodford county. M Dec. 23, 1850. S 12/25.

D. H. Henderson to Miss Mary Jane Tudor, of Lexington. M Dec. 17, 1850. S 12/25.

Robert Nelson, of Clark county, to Miss Eliza J. Nelson, daughter of William Nelson, of Montgomery county. M in Aberdeen, O., Dec. 27, 1850. S 1/1/1851.

Capt. J. K. Bishop, of Harrodsburg, to Miss Mary J. E., only daughter of

O. Garnett, of Boyle county. M Dec. 10, 1850. S 1/11/51.

Edwin P. Elliot, of Clark county, to Miss Lizzie Wood, of Madison county M Dec. 19, 1850. S 1/18/1851.

William H. Montague to Miss Ann Nutter, daughter of William Nutter, all of Fayette county. M Jan. 7, 1851. S 1/18.

William R. Cleland, of Mercer county, to Miss Louisa, daughter of Elijah McClanahan, of Fayette county. M Jan. 14, 1851. S 1/22.

1851

John O. Day to Miss Sarah M. Anderson, both of Cynthiana. M Jan. 9, 1851. S 1/22.

William S. Harper, formerly of Lexington, Ky., to Miss Ariadne M. Stine, daughter of the late Jacob R. Stine, of St. Louis, Mo. M in St. Louis, Jan. 8, 1851. S 1/22.

James R. Ellison to Miss Samaria Edginton, of Woodford county. M Jan. 5, 1851. S 1/22.

J. B. Morton, of Lexington, to Miss Sarah Frances, daughter of Jacob Embry, of Fayette county. M Jan. 21, 1851. S 1/29.

Joseph B. Stewart, of Louisville, to Miss Harriett, youngest daughter of Jacob Hughes, of Fayette county. M Jan. 21, 1851. S 1/29.

Thomas Lister to Miss Mary Eliza, daughter of Hugh Jeter, all of Lexington. M Jan. 23, 1851. S 1/29.

Tilford Alexander, of Bourbon county, to Miss Emily Otwell, of Scott county. M Jan. 16, 1851. S 1/29.

William H. Brand to Miss Frances, daughter of John McCaw, all of Lexington. M Jan. 28, 1851. S 2/5.

John C. Poulter to Miss Martha M. Moffett, both of Lexington. M Feb. 4, 1851. S 2/8.

David C. Holeman to Miss Nancy Collier, of Fayette county. M Jan. 23, 1851. S 2/8.

John A. Willis to Miss Margaret A. Roberts, both of Jessamine county. M Feb. 11, 1851. S 2/15.

Thomas P. Wendover, son of the late Sheriff Wendover, to Miss Mary McGinniss, daughter of Hugh McGinniss. M in New York, Feb. 16, 1851. S 2/15.

William H. Woodhouse, of Harrodsburg, to Miss Julia Ann Hukle, of Lexington. M Feb. 20, 1851. S 2/22.

J. H. Robards to Miss Amanda Trumble, both of Lexington. M Feb. 20, 1851. S 4/26.

Sanford B. Vanpelt to Mrs. Henrietta C. Hayes, both of Lexington. M Feb. 23, 1851. S 2/26.

Jesse H. Baker to Mrs. Mildred Anderson, both of Lexington. M Mar. 5, 1851. S 3/8.

Edward H. Hicks, formerly of Fayette county, Ky., to Miss Elizabeth Stowers, daughter of Col. James Stowers. M in Jefferson county, Miss., Feb. 5, 1851. S 3/8.

Sydney White to Miss Lavinia Jennings, of Madison county. M Mar. 11, 1851. S 3/15.

Hiram Ingels, of Lexington, to Miss Amanda R., daughter of Owen D. Winn, of Fayette county. M Apr. 3, 1851. S 4/5.

James W. Kennard, of Franklin county, Pa., to Miss Margaret Ann Mesmer, of Lexington, Ky. M latter place, Apr. 17, 1851. S 4/23.

Austin Dall, of Baltimore, Md., to Miss Mary A., second daughter of the late William M. Brand. M in Lexington, Ky., Apr. 23, 1851. S 4/26.

John Higgins to Miss Eliza Jane Skillman, both of Fayette county. M Apr. 24, 1851. S 4/26.

John A. Erdman to Miss Amanda Kise, both of Fayette county. M April 24, 1851. S 4/26.

Col. Jonathan Barritt to Mrs. Eliza T. Scott, both of Paris. M Apr. 20, 1851. S 4/26.

John S. Hupp, of Virginia, to Miss Amanda Bowman, of Fayette county. M Apr. 24, 1851. S 5/7.

Dr. W. D. Stone, of Lexington, to Miss Sidney A. Passmore, of Harrodsburg. M latter place, May 14, 1851. S 5/17.

George Lanckhart to Miss Susan Hardisty. M Apr. 22, 1851. S 5/24.

William H. Smott to Miss Martha J. Bunnell. M in Lexington, May 22, 1851. S 5/24.

Griffith S. Morgan to Mrs. Mary Brent. M in Lexington, May 29, 1851 S 5/31.

A. J. Viley to Miss Mary Louisa Peake, both of Scott county. M May 29, 1851. S 6/4.

Davis Burbank to Miss Martha R. Cocks, both of Lexington. M June 17. 1851. S 6/21.

James Brown, of Virginia, to Miss Margaret B., daughter of William L Todd, of Fayette county, Ky. M June 19, 1851. S 6/21.

William H. Ellis to Miss Zillah McCarthy, both of Lexington. M July 23 1851. S 7/26.

Dr. John Sutton to Mrs. Ellen Richmond, both of Georgetown. M in Lexington, Aug. 19, 1851. S 8/20.

David Shepherd to Miss Barbary Atkins. M Aug. 28, 1851. S 8/29

William Staley to Miss Elizabeth Sacra, both of Lexington. M Aug. 24, 1851. S 8/29.

John Parker, of Fayette county, to Miss Josephine Laudeman, of Lexington. M Sept. 3, 1851. S 9/2.

Alpheus B. Johnson, of Miss., to Miss Virginia, daughter of the late Gen Cornelius Haring, of Miss. M Sept. 2, 1851. S 9/5.

George Dunlap, of Fayette county, to Miss Mary L. Nichols, of Lincoln county. M in Aberdeen, O., Sept. 16, 1851. S 9/23.

T. P. Atticus Bibb to Miss Mary Scott Snead. M in Lexington, Sept. 26, 1851. S 9/26.

William A. Dishman to Miss Mary Frost, both of Lexington. M Sept. 30, 1852. S. 10/1.

Hiram B. Searcy to Miss Mary Jan Lewis, both of Lexington. M Oct. 8, 1852. S 10/8.

Thomas H. Irvine to Miss Turrissa Weaver, daughter of Mr. Francis Weaver, all of Lexington. M Oct. 6, 1852. S 10/12.

Dr. W. D. Letcher to Miss Margaret Hill, both of Jessamine county M Oct. 5, 1852. S 10/12.

Thomas J. Zimmerman, "typo" for the *Kentucky Statesman,* to Miss P. Elizabeth McRoberts, both of Lexington. M at the Lexington residence of David L. Zimmerman, Oct. 28, 1852. S 10/29.

John L. Marshall, of Bourbon county, to Miss Mary Turner, of Lexington. M latter place, Nov. 2, 1852. S 11/5.

James C. Short to Miss Davidella F. Murray, both of Lexington. M Nov. 3, 1852. S 11/5.

William M. Dickson, of Cincinnati, to Miss Annie M. Parker, daughter of Dr. John T. Parker, of Lexington, Ky. M Oct. 19, 1852. S 11/5.

James W. Tutt, of New Orleans, to Miss Sallie Chiles, of Fayette county, Ky. M Nov. 10, 1852. S 11/12.

Dr. John T. Parker, of Lexington, to Mrs. Francis M. Taliaferro, of Newport. M Oct. 26, 1852. S 11/12. See above.

Jacob Fox, of Louisville, to Miss Mariam Epperson, of Lexington. M latter place, Nov. 23, 1852. S 11/23.

Samuel Muir, of Fayette county, to Miss Ann, daughter of Thomas Muir, of Jessamine county. M Nov. 18, 1852. S 11/23.

William M. Green, of Paris, to Miss Rachel Lyon, of Bourbon county. M at Phoenix Hotel, Lexington. Nov. 29, 1852. S 11/30.

John E. Aubrey to Miss Sarah F. Wilson, both of Lexington. M Dec. 4, 1852. S 12/10.

Henry L. Payne, of Fayette county, to Miss Sarah Pointdexter (or Poindexter), of Lexington. M Dec. 9, 1852. S 12/14.

William Lawson Moore, merchant of Harrodsburg, to Miss Virginia L., daughter of Capt. John Neet, of Woodford county. M Dec. 9, 1852. S 12/21.

G. W. McConnell, of Woodford county, to Miss Mag, daughter of Capt. Samuel G. Herndon, of Mt. Sterling. M latter place, Dec. 7, 1852. S 12/21.

William McMains, of Ind., to Miss Mary J. McMains, of Lexington, Ky. M latter place, Dec. 21, 1852. S 12/21.

David Hall, of Jefferson county, to Miss Ann Eliza, eldest daughter of Col. J. Delph, of Fayette county. M in Lexington, Dec. 21, 1852. S 12/21.

Thomas Hughes to Mrs. Sarah Atchison, both of Fayette county. M at Russell's Cave, Dec. 21, 1852. S 12/24.

David D. Laudeman (also Laudaman) to Miss Elizabeth Montague, both of Fayette county. M Dec. 23, 1852. S 12/24.

J. H. McDowell, of Cincinnati, to Miss Belle, daughter of Col. William Rhodes, of Madison county, Ky. M near Richmond, Dec. 22, 1852. S 12/28.

Adam L. Childers, of Fayette county, to Miss Susannah McLeod, of Bourbon county. M Dec. 1852. S 12/31.

Charles McDaniel to Miss Malinda Dawson, both of Bourbon county. M Dec. 23, 1852. S 12/31.

Robert M. Buckner, of Louisville, to Miss Willina J. Abbott, daughter of P. H. Abbott, of Bourbon county. M Dec. 23, 1852. S 12/31.

Dr. William Robertson, of Jessamine county, to Miss Ann D. Browning. M at the Lexington residence of Mr. M. E. Browning, Jan. 6, 1853. S 1/11.

Benjamin Higginbottom to Miss Rachel A. Murray, both of Fayette county. M Jan. 4, 1853. S 1/14.

Henry R. French, of Ky., to Miss Mary Ann Hamilton, of Baltimore, Md. M Jan. 4, 1853. S 1/18.

John P. Gaines, Governor of Oregon, to Miss Margaret B. Wands, formerly of Albany, N.Y. M in Portland, Oregon Territory, Nov. 25, 1852. S. 1/21/1853.

W. E. Garvin, of Louisville to Miss Lucy R., daughter of Dr. J. A. Tomlinson, of Harrodsburg. M Jan. 19, 1853. S 1/25.

1853

Harvey R. Brown, of Louisville, to Miss Howard Ellen Parrish of Fayette county. M Feb. 1, 1853. S 2/1.

O. W. Delong to Miss Bettie Downing, both of Lexington. M Jan. 20, 1853. S 2/1.

Fleming Hughes to Miss Caroline Offutt, both of Lexington. M Jan. 20, 1853. S 2/1.

Alexander Julian, of Franklin county, to Miss Bettie Laughlin, of Winchester. M latter place, Feb. 10, 1853. S 2/18.

Simeon Haynes to Miss Lucretia Griggs, both of Fayette county. M Feb. 15, 1853. S 2/18.

Robert J. Breckinridge, M.D., to Miss Kate, daughter of A. D. Hunt, all of Louisville. M Feb. 15, 1853. S 2/18.

James W. Nutter, of Fayette county, to Miss Mary F., daughter of Stephen Houston, of Scott county. M Feb. 17, 1853. S 3/1.

Josiah Powell, of Madison county, to Miss Mary A. E. J. Searcy, of Fayette county. M Feb. 19, 1853. S 3/1.

William B. Brown to Miss Leona R., daughter of Robert Y. Thompson. M in Saline county, Mo., Feb. 14, 1853. S 3/8.

Dr. Richard Gano to Miss Mat.(ilda?) Welch, daughter of Dr. Thomas Welch, of Crab Orchard. M Mar. 15, 1853. S 3/22.

Charles Stewart to Miss Louisa Lewis, both of Lexington. M Mar. 27, 1853. S 3/29.

B. G. Caulfield, of Lexington, to Miss Sue Walker, daughter of David Walker, of Washington county. M at Belmont, near Springfield, Mar. 31, 1853. S 4/1.

A. M. Taylor to Miss Margaret E., daughter of J. Faulconer, all of Fayette county. M Mar. 31, 1853. S 4/12.

Hon. Ben Edwards Grey, late member of Congress from Kentucky, to Mrs. Eliza Frances Carson, Daughter of Col. T. R. Goldsby, of Sarmmerville, Alabama. M Mar. 22, 1853. S 4/12.

Charles C. Nourse, of Keosauqua, Iowa, to Miss Rebecca McMeekin, of Lexington, Ky. M Apr. 14, 1853. S 4/26.

Elias B. Johnson to Miss Sarah Virginia Keene, both of Scott county. M Apr. 26, 1853. S 4/29.

Dr. Thomas J. Wilkinson, of Madison county, to Miss Ann M., daughter of James Grigsby, of Montgomery county. M Apr. 21, 1853. S 5/3.

Thompson B. Field, of Mo., to Miss Lucy H. Graves, of Fayette county, Ky. M Apr. 27, 1853. S 5/3.

Dr. Robert T. Bryan, of Paris, to Miss Mary Ellen Offutt, of Fayette county. M May 4, 1853. S 5/13.

Jacob Rowe to Miss Mary Elizabeth Kerl, both of Bourbon county. M May 11, 1853. S 5/13.

William C. Magowan, of Montgomery county, to Miss Carrie Davis, daughter of the Hon. Garrett Davis, of Paris. M May 17, 1853. S 5/20.

Robert Lackey, of Bourbon county, to Miss Virginia E. Tracy, daughter of Gen. Obediah Tracy, of Clark county. M Apr. 20, 1853. S 5/20.

Charles E. Perry to Miss Bettie Toppass, both of Versailles. M May 20, 1853. S 5/27.

Albert G. Scearce, of Versailles, to Miss Mary Jane Rice, daughter of James Rice, of Woodford county. M May 26, 1853. S 5/27.

David P. King to Miss Sarah F. Jeter, both of Lexington. M May 24, 1853. S 5/31.

John C. Elrod to Mrs. Eugenia Lamkins, both of Lexington. M May 30, 1853. S 5/31.

Jacob Small to Miss Julia F. Downing, of Fayette county. M May 12, 1853. S 5/31.

Boswell Hulett to Miss Elizabeth Allen, both of Fayette county. M May 30, 1853. S 6/7.

Dr. John D. Ray, of Paris, to Miss Mollie E., daughter of Reuben Hutchcraft, of Bourbon county. M June 2, 1853. S 6/10.

James R. Cochran, of Harrodsburg, to Miss Catharine N. Manning, of Woodford county. M June 9, 1853. S 6/14.

James B. Woodruff to Miss Ann Eliza Wood, both of Lexington. M June 16, 1853. S 6/17.

William R. James to Miss Mary Ann Webb. M June 14, 1853. S 6/17.

William W. Cleary, of Lexington, to Miss Annie C., daughter of P. Wherritt, of Cynthiana. M latter place, June 14, 1853. S 6/17.

Dr. J. D. McFadden to Miss Malinda Douley, of Athens. M June 21, 1853. S 6/21.

John B. Watkins to Miss Elizabeth Tucker. M at the Fayette county residence of John Tucker, June 17, 1853. S 6/21

William A. Neil, of Columbus, Ohio, to Miss Mary L. Nevins. M at the Lexington, Ky., residence of Mr. E. Macallister, June 23, 1853. S 6/24.

John N. Wilson, of Franklin county, to Miss Laura A. Dillon of Woodford county. M latter place, at the residence of R. C. Graves, June 30, 1853. S 7/1.

Harrison Taylor, of Fayette county, to Miss Joannah Cullen, of Georgetown. M June 29, 1853. S 7/5.

Robert W. Bush, M.D., to Miss Lucy Webb. M in Lexington, July 5, 1853. S 7/8.

Thomas N. Arnold, of Covington, to Miss Fanny Pugh, of Harrison county. M at the Scott county residence of E. F. Cantrill, July 1, 1853. S 7/12.

John Reed, of Mason county, to Miss Catherine G. Hunt, second daughter of the late Charlton Hunt, of Lexington. M latter place, at Christ Church, July 12, 1853. S 7/15.

Augustus Clark, of Lexington, to Miss Sarah Felix, daughter of Josiah Felix, of Woodford county. M latter place, July 14, 1853. S 7/19.

William A. Osburn, of Georgia, to Miss Pauline M., daughter of Thomas Jones, of Bourbon county, Ky. M July 21, 1853. S 7/26.

Zachariah Gibbons to Miss Rhoda Ann Elder, eldest daughter of A. W. Elder, all of Lexington. M July 21, 1853. S 7/26.

Henry Clay Waller, of Nicholasville, to Miss Elizabeth L. Redmond, of Bourbon county. M latter place, July 21, 1853. S 7/26.

Eugene Erwin, of Lexington, Ky., to Miss Josephine, only daughter of Col. William H. Russell, of California. M July 16, 1953, at the Calloway county, Mo., residence of Judge Freeland. S 7/26.

W. J. Hughes, of Franklin county, to Miss Sarah L. Thompson, of Lexington. M Aug. 4, 1853. S 8/5.

Richard Mason to Miss Elizabeth Schooley, both of Lexington. M Aug. 11, 1853. S 8/12.

Rev. John Barker, D.D., President of Allegheny College, Meadville, Pa., to Mrs. Marianne J. Asa, of Lexington, Ky. M at latter place, Aug. 10, 1853. S 8/12.

John B. Herndon to Miss Mary R., eldest daughter of William S. Forman. M at Desha Glen, Mason county, Aug. 16, 1853. S 8/19.

John M. Ready, of Versailles, to Miss Dulcenia Bower, of Garrard county. M at the Court House, Lexington, Sept. 1, 1853. S 9/2.

1853

Rev. B. T. Quinn, of Scott county, to Miss Carelia, daughter of Gen. Milton Stapp, of Madison, Indiana. M latter place, Sept. 1, 1853. S 9/9.

Thomas Porter, Jr., to Miss Virginia, daughter of Lewis C. Pearce, all of Maysville. M Sept. 1, 1853. S 9/9.

Dr. John T. Fleming, of Fleming county, to Miss Adeline, daughter of the late Samuel Budlong, of Westfield, Chataque county, N. Y. M. Aug. 25, 1853. S 9/9.

Albert G. Robertson, of St. Louis, to Miss Sallie E. Davis, of Clark county, Ky. M in Aberdeen, Ohio, Sept. 5, 1853. S 9/13.

Benjamin Scott, of Lexington, to Miss Amanda Fulton, of Louisville. M latter place, Sept. 17, 1853. S 9/20.

David L. Shely to Miss Elizabeth Shely, both of Lexington. M Sept. 20, 1853. S 9/23.

Marius C. Foushee (or Faushee) to Miss Emily R. Ball, both of Versailles. M Sept. 13, 1853. S 9/23.

William A. Dishman to Miss Mary Frost, both of Lexington. M Sept. 30, 1853. S 10/1.

Hiram B. Searcy to Miss Mary Jane Lewis, both of Lexington. M Oct. 8, 1853. S 10/8.

John C. Snyder to Mrs. Elizabeth Ann Snyder, both of Paris. M Oct. 6, 1853. S 10/7.

Thomas M. Gibson to Susanna T. Wirt, both of Lexington. M Oct. 13, 1853. S 10/14.

John McAnespy to Miss Belle Gibbons, both of Lexington. M Oct. 13, 1853. S 10/17.

William A. Pullum to Miss Emily Shrewsbury, both of Lexington. M. Oct. 4, 1853. S 10/17.

James Norton, of New Orleans, to Miss Ann S., youngest daughter of Major John H. Hanly, of Cliff Cottage, Jessamine county, Ky. M Oct. 18, 1853. S 10/21.

Dr. A. B. Duke, of Georgetown, to Miss Charlotte Postelle, eldest daughter of Remus Payne, of Locust Grove, Scott County. M Oct. 20, 1853. S 10/21.

Thomas K. Letcher, of Garrard county, to Miss Mary H. Brown, of Jessamine county. M in Nicholasville, Oct. 5, 1853. S 10/25.

Joseph D. Fritylen to Miss A. K. Shelby, of Jessamine county. M Oct. 13, 1853. S 10/25.

Col. Thomas H. Payne to Miss Maria, daughter of Willa Viley, all of Fayette county. M Oct. 25, 1853. S 10/28.

Stephen Chipley Jones to Miss Dora Penny, both of Louisville. M at the Lexington residence of Mrs. D. Megowan, the bride's grandmother. Oct. 27, 1853. S 10/28.

Humphrey J. Lipscomb, son of Gen. W. S. Lipscomb, of Fayette county, to Miss Ann M. Hocker, daughter of Col. Joseph E. Hocker, of Lebanon, Iowa. M at the Madison county residence of Col. Nicholas Hocker, Oct. 27, 1853. S 11/1.

John Fitzgerald to Miss Catharine Herbert, both of Lexington, M at St. Peter's Church, Lexington, Oct. 30, 1853. S 11/1.

John C. Wickliffe, of Bardstown, to Miss Eleanor Hunt, daughter of the late Richard A. Curd M in Lexington, Nov. 2, 1953. S 11/4.

Dr. James Thompson, of Mason county, to Miss Lucy Gaines, of Woodford county. M latter place, Oct. 25, 1853. S 11/4.

Edmund W. Scott to Miss Elizabeth A. Valentine, both of Versailles. M there Oct. 27, 1853. S 11/4.

Samuel McGinnis to Miss Joanna Green, both of Versailles. M there Nov. 3, 1853. S 11/4.

James R. Mitten to Miss Cordelia Wilgus. M in Lexington, Nov. 17, 1853. S 11/18.

Samuel W. Reynolds to Miss Susan Barbee, both of Lexington. M Dec. 1, 1853. S 12/6.

H. R. French, editor of the *Georgetown Herald,* to Miss Lizzie V. Gault, both of Georgetown. M in Lexington, Dec. 27, 1853. S 12/27.

Jonathan W. Hunt to Miss Elizabeth D. Gay, daughter of Dunlap Gay, all of Clarke county. M Dec. 21, 1853. S 12/27.

William C. Aubrey to Miss Maria Jane Smith. M in Lexington, Dec. 31, 1853. S 1/6/1854.

Benjamin F. Bassett to Miss Mary Jane, daughter of Dr. Lloyd Warfield, all of Lexington. M Dec. 27, 1853. S 1/24.

Major Sebastian C. Paine, of Desoto county, Miss., to Miss Martha Ann Sheppard, of Lexington, Ky. M former place, Nov. 23, 1853. S 1/24/1854.

Allen Moore to Mrs. Elizabeth Sebastian, both of Fayette county. M Jan. 1, 1854. S. 1/3.

John James to Miss Elizabeth Danly. M in Lexington Jan. 4, 1854. S 1/6.

1854

Charles T. Craig, of Lexington, to Miss Sallie F., daughter of Mr. Davenport, of Nicholasville. M in Harrodsburg, Jan. 10, 1854. S 1/20.

William McCracken to Miss Kate Shivell, both of Lexington. M Jan. 12, 1854. S 1/24.

W. G. Budd, of Paris, to Miss Mary Stevenson, of Lexington. M Jan. 24, 1854. S 1/24.

Rodes T. Wiglesworth, of Harrison county, to Miss Lucy Ann Devers, of Fayette county. M Jan. 24, 1854. S 1/24.

John B. Rice, of Fayette county, to Miss Eleanor Easley, of Jessamine county. M Jan. 19, 1854. S 1/24.

William T. Hearne to Miss Margaret Hawkins, both of Bourbon county. M Jan. 24, 1854. S 1/27.

Joseph A. Daly, of Fayette county, to Miss Martha A. Montague, of Henry county. M latter place, Jan. 26, 1854. S 1/27.

Dandridge C. Freeman, of Franklin county, to Miss Mary Ann Giltner, daughter of John Giltner, of Bourbon county. M Jan. 18, 1854. S 2/7.

Jefferson S. Polk to Miss Julia A., only daughter of the late John Herndon, of Scott family. M Jan. 25, 1854. S 2/7.

Herod Patrick to Mrs. Malinda Utterback. M near Sharpsburg, Ky., Jan. 17, 1854. S 2/7.

James H. Rose, of Jessamine county, to Miss Mary Jane Morgan, daughter of George W. Morgan, of Lexington. M Feb. 7, 1854. S 2/10.

C. L. S. Todd, of New Orleans, to Miss Annie M. Stout, formerly of Lexington, Ky. M at New Albany, Ind., Feb 11, 1854. S. 2/17.

Isaac Shelby, son of Gen. James Shelby, dec'd., of Fayette county, to Miss Sarah McClure, of Jessamine county. M Feb. 22, 1854. S 2/24.

Daniel Barbee, of Baton Rouge, La., to Miss Isabel, daughter of Daniel Bradford, dec'd., of Lexington, Ky. M Jan. 17, 1854. S 1/17 and 2/24.

Thomas Berry to Miss Christina Brown, both of Lexington. M Feb. 27, 1854. S 2/28.

Francis M. Owings. Died at the Fayette county residence of his brother, Feb. 26, 1854, aged 23 years. S 3/7.

Edwin Spotswood, of Glasgow, Mo., to Miss Sallie P., daughter of F. Montmollin, of Lexington, Ky. M Mar. 9, 1854. S 3/10.

George Uttinger, of Fayette county, to Miss Ellen Haligan, formerly of Mercer county. M Mar. 9, 1854. S 3/14.

Thomas L. Coons to Miss Phebe True, both of Fayette county. M Mar. 16, 1854. S 3/17.

Alexander C. Hicks to Miss Martha E. Ewing, both of Fayette county. M Mar. 16, 1854. S 3/17.

James S. Darnaby (Darnably), of Fayette county, to Miss Mary Ellen Smith, of Clark county. M Mar. 16, 1854. S 3/17.

Dr. D. L. Price, of Fayette county, to Miss Ann M. Brassfield, of Woodford county. M Mar. 14, 1854. S 3/17.

Abire Merrill to Miss Jane Awbry. M Mar. 9, 1854. S 3/17.

B. A. Baxter to Miss Ann Hayman. M Feb. 23, 1854. S 3/17.

Leonard Kingsley, of Durhamville, N. Y., to Mrs. Augusta Thompson, of Shelbyville, Ky. M at Yonkers, N. Y., Mar. 20, 1854. S 3/31.

Bernard McHugh, of Woodford county, to Miss Hannah Freame, of Lexington. M latter place, Mar. 27, 1854. S 3/31.

Corelius Anderson, of Garrard county, to Miss Mary Ellen Murphy, of Fayette county. M latter place, near Lexington, on Mar. 30, 1854. S 3/31.

John Estes to Mrs. Mary Howe, both of Lexington. M Apr. 13, 1854. S 4/14.

James Morgan to Miss Mary Ann Thompson, both of Lexington. M Apr. 13, 1854. S 4/14.

James W. Price to Miss Elizabeth Williams, both of Lexington. M Apr. 6, 1854. S 4/14.

Benjamin Matthews, of Fayette county, to Miss Mattie E., Daughter of Thomas Smith, of Henry county. M latter place, Apr. 13, 1854. S 4/18.

William Emison to Miss Lucy, daughter of Robert P. Snell, of Scott county. M Apr. 18, 1854. S 4/25.

John Patrick, of Clark county, to Miss Sarah E. McCoy. M. in Sandersville, Fayette county, Apr. 25, 1854. S 4/28.

John W. Power to Miss Sarah A. Finch, both of Scott county. M at the residence of John S. Getty, May 2, 1854. S 5/9.

Benjamin Turner to Isabella Hedges. M in Lexington, May 5, 1854. S 5/12.

Dr. Samuel L. Marshall, editor of the *Express,* to Miss Mary C., eldest daughter of Col. Thomas B. Stevenson, of Maysville. M there, May 10, 1854. S 5/23.

Robert Chenault, of Madison county, to Miss Josephine Cavins, of Fayette county. M May 10, 1854. S 5/23.

W. H. Daniel, of N. A., to Miss Hattie M. Browning, daughter of Dr. M. C. Browning, of Lexington, Ky. M at New Albany, Iowa, May 11, 1854. S 5/23.

Henry Pilcher, Jr., to Harriet S. Wendover, daughter of A. Wendover, dec'd., in St. Louis, May 4, 1854. S 5/26.

William Pilcher to Julia S. Wendover, daughter of James A. Wendover, dec'd. M in St. Louis, May 4, 1854. See above. S 5/26.

Edward B. Savill to Miss Elizabeth Yates, both of Lexington. M May 16, 1854. S 5/30.

Loyd Tevis to Miss Susan G., daughter of Lewis Sanders, Jr. M in Sacramento in Apr. or May, 1854. S 5/30.

Rev. B. T. Crouch, son of Rev. B. T. Crouch, of LaGrange, Ky., to Mrs. Mary E. Bailes, of Fulton, Mo. M in Sacramento City, Apr. 15, 1854. S 5/30.

Sanford Strange to Miss Elizabeth Geers. M in Lexington, June 6, 1854. S 6/9.

Christopher T. Clark to Miss Ann Hardwick, both of Stanton, Powell county. M June 3, 1854. S 6/9.

J. Stoddard Johnston, of Louisville, to Miss Eliza, daughter of George W. Johnson, of Scott county. M June 13, 1854. S 6/16.

Robert Knox to Miss Mary Jane French, both of Powell county. M June 8, 1854. S 6/16.

Andrew J. McMains to Miss Martha Williams, both of Lexington. M June 15, 1854. S 6/16.

James E. Darnaby to Miss Mildred J. McCann, both of Fayette county. M June 8, 1854. S 6/27.

John Ackman to Miss Margaret Eads, both of Fayette county. M July 2, 1854. S 7/4.

Robert L. Bass, proprietor of the Oglethorpe House, Columbus, Ga., to Miss Margaret A. Rowland, of Versailles, Ky. M latter place, in July, 1854. S 7/7.

Franklin Massie, of Paris, to Miss Elizabeth J. Kenney, of Jessamine county. M July 4, 1854. S 7/7.

Dr. Curren Smith to Miss Sallie, daughter of Judge Goodloe. M at Richmond, July 5, 1854. S 7/11.

Charles F. Voss to Miss Mary E. Hickey, both of Lexington. M July 19, 1854. S 7/21.

William Quarrel to Mrs. Mary Ann Wheat. M Aug. 4, 1854. S 8/8.

Rev. James W. Gunn, of Lexington, Ky., to Miss M. C. Johnson, of Troy, Ohio. M latter place, Aug. 9, 1854. S 8/15.

Dr. G. H. Whitney, of Bourbon county, to Miss H. D. Moore, of Fayette county. M Aug. 15, 1854. S 8/18.

John E. Gibson, of Jackson county, Mo., to Miss Elizabeth, daughter of Asa McConathy, of Fayette county, Ky. M latter place, Aug. 24, 1854. S 8/29.

J. B. Shayp (Sharp) to Miss Louisa Chowning. M at the Lexington residence of James McMains, Sept. 7, 1854. S 9/8.

Andrew Darling, of Louisville, to Miss Eliza Jane, daughter of Peter Troutman, of Bourbon county. M Sept. 5, 1854. S 9/8.

John H. Wilson to Miss Mary J. McLear, both of Fayette county. M Sept. 12, 1854. S 9/15.

L. Beecher Todd, M. D., to S. Fannie, daughter of Stephen Swift, all of Lexington. M Oct. 3, 1854. S 10/6.

Benjamin Johnson to R. Charlton, youngest daughter of the late Charleton Hunt, all of Lexington. M Oct. 4, 1854. S 10/6.

Dr. H. B. Blackburn, of Lake Providence, La., to Miss Mary C., daughter of Joseph Bryan, of Fayette county, Ky. M Oct. 17, 1854. S 10/17.

James Bruin to Miss Elizabeth Williams, both of Lexington. M Oct. 19, 1854. S 10/20.

Robert H. Perry to Mrs. Elizabeth Morris, both of Franklin county. M Oct. 19, 1854. S 10/24.

Charles H. Harney to Mary P. Wallace, both of Lexington. M Oct. 14, 1854. S 10/27.

George M. Barkley, of Jessamine county, to Miss Fannie A., only daughter of William S. Scott, of Nicholasville. M Oct. 25, 1854. S 10/31.

David L. Zimmerman, of Lexington, to Mrs. Cordelia Stone, of Fayette county. M Oct. 31, 1854. S 10/31.

B. N. Grehan, of Scott county, to Miss Martha A. Gill, of Fayette county. M Oct. 31, 1854. S 10/31.

John Q. A. Hayman to Mrs. Susan L. Duce, both of Lexington. M Oct. 31, 1854. S 10/31.

James F. Schenck, of Iowa, to Miss Maria C. Bell, formerly of Lexington, Ky. M in Hudson city, Oct. 12, 1854. S 11/3.

John A. Hawkins, of Knox county, Mo., to Miss Susan M. Burrus, of Mercer county, Ky. M Nov. 7, 1854. S 11/10.

William T. Stewart to Miss Kate A. Elgin. M in Fayette county, Nov. 9, 1854. S 11/10.

Richard S. Moxley, of Louisville, to Miss Mary J. Davidson, of Lexington. M Nov. 9, 1854. S 11/10.

Richard Diamond to Miss Mary Rutherford. M Nov. 10, 1854. S 11/14.

N. B. Milton, of Nelson county, to Miss Martha McIntire, of Lexington. M Oct. 31, 1854. S 11/14.

Edward C. Carter to Miss Lucie Isabella Hicks, daughter of B. A. Hicks, all of Lexington. M Nov. 15, 1854. S 11/17.

Parker B. Bryant, of Jessamine county, to Miss Mattie L. Nutter, of Fayette county. M Nov. 14, 1854. S 11/17.

Gustavus Yarbough to Miss Anna M. Baldwin, both of Lexington. M Nov. 14, 1854. S 11/17.

Arrabia Hutcherson to Miss Susan Nivens, both of Anderson county. M Nov. 16, 1854. S 11/21.

Napoleon B. Carpenter to Miss Anne E., eldest daughter of Charles R. Thompson, all of Lexington. M Nov. 21, 1854. S 11/21.

William J. Norman to Miss Joanna Jones, both of Lexington. M Nov. 14, 1854. S 11/24.

Henry C. Rhorer, of Jessamine county, to Miss Mattie J. Hoover, of Monroe county, Ind. M Nov. 5, 1854. S 11/28.

Willis Price to Martha B., daughter of Benjamin McCann, of Fayette county. M Nov. 29, 1854. S 12/1.

Charles S. French, of Montgomery county, to Miss Margaret H. Moore, daughter of the late Thomas R. Moore, of Clarke county. M Jan. 2, 1855. OR 1/10.

T. Simpson, of Woodford county, to Mrs. Elizabeth White, of Montgomery county. M Dec. 28, 1854. OR 1/10/1855.

Warren Shaw to Miss Nannie Burton, both of Lexington. M Jan. 9, 1855. OR 1/13.

Green B. Milleon, of Madison county, to Mrs. Sarah A. Newman, of Jessamine county. M Jan. 7, 1855. OR 1/13.

1855

Andrew Sheehan to Mrs. Nancy Kennedy. M Jan. 8, 1855. OR 1/13.

Robert McMichael to Miss Frances Mason. M Jan. 10, 1855. OR 1/13.

T. D. Bayse, of Simpsonville, to Miss Mary Outten, of Fayette county, M Jan. 11, 1855. OR 1/13.

Charles Snowden Fairfax, of Virginia, to Ada, daughter of the late Joseph S. Bennam (Benham?). M at the Louisville, Ky., residence of George D. Prentice, Jan. 10, 1855. OR 1/17.

John B. Huston, of Winchester, to Mrs. Bettie Allen, daughter of the late Samuel G. Jackson, of Fayette county. M at the Frankfort residence of Mrs. Jackson, Dec. 20, 1854. OR 1/17/1855.

James M. Land to Miss Zantippe Brumfield, both of Jessamine county. M Jan. 3, 1855. OR 1/17.

Milton C. Smith to Miss Arabella Hill, of Jessamine county. M Jan. 11, 1855. OR 1/17.

Robert S. Morrow, of Paris, to Miss Sarah Belle, youngest daughter of Nat. Poyntz, of Maysville. M Jan. 18, 1855. OR 1/24.

P. F. Gatewood to Miss Kate Smith, both of Mt. Sterling. M Jan. 11, 1855. OR 1/24.

E. F. Wetmore, of Versailles, to Miss Lucy F. Bennett, of Lexington. M Jan. 23, 1855. OR 1/24.

Stephen S. Brown to Miss Caroline A. Bang, both of Versailles. M Jan. 17, 1855. OR 1/24.

James W. Douglass to Miss Rebecca E. White, both of Nicholasville. M there Jan. 21, 1855. OR 1/24.

Dr. C. W. Dudley to Mrs. Margaret A. Erwin, daughter of Capt. Henry

Johnson, all of Lexington. M at Lake Washington, Miss., on Jan. 16, 1855. OR 1/17.

James A. Craig to Miss F. Ellen, daughter of Jefferson Graves. M in Scott county, Jan. 11, 1855. OR 1/27.

Nathaniel Cropper to Mrs. Margaret Harlow, both of Lexington. M Jan. 25, 1855. OR 1/27.

Alexander G. Morgan to Miss Margaret, daughter of the late Col. T. A. Russell, all of Fayette county. M Jan. 25, 1855. OR 1/31.

William D. Calloway to Miss Lizzie, daughter of James M. Todd, all of Shelby county. M Jan. 24, 1855. OR 2/3.

Thomas M. Redd, of Woodford county, to Miss Mootie, daughter of George H. Bowman, of Fayette county. M Jan. 30, 1855. OR 2/7.

Joseph Soward, of Cynthiana, to Miss Mary Seuvir, of Fayette county. M Feb. 8, 1855. OR 2/10.

Patrick Joyes to Miss Florence, daughter of the late Chapman Coleman, all of Louisville. M February 5, 1855. OR 2/10.

George H. Heifner, of Fayette county, to Miss Eliza J. Horine, daughter of David Horine, of Jessamine county. M latter place, Feb. 15, 1855. OR 2/17.

William B. Kenney, of Fayette county, to Miss Mary K. Throckmorton, of Bourbon county. M Feb. 20, 1855. OR 2/21.

John S. Stewart to Miss Georgia A. Williams. M at Lexington, Mo., Jan. 28, 1855. OR 3/3.

Grant Green, of Frankfort, to Miss Kate S., daughter of the late Dabney C. Overton, of Fayette county. M Feb. 28, 1855. OR 3/3.

Noah J. Patterson, of Harrison county, to Miss Sarah Allen Fleming, daughter of the late Leonard J. Fleming of Woodford county. M Feb. 27, 1855. OR 3/3.

———————— McMinimy to Miss Ann Ragan, both of Sandersville, Ky. M Mar. 1, 1855. OR 3/3.

J. C. Chance to Miss Augusta A. Mitchell, daughter of Prof. Thomas D. Mitchell, of West Philadelphia, formerly of Transylvania University, Lexington. M in Philadelphia, Feb. 15, 1855. OR 3/7.

W. A. Hood to Miss Susan G. Howell, both of Montgomery county. M Feb. 27, 1855. OR 3/7.

Richard H. Jenkins, formerly of Georgetown, Ky., to Miss Elizabeth B., daughter of Robert F. Thompson, formerly of Fayette county. M at Plum Valley, Saline county, Mo., Feb. 5, 1855. OR 3/10.

Charles A. Farra to Miss Linis A. Neal, both of Jessamine county. M Mar. 1, 1855. OR 3/10.

Theodore Elbert, of Bourbon county, to Mrs. Mary Poor, of Nicholasville. M Mar. 8, 1855. OR 3/10.

Frank Fitch, of the firm George W. Norton & Fitch, Lexington, Ky., to Miss Fannie, daughter of Fielding S. Gant, of New York. M at Yonkers, N. Y., Mar. 1, 1855. OR 3/14.

C. H. Low, of Fayette county, to Miss Mollie A., daughter of Charles

Harris, of Montgomery county. M Feb. 22, 1825. OR 3/14.

Thomas M. McIlvain, of Nicholas county, to Miss Sarah E. Deboe, of Jessamine county. M Mar. 13, 1855. OR 3/17.

Thomas C. Vanmeter, of Clark county, to Miss Orpah, daughter of Whitaker H. Campbell, of Garrard county. M latter place, Mar. 13, 1855. OR 3/17.

James A. Farra to Miss Margaret, daughter of S. Higgins Lewis, all of Fayette county. M Mar. 15, 1855. OR 3/17.

George Cleighton to Miss Martha E. Kidd, both of Lexington. M Mar. 15, 1855. OR 3/17.

James F. Wilson to Miss Eliza Richardson, both of Lexington. M Mar. 15, 1855. OR 3/21.

J. T. Christopher, of Woodford county, to Miss Judith A., daughter of Culvin Sanders, of Shelby county. M Mar. 15, 1855. OR 3/28.

George S. Allison, of Louisville, to Miss Marianne W. Pinckard, of Lexington. M Mar. 20, 1855. OR 3/31.

William Darby to Miss Bettie Hutchinson, both of Paris. M in Aberdeen, Ohio, Mar. 22, 1855. OR 3/31.

George O. Hart to Miss Addie Hunter, daughter of Dr. John B. Stout, of Franklin county, formerly of Lexington. M at New Albany, Iowa, Mar. 13, 1855. OR 4/4.

William A. McQuie, of Pike county, Mo., to Miss Fannie E., eldest daughter of John Lingenfelter, of Fayette county, Ky. M Mar. 28, 1855. OR 4/7.

W. G. Wood, of Fayette county, to Miss Ellen C. Wheat, of Paris. M Mar. 29, 1855. OR 4/7.

Edward Perkins to Mrs. Mary Jane Perkins, both of Fayette county. M Apr. 10, 1855. OR 4/11.

Dr. William B. Harlan, of the Crab Orchard Springs, to Miss Sarah Middleton, daughter of Samuel O. Middleton, of Lincoln county. M latter place, Mar. 30, 1855. OR 4/11.

William F. Spears to Miss Ellen, daughter of the late Samuel Williams, all of Paris. M Apr. 5, 1855. OR 4/14.

Jes. (James?) Compton, of the Parish of Rapides, La., to Miss Annie, eldest daughter of John Shelby, of Lincoln county, Ky. M in Aberdeen, Ohio, Apr. 7, 1855. OR 4/14.

Rev. A. W. Robbins to Miss Julia Ann Rice, M at the Jessamine county home of John Vince, Apr. 12, 1855. OR 4/18.

William J. Higgins to Miss Lydia S., daughter of William Darnaby, all of Fayette county. M Apr. 11, 1855. OR 3/25.

Carter Henry Harrison, of Lexington, to Miss Sophronisba S. Preston, of Henderson county. M Apr. 12, 1855. OR 4/25.

Samuel C. Middleton, formerly of Woodford county, Ky., to Miss Mary E. Birchead, of Washington City. M latter place Apr. 17, 1855. OR 4/25.

William A. Gunn, of Lexington, to Miss Mary D. O'Niel, of Kingston.

M Apr. 24, 1855. OR 5/2.

William E. Burr to Miss Harriet H. Brand, daughter of the late William M. Brand, all of Lexington. M Apr. 24, 1855. OR 5/2.

M. K. Hughes, of Sacramento City, Cal. to Miss Martha R., daughter of the late Col. John Mosely, of Jessamine county, Ky. M Apr. 26, 1855. OR 5/2.

Gilbert McMaster, of Cincinnati, to Miss Paulina Lewis, of Scott county. M Apr. 17, 1855. OR 5/2.

R. C. Cluke, of Mt. Sterling, to Miss Kate K., daughter of Harvey Kerr, of Bourbon county. M May 1, 1855. OR 5/5.

James Funk to Miss Mary Martin, of Fayette county. M May 8, 1855. OR 5/9.

Milton J. McCarty to Miss Josephine Morgan, of Lexington. M May 3, 1855. OR 5/9.

James Hughes to Miss Ann Horan, of Lexington. M May 9, 1855. OR 5/12.

David J. Field to Miss Lucy Cunningham, both of Lexington. M May 8, 1855. OR 5/12.

Isaac W. Scott to Miss Sarah T. Pickett, both of Lexington. M May 5, 1855. OR 5/16/1855.

B. B. Crenshaw, of Fayette county, to Mrs. Mary Ann Squires, of Nicholas county. M May 17, 1855. OR 5/9.

James W. Estill, of Madison county, to Miss Nancy E. Scott, of Jessamine county. M May 8, 1855. OR 5/19.

Oscar Turner, of Ballard county, to Miss Eugenie C. Gardner, daughter of Major Alfred Gardner, of Weakley county, Tenn. M at Louisville Hotel, May 20, 1855. Oscar Turner was at one time a resident of Lexington. OR 5/23.

Randall G. Higgins, of Arkansas to Miss Sallie Maury, eldest daughter of the late Judge Maury, of Airslie, near Natchez, Miss. M latter place, Apr. 17, 1855. OR 5/26.

Samuel R. Shultz, of Lexington, to Miss Elizabeth Love, of Georgetown. M latter place, May 17, 1855. OR 5/26.

John M. Sharp, of Kentucky, to Kate Collins, of Chicago. M latter place, May 15, 1855. OR 5/26.

William P. Talbott of Danville, to Miss Mary F. Graves, daughter of Joseph Graves, of Fayette county. M in Aberdeen, O., May 29, 1855. OR 6/2.

C. C. Rogers to Miss Lucinda Scott, daughter of Willoughby Scott, all of Bourbon county. M May 29, 1855. OR 6/2.

D. Kean, of Midway, Woodford county, to Miss Zalina Vallandingham, of Frankfort. M latter place, May 28, 1855. OR 6/2.

William Downing to Miss Mary J. Ewing, both of Fayette county. M May 29, 1855. OR 6/6.

William R. Snyder to Miss Rebecca J. Hoagland, both of Lexington. M June 5, 1855. OR 6/6.

Thomas Underwood to Miss Maria Jane Wright, both of Fayette county. M June 5, 1855. OR 6/9.

Charles Coleman to Miss Sarah Jane Bailey, of Fayette county. M June 6, 1855. OR 6/9.

George W. Wicks, of the Louisville firm of Nock, Wicks & Co., to Miss Mary E. Dean, of Richmond. M June 5, 1855, at the latter place. OR 6/13.

Rev. George E. Thrall to Miss Thomasine Gist, step-daughter of the Hon. Lewis C. Levin. M at Philadelphia, June 6, 1855. OR 6/13.

Dr. John Lyle to Miss Bettie Garrard, both of Bourbon county. M June 7, 1855. OR 6/13.

John Hukill to Miss Sarah C. Robertson, both of Fayette county. M June 14, 1855. S 6/15.

Calvin M. McClung, of St. Louis, to Miss Kitty G., eldest daughter of the late Col. C. C. Morgan, of Lexington, Ky. M in Christ Church, Lexington, June 14, 1855. OR 6/16.

Judge James H. Embry, of Richmond, to Miss Eliza S. Pearce, daughter of Capt. Samuel C. Pearce, of Maysville. M June 12 1855. OR 6/16.

Augustus Payne, of Scott county, to Miss Nancy Haggin, daughter of Samuel Haggin, of Fayette county. M June 11, 1855. OR 6/16.

Robert H. Chilton to Miss Nannie McMurtry. M in Jessamine county, June 10, 1855. OR 6/20.

A. J. Eades, of Clark county, to Miss Frances Moore, of Lexington. M June 13, 1855. OR 6/20.

Frank H. Clark, of Jefferson county, to Miss Annie R. Hawkins, of Cass county. M April 1, 1855. Frank H. Clark was graduated from Transylvania Law Class about 1852. He was editor of the Jefferson, Texas, *Jefferson Herald* at the time of his marriage to Miss Hawkins. S 6/22.

Joseph B. Kinkead, of Louisville, to Miss Lucy, daughter of Dr. C. W. Short, of Jefferson county. M June 20, 1855. OR 6/23.

James H. Birch, of Plattsburg, Mo., to Miss Mary Bassett, of Harrison county, Ky. M near Cynthiana, June 26, 1855. OR 6/27.

J. W. Bowie, of Paris, to Miss Bettie A. Eden, of Lexington. M June 21, 1855. OR 6/30.

Lucius Williamson to Miss Frances McCoy, both of Sandersville. M July 3, 1855. OR 7/4.

J. M. Heath to Miss Mary E. Ford of Louisville. M in Hawesville, Ky., June 25, 1855. OR 7/4.

Thomas H. Fox, of Springfield, to Mrs. H. Clay Wilson, of Montgomery county. M June 20, 1855. OR 7/4.

Hon. Henry Daniel to Mrs. Polly Cravens, both of Montgomery county. M June 21, 1855. OR 7/4.

Hugh T. Brent, of Paris, to Miss Carrie A. Russell, daughter of D. A. Russell, of Danville. M June 28, 1855. OR 7/4.

Rev. John N. Norton, Rector of Accension Church, Frankfort, to Miss Mary Louisa, only daughter of George W. Sutton, of Lexington. M July 4, 1855. OR 7/7.

Rev. John A. Merrick, Rector of St. Peter's Church, Paris, to Miss Amelia

Timberlake, of Paris. M June 24, 1855. OR 7/7.

Richard S. Henderson to Mrs. Jane Maria Wiggington, daughter of Charles Talbott, all of Paris. M July 1, 1855. OR 7/7.

Andrew Jackson to Miss Sabina Jane Hall, daughter of John G. Hall, all of Lexington. M July 10, 1855. S 7/10.

James Green to Miss Margaret Bledsoe, both of Sandersville. M July 19, 1855. OR 7/25.

Martin B. Frazer to Miss Catherine Trimble, both of Jessamine county. M at the Jessamine county residence of John Messick, July 19, 1855. OR 7/25.

James L. Allen to Miss Sallie A., daughter of John McCaw, all of Lexington. M July 25, 1855. OR 7/25.

James Kenney to Miss Eleanora, daughter of H. C. Graves, all Scott county. M July 24, 1855. OR 8/4.

John M. Snell to Miss Mary E., daughter of Benjamin Finnell, of Georgetown. M in Aberdeen, O., in July, 1855. OR 8/4.

William Preston Gibson, of Terrebonne, to Miss Eldie (or Elodie) Mary Humphreys, daughter of the late Dr. Alexander Humphreys, of the Parrish of St. James, La. M latter place, July 19, 1855. OR 8/8.

Rev. Henry E. Thomas, of Georgetown, to Miss Annie A. Hodges, senior proprietor of the *Frankfort Commonwealth*. M Aug. 7, 1855. OR 8/18.

C. G. Dennis, of Nicholasville, to Miss Mollie J. Story of Lexington. M Aug. 21, 1855. OR 8/25.

Frederick Yeiser, of Lexington, Ky., to Miss Clara Morris of Indianapolis. M latter place, Aug. 21, 1855. OR 9/1.

Samuel Larimer to Miss Hetty Ann Hendricks, both of Lexington. M Aug. 28, 1855. OR 9/1.

Richard P. Harrison, of New Orleans, to Miss Mary K. Hunt. M at the Louisville residence of Abram Hunt, Sept. 5, 1855. OR 9/8.

James F. Nicholas to Miss Eleanora Estill, both of Fayette county. M Sept. 10, 1855. OR 9/15.

James Johnson, of Fayette county, to Miss Arminta Redman, of Lexington. M Sept. 19, 1855. OR 9/22.

Byron Cates, of Paris, to Miss Molly, daughter of Thomas Y. Brent. M in Louisville, Sept. 12, 1855. OR 9/26.

Will Winn, of Winchester, to Miss Carrie S., daughter of Abner Hord, of Mason county. M Aug. 28, 1855. OR 9/26.

Col. George D. Southall, of Memphis, to Miss Belle Chamlin, of Mt. Sterling. M Sept. 5, 1855. OR 9/26.

William H. Jennings, of St. Louis, to Miss Hannah Jane Welch, daughter of Dr. Thomas Welch. M at Crab Orchard, Ky., Sept. 25, 1855. OR 9/29.

Rev. John T. Edgar, of Nashville, to Mrs. Ann Crittenden. M at the Franklin county, Ky., residence of the bride's father, John Morris, Sept. 20, 1855. OR 9/29.

Milford Berry, of Nicholas county, to Mrs. Eliza Ann Robertson, daughter of John Judy, of Clarke county. M Aug. 28, 1855. OR 10/3.

W. T. Bartley to Mrs. Emily B. Tilford, daughter of Captain Henry Johnson, of Miss. M at Louisville, Ky., Sept. 27, 1855. OR 10/3.

George E. Moore, of Versailles, to Miss Ann M. Railey, of Woodford county. M Sept. 25, 1855. OR 10/6.

James T. Thornton, of Cass county, Mo., to Miss Mary H., daughter of Judge James Simpson, of Winchester, Ky. M Oct. 2, 1855. OR 10/6.

Stephen P. Waller to Mrs. Fannie Neal, daughter of the late James Barkley, Sr., of Jessamine county. M Oct. 2, 1855. OR 10/10.

Mason S. Neal, of Jessamine county, to Miss Mary M., daughter of Berry Hollins, of Midway, Woodford county. M at latter place, Oct. 2, 1855. OR 10/10.

William R. Lewis to Miss Mary A. Boone, both of Fayette county. M at the residence of E. H. Arnett, Sept. 27, 1855. OR 10/10.

A. G. Karsner to Mrs. Fannie Price, both of Jessamine county. M at the Jessamine county residence of Cleba Price, Oct. 2, 1855. OR 10/13.

Samuel S. Bush, of Gallatin, Tenn., to Miss Mary Ann Cornelia, daughter of Judge Z. Wheat, and grandaughter of the Hon. Ben. Monroe, of Frankort, Ky. M latter place, Oct. 9, 1855. OR 10/13.

John J. Grigsby, of St. Louis, to Miss Martha Ann Elbert, of Fayette county, Ky. M at the residence of her father, in Fayette county, Oct. 18, 1855. OR 10/20.

T. B. Burbridge, of Scott county, to Miss Susan E., daughter of the late William Henry, of Christian county. M in Hopkinsville, Oct. 3, 1855. OR 10/20.

William N. Beckham, of Shelby county, to Miss Julia T., youngest daughter of the Hon. C. A. Wickliffe. M at Wickland, near Bardstown, Oct. 16, 1855. OR 10/20.

James E. Ford, of Bourbon county, to Miss Harriet, daughter of Presley Simpson, of the city of Washington. M at latter place, Oct. 18, 1855. OR 10/25.

Dr. John S. Carter, of New Orleans, to Miss Letitia S., daughter of Col. Charles S. Todd, of Shelby county, Ky. M Oct. 18, 1855. OR 10/31.

Samuel Downing, of Fayette county, to Miss Mag. Leslie Combs, daughter of Gen. Leslie Combs, of Lexington. M at Christ Church, here, Oct. 30, 1855. OR 11/3.

William McDonald, of Bourbon county, to Miss Adelaide Keiser, of Fayette county. M at Athens, Oct. 30, 1855. OR 11/3.

Col. Daniel Garrard, aged 75 years, of Clay county, to Miss Mary F. Adkins, aged 24, of Knox county. M latter place, Oct. 16, 1855. OR 11/7.

Thomas S. Redd to Mrs. Eliza O. Bullock, of Fayette county. M Nov. 8, 1855. OR 11/14.

Benj. Bland, of New Orleans, to Miss Juliana W. Marshall, youngest daughter of the late Gen. Thomas Marshall, of Lewis county, Ky. M in Fleming county, Nov. 6, 1855. OR 11/14.

John M. Caffery, of Lexington, to Miss Harriet Agnes Fielding, of New York. M in Louisville, Nov. 6, 1855. OR 11/14.

Benoni Macklin, of Franklin county, to Miss Helen Harper, of Woodford county. M latter place, at the residence of John Utterback, Nov. 6, 1855. OR 11/14.

W. E. Arthur, to Ada, daughter of the late Hon. W. W. Southgate, all of Covington. M Nov. 6, 1855. OR 11/14.

G. W. Searcy, of Fayette county, to Miss Mary C., daughter of J. C. Hall, of Lexington. M Nov. 13, 1855. OR 11/17.

William A. Anderson, of Lafayette county, Mo., to Miss Bettie S. Wallace, daughter of Salene Wallace, of Madison county, Ky. M Nov. 8, 1855. OR 11/17.

B. F. Blackburn, of Woodford county, Ky., to Miss D. B. Hamilton, of Chicago. M Nov. 1, 1855. See below. OR 11/17.

John G. Keenon, M. D., of Frankfort, Ky., to Miss Ellen Hamilton, daughter of Col. R. J. Hamilton, and sister of above? M at Chicago, Nov. 1, 1855. "Miss Ellen Hamilton that was (says the Chicago *Democrat*,) though but a bride of 22 years—there is no harm in telling, now that she is a bride, is the oldest native inhabitant of Chicago." OR 11/17.

John T. Hughes to Miss Sarah De Hart, of Louisville. M Nov. 15, 1855. OR 11/21.

Joel P. Williams, of Harrodsburg, to Miss Martha A. Stone, daughter of David Stone, of Fayette county. M latter place, Nov. 13, 1855. OR 11/21.

Ewing M. Sloan, of Westport, Mo., to Miss M. Helen, daughter of Dr. Joseph Chew, of Richmond, Mo. M Nov. 6, 1855. OR 11/21.

James W. Ratcliffe to Miss Louisiana Ann, daughter of Elder Samuel Jones, all of Bath county. M Oct. 18, 1855. OR 11/21.

Charles B. Hicks to Miss Mary D. Flint. M Nov. 20, 1855, at the residence of her grandfather, James Carter, all of Fayette county. OR 11/21.

John McNevins to Miss Mary E. Mosely, both of Anderson county. M. Nov. 15, 1855, in Camdenville. OR 11/21.

James Blackburn, of Chicago, to Miss Emma, daughter of the late Samuel D. Everett, of Montgomery county, Ky. The groom was "recently of Woodford county, Ky." M Nov. 20, 1855. OR 11/24.

Lucien B. Dickinson, of Georgetown, to Miss Mary Jane Leathers, of Covington. M at the Covington residence of C. B. Sandford, Nov. 15, 1855. OR 11/21.

William N. Hood, of Scott county, to Miss Clara R., daughter of the late William Hickman, of Bourbon county. M Nov. 20, 1855. OR 11/24.

Edward C. Breck, of Savannah, to Miss Letitia, daughter of the Hon. David Todd. M in Booneville, Mo., Nov. 8, 1855. OR 11/24.

D. W. Bell to Miss Ellen P., eldest daughter of Elisha Warfield, all of Lexington. M Nov. 27, 1855. OR 11/28.

Hon. George E. Pugh, U. S. Senator from Ohio, to Miss Theresa Chalfant, both of Cincinnati. M Nov. 22, 1855. OR 11/28.

Thomas Sutton to Miss Annie M. Johnson, both of Lexington. M Nov. 29, 1855. OR 12/1.

Clayton C. Bell to Miss Alivia P. Moseley, both of Irvine, Ky. M there Nov. 27, 1855. OR 12/1.

John Lair, of Harrison county, to Miss Maria S. Varnon, of Bourbon county. M Nov. 22, 1855. OR 12/1.

Dr. Temple E. Gayle to Miss Angelina Offutt, of Scott county. M Nov. 22, 1855. OR 12/1.

Henry C. Dunlap, of Lexington, Ky., to Miss La Belle Boyce, of Wheeling, Va. M latter place, Nov. 20, 1855. OR 12/5.

Hamilton Pope, of Louisville, to Miss Henrietta Prather. M in Springfield, Nov. 23, 1855. OR 12/5.

Gabriel Martin to Miss Eda Griggs both of Fayette county. M in Sandersville, Dec. 4, 1855. OR 12/8.

G. Silas Cowgill, of Fayette county, to Miss Emaline Robb, of Jessamine county. M Dec. 6, 1855. OR 12/8.

John D. Williams, of Rochester, to Miss Samuella R., daughter of Leonard Taylor, of Lexington. M Dec. 6, 1855. OR 12/8.

Lunceford Talbott, of Bourbon county, to Miss Mary C., daughter of Major T. Young. M in Bath county, Dec. 5, 1855. OR 12/12.

Thomas W. Lewis, of Clarke county, to Miss Paulina L., daughter of Johnson Young. M Dec. 5, 1855. OR 12/12.

Capt. Caleb Thompson Worley, recently of Jessamine county, Ky., to Miss Lizzie, daughter of Jefferson Garth, of Columbia, Mo. M latter place, Dec. 4, 1855. OR 12/15.

J. S. Eshom, of California, to Miss Cordelia, daughter of the late Col. John Williams, of Mt. Sterling, Ky. M Dec. 12, 1855. OR 12/19.

Dudley Carptenter, of Woodford county, to Miss Martha J. Murrain, of Jessamine county. M at the Jessamine county residence of William Murrain, Nov. 28, 1855. OR 12/19.

1856

J. R. Gibbaney to Miss Mary C. Rollins. M in Lexington, Dec. 20, 1855. OR 12/22.

John J. Craig, of Boyle county, to Miss Amanda A. Goodloe, daughter of Judge William C. Goodloe, of Madison county. M at the residence of Ex-Jovernor Owsley, Dec. 18, 1855. OR 12/22

H. Wallace Bosworth to Miss Marian Wilson, both of Lexington. M Oct. 1, 1856. S 10/3.

George E. Darnaby to Miss Mary E., eldest daughter of G. Washington Allen, of Jessamine county. M Sept. 30, 1856. S 10/3.

Dr. William Webb, of St. Louis, to Miss Mary A. Castleman, daughter of the late David Castleman. M at Castleton, Fayette county. Oct. 2, 1856. S 10/7.

William Lewis to Miss Susan Ann McCarty. M in Lexington, Oct. 8, 1856. S 10/10.

E. J. Orear, of Salem county, Mo., to Miss Julia E. Orear. M Oct. 13,

1856. S 10/14.

John A. Lytle to Miss Jane G. Brockway, both of Springfield, Illinois. They were formerly of Bourbon county, Ky. M latter place, Sept. 29, 1856. S 10/14.

Washington C. Houghton to Miss Margaret Harney, of Lexington. M Oct. 14, 1856. S 10/21.

William Purnell, of Keokuk, Iowa, to Miss Mary T. Gillmore, of Fayette county, Ky. M Oct. 21, 1856, at the residence of Andrew Gillmore. S 10/21.

Woodford Taylor, of Bloomington, Ill., to Miss Maria Louise Price. M in Nicholasville, Ky., Oct. 23, 1856. S 10/28.

John B. Wallace to Miss Lucy Sims, both of Nicholasville. M at the residence of John Sims, Oct. 28, 1856. S 11/7.

Daniel McCarty to Mrs. Mary Puthuff, both of Sandersville. M Nov. 6, 1856. S 11/7.

William Adams to Miss Elizabeth Halligan, both of Fayette county. M Nov. 9, 1856. S 11/11.

A. S. Welch, of Lexington, to Miss Priscie, daughter of Dr. Abraham Addams, of Cynthiana. M Nov. 6, 1856. S 11/18.

William M. Thompson, of Scott county, to Miss Mary E., daughter of Abraham F. Dudley, of Fayette county. M Nov. 4, 1856. S 11/18.

Stephen E. Jones, of Iowa, to Miss Mattie, only daughter of the late Col. William R. McKee, of Lexington, Ky. M Nov. 12, 1856. S 11/18.

Peter A. White, of Cincinnati, to Miss Margaret H., eldest daughter of the late Aaron K. Woolley, of Lexington, Ky. M in the latter place, Nov. 18, 1856. S 11/21.

Dr. Henry B. Kidd, of Yazoo City, Miss., to Miss Lucy A. Thornton, of Salvisa, Mercer county, Ky. M latter place on 19th of Nov., 1856. S 11/21.

Charles W. Woolley, of Lexington, Ky., to Miss Mary F., daughter of Jacob Strader, of Cincinnati. M latter place on 12th of Nov., 1856. S. 11/28.

J. F. Thompson to Miss Julia G. Norlon, both of Lexington. M Nov. 25, 1856. S 11/28.

James Scrugham to Miss Joanna Foreman, both of Lexington. M Nov. 27, 1856. S 12/2.

John McGinnis, president of the Bank of Quincy, Quincy, Ill., to Miss Lydia, daughter of Gov. Joel A. Matteson, of Springfield, Ill. M at the residence of the brides father, Nov. 27, 1856. S 12/2.

Dwight Brown, of Lexington, Ky., to Miss Carrie E. Weeks, of Saratoga Springs, N. Y. M latter place, Nov. 25, 1856. S 11/5

F. Montmollin, Jr., to Miss Mary Parker, both of Lexington. M Dec. 16, 1856. S 12/16.

Howard Combs, of Quincy, Ill., to Miss Mary Loud, of Lexington, Ky. M Dec. 16, 1856. S 12/19.

T. F. Gorham to Miss Emily E. Ross, both of Fayette county. M Dec. 18, 1856. S 12/23.

John P. Knight to Miss Adelaide L., daughter of Walter C. Young, all of

Jessamine county. M Jan. 6, 1857. OR 1/10.

George Shackelford to Miss Lizzie J. Sweeney, both of Paris. M at the Bath county residence of Gen. W. M. Sudduth, Jan. 6, 1857. OR 1/10.

Harrison Taylor, of Fayette county, to Miss Margaret Lawless, of Nicholasville. M at latter place, at the residence of Henry Beddow, Jan. 13, 1857. OR 1/14.

Col. Hyman C. Gratz, of Woodford county, to Miss Laura Hamilton, daughter of the late Alexander Hamilton, of that county. M at Highland, the Woodford county residence of the bride's mother, Jan. 13, 1857. OR 1/17.

Noah D. Ferguson to Miss Sally Elizabeth, daughter of Gen. James Dudley, all of Fayette county. M Jan. 14, 1857. OR 1/17.

Col. R. H. Hutchcraft, of Bourbon county, to Miss Sue Croxton, daughter of Henry Croxton, of Clarke county. M Jan. 13, 1857. OR 1/21.

1857

G. A. Pratt, of Mass., to Miss Sallie G. Clarendon, of Vermont, both of the Lexington, Ky., Theatre. M Jan. 21, 1857. OR 1/24.

Fountain Worsham to Miss Mary Ann Jenkins, both of Lexington. M Jan. 22, 1857. OR 1/24.

Scion Kimball, of Madison county, to Miss Martha F. Walker, of Fayette county. M Jan. 6, 1857. OR 1/24.

James W. Ingles to Miss Mary Davis, both of Paris. M Jan. 20, 1857. OR 1/24.

John W. Cassel to Miss Mary A. Leeds, both of Fayette county. M at the house of Dr. Roberts, Jan. 20, 1857. OR 1/24.

Rev. Joseph Nickol, of Morgan county, to Miss Zarilda E., daughter of Whitfield White, of Owsley county. M at Magnolia Cottage, in latter place, Dec. 24, 1856. OR 2/4/1857.

Watson M. Gay, of Clarke county, to Miss Nannie C. Owen, of Bourbon county. M Jan. 22, 1857. OR 2/4.

W. G. Barbour, of Winchester, to Miss Agnes, daughter of the late Major Ben. P. Grey. M at the Woodford county residence of the brides mother, Jan. 27, 1857. OR 2/4.

Milton G. Thompson to Miss Mary Foreman, both of Lexington. M Feb. 10, 1857. OR 2/11.

William F. Miller to Miss Mary Frances Kidd, both of Lexington. M Feb. 10, 1857. OR 2/11.

James W. Peel to Miss Susan McCoy. M Feb. 13, 1857, in Lexington. OR 2/11.

John P. Innes, of Fayette county, to Miss Lummie Davis, of Woodford county. M latter place, Feb. 11, 1857. OR 2/14.

Charles Alexander, of Woodford county, to Miss Mollie M. Daniel, of Jessamine. M Feb. 5, 1857. OR 2/14.

Captain James M. Hawes, of the U. S. Army, and son of the Hon. R. Hawes, of Paris, Ky., to Miss Maria J., daughter of Gen. James Southgate, of Covington. M at Christ Church, in Cincinnati, Feb. 3, 1857. OR 2/14.

John Arnsparger to Miss Maria Offutt. M in Fayette county, Feb. 5, 1857. OR 2/18.

Dr. Easom Fitgarrel, of Carlinville, Ill., and formerly of Kentucky, to Miss Sue. G. Taylor, daughter of Stark Taylor, of Fayette county, Ky. M at the residence of the brides brother, in the former place, Feb. 12, 1857. OR 2/25.

Dr. S. Woodson Coleman, of Oldham county, to Miss Mattie E. Calluway (Calloway?), of Henry county. M Jan. 17, 1857. OR 2/25.

1857

James D. Bollin to Miss Joanna Farrell, both, of Lexington. M Feb. 22, 1857. OR 2/25.

Samuel T. Dobyn to Miss Sarah T., daughter of Samuel T. Green, all of Montgomery county. M Feb. 19, 1857. OR 2/25.

Col. Barton W. Stnone (Stone?), of Dallas, Texas, to Miss Sue E. Smith, of Montgomery county, Ky. M Feb. 24, 1857. OR 2/28.

Allen T. Rice, of Fayette county, to Miss Lucy J. Ryman, of Jessamine county. M in Lexington, Feb. 1, 1857. OR 2/28.

Oscar F. Taylor, of Bourbon county, to Miss Cordelia, youngest daughter of Louis Sugget, of Lexington. M Feb. 26, 1857. OR 2/28.

Dr. J. K. Morton to Miss Ada Montmollin, daughter of Mr. F. Montmollin, all of Lexington. M Feb. 26, 1857. OR 2/28.

Edward R. Bryan, of Fayette county, to Miss Mary B. Williams, of Scott county. M latter place, Feb. 25, 1857. OR 2/28.

George C. Young, of Johnson county, Mo., to Miss Mary Elizabeth Mahin, daughter of J. M. Mahin, of Woodford county. M Mar. 3, 1857. OR 3/4.

William C. Nichols to Miss Mary E. White, eldest daughter of Jacob White, all of Lexington. M Mar. 3, 1857. OR 3/4.

Josiah H. Nettles, of Clinton, La., to Miss Elizabeth V. Elbert, of Lexington, Ky. M latter place, Mar. 3, 1857. OR 3/7.

John Roseli to Miss Paulina Coons, both of Lexington. M Mar. 5, 1857. OR 3/7.

Edward Tuttle to Miss Amanda Murry, both of Lexington. M Mar. 5, 1857. OR 3/7.

James Y. Kelly, clerk of the Scott Circuit Court, to Miss Kitty Osborne, both of Georgetown, Ky. M in Greenfield, Ind., Feb. 24, 1857. OR 3/7.

William Richardson, of Louisville, to Miss Mary Ann Lindsley, of New Albany, Ind. M latter place, Feb. 26, 1857. OR 3/7.

Richard Hawes, Jr., of Daviess county, to Miss Millie Davis, daughter of J. Dudley Davis; M in Scott county on 3rd of March, 1857. OR 3/7.

John T. Wornall, of Harrison county, to Miss Anna Ewalt, daughter of Samuel Ewalt, of Fayette county. M Feb. 26, 1857. OR 3/7.

Charles W. Field, of the U. S. Army, to Miss Moninia Mason, daughter of

W. Roy Mason. M at Cleveland, King George county, Mar. 10, 1857. OR 3/7.

John Staley to Miss Harriett Jane Holland, both of Lexington. M Jan. 1, 1857. OR 1/7.

Dr. M. Goldsmith Jones, of Hillsborough, Ohio, to Miss Mary R., daughter of L. M. Stone, of Bath county, Ky. M Dec. 23, 1856. OR 1/7/1857.

Hon. John P. Campbell, Representative in Congress from Kentucky, to Miss Mary Boyd, third daughter of the Hon. Charles James Faulkner, of Virginia. M near Martinsville, Va., Dec. 24, 1856. OR 1/7/1857.

D. D. Dykeman to Miss Mary Eliza Tomblinson, both of Logansport, Ind. M there Dec. 30, 1856. OR 1/7/1857.

Col. Anderson Taylor to Mrs. Sarah Dorsey, both of Woodford county. M Feb. 26, 1857. OR 3/11.

James Grubb, of Lexington, to Miss Jennie F. Colvin, daughter of John D. Colvin, of Versailles. M latter place Mar. 10, 1857. OR 3/8.

Robert Prewitt, of Fayette county, to Miss Lizzie Howell, of Montgomery county. M Mar. 11, 1857. OR 3/18.

Joseph D. Lisle, of Jackson county, Mo., to Miss Mag. S. Caldwell, daughter of John Caldwell, formerly of Fayette county, Ky. M former place, Feb. 19, 1857. OR 3/18.

Dr. John P. Henry to Miss Arabella M., only daughter of William W. Graves, all of Lexington. M Mar. 16, 1857. OR 3/21.

Benjamin F. Dillon, formerly of Fayette county, Ky., to Mrs. Elizabeth White, formerly of Virginia. M in Fillmore, Anderson county, Mo., Jan. 20, 1857. OR 3/25.

Lyman T. Shoemaker, of New York state, to Miss Elizabeth Little, of Woodfird county, Ky. M latter place, at the residence of William Vance, Mar. 23, 1857. OR 3/28.

Leo L. Lewis to Miss America G. Kay, both of Fayette county. M Mar. 31, 1857. OR 4/1.

James H. Bean to Miss Maria Duerson, both of Clarke county. M Mar. 26, 1857. OR 4/8.

J. G. McComas, of Paris, to Miss Sarah, daughter of John Frost, of Lexington. M Apr. 7, 1857. OR 4/11.

James Nixon to Miss Susan Worsham, both of Lexington. M Apr. 7, 1857. OR 4/11.

Jacob Jacoby, of Bourbon county, to Miss Charity C. Haynes, of Fayette county. M Apr. 3, 1857. OR 4/11.

Charles Kimbrough to Miss Mary E., daughter of Benson Roberts, both of Harrison county. M Apr. 4, 1857. OR 4/11.

H. J. Robinson to Miss Mildred Ann Carroll, both of Lexington. M Apr. 16, 1857. OR 4/18.

Charles Bevercomb to Miss Jane, daughter of William Warren, all of Fayette county. M Apr. 11, 1857. OR 4/18.

Charlton M. Metcalfe, of Cincinnati, to Miss Maggie, eldest daughter of M. Keen, of Louisville. M Apr. 14, 1857, at the Louisville Hotel. OR 4/18.

Werter Combs to Mrs. Kitty Ann Combs, both of Clarke county. M Apr.

24, 1857. OR 4/25.

Benjamin P. Gough, of Clarke county, to Miss Ann Prewitt, of Montgomery county. M Apr. 9, 1857. OR 4/25.

In Danville, Apr. 23, 1857, by the Rev. John C. Young, Gelon H. Rout, of Lincoln county, to Miss Mary Young; and at the same time, by the same, Rutherford Douglass to Miss Caroline J. Young, both brides the daughters of the officiating minister. OR 4/29.

John Young Brown, of Elizabethtown, to Miss Lucie, daughter of Col. Thomas Barbee, of Boyle county. M Apr. 23, 1857. OR 4/29.

Edward J. Holland to Miss Amanda F. Harris, both of Lexington. M Apr. 30, 1857. OR 5/2.

John M. Hunt, of Fayette county, to Mrs. Huldah J. Stephens, of Nicholasville, M Apr. 30, 1857. OR 5/2.

Charles H. Powell, of Henderson, to Miss Carrie, daughter of Richard Butler, of Carrollton. M Apr. 29, 1857. OR 5/2.

Isaac W. Scott, M. D., formerly of Lexington, Ky., to Miss Mary F., daughter of the late George Buchannan, all of St. Louis. M latter place, Apr. 30, 1857. OR 5/9.

Rev. W. C. Piper to Miss Mollie L. Simms, daughter of John G. Simms, of Nicholasville. M in May, 1857. OR 5/9.

John S. Shields, of Paducah, to Miss Carrie Bradford Turner, formerly of Lexington. M former place, Apr. 28, 1857. OR 5/23.

Henry Clay McDowell to Miss Nannie, daughter of the late Col. Henry Clay, Jr., and granddaughter af the "lamented Sage of Ashland." M at Oaklea, Oldham county, May 21, 1857. OR 5/27.

D. Ephraim Noble to Mrs. Mary Bruen, both of Lexington. M May 28, 1857. OR 5/30.

Nathaniel P. Rogers to Mrs. Eveline Bayless, both of Bourbon county. M May 15, 1857. OR 5/30.

Dr. John Welch, of Nicholasville, to Miss Mary E. Downing, daughter of A. Downing, of Salvisa, Ky. M latter place, May 21, 1857. OR 6/3.

H. H. Davis, of Harrodsburg, to Miss Courtney H. Prewitt, of Nicholasville. M May 21, 1857. OR 6/3.

Jos(eph) C. Oldham, of Jefferson county, to Miss George Ann Anderson, of Jessamine county. M at the residence of Mrs. Mary McDowell, in latter place, June 4, 1857. OR 6/6.

Richard Atkinson, of Louisville, to Miss Mary Ellen Craig, daughter of Parker Craig, of Lexington. M June 2, 1857. OR 6/6.

William Johnston to Miss Emily Ward, daughter of Robert J. Ward, all of Louisville. M June 2, 1857. OR 6/6.

William S. Simpson to Miss Henrietta O. Griffing, both of Paris. M at the residence of W. D. Griffing, there, June 3, 1857. OR 6/6.

John Lees to Miss Susan M. Van Pelt, both of Lexington. M June 9, 1857. OR 6/10.

Col. R. R. Bolling, of Danville, to Miss Eddie, daughter of W. S. Scott, of

Paris. M June 9, 1857. OR 6/13.

John B. Smedley to Miss Mary Ellen Hickey, both of Fayette county. M. June 11, 1857. OR 6/13/1857.

Morton Moore, of Franklin county, to Miss Amanda Sallie, of Fayette county. M June 11, 1857. OR 6/13.

William E. Rogers to Miss Maggie K., daughter of H. W. Varnon, both of Bourbon county. M in Paris, June 10, 1857. OR 6/20.

Col. John McMullin, of California, to Miss Eliza F., youngest daughter of Gen. Daniel Morgan, of Fleming county, Ky. M June 18, 1857. OR 6/24.

Edward M. Turner to Miss Lucy Jane Frances, both of Lexington. M June 24, 1857. OR 6/27.

John W. Reineking, of New Albany, Ind., to Miss Eunice Bruce Stout, youngest daughter of John B. Stout, M. D., formerly of Lexington, Ky. M former place, June 2, 1857. OR 7/1.

Marshall Key, of Mason county, to Mrs. Helen M. Martin, of Louisville. M June 24, 1857. OR 7/1.

Archer Bankhead to Miss Mary Chambers, daughter of the late Col. A. B. Chambers, of St. Louis. M at Oakland, near Bowling Green, Mo., June 10, 1857. OR 7/4.

John Everett, of Mt. Sterling, Ky., to Miss Laura R., daughter of J. S. Chenowith, of Cincinnati. M July 1, 1857. OR 7/4.

C. H. Klaranaar to Miss Maggie Norris, both of Lexington. M July 2, 1857. OR 7/8.

F. M. Murray, formerly of Louisville, to Miss Margaret Grimes, daughter of Owen W. Grimes. M in Paducah, June 25, 1857. OR 7/8.

Dr. Mat. R. Harper, of Midway, to Miss Georgia, daughter of George Parker, of Bourbon county. M June 30, 1857. OR 7/8.

William F. Baird, of Cincinnati, to Miss Annie M. Offutt, of Scott county, Ky. M June 30, 1857. OR 7/8.

Sidney Christian to Miss Mary F. Halsell, of Fayette county. M July 6, 1857. OR 7/11.

Dr. John T. Russell to Miss Fannie E., daughter of John Giltner, of Bourbon county. M July 7, 1857. OR 7/11.

M. C. Hastings, of Georgetown, to Miss M. A. Riddle, daughter of Northan Riddle, of Fayette county. M in Aberdeen,* Ohio, July 5, 1857. OR 7/11.

George Clugston to Miss Laura G. Cromwell. M July 12, 1857. OR 7/15.

Joseph Ohaver to Mrs. Mary Jeter, both of Lexington. M July 13, 1857. OR 7/15.

Hamilton Davis, of Fayette county, to Mrs. Mary Aubrey, of Lexington. M in July, 1857. OR 7/15.

William Hukill to Miss Susan Robertson, both of Lexington. M July 16, 1857. OR 7/18.

Richard Ten Broeck, of New York, to Miss Patty D. Anderson, of Louisville, Ky. M at St. Mary's Church, Andover, Hants, England, June 16, 1857.

OR 7/18.

Thomas A. Peters, formerly of Paris, to Miss Margaret A. Puthuff, daughter of John Puthuff, of Fayette county. M July 20, 1857. OR 7/22.

J. E. Delph to Miss Mary A. Rose, both of Fayette county. M July 16, 1857. OR 7/22.

Anderson W. Jackson to Mrs. Nancy H. Martin, of Fayette county. M July 16, 1857. OR 7/22.

Joseph Milward, of Lexington, to Mrs. Keturah H. Gruelle, of Versailles. M latter place, at the residence of Mr. A. Thornton, July 29, 1857. OR 8/1.

Mahlon Pruden to Miss Martha Jane Lawrence, both of Lexington. M Aug. 2, 1857. OR 8/5.

John Blount, of Danville, to Miss Lucretia Ann Hoagland, of Lexington. M here by the Rev. Samuel B. Cheek, Aug. 5, 1857. "All were mutes." OR 8/8.

John B. Temple to Miss Bland Broadhead, both of Frankfort. M at the residence of Col. Orlando Brown, Aug. 5, 1857. OR 8/2.

W. J. Owens, of Lexington, to Miss Kate C. White, of Crab Orchard. M latter place, Aug. 5, 1857. OR 8/12.

George D. Hinkle, of Louisville, to Miss Mary H., daughter of John Clark, of Fayette county. M latter place, July 30, 1857. OR 8/15

Benjamin J. Downing to Miss Mary Ann Breckinridge, both of Lexington. M Aug. 2, 1857. OR 8/22.

Rev. T. N. Ralston, of Lexington Methodist Episcopal Church, South, to Miss Mary W. Phister, only daughter of Conrad M. Phister, of Maysville. M latter place, Aug. 12, 1857. OR 8/22.

Dr. William Brother, of Madison county, to Miss Kate Wilson, daughter of the late William Wilson, of Lexington. M Aug. 20, 1857. OR 8/26.

Charles Blanche to Miss Margaret Kriesel, both of Lexington. M Aug. 22, 1857. OR 8/26.

Samuel M. Boone, of Fayette county, to Miss Mary W., daughter of Col. G. S. Caldwell, of Boyle county. M Aug. 18, 1857. OR 8/26.

William Ford to Miss Sarah Ann Haley, both of Fayette county. M Aug. 20, 1857. OR 8/29.

Levi Grow to Miss Margaret E. Sanford, both of Keene, Jessamine county. M Aug. 26, 1857. OR 8/29.

Benjamin G. Chinn, son of Dr. J. G. Chinn, of Lexington, Ky., to Miss Britty Buford, daughter of M. T. and E. Buford. M in Lafayette county, Mo., Aug. 19, 1857. OR 8/29.

Henry P. Prewitt, of Scott county, to Miss Annie R. Bryan. M at the Fayette county residence of Samuel Bryan, Aug. 13, 1857. OR 9/2.

W. T. Hieronymus, of La., to Miss Emma, daughter of A. M. Cooper, of Louisville, Ky. M Sept. 3, 1857. OR 9/9.

Richard M. Price, of Shelby county, to Miss Margaret A. Wallace, daughter of Major John H. Wallace, of Fayette county. M Sept. 8, 1857. OR 9/9.

James Miller to Miss Nannie Shurlock, both of Versailles. M Sept. 8, 1857.

OR 9/9.

Levi Barkley, of Marion county, to Mrs. Mary A. Bronaugh, of Jessamine county, Ky. M at the residence of Henry B. Dunn, near Philadelphia, Mo., Sept. 1, 1857. OR 9/12.

John H. Martin to Miss Anna M. Richardson, both of Louisville. M Sept. 7, 1857. OR 9/12.

Henry W. Lansing to Miss Mary J., daughter of Dr. McDowell, all of Chillicothe, Mo. M at the residence of Mrs. P. McDowell, near Nicholasville, Ky., Sept. 8, 1857. OR 9/12.

Samuel H. Lewis, of Fayette county, to Miss Jessie Willmore, of Jessamine county. M in Aberdeen, Ohio, Aug. 24, 1857. OR 9/16.

John H. Dills to Miss Julia Ellen, daughter of General Lucius Desha, all of Harrison county. M Sept. 15, 1857. OR 9/19.

William Cook to Miss Mary Howe, both of Lexington. M Sept. 16, 1857. OR 9/23.

John C. Bonnycastle, U.S.A., to Miss Harriet B. Everett, daughter of Isaac Everett, of Jefferson county. M Sept. 22, 1857. OR 9/26.

Alfred W. Douglass to Miss Eliza Laffoon, of Jessamine county. M Oct. 1, 1857. OR 10/3.

William H. Woolums to Miss Ann Maria Sinclair, both of Lexington. M Sept. 29, 1857. OR 10/3.

A. B. D. Allen, of Chicago, to Miss Jennie Duvall, daughter of Alexander Duvall, of Lexington, Ky. M Oct. 1, 1857. OR 10/3.

Rev. William C. Handy, of Somerset county, Maryland, to Miss Marie Preston, daughter of the Rev. Dr. R. J. Breckinridge. M at Braedabane, Fayette county, Oct. 1, 1857. OR 10/3.

Dr. Thomas E. Broaddus to Miss Kate Gaines Mahan, both of Kentucky. M at the Meghee Methodist Church, New Orleans, Oct 1, 1857. OR 10/14.

Charles Edwin Erwin to Eveline A., youngest daughter of Beverly A. Hicks, of Fayette county. M Oct. 13, 1857. OR 10/17.

William W. Lonney, of Lexington, to Miss Catharine E., daughter of Hugh Paul, of Woodford county. M Oct. 15, 1857. OR 10/17.

Benijah Bosworth to Miss Mary Cloud, both of Fayette county. M Oct. 15, 1857. OR 10/17.

George V. Ward, of Scott county, to Miss Maria L. Williams, daughter of Minor Williams, formerly of Scott county, Ky. M in Randolph county, Mo., Sept. 27, 1857. OR 10/17.

J. P. Shortridge, of New Orleans, to Miss Mary, eldest daughter of Richard M. Johnson. M Oct. 1, 1857. OR 10/17.

Lieut. William T. Welcker, U.S.A., to Miss Katy Adair, daughter of Gen. John Adair. M at Astoria, Oregon Territory, July 23, 1857. OR 10/17.

Daniel M. Griffith, of Owensboro, to Miss Jennie S., daughter of Col. C. S. Todd, of Shelby county. M latter place, Oct. 14, 1857. OR 10/21.

A. W. Long, of Mo., to Clara M., fourth daughter of R. Malone Raymond, of Cincinnati, formerly of Dublin, Ireland. M in St. Louis, at Barnum's Hotel, in October (?), 1857. The groom was formerly from Versailles, Ky. OR 10/21.

Charles G. Wintersmith, of Elizabethtown, to Miss Emily, daughter of Ralph Cotton. M in Nelson county, Oct. 15, 1857. OR 10/21.

C. W. Browne to Miss Lucie A. Harris, both of Jessamine county. M Nov. 7, 1857. OR 11/11.

G. B. Hill to Miss Martha A. Overstreet, both of Jessamine county. M Nov. 3, 1857. OR 11/11.

J. W. Harris, of Jessamine county, to Miss Bettie Walter, of Garrard county. M Nov. 4, 1857. OR 11/11.

A. Keene Richards to Miss Sallie, daughter of the late Edmond P. Pope, of Louisville. M in Scott county, Oct. 15, 1857. OR 10/24.

John Roach, of Indianapolis, to Miss Maria Wright, of Fayette county, Ky. M Oct. 20, 1857. OR 10/24.

Col. Matt. Martin, of Shelbyville, Tenn., to Miss Amelia E., daughter of the Rev. M. M. Henkle. M in Murfreesboro, Tenn., Oct. 15, 1857. OR 10/24.

Thomas J. Montague, of Fayette county, to Miss Joanna E. Wolverton, daughter of Silas Wolverton, of Lexington. M Oct. 27, 1857. OR 10/28.

James Searees to Miss Lizzie Wallace, both of Lexington. M Oct. 27, 1857. OR 10/31.

John E. Frazer, of Fayette county, Ky., to Miss Maria L. Hanly, daughter of T. B. Hanly, of Arkansas, and granddaughter of Major John H. Hanly. M in Jessamine county, Ky., Oct. 22, 1857. OR 11/4.

Charles P. Talbott, Representative elect from Bourbon county, to Miss Bettie, daughter of Wesley Sparks, of Harrison and formerly of Bourbon county. M Oct. 31, 1857. OR 11/7.

J. M. Daniels to Miss Rosaline Bowie, both of Lexington. M Nov. 5, 1857. OR 11/11.

Edmund J. Thomas to Miss Mary R. Timberlake, daughter of H. H. Timberlake, of Louisville. M November 3, 1857. OR 11/11.

Thomas A. Hoover to Mary C. Smith, of Jessamine county. M Nov. 10, 1857. OR 11/14.

John G. Troutman, of Bourbon county, to Miss Esther Mary Logan, daughter of David Logan, of Fayette county. M latter place, Nov. 10, 1857. OR 11/14.

Brice C. Randall, M. D., to Eleanora, daughter of James March. M in Lexington, Nov. 10, 1857. OR 11/14.

William F. Pullen to Miss Mary Hanna Neale. M in Georgetown, Scott county, Nov. 11, 1857. OR 11/14.

Noah D. Bell, of Keokuk, Iowa, formerly of Lexington, Kentucky, to Miss Harriet G., eldest daughter of William P. Warfield, of Memphis, Tenn. M latter place, Nov. 10, 1857. OR 11/18.

John Hammon, of Mortonsville, Mo., to Mrs. Margaret J. Kidd, of Lexington, Ky. M Nov. 12, 1857. OR 11/21.

Richard T. Elmore to Mrs. Cyrenia Waller, both of Jessamine county. M

Nov. 12, 1857. OR 11/21.

Horace H. Brand to Miss Rebecca Wilson, eldest daughter of B. S. Wilson, all of Boonville, Mo. M Nov. 5, 1857. OR 11/25.

Matthew A. Kenney, of Fayette county, Ky., to Miss Harriet B. Stacy, daughter of Matthew Stacy, of Jacksonville, Ill. M latter place, Nov. 5, 1857. OR 11/14.

John R. Sharpe, of Maysville, to Miss Lizzie, eldest daughter of George W. Norten. M Oct. (?) 27, 1857. OR 11/25.

Robert Scott, of Spencer county, to Miss Sarah J. Lindsay, of Jessamine county. M Nov. 25, 1857. OR 11/28.

Benjamin M. Chambers to Miss Melissa Cannon, both of Scott county. M Nov. 27, 1857. OR 11/28.

Wesley Fowler, of Madison county, to Miss Mary Mildred Carr, of Fayette. M Nov. 27, 1857. OR 11/28.

Daniel Scott, of the "National House," Winchester, to Miss Sallie Watts, of the same place. M there, Nov. 25, 1857. OR 11/28.

Dr. Lewis Craig, of New Jersey, to Miss Mary D., daughter of G. Drummond Hunt, of Fayette county, Ky. M Dec. 1, 1857. OR 12/2.

James March to Mrs. Harriet A. Dunlap, both of Lexington. M Dec. 1, 1857. OR 12/2.

Honorable Z. Wheat, one of the Judges of the Appellate Court of Kentucky, to Miss Anna M., daughter of Dr. Ben. Logan, of Shelby county. M there Dec. 1, 1857. OR 12/5.

Charles H. Christian, of the Isle of Man, England, to Miss Harriet Chester, daughter of Bishop Smith. M at Kalerama, Dec. 2, 1857. OR 12/5.

Major A. Bean, of Clark county, Ky., to Miss Anna W., daughter of George Buckner, of Lexington, Mo., formerly of Covington, Kentucky. M at the former place, Nov. 26, 1857. OR 12/9.

Dr. J. J. Sturgus, of Cleveland, Ohio, formerly of Fayette county, Ky., to Miss Maria E. McNulty, of Mansfield, Ohio. M latter place, Dec. 1, 1857. OR 12/9.

James W. T. Elliott to Miss Margaret Harrison, both of Lexington. M Dec. 10, 1857. OR 12/12.

William G. Cogar, of Jessamine county, to Mrs. Kitty A. Fretwell, daughter of John Hildreth, of Bourbon county. M Dec. 8, 1857. OR 12/12.

John G. Peck, of Lexington, to Miss Elizabeth B. Smith, of Louisville. M Dec. 9, 1857. OR 12/12.

William H. Hoover, of Jessamine county, to Miss Sarah A. Evans, of Garrard county. M Nov. 26, 1857. OR 12/16.

E. S. Craig, of Louisville, to Miss Eliza P. Mason, of Nelson county. M Dec 10, 1857. OR 12/16.

Major W. H. Lee, of Mississippi, to Miss Emma, daughter of Dr. J. W. Knight, of Louisville, Ky. M Dec. 9, 1857. OR 12/16.

Joseph Downing to Miss Lucy Wilson, both of Fayette county. M December 15, 1857. OR 12/16.

Ben. Warfield, of Fayette county, to Miss Eliza, eldest daughter of the late John O. Cochran, of Louisville. M Dec. 17, 1857. OR 12/19.

James P. Rogers to Miss Emeline D. Fontaine, daughter of A. B. Fontaine, all of Louisville. M Dec. 17, 1857. OR 12/19.

Cuthbert Powell, of Paducah, to Miss Sue, second daughter of the Hon. Archibald Dixon. M in Henderson, Ky., Dec. 17, 1857. OR 12/23.

Richard Higgins, of Lexington, Ky., to Miss Lizzie Gibson, daughter of Gideon Gibson, of Warren county, Miss. M Dec. 8, 1857. OR 12/26.

R. J. Aubry to Mrs. Sarah A. Briggs, both of Lexington. M Dec. 22, 1857. OR 12/26.

John M. Fishback to Miss Julia, daughter of John D. Gault, all of Clark county. M Dec. 17, 1857. OR 12/26.

James E. Evans, of Winchester, Ky., to Miss Maggie A., eldest daughter of John Stillfield, formerly of Lexington, Ky. M in Clinton county, Mo., Dec. 10, 1857. OR 1/2/1858.

John Payne, of Woodford county, to Miss Fannie Halley, daughter of Samuel H. Halley, of Scott county. M Dec. 15, 1857. OR 1/6/1858.

George Steinhaver, of Jessamine county, to Miss Catherine Viwi, of Lexington. M Dec. 20, 1857. OR 1/6/1858.

William McDowell to Miss Henrietta, daughter of William Simpson. M near Nicholasville, Dec. 31, 1857. OR 1/6/1858.

Col. John Allen, of Shelby county, to Miss Ruth Thomas, of Spencer county M Dec. 20, 1857. OR 1/6/1858.

John Taylor Moore, of Scott county, to Miss Mollie Muir, of Fayette county. M Dec. 24, 1857. OR 1/9/1858.

Charles W. Dodd, of Lexington, to Miss Elizabeth Butler, of Cincinnati. M Dec. 31, 1857. OR 1/9/1858.

B. F. Watts, of Fayette county, to Miss Emma J. Cotts, formerly of Mass. M at the Spencer House, Cincinnati, Dec. 4, 1857. OR 1/9/58.

J. E. Moorman, of Springfield, Ohio, to Miss Sophronia, daughter of M. M. Hersman, formerly of Fayette county, Ky. M in Versailles, Illinois, Dec. 31, 1857. OR 1/13/1858.

A. A. Ward to Miss Lizzie Ware, both of Cynthiana. M Dec. 30, 1857. OR 1/16/1858.

Thomas Turner, of Mt. Sterling, to Miss Henrietta Robinson, of Montgomery county. M former place at the residence of the bride's father, Dec. 31, 1857. OR 1/20/1858.

R. T. Posey to Miss Letitia Shelby Russell, daughter of Robert H. Russell, all of Burnett county, Texas. M Dec. 30, 1857, at the residence of Antoine Come, in St. Mary's Parish, La. The bride was the granddaughter of Col. C. S. Todd, of Shelby county, Ky. OR 1/23/1858.

Andrew M. Stephenson, formerly of Woodford county, Ky., to Miss Maria E. Gardner, formerly of Arkansas. M in Suisum, California, Dec. 3, 1857. OR 1/27/1858.

James C. Barkley, formerly of Lexington, Ky., to Miss Linna C. Warren, daughter of Thomas Warren, of Chillicothe, Mo. M at latter place, Dec. 24, 1857. OR 2/13/1858.

Col. W. H. Bronston, of Richmond, to Miss Nannie Baily, of Newport. M Jan. 5, 1858. OR 1/9.

Joseph Bryan, of Fayette county, to Miss Mary M. Gist, of New Castle, Ky. M Jan. 5, 1858. OR 1/19.

John C. Marshall to Mrs. Susan M. Crutchfield, daughter of Thomas Winn, of Hickman county. M in Louisville, Jan. 13, 1858. OR 1/16.

W. S. Downey, of Clark county, to Mrs. Emma J. Burbridge, of Scott county. M Jan. 20, 1858. OR 1/23.

Benjamin F. Nunnelly, of Lexington, to Miss Mary S. Ball, of Versailles. M latter place, at the residence of Mrs. Susan Ball, on January 21, 1858. OR 1/23.

Porter D. Hunt to Miss Anna M. Beard, both of Cincinnati. M Jan. 19, 1858. OR 1/23.

Jesse Moore to Miss Priscilla C. Wharton, both of Woodford county. M Jan. 21, 1858, at the residence of Joseph Wharton. OR 1/27.

Lieut. Thomas F. Smith, of the United States Army, to Miss Blanche Weissinger, daughter of the late G. W. Weissinger, of Louisville. M Jan. 21, 1858. OR 1/28.

Henry W. Gray to Miss Mary E. Peers, daughter of the late Rev. Benjamin P. Peers, for many years a resident of Lexington. M at the Christ Church, Louisville, Jan. 21, 1858. OR 1/27.

Rev. W. W. Hill, of Louisville, to Miss M. J. Smith, daughter of the late Rev. James T. Smith. M in Danville, Jan. 21, 1858. OR 1/27.

William M. Drake, of Jessamine county, to Miss Martha J., daughter of David Crozer, of Danville. M Jan. 21, 1858. OR 1/27.

Edward E. Eagle to Miss Nannie Rodes, daughter of Waller Rodes, all of Fayette county. M Jan. 26, 1858. OR 1/27.

B. D. Johnson to Miss Betsy Ann Wilson, both of Jessamine county. M Jan. 7, 1858. OR 1/30.

Zachariah Ford to Miss Narcissa A. Reed, both of Woodford county. M Jan. 21, 1858. OR 1/30.

James W. Lillard, of Mercer county, to Miss Cynthia Ford, of Woodford county. M Jan. 21, 1858. OR 1/30.

O. J. Wilson to Miss Annabella Newman, late of Missouri. M Jan. 26, 1858. OR 1/30.

Ephraim Young to Miss Lizzie J. Wood, both of Jessamine county. M Jan. 26, 1858. OR 1/30.

Harvey W. Garrett, of Missouri, to Miss Maria Gill, of Fayette county, Ky. M at the residence of William B. Pettit, in the latter place, Feb. 2, 1858. OR 2/3.

James McIntyre, of Bourbon county, to Miss Bettie K. Lydick. M at the residence of Jacob Lydick, Feb. 4, 1858. OR 2/10.

Warren W. Bain, of Bourbon county, to Miss Fannie N. Causey, of Fayette. M Feb. 2, 1858. OR 2/13.

F. C. Wagner to Miss Martha Eaves, both of Lexington. M Feb. 14, 1858. OR 2/17.

David P. Logan to Miss Anna E., youngest daughter of Jesse Cunningham, of Hamilton county, Ohio. M Feb. 11, 1858. OR 2/17.

Stephen Lewis, of Fulton county, Illinois, to Miss Helen Johnson, daughter of General William Johnson, of Scott county, Ky. M Feb. 16, 1858. OR 2/20.

Clements Cook to Gertrude Jacob, both of Lexington. M Feb. 18, 1858. OR 2/20.

John A. Headley to Miss Susan M. Neal, both of Jessamine county. M at the residence of David Neal, there, Feb. 18, 1858.

Jos. C. S. Blackburn, of Woodford county, to Miss Theresa, daughter of Dr. C. Graham, of Danville. M at the latter place, Feb. 16, 1858. OR 2/24.

C. R. Johnson, of Arkansas, to Miss Marie Worthington, of Grand Lake. M latter place, Feb. 14, 1858. OR 2/24/1858.

J. F. Caulk to Miss Henrietta Peters, both of Montgomery county. M Feb. 23, 1858. OR 2/27.

Josiah Jordan, of Kiddville, Ky., to Miss Everin Scearce, of Mt. Sterling. M Feb. 25, 1858. OR 2/27.

J. D. Cooley to Miss America H. Scearce, both of Mount Sterling. M Feb. 25, 1858. OR 2/27. See above.

Alexander Thompson to Miss Eliza Dearinger, both of Jessamine county. M at the residence of Thomas Shields, on Feb. 23, 1858. OR 2/27.

E. H. Pahrish (Parrish?) to Miss Laura C. Poindexter, daughter of William Poindexter, all of Lexington. M Mar. 3, 1858. OR 3/6.

Benjamin Turner, of Winchester, to Miss A. G. Bryan, daughter of the late Samuel Bryan, of Fayette county. M Feb. 25, 1858. OR 3/6.

Reuben Baxter to Miss Margaret Sutton, both of Lexington. M Mar. 6, 1858. OR 3/10.

Robert McMichael to Miss Rebecca Nichols, both of Lexington. M Mar. 11, 1858. OR 3/13.

Thomas Dudley Carr, Deputy Sheriff of Fayette county, to Miss Sallie E., daughter of E. Clarke, of Lexington. M Feb. 24, 1858. OR 3/17.

G. J. Garth, of Scott county, to Miss Eddie A. Payne, daughter of Nathan Payne, of Fayette county. M in March, 1858. OR 3/20.

Prof. Charles H. Winston, of Transylvania University, Lexington, to Miss Nannie, daughter of Major John H. Steger, of Amelia county, Va. M March 16, 1858. OR 3/24.

Gabriel A. Jones to Miss Mary C., daughter of William A. Ellis, all of Louisville, and granddaughter of B. A. Hicks, of Fayette county. M at Aberdeen, Ohio, Mar. 15, 1858. OR 3/24.

Charles T. Wilson, of Cynthiana, to Miss Sallie T., daughter of John Williams, of Harrison county. M Mar. 9, 1858. OR 3/24.

Dr. L. J. Woollen, formerly of Madison, Ind., to Miss Mary, eldest daughter of George S. Van Pelt, of Wooster, Ind. M Mar. 18, 1858. OR 3/24.

Dr. Michael Faris, of Kirksville, Ky., to Miss Mary E. Mason, daughter of James F. Mason, of Houston county, Texas. M Mar. 23, 1858. OR 3/27 and 3/31.

Dr. E. O. Brown, of Brandenburg, to Miss Mary J. Crouch, daughter of the Rev. B. T. Crouch, officiating minister, of Oldham county. M Mar. 23, 1858. OR 3/31.

John P. Gray, of Springfield, Ill., to Miss Julia C. Keene, daughter of the late Marcellus Keene, of Scott county, Ky. M at the Fayette county residence of Mrs. Mary H. Cooper, Mar. 31, 1858. OR 4/3.

Robert S. Strader, of Cincinnati, to Miss Margaret G. Sims, daughter of John G. Sims, of Jessamine county, Ky. M Mar. 30, 1858. OR 4/3.

Ben. F. Ginn, of Harrison county, to Miss Mary A. Haviland, who lived at Havilandsville. M Mar. 30, 1858. OR 4/7.

James W. Johnson, of Lexington, to Miss Sardonia A. Easton, of Columbia, Mo. M Mar. 14, 1858. OR 4/7.

Capt. Joshua G. Barney, of Baltimore, Md., to Mrs. Kate B. Thruston. M in Louisville, Ky., Apr. 5, 1858. OR 4/10.

John W. Lee to Miss Frances A. Hardesty, both of Lexington. M Apr. 20, 1858. OR 4/21.

Thomas H. Parker to Miss Elizabeth A. Story, both of Lexington. M April 16, 1858. OR 4/21.

John E. Cromwell to Mrs. Elizabeth D. Metcalf, both of Fayette county. M April 20, 1858. OR 4/21.

Joshua McMichael to Miss Emma Oots, both of Lexington. M Apr. 21, 1858. OR 4/24.

Anthony McConnell to Miss Sidney F. Rees, both of Lexington. M Apr. 21, 1858. OR 4/24.

Major J. T. Tucker to Miss Mary Hood, daughter of Dr. A. Hood, all of Winchester. M Apr. 15, 1858. OR 4/24.

J. B. Steves, of Lexington, to Miss Mattie Elbert, daughter of Pollard Elbert, of Fayette county. M latter place, Apr. 27, 1858. OR 4/28.

J. H. Johnson, formerly editor of the *Cynthiana Age,* to Miss Bettie McMillan, daughter of Dr. A. F. McMillan, of Fayette county. M at the Spencer House, Cincinnati, Apr. 27, 1858. OR 5/1.

Dr. Theophilus Steele to Miss Sophonisba Preston, daughter of the officiating minister, Dr. R. J. Breckinridge. M at Braedalbane, Apr. 29, 1858. OR 5/1.

Rev. William Chauncey Langdon, of Philadelphia, to Miss H. Agnes Courtney, of Baltimore. M former place, Apr. 27, 1858. OR 5/5.

Theodore F. Candy to Miss Mary E. F. Wood, both of Lexington. M May 2, 1858. OR 5/5.

John A. Bell, editor of the *Georgetown Gazette,* to Miss Nolie Elliott. M at the Scott county residence of the bride's uncle, Dr. F. F. Elliott, May 6, 1858. OR 5/10.

Benjamin F. Hardesty to Miss Mary F., daughter of David L. Zimmerman, all of Lexington. M May 25, 1858. OR 5/26.

Charles J. Gilbert, of Fayette county, to Miss Mary E. Oots, daughter of Sampson Oots, of Lexington. M Apr. 25, 1858. OR 5/29.

George A. Shelby, of Lexington, to Miss Mary F. Allen, of Bourbon county. M May 27, 1858, at the Paris Hotel, Paris. OR 5/29.

L. A. Thomas, of Frankfort, Ky., to Miss Ellen M. Polk, of Shelby county, Ky. M in St. Louis, Mo., May 26, 1858. OR 6/2.

Henry Cohen to Miss S. M. Berry, niece of Carter Berry, both of Fayette county. M May 20, 1858. OR 6/9.

Dr. J. J. Wilson to Miss Mollie E. Boyd, both of Lexington. M June 10, 1858. OR 6/12.

Wilson David to Miss Ellen Sims, both of Bourbon county. M in Lexington, June 8, 1858. OR 6/12.

E. T. Stetson to Mrs. Mary A. Meeker, both of the ''Excelsior Dramatic Company''. M in Salvisa, Mercer county, June 7, 1858. OR 6/16.

Samuel F. Maguire, of Danville, to Miss Melinda J., daughter of John H. Wallace, of Fayette county. M June 17, 1858. OR 6/19.

Col. William E. McCann, of Fayette county, to Miss Bettie, daughter of James Anderson, of Garrard county. M June 23, 1858. OR 6/26.

Robert Dejarnett, of Fayette county, to Miss Eliza Ann, daughter of Robert Langston, of Bourbon county. M June 24, 1858. OR 7/3.

John McReynolds, of Osawatomie, Kansas, to Miss Sallie Louisa, only daughter of Percival Gaugh, of Bloomington, Illinois, and formerly of Lexington, Ky. M June 28, 1858. OR 7/7.

Ambrose Ellis to Miss Catharine T. Brown, both of Lexington. M July 6, 1858. OR 7/7.

D. D. Waldo, of New York, to Miss Mary M. Davis, of Frankfort, Ky. M July 5, 1858, at the residence of James C. Davis (of Fayette county, Ky.?). OR 7/7.

Rev. Herman H. Allen, of Cynthiana, to Miss Nannie J. Thayer, of Danville. M July 6, 1858, at the residence of the Hon. John L. Bridges. OR 7/10.

William H. Edwards to Miss Mary H. Ferguson, both of Woodford county. M there, at the residence of the bride's father, in July, 1858. OR 7/10.

Edmond R. Norris, of St. Louis, to Miss Ann E. Martin. M in Fayette county, Ky., July 1, 1858. OR 7/10.

John Robertson to Miss Mary Wilson, both of Lexington. M July 13, 1858. OR 7/14.

A. Harwood, formerly of Lexington, Ky., to Miss Isabella D., daughter of W. P. Boyd, late of Flemingsburg, Ky. M in Bloomington, Ill., June 22, 1858. OR 7/17.

Benjamin F. Dunn to Miss George Ann Horine, daughter of Dr. Henry

Horine, all of Lexington. M July 15, 1858. OR 7/17.

Col. Robert S. Bullock, of Fayette county, Ky., to Miss Mary Franklin, of Bloomington, Ill. M latter place, July 15, 1858. OR 7/24.

James F. Keiser to Miss Eleanor O., daughter of Col. B. B. Taylor, all of Lexington. M July 27, 1858. OR 7/28.

Dr. H. W. P. Junius, of Lexington, to Miss Margaret P. Elbert, of Fayette county. M July 29, 1858. OR 7/31.

Capt. J. O. Shelby to Miss Bettie Shelby, both of Lafayette county, Mo. M at Waverly, Mo., July 22, 1858. OR 7/31.

Alex F. Denny, of Huntsville, Mo., to Miss Sophia E. Pitts, daughter of the officiating minister, Rev. Y. R. Pitts. M in Scott county, Ky., July 20, 1858. OR 7/31.

James B. Hutchinson to Miss Sarah F. Robertson, both of Sandersville. M August 1, 1858. OR 8/4.

Charles H. Hutchinson to Miss Ann Maria Peel, both of Sandersville. M August 2, 1858. OR 8/4.

Alexander Green to Miss Sarah Ann Webb, both of Sandersville. M August 3, 1858. OR 8/4.

Col. J. D. Pollard, of Lexington, to Miss Nannie E. Horine, daughter of H. N. Horine, of Fayette county. M Aug. 10, 1858. OR 10/14.

B. Gratz Brown, editor of the *St. Louis Democrat,* to Miss Mary Gunn, of Jefferson city, Mo. M there, Aug. 12, 1858. OR 8/18.

Charles Ripley, of Louisville, Ky., to Mrs. Margaret Drake, daughter of the late Henry Breckinridge, of Jefferson county, Ky. M at the Washington City residence of Governor Floyd, Aug. 13, 1858. OR 8/21.

W. H. Roberts, of Elkton, Todd county, to Miss Martha A., daughter of Woodson Bryan, of Fayette county. M Aug. 26, 1858. OR 9/1.

Robert S. Hopkins, of Payne's Depot, Scott county, to Miss Alice V. Dunnington, of Bourbon county. M Aug. 31, 1858. OR 9/4.

William Masner to Miss Margaret Davis, daughter of George Davis, all of Lexington. M Sept. 2, 1858. OR 9/4.

R. P. Ashurst, of Lexington, Ky., to Miss Virginia, daughter of James H. Ware, of Lexington, Mo. M Sept. 7, 1858. OR 9/11.

Abraham Harp, of Fayette county, to Miss Mary J. Dennison, of Bourbon county. M Sept. 6, 1858. OR 9/11.

Daniel McIntyre, of Fayette county, to Miss Lucinda Lyter, of Bourbon county. M Sept. 8, 1858. OR 9/11.

William Henry Johnson, of Warren county, Miss., to Miss Lucy Berry, daughter of Capt. Henry Berry, of Fayette county, Ky. M Sept. 16, 1858. OR 9/22.

John H. Harrison, of New Orleans, to Miss Sallie H., daughter of Richard Allen, of Fayette county, Ky. M Sept. 22, 1858. OR 9/25.

Zeph Morris, of Lexington, to Miss M. E. Spence, of Warsaw, Ky. M latter place, Sept. 14, 1858. OR 9/25.

William Highfield, Conductor on the Lexington and Danville Railroad, to Miss Virginia Welch, of Nicholasville. M Sept. 21, 1858. OR 9/25.

W. B. Tarlton, of Fayette county, to Miss Sue Corbin, of Scott county. M Sept. 23, 1858. OR 9/29.

William Wilson to Miss Elizabeth Taylor. M in Grant county, Sept. 26, 1858. OR 9/29.

F. R. Neale, Jr., of Woodford county, to Miss Laura, daughter of William R. Logan, of Fayette county. M Sept. 28, 1858. OR 10/2.

Joseph S. Woolfolk, of Woodford county, to Mrs. Lucy D. Craig, of Lexington. M Sept. 30, 1858. OR 10/2.

John D. Smith, of Clark county, to Miss Mary, daughter of E. H. Parrish, of Scott county. M Sept. 29, 1858. OR 10/2.

James C. Davis, of Fayette county, to Miss Eliza A. Parrish, of Columbia, Mo. M at the Jessamine county, Ky., residence of John Robinson, Sept. 23, 1858. OR 10/6.

Dr. E. S. Talbert, of Lexington, Ky., to Miss Charlotte D., daughter of Col. Jonathan Brownell, of Little Compton, R. I. M Sept. 28, 1858. OR 10/9.

Thomas P. Dudley, Jr., of Madison county, son of Ambrose Dudley, to Miss Mollie S. Gentry, daughter of Dr. J. B. Gentry, of Frankfort. M on Sept. 23, 1858. OR 10/9.

Squire C. Gaines to Anna E. Thomson, both of Fayette county. M Oct 5, 1858. OR 10/9.

Alex. S. Miller, of Bourbon county, to Miss Ann C. Pelham, of Mason county. M Oct. 5, 1858. OR 10/9.

E. P. Byrne, of Woodville, Miss., to Miss Sue V., daughter of the Hon. John Joyes, of Louisville, Ky. M later place, Oct. 6, 1858. OR 10/13.

Samuel Walker, of Covington, to Miss Amanda, daughter of Governor C. S. Morehead. M at the Church of Ascension, Frankfort, October 7, 1858. OR 10/13.

George W. Bonnell to Miss Henrietta Downing, both of Lexington. M October 14, 1858. OR 10/16.

John McGilaway, of Philadelphia, to Miss Margaret Claney, of Lexington, Ky. M latter place. Oct. 11, 1858. OR 10/16.

Robert W. Brown, of Versailles, to Miss Mary C., daughter of John H Hart, of Fayette county. M at "Hartland Place," residence of the bride's father, October 14, 1858. OR 10/16.

William R. Taylor to Miss Emily Preston, both of Fayette county. M at the residence of John Hukill, Oct. 14, 1858. OR 10/16.

M. D. Armstrong, of Fayette county, to Miss Arte M. Lewis, daughter of John Lewis, of Lexington. M October 21, 1858. OR 10/23.

Jeremiah Tarlton to Miss Fannie D. Lawson, niece of David Lawson, both of Fayette county. M October 21, 1858. OR 10/23.

Gill Eve Belles to Miss Fannie A. Morehead, daughter of Charles R. Morehead, cashier of the Farmers' Bank, Lexington, Mo. M October 14, 1858. OR

10/23.

M. S. Dowden, of Lexington, to Miss Julia, daughter of Jesse Cannon, of Scott county. M Oct. 21, 1858. OR 10/23.

Edwin A. Ford, of Nashville, Tenn., to Miss Lida, daughter of Dr. Samuel Breck, of Huntsville, Ala. M at the Richmond, Ky., residence of the Hon. David Breck, Oct. 26, 1858. OR 10/30.

Abraham Langston, of Bourbon county, to Miss Emilia J. Dejarnett, daughter of G. H. Dejarnett, of Fayette county. M Oct. 28, 1858. OR 10/30.

James Vanmeter to Miss Fannie Lewis, daughter of Thornton Lewis, both of Clark county. M Oct. 28, 1858. OR 10/30.

James R. Dudley, of Missouri, to Miss Sarah W. Rodes, daughter of Waller Rodes, of Fayette county. M Oct. 28, 1858. OR 11/3.

William Robertson to Miss Elizabeth J. Lyons, both of Lexington. M October 28, 1858. OR 11/3.

Daniel Cowgill, of Fayette county, to Miss ————— Payne, of Woodford county. M October 21, 1858. OR 11/3.

Gen. Armstead Blackwell, of Clark county, to Miss Sally, daughter of F. G. Murphy, of near Bardstown. M latter place October 28, 1858. OR 11/3.

Samuel C. Bull to Miss Jacqueline Page, daughter of Thomas S. Page, all of Frankfort. M Oct 28, 1858. OR 11/3.

Darwin W. Johnson, of Scott county, to Miss Lucy Jacob, daughter of the late John J. Jacob, of Louisville. M at Ashland, residence of the Hon. James B. Clay, October 28, 1858. OR 11/3.

William Willis Penney, of Randolph county, Mo., son of John H. Penney, formerly of Lexington, Ky., to Miss Mary J. Morris, of Howard county, Mo., daughter of the late Judge John P. Morris, of Glasgow, Mo. M at the residence of Capt. J. Finks, Sept. 20, 1858. OR 11/3.

Otho W. Harding, of Shelby county, to Miss S. B. Morrow, daughter of P. B. Morrow, of Versailles. M in Jefferson county, Oct. 28, 1858. OR 11/3.

William H. Fagan to Miss Kittie, daughter of John W. Craig, all of Louisville. M November 2, 1858. OR 11/6.

John Maupin to Miss Mary Turley, both of Montgomery county. M October 14, 1858. OR 11/6.

Jesse Burbridge, of Pike county, Mo., to Miss Mary C., daughter of John Lingenfelter, of Fayette county, Ky. M Oct. 27, 1858. OR 11/6.

L. P. Milward to Miss Lizzie L., daughter of Jos(eph) B. Cooper, all of Lexington. M Nov. 4, 1858. OR 11/6.

Thomas W. Morton, of Paducah, to Miss Elizabeth Norton Clarke, daughter of John Clarke, of Fayette county. M Nov. 4, 1858. OR 11/10.

David B. Elrod, of Versailles, to Miss Carrie George, of Lexington. M October 26, 1858. OR 11/10.

W. W. Dowden, of Lexington, to Miss Nannie A., daughter of John Shryock, of Woodford county. M Nov. 11, 1858. OR 11/13.

Harvey C. Graves, Jr., of Fayette county, to Miss Maggie Kennedy, of Carlisle, Nicholas county. M September 30, 1858. OR 11/13.

E. F. Holloway, of Richmond, to Miss Rosa Moberly, daughter of William J. Moberly, of Mercer county. M Nov. 9, 1858. OR 11/17.

Elder John F. Johnson, of Monteray, Indiana, to Mrs. Rebecca T. Lewis, of Fayette county, Ky. M Nov. 18, 1858. OR 11/20.

Hugh W. Paul, of Woodford county, to Miss Catharine Lonney, of Lexington. M November 18, 1858. OR 11/20.

James H. Kitsen to Mrs. Amanda Tribble, both of Henry county. M November 14, 1858. OR 11/20.

P. B. Eubanks, of Clark county, to Miss Susan Maples, of Estill county. M at the Estill county residence of Isaac Mise, Nov. 16, 1858. OR 11/20.

George W. Alford, of Lexington, to Miss Laura V. Chiles, of Fayette county. M latter place, at the residence of D. S. Coleman, on November 18th, 1858. OR 11/20.

M. V. Daniels to Miss Elizabeth Hebener, both of Lexington. M Nov. 19, 1858. OR 11/24.

Edwin Murray to Miss Cordelia Wade, both of Lexington. M Nov. 16, 1858. OR 11/24.

John R. Wardle, of New Orleans, to Miss Susan M. Fleming, of Lexington, Ky. M. Dec. 2, 1858. OR 12/4.

Edmund Barr, of Fayette county, Ky., to Miss Fannie A. Montague, of Cincinnati. M latter place, Nov. 30, 1858. OR 12/4.

Rev. John W. Cracraft, of Gambier, Ohio, to Mrs. Louise D. Burrows, daughter of Col. Ambrose Dudley, of Cincinnati. M Dec. 1, 1858. OR 12/4.

John M. Rea to Miss Eliza Jane Foot, of Bourbon county. M Nov. 16, 1858. OR 12/4.

George T. Gaines, of Boone county, Ky., to Miss Sue R. Harrison, daughter of the officiating minister, Rev. J. C. Harrison. M in Covington, November 30, 1858. OR 12/8.

Ambrose J. Dudley to Miss Sue Gilbert, both of Madison county. M there, at the residence of J. G. Gilbert, Dec. 1, 1858. OR 12/8.

James M. Barkley to Miss Lucy A. Lancaster. M at Keene, Ky., Oct. 14, 1858. OR 12/8.

H. H. Vandyke, of Mercer county, to Miss Jane E. Lancaster, of Jessamine county. M at the residence of M. M. Lancaster, Nov. 11, 1858. OR 12/8.

F. S. Wilson to Miss Sarah A. Egbert, both of Woodford county. M Nov. 18, 1858. OR 12/8.

C. McDavitt, of Keene, to Miss Ellen Holbert, of Jessamine county. M. Nov. 25, 1858. OR 12/8.

James R. Page to Miss Mollie Ford, daughter of Col. A. G. Hodges, all of Frankfort. M there December 8, 1858. OR 12/11.

Lieut. George H. Mendell, U. S. Army, to Miss Ellen, daughter of General

John Adair, of Astoria, Oregon Territory, formerly of Kentucky. M at Astoria, October 8, 1858. OR 12/15.

1858

Dr. R. S. Smythe, of Virginia, to Miss Lucy V. Parrish, daughter of Caleb Parrish, of Clark County, Ky. M December 14, 1858. OR 12/18.

Dr. John Thruston to Miss Ellen Pope, daughter of the late Hon. Patrick H. Pope. M in Louisville, Dec. 13, 1858. OR 12/18.

George W. Johnston, of Woodford county, to Mrs. George Ann Willis, of Versailles. M Dec. 14, 1858. OR 12/18.

Moses G. Young, of Fayette county, to Miss Elizabeth McIsaacs, of Lexington. M latter place, Dec. 16, 1858. OR 12/18.

Jacob Ott to Miss Mollie Brisby, both of Lexington. M Dec. 15, 1858. OR 12/18.

James F. Wyatt to Miss Mary M., daughter of Henry Lancaster, all of Lexington. M December 16, 1858. OR 12/18.

J. P. Saseen, of Paducah, to Miss Mollie Towles, daughter of Thomas Towles, of Henderson. M latter place, Dec. 15, 1858. OR 12/22.

Edward P. Shelby, of Kentucky, to Miss Susan G., daughter of David P. Hart, of Buchanan county, Mo., formerly of Fayette county, Ky. M December 4, 1858. OR 12/22.

William F. Prewitt, of Montgomery county, to Miss Mary Gateskill, of Clark county. M Dec. 14, 1858. OR 12/22.

Rev. E. H. Rutherford, of Vicksburg, Miss., to Miss Jane R. Young, daughter of the late Rev. John C. Young. M in Danville, Ky.

George F. Miller to Mrs. Pernelia Noel, both of Lexington. M Dec. 21, 1858. OR 12/25.

Henry B. Bissell to Miss Ada, daughter of Robert Chalfant, both of Cincinnati. M December 21, 1858.

William S. Rule, of Lexington, to Miss Mary L. Barber, of Pennsylvania. M at the former place, Dec. 29, 1858. OR 1/4/59.

J. E. Wintermote, of Tennessee, to Miss Maria J. Vanpelt, of Lexington, Ky. M at the latter place Feb. 16, 1859. OR 2/18.

William Hukill, of Bourbon county, to Miss Elizabeth Mitchell, of Henry county. M Mar. 8, 1859. OR 3/11.

William H. Able, of Jefferson county, to Miss Catherine Able, of Henry county. M Mar. 8, 1859. S 3/11.

James N. Prather, of Mercer county, to Miss Nannie H., daughter of Dr. David Bell, of Lexington. M Mar. 17, 1859. S 3/22.

1859

William C. P. Breckinridge, son of Rev. R. J. Breckinridge, to Miss Lucretia, daughter of Thomas H. Clay. M at Mansfield, near Lexington, March 17, 1859. S 3/22.

M. H. Kendall to Miss Eliza, eldest daughter of the late Dr. H. B. Lary, of Louisiana, all of Bourbon county, Ky. M at the residence of Daniel Lary, Mar.

15, 1859. S 3/22.

James Shearer, Jr., to Miss Mary E. Simmons, both of Madison county. M there, at the residence of Josiah P. Simmons, Mar. 3, 1859. S 3/22.

Dr. Edmund J. Peckover, of Paris, to Miss Jennie E. Ridgley, daughter of Richard H. Ridgley, of Nicholasville. M at the Spencer House, Cincinnati, in March, 1859. S 3/22.

James O. Smith to Miss Sallie Burch, both of Scott county. M Mar. 10, 1859. S 3/29.

John C. Payne, of Scott county, to Miss Jennie L. Embry, of Fayette county. M Mar. 22, 1859. S 3/29.

Simon Straus, of Lexington, Ky., to Miss Regina Goldsmith, of Grunstadt, State of Rhine, Bavaria. M at Frankfort on the Meine, Germany, in March or April, 1859. S 4/26.

William R. Fleming, of Philadelphia, to Miss Lizzie W. Hood. M in Scott county, April 12, 1859. S 4/26.

William R. Logan, of Fayette county, to Mrs. Sena Muir, of Bourbon county. M Apr. 19, 1859. S 4/26.

James N. Campbell to Miss Lucy J. Ferguson, daughter of Mrs. N. K. Ferguson, all of Fayette county. M May 19, 1859. S 5/20.

Thomas Hewson, formerly of Madison, Ind., to Miss M. Kate Van Pelt, of Lexington, Ky. M at the latter place June 2, 1859. S 6/3.

H. B. Searcy, of Lexington, to Miss Sarah Allcott, of Covington. M June 8, 1859. S 6/10.

Samuel F. Maguire, of Danville, to Miss Malinda J. Wallace, of Fayette county. M June 17, 1859. S 6/18.

Felix L. Bosworth to Miss Sallie, only daughter of Dr. B. P. Drake, of Lexington. M June 21, 1859. S 6/21.

William W. Featherston to Miss Maggie J. Cassell, of Fayette county. M June 9, 1859. S 6/21.

Robert A. Athey, formerly of Lexington, to Miss Elizabeth J. Wallace, both of Covington. M June 30, 1859. S 7/7.

B. W. Symonds, late of Lexington, Ky., to Miss Hanna Dyer. M at the Galveston, Texas, residence of Joseph Osteman, July 14, 1859. S 7/19.

Capt. Ambrose P. Hill, of the U. S. Army, to Mrs. C. M. McClung. M July 19, 1859. S 7/26.

John Edge to Miss Mary Louisa Tipton, both of Lexington. M Aug. 4, 1859. S 8/9.

James W. Knight to Miss Eliza, daughter of Walter Young, both of Jessamine county. M Aug. 16, 1859. S 8/19.

Samuel W. Capps, of Scottsville, Macoupin county, Ill., and formerly of Fayette county, Ky., to Miss Abbie L. Smith, of Athensville, Green county, Ill. M in St. Louis, Mo., on Aug. 23, 1859. S 9/6.

John W. Cooper to Miss Kate Evens, eldest daughter of Joseph Evens, all of Fayette county. M Sept. 6, 1859. S 9/6.

Joseph Van Pelt, of Lexington, to Miss Sarah Ann Rucker, of Fayette county. M Sept. 18, 1859. S 9/23.

Col. Hart Gibson, of Woodford county, to Miss Mary Duncan, eldest daughter of Henry T. Duncan. M at "Duncanan," residence of the bride's father, near Lexington, Sept. 20, 1859. S 9/23.

Thomas Lyons to Miss Elizabeth Burton, both of Lexington. M Sept. 26, 1859. S 9/27.

Benjamin P. Freeman, of Mason, Ga., to Miss Catherine M. Shaw, daughter of the late Nat. Shaw, of Lexington, Ky. M Oct. 12, 1859. S 10/14.

Dr. Z. S. Gillespie, of Arkansas, to Miss Elleanor Bainbridge, daughter of Dr. Bell, of Lexington, Ky. M Oct. 19, 1859. S 10/21.

G. W. Miller, of Frankfort, to Miss Octavia Willis, of Lexington. M Oct. 27, 1859. S 10/28.

David C. Biggerstaff to Miss Mary E. Holland, both of Lexington. M Oct. 25, 1859. S 10/28.

W. D. Boswell to Miss Nannie V. Crutchfield, both of Lexington. M Nov. 3, 1859. S 11/4.

C. W. Lewis to Miss Lavina E. Johnson, both of Lexington. M Nov. 17, 1859. S 11/18.

William W. Pigg to Miss Joicy C. Sneed. M at Arrator, Pettis county, Mo., Nov. 12, 1850. S 11/18.

John E. Johnson to Miss Margaret A. Montague, both of Lexington. M Nov. 17, 1859. S 11/18.

Thomas B. Monroe, Jr., of Lexington, Ky., to Elizabeth, daughter of the Hon. R. C. Grier, of Philadelphia. M at the latter place Nov. 15, 1859. S 11/29.

1860

Richard Loud to Mrs. Mary Ann Coyner, both of Lexington. M Nov. 29, 1859. S 12/2.

Thomas J. Zimmerman to Miss Mary A. Peel, both of Lexington. M Dec. 8, 1859. S 12/13.

R. W. Cooper to Miss Elizabeth Smith, daughter of J. C. Smith, of Shelby county. M in December, 1859. S 12/16.

William W. McCoy, of Anderson county, to Miss Sallie A. Nicholas, of Lexington. M at the Lexington residence of Mr. E. Nichols, Jan. 5, 1860. S 1/6.

A. Kavanaugh to Miss Sarah Maupin, both of Madison county. M there, at the residence of D. C. Maupin, Jan. 3, 1860. S 1/6.

Stephen G. Roszel, of Baltimore, to Miss Maggie W. Morris, of Lexington, Ky. M Jan. 17, 1860. S 1/24.

John Lindsay to Miss Helen M., daughter of William G. Talbott. M at the Frankfort residence of Gen. Peter Dudley on Jan. 18, 1860. S 1/24.

W. H. Ireland, of Philadelphia, to Miss Arie E. Graves, daughter of Highland Graves. M at Mayslick, Ky., Dec. 22, 1859. S 1/24/1860.

Humphrey Marshall, Jr., to Miss Helen M. Fenwick, both of Lewis county. M Jan. 5, 1860. S 1/24.

William N. Moffett, of Cynthiana, to Miss Annie E. Vigus, of Lexington. M Jan. 25, 1860. S 1/27.

George Gessman to Miss Kate W. Miller. M in Frankfort on Jan. 24, 1860. S 1/27.

Robert Tanner, of Rapides Parish, La., to Miss Anna Adelia, daughter of Col. William Tanner. M near Mobile, Ala., Nov. 15, 1859. S 1/27.

J. B. Parisa, late of Shelby county, Ky., to Miss Hattie N. Johnson, of Clinton county, Mo. M Jan. 19, 1860. S 1/27.

John B. Campbell to Miss Ellen L. Swift, eldest daughter of Stephen Swift, of Lexington. M February 7, 1860. S' 2/10.

Thomas J. Shipp to Miss Margaret Moore, both of Bourbon county. M Feb. 7, 1860. S 2/10.

Jonathan Smith to Miss Sarah Maria, daughter of John Allison, of Bourbon county. M Feb. 3, 1860. S 2/10.

Thomas C. Froman, of Grundy county, Mo., to Miss Sally Walter, of Jessamine county, Ky. M Jan. 31, 1860. S 2/10.

Dr. John W. Whitney, of Lexington, to Miss Tomson B. Gray, of Woodford county, daughter of the late Benjamin P. Gray. M in Paducah, Feb. 9, 1860. S 2/14.

Charles L. Thompson, of St. Louis, to Miss Bettie H. Shackelford, daughter of W. H. Shackelford, of Boyle county, Ky. M at the Fayette county, Ky., residence of William Duke, Feb. 8, 1860. S 2/14.

E. S. Muir to Miss Maggie A. Tarlton, both of Fayette county. M Feb. 22, 1860. S 2/28.

E. D. Muir to Miss Bettie Chrisman, daughter of Gen. H. M. Chrisman, all of Jessamine county. M at the Nicholasville Methodist Church, Feb. 22, 1860. S 2/28.

A. J. Gorham to Miss Sallie E. Wallace, both of Fayette county. M Feb. 23, 1860. S 3/1.

Benjamin O. Leonard to Kate M. Brand, youngest daughter of the late William Brand, of Lexington. M at Booneville, Mo., Feb. 7, 1860. S 3/6.

Franklin B. Taylor to Miss Bettie, daughter of Peter Evans, all of Fayette county. M Mar. 20, 1860. S 3/23.

William J. Henry, of Harrison county, to Miss J. Jouett, of Fayette county. M Mar. 1, 1860. S 3/23.

Wesley Redhead, Postmaster of Des Moines, Iowa, to Miss Anna Seymour, formerly of Shelbyville, Ky. M at former place, April 5, 1860. S 4/24.

Col. R. H. Forrester, editor of the *Maysville Express*, to Mrs. Sally F. Hamilton, of Jefferson county. M Apr. 18, 1860. S' 4/27.

J. T. Hildreth, of Scott county, to Miss Victoria Goodwin, daughter of Lloyd K. Goodwin, of Fayette county. M Apr. 5, 1860. S 4/27.

J. M. Jones, of Potter county, Mo., to Miss Minervie Hanson, of Lexington, Ky. M Apr. 20, 1860. S 5/1.

Charles H. Pettel to Miss Hannah Shreve, daughter of Thomas Steele. M Apr. 26, 1860. S 5/1.

F. K. Colyer, of Lexington, to Miss A. C. Goodloe, of Woodford county. M latter place May 1, 1860. S 5/4

G. W. Hancock to Miss Mary T. Young, both of Lexington. M May 22, 1860. S 5/25.

D. M. Bright, of Lewisburg, Va., to Miss Laura M. Fields, of Frankfort, Ky. M latter place, at the Capital Hotel, May 22, 1860. S 5/25.

Abraham B. Bowman to Miss Maria E. Garth, both of Fayette county M June 20, 1860. S 6/22.

William Klarenaar to Mrs. Eliza Wilson. M at the Catholic Church, Lexington, July 1, 1860. S 7/10.

John Berry, of Woodford county, to Miss Anne M. Gaines, daughter of Elder T. N. Gaines, of Versailles. M latter place, July 3, 1860. S' 7/13.

John Wormsley to Miss Elizabeth A. Story, both of Lexington. M July 16, 1860. S 7/17.

Capt. J. S. Shaw, of St. Louis, to Miss Mary J. Elbert, of Lexington, Ky. M July 24, 1860. S 7/24.

James J. Lipscomb, of Fayette county, to Miss Elizabeth M. B. Uttinger, of Jessamine county. M Sept. 18, 1860. S 9/25.

Thomas Thompson to Miss Ann Maria Byrnes. M Sept. 3, 1860. S 9/25.

Charles J. Sheppard, of Arkansas, to Miss Florida N., daughter of Joseph Miller, of Lexington, Ky. M Sept. 27, 1860. S' 9/28.

John Sheppard to Miss Virginia K. Fogle, both of Lexington. M Oct. 4, 1860. S 10/5.

Bryan H. Allen to Miss Mary H. Higgins, both of Lexington. M Oct. 2, 1860. S 10/9.

Joseph H. Wilson to Miss Nettie Lewis, both of Lexington. M Oct. 11, 1860. S 10/16.

Green Taulbert to Miss Elizabeth Jane, daughter of Henry Combs, all of Breathitt county. M Sept. 12, 1860. S 10/16.

Orville Biggerstaff to Miss Nannie C. Donegan, both of Lexington. M Oct. 25, 1860. S 11/2.

Edward F. Pittman, of St. Louis, to Miss Anna Harrison, daughter of George B. Harrison, of Fayette county, Ky. M latter place, Nov. 13, 1860. S 11/16.

Osmar C. Sage, of Prattsville, N. Y., to Miss Mary E., daughter of J. W Norton, of Lexington, Ky. M latter place Nov. 15, 1860. S 11/23.

P. Farrel to Miss B. McLaughlin, both of Lexington. M Nov. 30, 1860. S 12/7.

B. W. Blincoe, of Lexington, to Miss Anna R. Curtis, daughter of John Curtis, of Fayette county. M Nov. 27, 1860. S 12/11.

Major James D. Blincoe, formerly of Lexington, Ky., to Miss Mollie B. Austin, daughter of Col. Morris Austin, all of Savannah, Miss. M Nov. 10, 1860. S 12/11.

H. T. Duncan, Jr., to Miss Lily Brand, eldest daughter of George W. Brand. M at the Lexington residence of E. Macalester, Dec. 13, 1860. S 12/18.

George W. Stapleton, of Glasgow, Mo., to Miss W. J. Cornelison, of Lexington, Ky. M at the Lexington residence of James M. White, Dec. 14, 1860. OR 12/19.

1861

George W. Hamilton of Brooksville, Ky., to Miss Mattie J. W. Haviland. M at Havilandsville, Harrison county, Dec. 5, 1860. OR 12/19.

George W. Robb to Miss Lizzie, daughter of A. W. Macklin, of Franklin county. M Dec. 13, 1860. OR 12/19.

John C. Berryman to Miss Helen J. Cooper, daughter of the late Rev. Spencer Cooper, all of Fayette county. M Dec. 17, 1860, at the First Methodist Church, Lexington. OR 12/19.

Matt. F. Johnson, of Chatham, Lake Washington, Miss., to Miss Narcissa, daughter of Dr. Richard Keene, dec'd., of Louisiana, and formerly of Georgetown, Ky. M at the Grand Lake, Arkansas, residence of Benjamin Johnson, Dec. 27, 1860. S 1/8/61.

Dr. W. D. Justice to Mrs. Sophia E. Scott, daughter of Henry Croxton, of Clark county. M Jan. 30, 1861. S 2/5.

Oliver W. Gaines, Jr., of Georgetown to Miss Mollie A. Collins, of Bourbon county. M Jan. 18, 1861. S 2/5.

Allen Bashford, of Paris, to Miss Mollie Rowland. M Feb. 6, 1861, at the residence of the late Milton Rowland. S 2/15.

Elisha J. Fitch, of Fleming county, to Miss Lavina Jane Stricklett, daughter of L. C. Stricklett, of Clarksburg, Ky. M latter place Jan. 23, 1861. S 2/22.

Col. G. H. Morrow, of Paducah, to Miss Sallie Robertson, of Mt. Sterling. M Feb. 12, 1861, S 2/22.

John Webb, of LaFayette county, Mo., to Miss Lucy Webb, formerly of Kentucky. M at Lexington, Mo., Feb. 7, 1861. S 2/26.

William A. White, of Georgetown, to Miss Jennie Norwood, eldest daughter of Major John Norwood, of Fleming county. M Feb. 26, 1861. S 3/8.

John E. Jones, of Gallatin county, to Mrs. _____ Samuels, of Owen county. M Feb. 24, 1861. S 3/8.

C. H. Wollums to Miss M. J. Sinclair, both of Lexington. M Mar. 19, 1861. S 3/22.

Charles H. Hogan to Miss Elizabeth Hogan, both of Lexington. M Mar. 28, 1861. S 3/29.

H. H. Daniel, of Nicholasville, to Miss Lavina Muir, of Jessamine county. M at the Burnett House, Cincinnati, Mar. 25, 1861. S 4/2.

Samuel S. Clay, of Bourboun county, to Miss Lizzie, daughter of John M. Kimbrough, of Harrison county. M Mar. 21, 1861. S 4/2.

Werter Combs to Miss Mary E. Hagen. M April 4, 1861. (The *Kentucky Statesman* lists the groom as Peter Combs.) OR 4/10.

Robert G. Butler, of Woodford county, to Miss Julia E. Sutton, of Bourbon county. M Apr. 18, 1861. S 4/19.

A. T. Parker to Miss Virginia Oots, both of Lexington. M Apr. 23, 1861. S 4/26.

Richard West, of Scott county, to Miss A. G. Barber, daughter of the late Bejamin Gray, of Woodford county. M May 2, 1861. S 5/3.

Andrew J. Loecher to Miss Nannie Newbold, both of Lexington. M Apr. 24, 1861. S 5/3.

J. D. Trapp to Miss Hetty Chinn, both of Lexington. M at the Spencer House, Cincinnati, June 4, 1861. S 6/7.

Andrew J. Stillfield, of Lexington, to Miss Elizabeth Henderson, of Frankfort. M latter place at the residence of the bride's brother, John Henderson, in June, 1861. S 6/21.

Major Thomas Hays to Miss Sallie H. Helm, daughter of Ex-Governor John L. Helm, of Hardin county. M there July 17, 1861. S 7/23.

J. J. Coons to Miss Kitty Darnaby. M in Fayette county on Aug. 1, 1861. S 8/6.

Samuel W. Turner to Miss Mary F. Schooler, both of Lexington. M Aug. 1, 1861. S 8/13.

Joshua M. Dill to Miss Jenny Day. M in Lexington Aug. 20, 1861. S' 8/23.

William C. P. Breckinridge to Miss Issa, eldest daughter of Dr. John R. Desha. M Sept. 19, 1861. S 9/20.

John R. Briggs, of Nashville, Tenn., to Miss Ellen Harris, daughter of William Harris, of Woodford county. M at Mt. Vernon, Nov. 14, 1861. OR 11/20.

N. Frazier, of Harrison county, to Miss Kate Dunlap, daughter of T. G. Dunlap, of Shelby county. M Nov. 5, 1861. OR 11/27.

Rev. Alexander Henry to Miss Emma S. Railey, eldest daughter of Randolph Railey, of Woodford county. M Nov. 13, 1861. OR 11/27.

Rev. Herman H. Allen to Miss Mary W. Marshall, daughter of Glass Marshall, of Fayette county. M Nov. 14, 1861. OR 11/27.

Joseph V. Morton, of Shelby county, to Miss Sarah Taliaferro, of Winchester. M latter place, Nov. 18, 1861. OR 11/27.

Charles H. Morton, of Charleston, Ill., to Miss Belle Price, daughter of the late Rev. Jacob F. Price. M in Clark county, Ky., Oct. 21, 1861. OR 11/27.

1861–1863

Charles Clarke, of Mason county, to Miss Mee J. Nunn, daughter of William Nunn, of Bourbon county. M at Forest Hill, residence of William Nunn, Nov. 20, 1861. OR 11/27.

John Daily to Mrs. A. Smith. M Dec. 25, 1861. OR 12/28.

James Hutson, of Jessamine county, to Miss Susan Rucker, of Lexington. M at the residence of C. S. Wade, Dec. 24, 1861. OR 12/28.

William F. Spurgeon to Miss Mattie L. Hair, daughter of the Rev. G. M. Hair, all of Fayette county. M at Walnut Hill, Dec. 31, 1861. OR 1/22/1862.

Lafayette Cruthcher, of Woodford county, to Miss Anna Graves, daughter of Joseph Graves, of Fayette county. M Jan. 9, 1862. OR 1/11.

D. B. Patterson, of Johnson county, La., (or Iowa?) to Miss Eliza Ann, daughter of John Beatty, of Bourbon county, Ky. M latter place, Jan. 14, 1862. OR 1/18.

James H. Kerr, of Fayette county, to Miss Annie E., daughter of Dr. John H. Brooks, of Bourbon county. M Jan. 16, 1862. OR 1/18.

L. W. Laudeman, of Lexington, to Miss M. L. Lowry, of Jessamine county. M Jan. 16, 1862. OR 1/18.

Hon. Charles G. Wintersmith to Miss Malvina N. Gorin, daughter of F. Gorin, of Louisville. M Jan. 16, 1862. OR 1/22.

George Fry to Miss Annie E. Scott, both of Clark county. M Jan. 21, 1862. OR 1/22.

J. R. Meloy to Miss Rebecca Rucker, both of Lexington. M Jan. 22, 1862. OR 1/25.

John M. Duke, Jr., to Miss Sallie T. Deweese, daughter of J. Coburn Deweese, all of Maysville. M Jan. 23, 1862. OR 1/29.

Josiah T. Ashurst to Miss Laura E. Suggett, of Scott county. M there, at the residence of Wickliffe Bradley, Jan. 26, 1862. OR 2/5.

H. Clay Hutchcraft to Miss Mary E. Cunningham, both of Bourbon county. M at the residence of Thomas Cunningham, Jan. 9, 1862. OR 2/5.

James T. Shackelford, of St. Louis. Mo., to Miss Mary C. Bates, of Clark county, Ky. M at the residence of James T. Woodward, Jan. 23, 1862. OR 2/5.

F. M. Timberlake, of Lexington, Ky., to Miss Mollie B. Fry, of Brunswick, New Jersey. M at the residence of P. S. Rule, Feb. 4, 1862. OR 2/8.

Elisha Frary to Miss Abby H. Stewart, daughter of George W. Stewart, of Lexington. M Feb. 6, 1862. OR 2/8.

W. H. Guyton, Jr., to Miss Maggie T. Harris, of Mercer county. M there Feb. 6, 1862. OR 2/12.

James K. Duke, Jr., to Miss Pauline, daughter of Henry Bruce, all of Covington. M Feb. 11, 1862. OR 2/15.

Charles M. Daly, of Fayette county, to Miss Lizzie O. Moore, of Owen county. M Feb. 13, 1862. OR 2/22.

Jo. Clark to Miss Kate Lewis, both of Lexington. M Feb. 20, 1862. OR 3/1.

Elijah B. O'Neal, of Jessamine county, to Miss Mary Towles, daughter of R. D. Towles, of Woodford county. M Feb. 26, 1862. OR 3/1.

Richard A. Barrett to Miss Mary Finney, daughter of the late William Finney, all of St. Louis, Mo. M there Feb. 27, 1862. OR 3/8.

James Brown, of Scott county, to Miss Lizzie H. Morris, of Fayette. M at the Lexington residence of James Morris, Mar. 19, 1862. OR 3/22.

Alexander Jeffrey to Mrs. Rosa Vertner Johnson. M May 1, 1862. OR 5/3.

Milton W. Hudson to Miss Sarah E. Anthony, both of Fayette county. M May 1, 1862. OR 5/3.

Samuel H. Jones, of New Jersey, to Miss E. Kate Jacob, daughter of the late John I. Jacob, of Louisville, Ky. M at Ashland, home of the Hon. James B. Clay, May 1, 1862. OR 5/7.

Isaac Webb to Miss Ben Ella Gray, daughter of the late Ben P. Gray, of Woodford county. M May 8, 1862. OR 5/10.

Theodore J. Dwight, of Davenport, Iowa, to Miss Helen V., daughter of the Hon. W. A. Richardson, of Quincy, Ill. M at the latter place Apr. 27, 1862. OR 5/10.

Alfred Carr to Miss Angelica C. Yeatman, daughter of James E. Yeatman, all of St. Louis, Mo. M Apr. 29, 1862. OR 5/10.·

Robert M. Ferguson to Miss Nannie N., daughter of the late Thomas Hughes, of Fayette county. M May 15, 1862. OR 5/17.

John S. Henry to Miss Mary Elizabeth Brockman, both of Hawesville, Ky. M May 7, 1862. (OR 5/24 lists the bride as Miss Lizzie Brockman.) OR 5/17.

James C. Dillon, of Fort Wayne, Ind., to Mrs. Anna Tower, of Covington Ky. M at latter place at the residence of A. F. Woodall, Sept. 29, 1862. OR 10/29.

Henry Edwards to Miss Mary A., daughter of Charles Hoffman. M in Bourbon county, home of the bridg, Nov. 20, 1862. OR 11/22.

W. Dudley Parrish to Miss Lizzie Kingsland. M in St. Louis, Mo., Oct. 23, 1862. OR 11/26.

Joshua Neale, of Newport, to Mrs. Amanda M. Stapleton. M in Winchester Dec. 10, 1862. OR 12/13.

John B. Trussell to Miss Margaret Holman. M in Winchester, Dec. 9, 1862. OR 12/3.

William B. Holloway, of Woodford county, to Miss Alice J. Chilton, of Mercer county. M Dec. 11, 1862. OR 12/17

1863

James R. Marrs, editor and proprietor of the *Danville Tribune*, to Miss Sallie E. Jackson, daughter of Joseph Jackson, all of Danville. M Nov. 3, 1863. OR 11/11.

John G. Simrall, Jr., to Miss Cornelia S. Smith, daughter of Thomas P. Smith, of Louisville. M Nov. 3, 1863. OR 11/14.

Dr. James M. Montmollin, of Lexington, to Miss Martha F. Young, daughter of the late Dr. Archibald Young, of Jessamine county. M Nov. 11, 1863. OR 11/14.

Dr. E. M. Norwood to Miss Priscilla Downing, daughter of Richard Downing, of near Lexington. M Nov. 19, 1863. OR 11/28.

John H. Zanone to Miss Susan Norris, daughter of William Prather, of Louisville. M Nov. 11, 1863. OR 11/14.

A. D. Bishop, of Cincinnati, to Miss A. P. Ficklin, daughter of William Ficklin, of Paris, Ky. M Nov. 5, 1863. OR 11/14.

Thomas Butler, of Jessamine county, to Miss Phebe Winn, of Missouri. M at the Fayette county, Ky., residence of James Clarke, Nov. 5, 1863. OR 11/18.

A. B. Bonta to Miss Lizzie T. McDonald. M near Harrodsburg, Nov. 19, 1863. OR 11/25.

Thomas I. Harris to Miss Kate S., daughter of Mrs. Catharine Johnson, all of Frankort. M Nov. 25, 1863. OR 12/2.

James M. Jones, of Whitley county, to Miss Eliza C., daughter of William B. Holeman, of Frankfort. M Nov. 26, 1863. OR 12/2.

L. B. Faught, of Lexington, to Miss Josephine Florence Richardson, of Covington. M latter place, at the residence of the bride's brother-in-law, B. Whitney, Nov. 29, 1863. OR 12/5.

Benjamin F. Bryant, of Jessamine county, to Miss Sallie Hall, daughter of John Hall, of Shelby county. M Nov. 24, 1863. OR 12/5.

Benjamin F. Rogers, of Bourbon county, Ky., to Miss Bettie, eldest daughter of the late Hon. John Jameson, of Missouri. M at the Calloway county, Mo., residence of the bride's mother, Nov. 2, 1863. OR 12/12.

Henry W. Dunn to Miss Peggie P. Robinson, eldest daughter of Benjamin F. Robinson, all of Garrard county. M Dec. 15, 1863. OR 12/23.

Eben Milton, Jr., to Miss Emma, daughter of the late David H. Merriweather (Merriwether). M at the Jefferson county residence of Charles Tilton, Dec. 15, 1863. OR 12/23.

John Milton to Miss Laura, daughter of Lewis Smyser. M on Dec. 17, 1863. OR 12/23.

R. R. Bacon to Miss Lizzie Sneed, daughter of the late Dr. W. C. Sneed, all of Frankfort. M Dec. 16, 1863. OR 12/23.

R, L. Brown, of Nashville, Tenn., to Miss Laura Pulliam. M at Walnut Grove, Allen county, Dec. 22, 1863. OR 1/2/1864.

D. P. Bedinger, Jr., to Miss Pattie F., daughter of Major William Holloway, of Richmond. M Dec. 22, 1863. OR 1/6/1864.

C. C. Stivers to Miss Minerva Christopher. M in Lexington, Dec. 20, 1863. OR 1/9/1864.

1864

Capt. William N. Danks, of Chicago, to Miss Susia Llewellyn. M in Lexington, Ky., Jan. 4, 1864. OR 1/6.

George Lancaster, of Lexington, to Miss Josie M. Stone, daughter of Col Kissey Stone, of Bourbon county. M Jan. 5, 1864. OR 1/9.

C. C. Barbee, of Georgetown, to Miss Mollie McCann, of Carroll county. M Jan. 7, 1864. OR 1/16.

George McD. Caldwell, of Illinois, to Miss Kittie Robards, of Jessamine county, Ky. M Jan. 6, 1864. OR 1/16.

Dr. Joseph P. Letcher, of Nicholasville, to Mrs. Florida M. Price, of Clark county. M at the Clark county residence of Mrs. M. P. Price, Jan. 21, 1864. OR 1/23.

Edward Sayre, of Illinois, to Miss Mary M. Lilly, of Lexington, Ky. M Jan. 27, 1864, at the residence of her father, on Broadway, Lexington.

OR 1/30.

P. C. Hollinshead, of Lexington, Ky., to Miss Ella Mills, of Yellow Springs, Ohio. M latter place, Feb. 3, 1864. OR 2/6.

Levi Royalty to Mrs. Letitia L. Myers, both of Lexington. M Feb. 4, 1864. OR 2/6.

James M. Brasley, of Jessamine county, to Miss Virginia F., daughter of Charles H. Wickliffe, of Lexington. M Feb. 10, 1864. OR 2/13.

Lieut. Hugh Lonney, of the 21st Kentucky Volunteers, to Miss Fannie Shepherd, both of Lexington. M Feb. 10, 1864. OR 2/13.

George W. Spencer to Mrs. Frances A. Tucker, both of Fayette county M Feb. 11, 1864. OR 2/13.

Corporal Marion Jenkins, of the 6th Kentucky Cavalry, to Miss Louisa Reynolds, both of Fayette county. M Feb. 11, 1864. OR 2/13.

Thomas Hawkins, of Jessamine county, to Mrs. Sarah W. Elgin, formerly of Fayette county. M. Feb. 7, 1864. OR 2/17.

George H. Cooke to Miss Dorothy Wright, both of Fayette county. M Feb. 11, 1864. OR 2/17.

Dr. A. B. Duke, of Scott county, to Miss Amy Armstrong, of Maysville. M latter place, Feb. 9, 1864. OR 2/20.

John Jenkins to Miss Carey Adams, both of Fayette county. M at the Lexington residence of the bride's sister, Mrs. Martha Norvell, Feb. 17, 1864 OR 2/20.

William F. Mahin, of Lafayette, Ind., to Miss Charlotte Richards, of Lex ington, Ky. M. latter place Feb. 26, 1864. OR 2/27.

Rev. Thomas C. Gunn, First Lieut. Company D, 21st Kentucky Infantry, to Miss Cattie Wagner, of Greensburg, Ky. M Feb. 16, 1864. OR 2/27.

Edward S. Stevenson, of Russellville, to Miss Mirian Hewett, of Louisville. M latter place, Feb. 24, 1864. OR 2/27.

Francis E. Cleveland, State Senator from Bracken and Harrison counties, to Miss Laura Harlan, daughter of the late Hon. James Harlan, of Frankfort. M Feb. 22, 1864. OR 2/27.

William Petitt to Miss E. J. Carr, daughter of D. T. Carr, all of Fayette county. M Feb. 24, 1864. OR 3/2.

John G. Kiser to Miss Josephine, eldest daughter of Lieut. D. F. Winchester, all of Lexington. M Mar. 16, 1864. OR 3/19.

Bryan Mullanphy Clemens, of St. Louis, to Miss Mary Ross Warfield, daughter of William P. Warfield, of Arkansas. M in Louisville, Ky., Mar. 17, 1864. OR 3/19.

W. B. Moore, of Frankfort, to Miss Annie M., daughter of Harrison Thomson, of Clark county. M latter place Apr. 12, 1864. OR 4/16 and 4/20.

Richard T. Downing, of Fayette county, to Miss Maria W., second daughter of William Russell, of Bardstown. M. Apr. 14, 1864. OR 4/20.

William H. Gentry, of Madison county, to Miss Lucy Ann Taylor, of Estill county. M Apr. 7, 1864. OR 4/16.

J. Lunsford Carter, of Fayette county, to Miss Sallie J. Smith, of Scott county. M Apr. 14, 1864. OR 4/23.

Thomas D. Chenault to Miss Callie Chenault, both of Madison county. M Apr. 19, 1864. OR 4/23.

A. Anawalt, of Weston, Va., to Mrs. Emma Shepherdson. M at the Jessamine county, Ky., residence of Mr. E. Young, Apr. 19, 1864. OR 4/23.

J. B. Soward to Miss Jane H., daughter of John Winter, of Georgetown. M Apr. 21, 1864. OR 4/23.

Lieut. Sebastian S. McFaden, U. S. Army, to Mrs. Matilda R. Welch, of Nicholasville. M Apr. 18, 1864. OR 4/23.

George Hopper, of the 1st Kentucky Cavalry (Col Wolford's), to Miss Mary Ann Ward. M in Waco, Madison county, Apr. 19, 1864. OR 4/27.

J. P. Smith, of Illinois, to Miss Annie P. O'Bannon. M in Fayette county, Apr. 28, 1864. OR 4/20.

Alfred Z. Royer, of Trimble county, to Miss Martha P. Castleman, daughter of Charles W. Castleman, of Fayette county. M May 11, 1864. OR 5/14.

Robert T. Miller, of Urbana, Ill., to Miss Eliza W. Hamilton, eldest daughter of James Hamilton, of Lexington, Ky. M May 12, 1864. OR 5/14.

Col. James Holloway, of Henderson, Ky., to Miss Mollie Williams, daughter of Col. John S. Williams. M at the Fayette county residence of Jacob Hughes, Apr. 19, 1864. OR 5/18.

William Harting, of Lexington, to Miss Jennie Hillenmeyer, of Fayette county. M May 12, 1864. OR 5/18.

Prof. E. Amende, of Paris, to Miss Mollie E. Finley. M at the Cynthiana residence of Col. C. Walton, May 16, 1864. OR 5/23.

John P. Montgomery, of Franklin county, to Miss Irene Cooke, of Fayette county. M May 19, 1864. OR 4/25.

Abner Wilson to Mary E. Weathers, both of Fayette county. M May 19, 1864. OR 5/25.

J. H. Wallingford, of Mason county, to Miss Amelia Stewart, of Clark county. M May 12, 1864. OR 5/28.

Elder James H. Wallingford, of Mason county, married Amanda Stuart, daughter of Mrs. Sally Stuart, of Clarke county. M latter place May 12, 1864. See p. 494. OR 6/15.

James Chorn, of Montgomery county, to Miss Mary W. Branham, daughter of Major Branham, of Bourbon county. M May 17, 1864. OR 6/15.

W. J. Hammond, of Indianapolis, to Miss Lizzie Mills, of Scott county, Ky. M latter place, at the residence of E. H. Parrish, June 1, 1864. OR 6/15.

Joseph B. Perkins, of Springfield, Ill., to Miss Ann Mary Price, of Clarke county, Ky. M June 8, 1864. OR 6/18.

Henry C. Laughlin, of Philadelphia, to Frances Spalding, daughter of the late W. W. Tetterman, of Pittsburg. M June 9, 1864. OR 6/25.

S. L. Shivel to Miss Maria E. Carcourt, both of Lexington. M. July 5,

1864. OR 7/6.

William Mateer to Miss Sarah A. Simpson. M in Madison county, July 13, 1864. OR 7/20.

B. N. Webster to Mrs. D. C. Broadwell, both of Lexington. M Aug. 2, 1864. OR 8/6.

Col. Lewis D. Watkins, of the 6th Kentucky Cavalry, to Miss Mary E., daughter of Major-General Lovell H. Rosseau, of Louisville. M there Aug. 4, 1864. OR 8/10.

Singleton Atchison to Miss Julia A. E. Marsh, of Lexington. M Aug. 23, 1864. OR 8/24.

Samuel F. Gray, of Lexington, to Miss Eliza Y. Springer, of Harrodsburg. M latter place, Aug. 4, 1864. OR 8/27.

Sergeant Joseph J. Landram, of the 4th Kentucky Infantry, to Miss Ida Pullen, daughter of William Pullen, of Fayette county. M Sept. 6, 1864. OR 9/7.

Cornelius V. Cowgill to Miss Margaret Waller, of Woodford county. M Sept. 7, 1864. OR 9/10.

John W. Moore, of Fayette county, to Miss Louisa H. Duncanson, of Richmond, Virginia. M in Lexington, Ky., Sept. 20, 1864. OR 9/24.

M. A. Peak to Miss Mary Alice Brisco, both of Scott county. M Sept. 25, 1864. OR 9/28.

Dr. R. Werthrop Saunders, of the British Army, to Miss Martha Overton Taylor, daughter of Col. James Taylor, of Newport, Ky. M Oct. 6, 1864. OR 10/12.

Thomas W. Roberts to Miss Virginia A. Payne, daughter of William Payne. M Oct. 13, 1864. OR 10/19.

1865

Richard Ellis to Miss Sue C. Wickliffe, daughter of Charles H. Wickliffe, M in Lexington, Feb. 2, 1865. OR 2/4.

M. H. Parker, of Fayette county, to Miss Anna M. Cooper, of Louisville. M latter place, Feb. 1, 1865. OR 2/4.

Benjamin Letcher, formerly of Lexington, then of Cincinnati, to Miss Mary R., Daughter of James Anderson, of Louisville. M Jan. 31, 1865. OR 2/4.

Col. W. P. Hart, of "Spring Hill," Woodford county, to Miss Rebecca C. Tevis, a granddaughter of Isaac Shelby. M at "Arcadia," in Lincoln county, Feb. 9, 1865. OR 2/11.

David Adams to Miss Laura E. Lillard, daughter of Stephen Lillard, all of Mercer county. M Feb. 9, 1865. OR 2/15.

J. G. Frazer to Miss Anna E. Bosworth, both of Fayette county. M at the Patterson, N. J., residence of L. R. Stelle, Feb. 1, 1865. OR 2/15.

R. M. Yeates, of Montgomery county, to Miss Ella Gradley, of Clarke county. M Feb. 7, 1865. OR 2/15.

George C. Everett to Miss Nannie Talbott, both of Mount Sterling. M Feb. 8, 1865. OR 2/15.

Eton C. Marton to Miss Martha F. Blincoe, both of Lexington. M Feb. 16, 1865. OR 2/18.

Henry F. Herndon, of Henry county, to Miss Nannie Withers, of Woodford county. M at the residence of Dr. James Crutcher, near New Castle, Ky., Feb. 14, 1865. OR 2/18.

Richard A. Pittman, of Nashville, to Miss Nannie B. Boyd, of Fayette county, Ky. M Feb. 16, 1865. OR 2/22.

D. B. Willes to Miss Sallie E. Simmons, both of Madison county. M Jan. 31, 1865. OR 2/22.

L. W. Clark to Miss Maggie Giltner, both of Bourbon county. M Jan. 26, 1865, at the Bourbon county residence of John Giltner. OR 2/22.

William Buckhart, of Louisville, to Miss Carrie McKenney, of Shelbyville. M latter place, Feb. 21, 1865. OR 2/25.

William H. Price, M. D., of Seymour, Ind., to Miss Lida McBroom, of Henry county, Ky. M Feb. 21, 1865. OR 3/1.

John S. Burrier to Miss Alice Craig, of Jessamine county. M Mar. 2, 1865. OR 3/4.

James M. Scott, of Scott county, to Miss Helen A. Freeland, youngest daughter of Egbert Freeland, formerly of Baltimore. M at the Fayette county residence of the bride's sister, Mrs. Robert J. Wilson, Feb. 8, 1865. OR 3/8.

Bishop H. H. Kavanaugh, of the M. E. Church South, to Mrs. Martha Lewis, of Louisiana. M Mar. 7, 1865. OR 3/11.

George R. Coons, of Fayette county, to Miss L. M. Higgins, of Franklin, Tenn. M in March, 1865. OR 3/11.

Capt. H. C. Oots to Miss Mollie Wilging. M Mar. 14, 1865. OR 3/15.

Benjamin Doom to Miss Mollie, youngest daughter of Felix G. Murphy, all of Nelson county. M at the Clarke county residence of Gen. A. Blackwell, Feb. 14, 1865. OR 3/15.

Henry Sizemore, of Tenn., to Miss Margaret A. Davis, of Jessamine county, Ky. M in Nicholasville, Mar. 4, 1865. OR 3/15.

Wesley Clarke to Mrs. Nancy Grant, the former of Jessamine county, the latter of Washington county. M Mar. 11, 1865. OR 3/15.

Gus A. Goldsmith, formerly of Lexington, Ky., to Miss Rachel Frank, of New York City. M latter place, Mar. 5, 1865. OR 3/22.

William Ogg to Miss Mary F. Duerson, both of Madison county. M Mar. 14, 1865. OR 3/22.

Joseph M. Downing to Miss Catharine Downing. M Mar. 16, 1865. OR 3/18.

James J. Spears to Miss Mary J. Faulconer, daughter of Joseph Faulconer, all of Boyle county. M Mar. 21, 1865. OR 3/29.

A. J. Reed, of Cincinnati, to Miss Hessie A. Johnston, of Madisonville, Tenn. M Mar. 25, 1865. OR 4/5.

J. A. Reynolds to Miss Mary J. McGaughey. M in Shelbyville, home of the bride, Apr. 6, 1865. OR 4/12.

H. Clay Prewitt to Miss Sarah M. Stone, daughter of James M. Stone, of Scott county. M Apr. 5, 1865. OR 4/12.

Jerome Buck, of New York City, to Kate McGrath, of Louisville, Ky. M Apr. 17, 1865, in Lexington, Ky. OR 4/19.

S. W. Reynolds to Miss Betty Sherlock. M in Versailles, Apr. 13, 1865. OR 4/19.

John Felix to Miss Sallie Baxter, both of Lexington. M Apr. 13, 1865. OR 4/19.

Capt. David H. Todd to Mrs. Susie Williamson, daughter of D. F. Turner, of Huntsville, Alabama. M at Marion, Ala., Apr. 4, 1865. OR 4/29.

Albert Fink to Miss Sallie, daughter of A. D. Hunt, all of Louisville. M Apr. 27, 1865. OR 5/3.

Col. John G. Eve, of Barbourville, to Miss M. E. Davidson, of Lexington. M May 9, 1865. OR 5/10.

George H. Dozier to Miss M. Florence Lowry, both of Lexington. M May 10, 1865. OR 5/13.

Charles S. Turner, of Madison county, Ky., to Miss Henrietta M. Campbell, of Daviess county, Ind. M at Washington, Ind., on May 10, 1865. OR 5/17.

J. C. Russell to Mrs. M. H. Roszell, daughter of J. R. and D. H. Morris. M in Lexington, May 16, 1865. OR 5/20.

E. Rumsey Wing, of Louisville, to Miss Louise R. Scott, daughter of Robert Scott, of Franklin county. M May 17, 1865. OR 5/20.

James M. Bland to Miss Julia A. Sandusky. M in Liberty, Mo., May 11, 1865. OR 5/20.

Capt. D. L. Cook to Miss M. Garner. M in Winchester, home of the bride, May 23, 1865. OR 5/31.

Henry C. Payne, of Scott county, to Miss Laura Prewitt, daughter of Alexander Prewitt, of Fayette county. M in latter place, May 31, 1865. OR 6/3.

W. R. Higgins to Miss Laura Webster, both of Lexington. M May 24, 1865. OR 6/7.

Frank Bissicks, of Nashville, Tenn., to Miss Julia Hunter, of Lexington, Ky. M at the latter place, at Christ Church, on June 6, 1865. OR 6/10.

Lieut. R(ichard) T(aylor) Jacob to Miss Laura Wilson, of Lexington. M here June 6, 1865. OR 6/10.

William Cassius Goodloe to Miss Mary Mann, both of Lexington. M here, at Christ Church, June 8, 1865. OR 6/10.

Henry Geovannole to Miss Kate Harris, both of Lexington. M June 22, 1865. OR 6/24.

G. W. Gray to Miss Margaret Hunter, both of Jessamine county. M June 15, 1865. OR 6/28.

William Vorhies, Jr., to Miss Ellen Funcan. M at the Lexington residence of the bride's father, June 22, 1865. OR 6/24.

Col. Wickliffe Cooper, of the 4th Kentucky Vet. Cav., to Miss Sallie S. Venable. M at the Shelby county residence of her father, June 28, 1865.

OR 7/5.

E. D. Hicks to Miss Theodosia, daughter of William Payne, of Scott county. M July 20, 1865. OR 7/22.

T. D. Mitchell to Miss Jennie Taylor, both of Lexington. M July 20, 1865. OR 7/29.

Lew. Sharpe to Miss Julia Vallandingham, both of the vicinity of Athens, Ky. M June 15, 1865. OR 8/2.

Sergt. A. W. Bell, of the Wisconsin Battery, to Mrs. Mary Diamond, of Lexington, Ky. M June 27, 1865. OR 8/2.

Elihu Sparks, of Casey county, to Miss Josephine Gill, of Jessamine county. M at the Buford House, Nicholasville, July 20, 1865. OR 8/9.

William H. Barbee, of Scott county, to Mrs. Fannie Quilling, of Franklin county. M. Aug. 24, 1865. OR 8/26.

Col. William T. Scott, of Lexington, to Miss Mary Y. Brown, daughter of Judge Mason Brown, of Frankfort. M at the latter place in August, 1865. OR 8/26.

J. M. Dillard, son of the Rev. R. T. Dillard, officiating minister, to Miss Nannie M. Carr, daughter of the late Thomas Carr, both of Fayette county. M Aug. 15, 1865. OR 9/13.

C. R. Estill to Miss Mary E. Carr, daughter of David Carr, all of Fayette county. M Sept. 5, 1865. OR 9/13.

H. C. Funk to Miss Laura Lydick, both of Fayette county. M there, at the residence of Jacob Lydick, Sept. 7, 1865. OR 9/13.

William Green to Miss Flora Overstreet, of Madison county. M Sept. 12, 1865. OR 9/13.

John Boggs to Miss Phebe Bratton, both of Lexington. M Sept. 12, 1865. OR 9/13.

N. A. Oldham to Miss Talitha Evans, both of Fayette county. M. Sept. 12, 1865. OR 9/16.

A. C. Griffith to Miss Sarah E. Blincoe, both of Lexington. M Sept. 14, 1865. OR 9/16.

F. M. Ambrose to Miss Mariah L. Minter, daughter of William P. Minter, both of Owsley county. M at Traveler's Rest, Ky., Sept. 12, 1865. OR 9/20

Eli Calvin Crow to Miss Mary J. Welch, both of Jessamine county M Sept. 14, 1865 at the residence of Mrs. Thomas Welch. OR 9/23.

T. G. Crockett, of Scott county, to Miss Emma Long. M at the Lexington residence of the bride's father, Sept. 28, 1865. OR 9/30.

J. H. Stoner, of Madison, Wisc., to Miss Bettie Milbourn, daughter of J. D. Milbourn, of Lexington, Ky. M at the residence of the bride's uncle, J. H. Stephens, in Illinois City, Ill., Sept. 5, 1865. OR 9/30.

Milo G. Featherston to Miss Belle Foley. M Sept. 28, 1865. OR 9/30.

B. T. Zimmerman, formerly of Danville, to Miss Lizzie Perkins. M in Fayette county, home of the bride, Sept. 28, 1865. OR 10/4.

Major A. S. Bloom, late of the 7th Kentucky Cavalry Vols., to Miss Eliza L. Dolin (or Doolin). M at the Lexington residence of the bride's father, Oct. 5, 1865. OR 10/7.

James A. Shrock, of Bloomington, Ill., to Miss Mattie L. Ricketts, of Fayette county. M Oct. 5, 1865. OR 10/7.

Col. Sanders D. Bruce to Mrs. Mary H. Hinkle, daughter of John Clarke, M Oct. 3, 1865. OR 10/7.

Joseph N. Reid to Miss Georgia A. Jones, both of Lexington. M Oct. 8, 1865. OR 10/11.

Charles Kastle to Miss Maggie C. Fowler, both of Lexington. M Oct. 4, 1865. OR 10/11.

H. C. Clay, of Bourbon county, to Miss Ara J. Grimes, of Clark county. M Oct. 3, 1865. OR 10/14.

William C. Arnett to Miss Mattie B., daughter of Captain William Dunlap, all of Woodford county. M there, at the New Union Meeting House, Oct. 10, 1865. OR 10/14.

N. B. Peeler, of Eminence College, to Miss Mary A., daughter of A. O. Redd, of Fayette county. M Oct. 10, 1865. OR 10/14.

Frederick H. Overton to Miss Martha A. Garland. M in St. Paul's Church, Henderson, Ky., Oct. 11, 1865. OR 10/18.

G. W. Davis to Miss Harriet Evans. M at Pleasant Hill, residence of the bride's mother in Jessamine county, Oct. 5, 1865. OR 10/18.

William M. Ford to Miss Alice E. Martin, both of Woodford county. M at the residence of the bride's father in Mortonsville, Ky., Oct. 10, 1865. OR 10/18.

George T. Mountjoy, of Anderson county, to Miss Martha E. Mosby, of Woodford county. M latter place Oct. 12, 1865. OR 10/18.

A. B. Kennedy to Miss Lizzie, daughter of Harrison Rankins, all of Scott county. M at Georgetown, Oct. 3, 1865. OR 10/18.

Willie B. Cassell to Miss Mary E. Wilson. M Oct. 18, 1865. OR 10/21.

John W. Buckner, of Covington, to Miss Mary A. Gano, only daughter of Elder John A. Gano. M Oct. 17, 1865. OR 10/21.

James D. Sutton to Miss P. F. Sallee. M Oct. 19, 1865. OR 10/21.

T. M. McNeeley, of Wheeling, Va., to Miss Mary E. Busbey, of Jessamine county, Ky. M Oct. 24, 1865. OR 10/25.

Rev. R. G. Brank, pastor of the Presbyterian Church at Lexington, to Miss Ruth Smith, daughter of Dr. J. R. Smith, of Lexington. M Oct. 17, 1865. OR 10/25.

Ben H. Smith to Miss Rachel F. Duvall, both of Clark county. M. Oct. 19, 1865. OR 10/25.

Capt. R. G. Potter, late of the 24th Kentucky Infantry Vols., to Miss N. Katie Gilbert, daughter of F. G. Gilbert, of near Manchester, Clay county.

M there Oct. 17, 1865. OR 10/25.

George W. Ryan to Miss Mag. Cardwell, both of Lexington. M Oct. 17, 1865. OR 10/28.

William H. Mundy, of Louisville, to Miss Laura R. Offutt, daughter of Col. E. N. Offutt, of Scott county. M Oct. 25, 1865. OR 10/28.

John G. Allen to Miss Sallie H. Emmal, both of Lexington. M Nov. 14, 1865. OR 11/15.

Wilson Fain to Miss Mary E. Vanpelt, both of Jessamine county. M Nov. 2, 1865. OR 11/15.

Claiborn T. Kearby, of Garrard county, to Miss Mary Jacobs, of Jessamine county. M Nov. 7, 1865. OR 11/15.

Newton Corman to Miss Elizabeth Heaston, both of Jessamine county. M Nov. 9, 1865. OR 11/15.

Joseph E. West, of Georgetown, to Miss Amelia L. Nutter, of Fayette county. M Oct. 25, 1865. OR 11/18.

J. Middleton, of Louisville, to Miss J. Thomas, of Henry county. M Nov. 14, 1865. OR 11/18.

W. G. Darnaby to Miss Lou. Stone, both of Fayette county. M Nov. 14, 1865. OR 11/22.

James C. Graves to Miss Laura, daughter of Thomas Graddy, all of Woodford county. M Nov. 8, 1865. OR 11/22.

David W. Young to Miss Mary Ann Hughes, both of Jessamine county. M Nov. 14, 1865.

Hardin H. Masters, of Jessamine, to Miss Lucy J. Bush, of Fayette county. M November 21, 1865. OR 11/25.

Col. John J. Curtis to Miss Sallie M. Spurr, daughter of Dr. R. J. Spurr, all of Fayette county. M Nov. 22, 1865. OR 11/25.

INDEX

212

Barnett, Charles 90
James G. 56
Marquis 26
Rebecca B. 90
Rosanna 106
Barney, Joshua G. 186
Barr, Edmund 191
Eliza 13
Elizabeth J. 99
Ibbey 42
Margaret 5
Maria 7
Mary 28
Mary H. 101
Nancy 91
Robert S. 32
Thomas J. 92
William V. 122
Zeralda Ann 84
Barret, Mary L. 17
Barrett, James 17
Richard A. 199
Richard F. 70
William F. 119
Barringer, Henry V. 141
Barritt, Jonathan 154
Barrow, David 127
Barry, A. J. 151
Catharine A. 94
Mary Catherine 80
Susan 36
William T. 8
Bartlett, Thomas H. 52
Edward B. 78
John C. 13
Margaret 19
P. 46
Thomasella V. 142
Bartley, W. T. 169
Barton, Abraham S. 13
Edmonia 104
Eliza 9, 44
John 70
Mary S. 75
Rachel 48
Bartow, Mary D. 66
Bascom, H. B. 98
Hannah H. 136
Basey, Sarah 23
Bashford, Allen 197
Francis 112
Baskett, Sarah 139
Bass, Robert L. 162
Bassett, Benjamin F.160
James H. 146
Mary 168
Bateman, John 64
Bates, John 51
Mary C. 199
Sarah F. 75

Battaile, Sarah 94
Baxter, B. A. 161
Emaline 78
Rebecca 42
Reuben 185
Sallie 206
Thomas B. 135
Bayles, Jesse 94
Samuel 20
Bayless, Eliza M. 58
Eveline 177
Jesse 76
Sol. D. 145
S. M. 143
Baylor, Betsey D. 68
Courtney 19
Jane 58
John Walker 6
Mary Jane 42, 58
Bayse, T. D. 164
Beach, Elisha A. 118
Jerusher 128
Paulina 87
William 103
Bealer, George 54
Beall, Mary 60
Bean, James 149
James H. 176
Major A. 182
Nancy 93
Samuel C. 94
Beard, Ann 12
Anna M. 184
Henry 16
Isabella 89
Joseph 106
Martha 16
O.H.P. 143
Bearding, Robert S. 146
Beasley, James A. 133
Beatty,Charles Clinton 50
Eliza Ann 199
George E. 145
Helen P. 146
J. Charleton 55
W. R. 104
Beauchamp, Ann Aliza 125
Elizabeth 42
H. M. 140
Beck, Lavina 34
Beckett, Samuel R. 65
Beckham, William N. 170
Beckley, Alfred 70
Beckman, Frederick 37
Bedford, Archibald C. 59
Franklin P. 141
Henry 57
Mary C. 51
Nancy 63
P. P. 57

Bedford, Susan 67
Bedinger, B. F. 26
D. P. Jr. 201
Olivia 145
Beebe, Boswell 136
Beech, Mary 103
Bell, A. W. 207
Benjamin 44
Catherine R. 112
Clayton C. 172
D. W. 171
Eliza M. 136
Henderson 36
John 8, 57, 84
John A. 186
John Henderson 48
Marcia 31
Margaret J. 107
Maria C. 163
Martha Jane 126
Mary Jane 70
Nannie H. 192
Noah D. 181
Peggy 8
Samuel 76, 97
Sarah Ellen 105
Theodore S. 74
Thomas 49
Virginia 111
William 83, 119
William E. 134
Belle, Mary Anne 32
Belles, Gill Eve 189
Belt, Osborn 105
Benham, Harriet 83
Bennam, Ada 164
Bennets, Susan Jane 150
Bennett, James 107
L. E. 142
Lemuel 62
Lucy F. 164
Sophia 34
Bentley, Mary 120
Benton, Eliza P. C. 126
Bentwell, B. J. 77
Bergin, Cornelius S. 127
Berkley, Edward F. 99
Bernaugh, Atterson 109
Berry, Mrs. 43
Ben Jr. 122
Elizabeth A. 151
Fanny 145
Frances Jane 59
James 98, 145
John 196
Lucy 188
Milford 169
Nancy 76
Newton 93
R. B. 91

Berry, S. M. 187
  Samuel O. 126
  Thomas 161
  Virginia 133
Berryman, Arthur 75
  Charles 41
  Edwin Upshaw 47
  Eliza 68
  John C. 197
  Mary R. 59
  Thomas 11
Besore, John 147
Best, Amanda 97
  Elizabeth C. 127
Bevercomb, Charles 176
Bevins, Sally Ann 82
Bevis, John L. 17
Bex, John A. 134
Beynroth, Charles E. 61
Bibb, Charles S.
  Emily 144
  Susan 57
Bibbs, T. P. Atticus 154
Bickley, Margaret 40
Biddle, Thomas 33
Biggerstaff, David C. 194
  Orville 196
Bilbro, Charles D. 72
Biles, William M. 123
Birch, James H. 39, 168
  W. F. 44
Birchead, Mary E. 166
Bird, Mary 27
Birney, Ann 11
Biship, Margaret 34
Bishop, A.D. 200
  A. K. 109
  Emeline 86
  J. K. 152
  Mary E. 110
Bissell, Henry B. 192
Bissicks, Frank 206
Bivings, Entima 45
Black, Emily E. 134
  Matilda 122
  Sarah 122
Blackburn, B. F. 171
  C. S. 185
  Churchill H. 129
  H. B. 163
  Henrietta 29
  James 171
  Luke P. 85
  Mary P. 93
  Prudence 111
  S. E. 50
  William E. 115
Blackwell, Armstead 190
  Mary Ann Frances 110
  Thomas 56

Blackwood, Eudora 101
Blain, Ellen S. 130
  Jacob 101
  Mary 47
  Robert, Jr. 112
Blair, Alexander 94
  Ann America 28
  Francis P., Jr. 129
  Maria W. 56
  Montgomery 119
  O. Jane 104
  William W. 18
Blake, Daniel 66
Blakemore, James 123
Blakey, Sally 40
Blancagniel,
  Estelle Florinde 119
Blanchard, Horatio F. 51
Blanche, Charles 179
Bland, Benjamin 170
  James M. 206
  Mary 47
Blanton, Alexander 140
  Richard 24
Bledsoe, Agnes 99
  Ann 149
  Dulcinea M. 49
  George Ann 149
  Hiram 24
  Hiram M. 99
  Joseph H. 58
  Judith Ann 38
  Margaret 169
  Mary Jane 145
  Sarah Gist 47
  Virginia L. 37
Blevens, Hugh A. 23
Blewitt, B. T. 135
Blincoe, B. W. 196
  James D. 196
  Martha F. 205
  Sarah E. 207
Block, Eliza Ann 113
  Louisa 58
Bloom, A. S. 208
Blount, John 179
  Owen C. 52
Blow, Charlotte T. 69
Blythe, Samuel D. 70
Boardman, Horace 121
  James 13
Bodkey, Judith Ann 114
Bodley, Charles S. 109
  Henry Innes 46
  John F. 88
  Judith Ann 114
  Maria Innes 73
Boggs, Eliza 15
  John 207
  Sophia H. 76

Boggs, Thomas 145
Bohannon, Albert 90
  Martha 27
  Mary Ellen 69
  Richard A. 66
Bohon, Dorinda 68
Boice, Eliza 45
Bollin, James D. 175
Bolling, R. R. 177
Bond, Emily 123
  Emily A. 147
Bonds, Archibald 107
Boner, Jane Elizabeth 81
Bonnell, George W. 189
Bonnycastle, John C. 180
Bonta, A.B. 201
Bontwell, B. J. 77
Booker, Henrietta Maria 119
  Martha R. 93
Boon, Nelson 73
Boone, Mary A. 170
  Samuel M. 179
Boot, Timothy 62
Booth, Matilda 17
Boston, John 148
Boswell, Ann Maria 58
  B. J. 107
  Charles S. 111
  Davidella 85
  Elizabeth A. 92
  Elvira D. 78
  Florida P.
  Frances P. 139
  George 26, 59
  H. 15
  Hartwell 55
  J. Kinley 126
  Julia 106
  Laura 96
  Mary 147
  Thomas E. 76
  W. D. 194
Bosworth, Adne 111
  Anna E. 204
  Benijah 180
  Edward Ann 123
  Eliza 50
  Felix L. 193
  H. Wallace 172
  Mary L. 130
  Sarah E. 104
  Sarah H. 15
  Sarah Jane 120
Bourn, Francis 134
Bourne, Mary Ann 101
Bower, Dulcenia 158
Bowie, J. W. 168
  Rosaline 181
Bowling, J. B. 21
Bowman, Abraham 12

Brockman,
   William 97, 118
Brockway, Jane G. 173
   Mary 151
Bronaugh, Mary A. 180
Bronson, Minerva 65
Bronston, Semira M. 141
   W. H. 184
Brook, Benjamin M. 13
   Frances 30
Brooking, Henrietta 134
   Laura S. 68
   Lavinia 145
   Samuel T. 84
Brooks, Annie E. 199
   Eliza Jane 74
   Margaret A. 81
   P. 49
   Rebecca 138
   S. T. 146
Brother, William 179
Brothers, Henry 19
Brough, John 78
Broun, Elizabeth 39
Brown, A.V. 113
   Ann M. 101
   B. Gratz 188
   Catherine T. 187
   Charlotte 25
   Christina 161
   Dwight 173
   E.O. 186
   Elias 35
   Elisha Warfield 102
   Elizabeth 69
   Elizabeth Ann 23
   F. Gratz 188
   Frances 36
   Francis G. 85
   George W. 54
   George Washington 39
   Harriet S. 119
   Harvey R. 156
   Henry B. 104
   James 154, 199
   John 5
   John P. 77
   John Young 177
   Jonathan 42
   Joseph 62
   Lloyd W. 129
   Louisa V. 49
   Martha 96
   Mary 31
   Mary H. 159
   Mary Jane 144
   Mary Y. 207
   Mason 38, 85, 144
   Matilda 9
   Moreau 101

Brown, Nancy 74
   Nancy D. 83
   Preston M.
   R. L. 201
   Rachel 81
   Rachel Ann 136
   Richard 72
   Robert 34
   Robert W. 189
   Sally 10
   Samuel 70
   Samuel F. 141
   Sarah J. 70
   Scott 58
   Stephen S. 164
   Susan Catherine 69
   T. R. 101
   Thomas Jefferson 56
   William 8, 66, 101
   William, Jr. 72, 81
   William B. 156
Browne, C. W. 181
Browning, Ann D. 156
   Daniel 23
   Harriet 31
   Hattie M. 162
   M. D. 101
   Marcus E. 145
   Orville H. 86
   Tabitha Ann 73
Brownwell, Charlotte 189
Bruce, B. G. 146
   Helvia 17
   James M. 130
   Margaret A. 89
   Pauline 199
   Rebecca 139
   Sanders D. 208, 132
Brueb, Amanda 106
Bruen, Elizabeth L. 91
   Joseph 22
   Mary 177
   William 116
Bruin, James 163
Brumfield, Zantippe 164
Brunot, W. 21
Bryan, A.G. 185
   Agatha 7
   Annie R. 179
   Daniel 140
   Edward R. 175
   Elijah C. 140
   Elizabeth 24, 26
   George 63
   Joseph 184
   Martha A. 188
   Martha G. 78
   Mary 98, 124
   Mary C. 163
   Mary J. 149

Bryan, Robert T. 157
   Sarah Ann 70
   Susan 90
   Talbott M. 145
   Thomas 78
   W. 93
   William 60
Bryant, Benjamin F. 201
   E. 29
   G. P. 63
   Parker B. 163
   Polly Ann 86
Bryon, Abram Clay 141
   Agatha 9
Bryson, William 46
Buchanan, Emmeline O. 134
   George 80
   Joseph 14
   Robert R. 31
Buchannan, Mary F. 177
   Thomas H. 74
Buchanon, Jane 48
Bucholts, Francis 81
Buck, Miss 8
   Jerome 206
   Peter C. 12
   Walter A. 107
Buckhart, George 74
   William 205
Bucklin, Amelia S. 117
Buckner, Miss 70
   Anna W. 182
   Eleanor E. 147
   John W. 208
   Mary E. 133
   Robert M. 156
   Sally Ann 98
   William T. 126, 142
Budd, T. L. 102
   W. G. 160
Budlong, Adeline 158
Buffington, Lewis 80
Buford, Britty 179
   Charles 28
   Henry 109
   John 37
   Martha M. 118
   Mary 28
   Patsy 125
   Sarah S. 56
Bull, J. Preston 129
   J. Randolph 142
   John 13
   Samuel C. 190
Bullitt, Amanthus 55
   Eloise 103
   Mary Ann 40
   Owen G. 133
Bullock, Dorothy 8
   Eliza 105

Bullock, Eliza O. 170
Elizabeth 7, 14
James M. 135
Mary Ann 60
Mildred D. 120
Robert S. 188
Waller 84
William F. 54
Bunnell, Jesse 50
Martha J. 154
Mary 139
Bucholts, Francis 81
Burbank, Davis 154
Elmira 150
Burbridge, B. L. 112
Elizabeth 83
Emma J. 184
Jesse 190
John B. 134
Matilda J. 123
Oscar H. 116
Robert 23
T. B. 170
Thomas 20
Burch, George W. 122
J. K. 101
Janetta 122
Lucinda 70
Malvina 129
Mary F. 91
Sallie 193
Burdett, Nelson 22
Burdsal, Elijah 113
Burke, Glendy 106
Burkley, Levin 117
Burnam, A. J. 125
Burns, Phenix 46
Rosanna 82
Burnsides, Clarissa 32
Burr, William E. 167
Burrell, Bethia 7
Burrier, Jacob 105
John S. 205
Burris, G. W. 115
Burrows, Louise D. 191
Burrus, Susan M. 163
Burt, James 133
Burton, Charles F. 41
Elizabeth 194
Kitty Ann 48
Nannie 164
Smith 115
William 150
Busbey, Mary E. 208
Busby, Samuel 94
Bush, Barbary J. 137
Frederick 120
John P. 148
Lucy J. 209
Lydia Ann 99

Bush, Mahala J. 123
Mary Jane 121
Mary P. 124
Robert W. 158
Samuel S. 170
Sarah B. 106
Thomas G. 90
William M. 137
Buster, Robert 10
Butler, Bettie F. 128
Carrie 177
Catherine H. 125
Charles T. 123
Elizabeth 183
Eveline 98
Jane 47
Juliann 74
Lucy Ann 19
Percival 32
Robert G. 198
Thomas 200
William O. 16
Zebulon 58
Buzzard, Solomon 58
Byandywine, Philip 44
Bybee, J. N. 30
Byrne, E. P. 189
Byrnes, Ann Maria 196
Elizabeth V. 124
Emily Caroline 104
Byrns, Susan 59
Bywater, Robert 12

C

Cabell, Charles J. 92
Sophonisba 11
Cable, James E. 66
P. L. 129
Caffery, John M. 170
Cahill, Edwin 80
William 9
Caldwell, Eliza H. 86
Elizabeth 63
George McD. 201
Mag. S. 176
Mary W. 179
Paulina D. 33
Sarah 82
Thomas Leaming 30
Calendar, Jane 30
Robert 78
Calhoun, Anna 96
Callahan, Joseph 88
Calloway, William 165
Calluway (Calloway?)
Mattie E. 175
Calmes, Nancy 38
Calvert, Obadiah 57
Cammack, John P. 59
Camp, Catharine 17

Campbell, Anderson 43
Ann 23
Ann Eliza 52
Arthur 10
Bettie 138
C. A. 112
Cynthia Ann 150
D. R. 125
Eliza Ann 52
Harriett Ann 44
Henrietta M. 206
Hugh 76
James B. 97
James N. 193
John B. 195
John P. 104, 176
John T. 73
M. E. 128
Margaret 62
Marian F. 18
Martha M. 103
Mary 18
Minerva 46
Moses 41
Orpah 166
Polly 32
Robert 82
Robert T. 25
Sarah Jane 96
William 104, 118
Camper, Peter 49
Campfield, Harriet 76
Camplin, Mary Ann 123
Candy, John 77
Theodore F. 186
Cannon, A. E. 146
John W. 129
Julia 190
Mary 62
Melissa 182
Canon, James A. 15
Mary 142
Capers, F. W. 136
Caperton, William H. 24
Caplinger, George W. 83
Capps, Samuel W. 193
Caps, Charles W. 139
Carcourt, Maria E. 203
Cardwell, Mag. 209
Carey, Elizabeth 42
Carl, Nelson 148
Carles, William 10
Carlisle, Elizabeth F. 83
George 78
Carneal, Alice 94
Sallie 106
Caroline, Eleanor 79
Carpenter, Dudley 172
Elizabeth 34
Horace 28

Clark, James S. 96
  Jo. 199
  Julia 142
  L.W. 205
  Lucinda 90
  Mary H. 179
  Nancy A. 97
  Polly 17
  Robert C. 103, 107
  Sarah J. 125
Clarke, Catharine M. 84
  Charles 198
  Charlotte 94
  Elizabeth 8, 33
  Elizabeth Norton 190
  Enoch 69
  Harriet 142
  James S. 96
  Jo. 199
  Mary 30, 99
  Patsy 8
  Richard 30
  Sallie E. 185
  Susan 75
  Wesley 205
Clarkem, Harriet 142
Clarkson, Julius M. 39
Clary, John R. 56
Clay, Ann B. 33
  Brutus J. 64
  Cassius M. 73
  Cypian 103
  Elizabeth 63, 122
  H.C. 208
  Henry, Jr. 43, 72
  Isabella 91
  Lucretia 192
  Mary Ann 85
  Mary E. 142
  Nannie 177
  Paulina G. 24
  Porter 6
  Sally 65
  Samuel 90
  Samuel S. 197
  Sidney P. 31
  Susan 88
  Susan H. 30
  Sydney P. 51
  Thomas H. 92
  W. Green 57
Cleaighton, George 166
Clear, Samuel 100
Cleary, William W. 157
Cleaveland, William 46
Cleland, William R. 153
Clemens,
  Bryan Mullanphy 202
Clements, Thomas H. 30
Clemerson, John 149

Clemson, Thomas C. 96
Cleneay, Joseph 6
Cleveland, Francis 202
  John T. 34
Clifford, John 6
  Mary Jane 30
  Sarah 27
Cline, David 55
Clinger, Daniel 137
Clinkenbeard, Isaac 51
Clopper, Ruth H. 13
Clore, Elizabeth 122
Cloud, Mary 180
Clugston, George 178
  Mary J. 111
Cluke, R.C. 167
Coats, Matilda 61
Cobb, Elizabeth 49
Coburn, James W. 11
  John 55
  Matilda 131
Cochran,
  Catherine L.A. 72
  Eliza 183
  J.O. 84
  J.W. 95
  James 46
  James R. 157
  John B. 135
  John C. 152
  Lucy Ann 12
  Robert H. 93
  Samuel 47
Cock, John A. 15
  Sarah E. 20
Cocks, Martha R. 154
Coffey, George W. 87
Coffman, Leonard, Jr. 53
Cogar, William G. 182
Coggshell, John B. 127
Coghlan, Cornelius 59
Cogshell, Ann Eliza 100
Cogwill, G. F. 110
  James 81
  Mary 116
Cohen, Alfred 113
  Henry 187
Coke, Richard H. 104
Coleman, Ann Mary 54
  Catharine E. 65
  Chapman 62
  Charles 168
  David S. 137
  Drucilla S. 130
  Eliza 33
  Florence 165
  Jane Amanda 116
  John B. 67
  John W. 30
  Mary E. 113

Coleman, Mary M. 109
  Nicholas D. 46
  S. Woodson 175
  T.C. 144
  William 12
Colleir, Nancy 153
Collier, Elizabeth B. 77
  James 92
  Joseph 44
  Nancy 81, 153
Collins, Elizabeth 124
  Hester 111
  Kate 167
  Lewis 32
  Mollie A. 197
  Orvie 23
  Sarah Elizabeth 124
  Whitfield 97
Colquitt, Elizabeth H. 120
Colter, Sarah 24
Colvin, Jennie F. 176
Colyer, F.K. 196
Combs, Abby 116
  Elizabeth Jane 196
  Howard 173
  John 25
  Kitty Ann 176
  La Belle 132
  Leslie 19, 142
  Mag. Leslie 170
  Mary Rebecca 117
  Sarah 85
  Susan E. 113
  Werter 176, 197
Comfort, William 19
Comingo, A. 134
Compton, Jes.(James) 166
Comstock, Nancy 14
Conn, Catharine 50, 126
  Thomas 131
Connell, Mary Ann 56
Connellee, S.T. 115
Conover, Amaryllis A.A. 99
  Henrietta 73
  James F. 70
Cook, Mr. 100
  Charlotte 65
  Clements 185
  D.L. 206
  Isaac 91
  James D. 131
  James M. 87
  James W. 116
  John 140
  John W. 54
  Mary M. 77
  Pamilia 68
  Rebecca 11
  Reuben 137
  Stephen 42

Grimes, John 21, 66, 69
  John A. 9
  Leannah 79
  Louretta 84
  Mahala 45
  Margaret 178
  Mitchell 148
  O. 36
  Sidney S. 80
  Verlinda A. 95
  William 79
  William H. 134
Grinstead, Mr. 24
  Robert 146
Grisby, Ann M. 157
  Elizabeth Maria 60
  J. Warren 152
  John J. 170
Grissim, John D. 113
Griswold, Henry A. 149
Groggs, Eda 172
Groom, B.B. 122
Grooms, Julian E. 110
  Louisa M. 95
  Matilda B. 78
Grosh, Sophia 6
Grosjean, John C. 17
Grosvenor, Almira 28
  Laura C. 51
Grow, Levi 179
  Nancy 150
Grubb, James 176
Gruelle, Keturah H. 179
  P.W. 134
Grugett, Eliza A. 16
Grundy, Robert C. 102
Guibert, Henry 20
Gunkle, John 147
Gunn, James W. 162
  Mary 188
  Thomas C. 202
  William A. 166
Gunnell, T. Allen 126
Gurin, Betrand 13
Gurley, Mary 73
Guthrie, Mary E. 104
Guyton, Ann J. 108
  W.H. Jr. 199
Gwartney, Michael 145
Gwin, George W. 57

H

Hackney, Nancy 77
Haden, Mary 52
Hagan, Sarah 137
Hagar, Upton L. 104
Hagen, Mary E. 197
Hager, Jonthan S. 59
  Upton L. 104
Haggard, David R. 138

Haggin, Miss 49
  Elizabeth 36
  James 5
  James B. 124
  Nancy 168
  Susan E. 140
Hailey, Agnes W. 78
  Elizabeth 53
  Sarah 78
Haily, Ambrose 78
Haines, Thomas 48
Hair, Mattie L. 198
Haldeman, W.H. 108
Hale, Abram 130
  Antoinette Caroline 51
  Cassandra 107
  Frances Jane 129
  Garland B. 83
Haley, Randolph J. 139
  Sarah Ann 179
Haligan, Ellen 161
Hall, Rev. Mr. 31
  Amanda 57
  Augustus 63
  B.F. 88
  Ben. E. 147
  C.W. 55
  Catherine 36
  David 155
  Florida P. 111
  Jacob 11
  James 148
  John 29, 40
  John R. 128
  Martha Ann 96
  Mary Ann 69, 89
  Mary C. 171
  Mary J. 81
  Sabina Jane 169
  Sallie 201
  Samuel 132
  Samuel B. 82
  W.W. 123
Hallack, Elvira 72
  Lloyd P. 83
  Mary A. 126
  Sarah Elvira 72
Haller, Lewis 10
Halley, Elizabeth T. 150
  Fannie 183
  Sarah Ann 90
Halligan, Elizabeth 173
Halsell, Mary F. 178
Halstead, Joseph S. 124
  Sarah C. 39
Hamilton, A.W. 149
  Ann 49
  Charles 71
  D.B. 171
  Eliza W. 203

Hamilton, Ellen 171
  George W. 196
  Jane 135
  John 14
  Laura 174
  Mary Ann 49, 100, 156
  Matilda 20
  Robert 47, 141
  Sally F. 195
  Thomas J. 22
  William 8
Hammett, Martha I. 92
Hammon, John 181
Hammond, Abby V. 38
  Smallwood C. 86
  W.J. 203
Hamon, A.D. 138
Hampton, Henry 102
  Mary A. 100
  Mary H. 133
  Wade, Jr. 95
Hancock, Ann 43
  G.W. 196
Handy, John 39
  William C. 180
Haney, Judith B. 61
Hankins, Maria M. 106
Hanley, Margaret E. 148
  Mary E. 137
  Thomas H. 79
Hanly, Ann S. 159
  M.C. 118
  Maria L. 181
Hann, Alexander R. 75
Hanna, John H. 22
  Mary 20
  Sophia 18
Hanson, Arabella 67
  Maria 44
  Matilda R. 139
  Minervie 195
  Richard H. 143
  Samuel 131
  Serena 58
Happy, Nancy 40
  William W. 59
Harbin, John B. 26
Harbinson, Paulina C. 68
Harcourt, Richard 81
Hardesty, Benjamin F. 187
  Frances A. 186
  Susan 141
Hardin, Davis 10
  Elizabeth 119
  Emily 60
  George W. 21
  Jane T. 136
  John J. 62, 64
  Lucinda 60
  Mark 9

Hays, Thomas 198
  William 5
Hazelwood, Nancy 123
Hazelrigg, Sarah 43
Hazelriggs, Elizabeth 120
Hazen, Charles C. 128
Head, Mary Jane 94
Headdington,
  Mary 86
Headington, Angelina 87
  Pamela 140
Headley, Hamilton A. 131
  John A. 185
Headly, Marshall 97
Hearb, Minerva Ann 55
Hearne, Ann B. 145
  Minds 79
  William T. 160
Heaston, Elizabeth 209
Heath, J. M. 168
Heathman, James 53
Hebner, Elizabeth 191
Hedge, Avis W. 135
  James 62
Hedger, William 124
Hedges, Isabella 161
Hedington, C. M. 76
Heifner, George H. 165
Helm, John L. 60
  Joseph D. 124
  Leah 100
  Martha 142
  Sallie H. 198
Hemingway, Thomas 54
Hemphill, Lucy 133
Henderson, Mr. 30
  D. H. 152
  Daniel 68
  Elizabeth 198
  Howard M. 72
  James 141
  James H. 102
  Nancy 7, 41
  Nancy W. 118
  Richard S. 169
  Samuel H. 124
  Sarah 63
  William 54
  William W. 109
Hendley, Mary E. B. 59
Hendrick, Elizabeth 96
  Martha M. 123
Hendricks, Hetty Ann 169
Hendrix, Samuel 109
Hendron, Wiatt 61
Henkle, Amelia E. 181
Henry, Alexander 198
  Celinda 58
  James P. 111
  John F. 18, 51

Henry, John P. 176
  John R. 61
  John S. 200
  Lucy C. 67
  Martha 13
  Mary W. 75
  Samuel G. 52
  Susan E. 170
  William 6, 77, 91
  William J. 195
Hensley, Maria A. 81
Heran, John M. 26
Herbert, Catharine 159
Herndon, Miss 19
  Augustus G. 5
  Eliza 73
  Eliza G. 50
  Frazer D. 73
  Harriet 23
  Henry F. 205
  John 75
  John B. 158
  Julia A. 160
  Mag. 155
  Mary 120
  Reuben 79
  Willina S. 98
Herring, Ellen 89
Herriott, Agnes C. E. 141
  Ephraim A. 141
  Harriett Ann 97
  Isabelle Eleanor 98
  John 116
  Ursula Emarine 116
Hersman, Matthew 37
  Sophronia 183
Herspurger, Henry 137
Hertzog, Ann 69
  Hypolite 131
Hervey, Joseph H. 14
  Mary 57
  William R. 98
Hewett, John M. 96
  John M. Sr. 87
  Mirian 202
  R. C. 130
  Susanna F. 74
Hewitt, James 45
Hewson, Thomas 193
Hicka, Sanford 109
Hickey, Frances 13
  Johanna 28
  Margaret 62
  Mary E. 162
  Mary Ellen 178
  Mary Jane 124
  Thomas 42
  Thomas M. 42, 94
  William J. 97
Hicklin, Sarah A. 144

Hickman, Albert 55
  Ann M. 144
  Caroline 132
  Catharine C. 49
  Clara R. 171
  D. M. 18
  Edwin C. 97
  J. T. 123
  James L. 19
  Lydia 64
  Maria T. 126
  Mary Agnes 136
  Sarah C. 150
  Thomas B. 47
Hicks, Alexander C. 161
  Charles B. 171
  E. D. 207
  Edward H. 153
  Eveline A. 180
  Jane H. 144
  Lucie Isabella 163
  Martha Beverley 93
  Mary Eliza 79
  Samuel 52
  Sanford 109
Hieatt, Sally 41
Hieronymus, W. T. 179
Higbee, Benjamin W. 82
  James P. 152
  John Jr. 33
  Sarah E. 152
Higginbottom, Benjamin 156
Higgins, America 33
  Caroline Virginia 51
  H. J. 99
  John 154
  L. M. 205
  Margaret 61
  Mary Ann A. 54
  Mary H. 196
  Randall G. 167
  Richard 77, 183
  Richard Jr. 70, 128
  Sinia 19
  W. R. 206
  W. W. 77
  William J. 166
  Wyatt K. 92
Highbee (Higbee), Emily 132
Highfield, William 189
Hildreth, J. T. 195
  Harriet 73
Hill, Ambrose P. 193
  Arabella 164
  Catharine 88
  Elizabeth 83
  G. B. 181
  Jane 152
  John 132
  Margaret 155

James, William 61
William R. 157
Jameso, Judith Ann 139
Jameson, Bettie 201
Eliza M. 147
James 35
Judith Ann 139
Jamison, Minerva 85
January, Andrew M. 16
Clementina 132
Clementina E. 37
Clementine 132
Eliza 29
Mary Eliza 132
Nancy 22
Peter 22
Robert W. 21
Samuel F. 137
Sarah Ann 102
Jarman, Mary 62
Jarvis, Margaret 110
Jeanes, Nancy 31
Jeffrey, Alexander 199
Jeffries, Derrick 100
Jenkins, Aliza Ann 60
America 114
Bushrod 60
Cordelia C. 81
Eliza Ann 60
Francis 73
John 202
John F. 29
Jonathan 43
Marion 202
Mary Ann 174
Matthew 44
Richard H. 165
Sally 97
Theoderick 30
Jennings, Miss 46
Elvina 122
J. Madison 97
Jane E. 148
Lavinia 154
Sally 61
Uriah 61
William H. 169
William R. 38
Jerman, Eliza 56
Sarah 44
Jesse, Benjamin A. 93
Mary E. 93
Jessup, Genl. 30
Jeter, Jane Catherine 138
Mary 178
Mary Eliza 153
Sarah F. 157
John, John H. 90
Johnson, Adeline J. 72
Alpheus B. 154

Johnson, Amanda F. 112
Amy 72
Ann A. 26
Ann Delia 113
Annie M. 171
B. D. 184
Benjamin 12, 163
Benjamin B. 61
Betsey 108
C. R. 185
Catharine Ann 75
Darwin W. 190
David D. 106
Dulciena 144
Elias B. 157
Eliza 18, 162
Eliza J.D. 11
Eliza M. 88
Elizabeth J. 57
Ellen 25
Evelyn 110
George W. 75
Green 69
Hattie N. 195
Helen 185
Henry 16, 151
Imogene 72
J.H. 186
James 51
James 76, 87, 169
James A. 130
James T. 79, 119
James W. 186
Jane Mary 138
John E. 194
John F. 191
John T. 12
Joseph 56
Julia 151
Kate S. 201
L.G. 64
Lavina E. 194
Louisa 132
M.C. 162
Madison B. 53
Margaret Ann 130
Mary 180
Mary E. 52, 85
Mary H. 112
Matt. F. 197
Nancy 76
Nancy B. 88
Nelson C. 39
Paulina M. 101
Payton 101
Richard M., Jr. 88
Rosa Vertner 199
Rosamond Clarke 78
Sarah D. 87
Thomas B. 51

Johnson, William G. 59
William Henry 188
Zephariah 65
Johnston, Albert S. 53
Eliza 39
George W. 192
Hessie A. 205
J. Stoddard 162
Mary Elizabeth 142
William 132, 177
Jonas, Abraham 58
Jones, Anna R. 152
Augusta D. 83
Cassandra 10
Daniel D. 54
Elizabeth 45
Fanny 57
Frances 56
Frederick A. 135
Gabriel A. 185
George 64
Georgia A. 208
J.M. 195
James M. 201
Joanna 164
John E. 197
John H. 90
John H., Jr. 89
Joseph, Sr. 56
Louisiana Ann 171
M. Goldsmith 176
Mary Ann 95
Mary C. 82
Nancy 62
Pauline M. 158
Richard 24
Roger 131
Sallie Jane 132
Samuel H. 199
Stephen Chipley 159
Stephen E. 173
William 35
William C. 126
William D. 96
Willis F. 118
Jons, William 35
Jordan, Mrs. 19
J.C. 75
John, Jr. 10
Josiah 185
Rachel 68
Jouett, J. 195
Matthew H. 13
Sarah B. 148
Jouette, Charles 10
Jouitt, Sarah B. 72
Joyce, John 68
Joyes, Patrick 165
Sue V. 189
Thomas 22

Martin, Nancy H. 179
  Nancy O. 39
  Orville B. 43
  Patsey W. 43
  Rachel 24
  Richard 36
  Solon D. 127
  Sophia 39
  Thomas B. 23
  Thomas S. 124
  Urena 146
Marton, Eton C. 205
Masner, William
Mason, Darius A. 128
  Eliza P. 182
  Frances 164
  James 19
  Lucy B. 135
  Margaret 5
  Mary E. 186
  Mary Thompson 12
  Moninia 175
  Richard 158
  Susan T. 58
Massey, James H. 100
Massie, Elizabeth 29
  Franklin 162
  Mary L. 59
  Sarah 126
Masstin, Elizabeth 77
Masters, Hardin H. 209
  John 96
Masterson, Joseph 54
Maston, Richard 25
Mateer, William 204
Mathers, James G. 85
Matson, Eliza 36
  Louisa Jane 116
  Rebecca 116
Mattack, Hannah 123
Matteson, Lydia 173
Matterson, Francis I. 105
  Lydia 173
Matthews, Alicia A. 52
  Amelia P. 55
  Benjamin 161
  Dianna M. 92
  Howard 113
  Marshall M. 110
  Mary A. 144
  William H. 147
Mattingly, Ignatius 65
Maupin, John 190
  Sarah 194
Maury, Abraham P. 40
  Sallie 167
  Sarah Ann S. 99
Mauze 35
Maxwell, J. L. 33
May, Juliet 6

May, Spicey 50
  William 63
Mayduell, Ann Maria 119
Mayes, Daniel 74
Mayo, Mary A. 57
Mazureau, Polixene 43
Meade, Coules G. 123
  Eliza 7
  Nancy 6
Meeker, Mary A. 187
Megee, Margaret J. 149
Meglone, Montgomery 90
Megowen, David 10
  Ellen 111
  Jane W. 65
  Joseph R. 117
  Julia O. 71
  Julia S. 27
  Marg. S. 68
  Mary A. 59
  Robert W. 147
  W.S.D. 88
Meloy, J. R. 199
Menard, Elziere 40
Mendell, George H. 191
Menefee, Richard H. 72
Mengies, Sallie 134
Menifee, Mary B. 103
Mentelle, Babet 33
  Louisa 151
  Mary 92
Mercer, Margaret 19
Merchant, Nancy Ann 91
Meredith, Elizabeth 94
Mergalf, Elizabeth 108
Meriweather, A.G. 50
Merrell, Azariah M. 91
  David J. 131
  Martha 107
  Sarah 13
Merrick, John A. 168
  William Matthews 108
Merrill, Abire 161
  Micajah 129
  Nancy 48
  Wilson 18
Merritt, Rebecca 88
Merriweather,
  (Merriwether)
  Emma 201
  Catherine H. 140
  David 108
Mesmer, Margaret 154
Messick, John 133
Metcalf, Elizabeth 186
  George 93
  Lucy A. 95
  Thomas L. 42
Metcalfe, Charlton 176
  Mary Ann 104

Metcalfe, William 147
Meteer, James 83
Metgalf, Elizabeth 108
Michael, Robert 143
Middleton, J. 209
  Samuel C. 166
  Sarah 166
Milam, Ben. 139
Milbourn, Bettie 207
Miles, Ann B. 85
Milleon, Green B. 164
Miller, James 49
  Adrew K. 72
  Alex. S. 189
  Andrew 120
  Catherine 95
  Dudley V. 148
  Eglentine 64
  Eliza B. 148
  Elizabeth 49
  Elizabeth H. 84
  F.M. 117
  Florida N. 196
  G.W. 194
  G.Washington 125
  George F. 192
  Isaac 113
  Isaac C. 99
  Isabella 140
  J. 63
  James 179
  James I. 38
  Joanna 95
  John 28
  John T. 121
  Kate W. 195
  L.R. 139
  Macy 119
  Margaret 41
  Margaret B. 137
  Mary 119
  Mary F. 62
  Maurice L. 32
  Nancy 75
  Robert T. 203
  Sarah 84
  William F. 174
Millikin, Mary 52
Mills, Ella 202
  Lizzie 203
  Martha 64
  Sally 56
  Thornton A. 134
Milton, Ann 21
  Bettie J. 151
  Eben, Jr. 201
  Elizabeth 143
  John 45, 201
  N.B. 163
  William E. 140

Milward, Joseph 40, 179
  L. P. 190
Minter, Mariah L. 207
Mitchael, Robert 143
Mitchell, A.I. 13
  A.S. 114
  Alexander 60
  Alexander J. 117
  Andrew 50
  Augusta A. 165
  Edward 69
  Elizabeth 192
  J.W.S. 75
  James H. 147
  John 46
  Margaret 35
  Martha 96
  Mildred R. 90
  Rebecca 30
  Samuel G. 7
  T.D. 207
  Thomas J. 120
Mitchum, John 94
  Susan 108
Mitten, James R. 160
Mixer, Nathan 41
Moberly, Daniel 62
  Lavina 23
  Rosa 191
Moffett, Emily B. 114
  Mariah 72
  Martha M. 153
  Mary H. 135
  Susan 112
  William N. 195
Moffitt, Eliza Jane 102
Monroe, J.J. 42
  James 148
  Jane 140
  John A. 130
  Thomas B., Jr. 194
Montague, Elizabeth 155
  Fannie A. 191
  Frances 140
  Margaret A. 194
  Martha 136
  Martha A. 160
  Thomas J. 181
  William H. 153
Montgomery, David 15
  Elizabeth T. 72
  John P. 203
  Larkin 137
  Mary W. 108
  Theresa E. 110
Montmollin, Ada 175
  F., Jr. 173
  James M. 200
  Sallie P. 161
Moody, Eliza Ann 126, 149

Moody, William H. 85
Moore, Alexander 76,141
  Allen 160
  Benjamin F. 145
  Eliza C. 103
  Frances 168
  George 81, 122
  George E. 170
  H.D. 162
  Hannah A.K. 113
  J.L. 76
  James 123
  Jane 104
  Jane Elizabeth 72
  Jane W. 41
  Jesse 184
  John H. 29, 134
  John Taylor 183
  John W. 204
  Joseph A. 46
  Lizzie O. 199
  Louia T. 61
  Madison M. 144
  Margaret 195
  Margaret H. 164
  Margaret L. 110
  Mary Ann S. 57
  Mary E. 70
  Morton 178
  N.D. 133
  Nancy 13
  Nancy T. 60
  Rebecca 118
  Samuel 84
  Sarah 56, 82
  Sarah R.L. 32
  Sophia 61
  Susan 20, 144
  Thomas J. 62, 151
  Thomas L. 54
  Thomas P. 18, 100
  W.B. 202
  William 98
  William H. 100
  William Lawson 155
  William P. 100
  Y., Jr. 48
  Z. 7
Moorehead, Elizabeth 86
Moorman, J.E. 183
Morehead, Amanda 189
  Charles D. 53
  Charles S. 33, 67
  Elizabeth 61
  Fannie A. 189
  Henry 51, 63, 115
  Lucy A. 121
  Octavia 57
  P.C. 63
Moreland, Alexander 107

Morgan,
  Alexander G. 33,165
  Calvin C. 33
  Eliza F. 178
  George 84
  Griffith S. 154
  James 161
  James A. 125
  John 139
  Josephine 167
  Kitty G. 168
  Mary A. 83
  Mary Jane 160
  Mildred D. 106
  Phebe 73, 146
Morin, Anne 18
Morrell, Jerusha M. 107
Morris, Ann 31
  Ann Crittenden 169
  Caleb 85
  Clara 169
  Daniel 76
  Elizabeth 163
  John P. 34
  Lizzie H. 199
  Maggie W. 194
  Mary J. 190
  Zeph 188
Morrison, Eliza 50
  Emily 67
  James N. 146
  John G. 88
  Kate Louisa 138
  Zerilda A. 64
Morrow, G.H. 197
  Louann B. 79
  Louisa Caroline 67
  P.B. 136
  Robert S. 164
  S.B. 190
Morton, Abraham B. 25
  Amanda P. 55
  America 33
  Catherine 25
  Charles H. 198
  E.S. 80
  Elijah 27
  Elizabeth 8
  George W. 51
  Henry C. 111
  Isabella 143
  J.B. 153
  J.K. 175
  Jane 10
  John 77
  Joseph V. 198
  Lucy 134
  Margaret B. 149
  Mary 8
  Mary E. 104

Morton, Molly 6
  Thomas W. 190
Mosby, Martha E. 208
  Rebecca 51
  Susan P. 85
Moseby, Benjamin 9
Moseley, Alivia P. 172
  John Ann 137
Mosely, Martha R. 167
  Mary E. 171
  John 137
  Samuel H. 106
Moss, Belary 33
  Bettie 129
  Elizabeth 44
  John 149
  Sarah Ann 140
Motley, Martha Ann 65
Mott, Mary Ellen 102
Mount, Samuel 15
Mountjoy, George T. 208
  Hannah 44
Moxley, Mary 145
  Richard S. 163
Moyers, Mary Ann 41
Muckledroy, John 34
Muir, Ann 155
  E. D. 195
  E. S. 195
  Lavina 197
  Mary A. 144
  Mollie 183
  Samuel 155
  Sena 193
Mulanphy, Ann 33
Mullay, John C. 88
  Julia Cecelia 118
Mullens, James 66
Mullikin, Polly 65
Mullins, Charles A. 81
  Lewis G. 27
Mundy, William H. 209
Munford, Matilda B. 39
Munsel, Luke 32
Murat, Achille 44
  Lucian 67
Murdock, Eleanor 47
  Mary Ann 58
Murphy, Francis 30
  James 124
  John 48
  Mary Ellen 161
  Mollie 205
  Sally 190
  William 8
Murrain, Martha J. 172
  Octavia R. 146
Murray, David 55, 74
  Davidella F. 155
  Edwin 191

Murray, F. M. 178
  Rachel A. 156
  William 138
Murrell, William 23
Murrian, Octavia R. 146
Murry, Amanda 175
Mussey, John B. 100
Myers, Caroline 55
  Julian 70
  Letitia L. 202
  Modoline Barbary 42
Myles, Ann Eliza 117

N

Naghel, E. F. 150
  E. Q. 151
Nall, Sarah 22
Narsh, Frederick 91
Nash, Miss 75
  Maria 22
  Mary Virginia Stith 46
Neal, Eliza Ann 121
  Fannie 170
  George 16
  J. M. 98
  Linis A. 165
  Mary Ann 98
  Mason S. 170
  Susan M. 185
Neale, F. R., Jr. 189
  Joshua 200
  Mary Hanna 181
Neet, John 69
  Virginia L. 155
Neil, William A. 158
Neiss, Ann H. 74
Nelson, Anna 103
  Eliza J. 152
  James 65
  M. A. W. H. 144
  Robert 43, 152
Nesbit, Martha 66
Netherland, Betsey 50
  Sallie J. 141
Nettles, Josiah H. 175
Neville, Amelia 70
Nevins, Mary L. 158
New, Ann L. 33
  Eliza C. 20
  Rebecca Ann 125
  Walter 19
Newbold, Nannie 198
Newcomer, George W. 85
Newland, Silas 44
Newman, Annabella 184
  David 123
  Sarah A. 164
Newsom, Mary Ann 40
Newton, A. O. 100
  Lucinda 45

Nicholas, Elizabeth 13
  George Ann 9
  Henry 78
  Hetty 20
  James F. 169
  Margaretta G. 13
  Maria 6
  Samuel S. 55
Nichols, Charlotte A. 128
  Frances 103
  Mary L. 154
  Rebecca 185
  Sallie A. 194
  Walter 110
  William C. 175
Nicholson, Thomas J. 135
  William P. 26
Nickol, Joseph 174
Nifong, Joseph 123
Nivens, Susan 163
Nixon, James 176
Noble, Ann Jane 140
  D. Ephraim 177
  Elijah 10
  George W. 110
  Thomas Hart 78
Noel, Ann Maria 36
  Frances Brown 36
  Pernelia 192
Nolan, J. T. 89
  Joshua 144
Noland, Joshua 152
Noorwood, Joseph G. 54
Norlon, Julia G. 173
Norman, Sophia 31
  William J. 164
Norris, Edmond R. 187
  Maggie 178
  Susan 200
Norten, Lizzie 182
Norton, Charles C. 111
  Elizabeth 130
  George W. 81
  James 159
  John N. 168
  Mary E. 196
  Sarah 117
  Susan G. 42
Norvell, Joshua 18
  Moses 14
Norwood, E. M. 200
  Jennie 197
  Joseph G. 54
  Minerva 142
Nourse, Charles C. 157
Nuckols, Mary Ann 123
Nunn, Mee J. 198
Nunnelly, Ashurst 134
  Benjamin F. 184
Nunnelley, Dudley 143

Nuttall, Thomas 28
Nutter, Amelia L. 209
 Ann 153
 James 15, 84
 James W. 156
 John 115
 John R. 92
 Mary Jane 92
 Mattie L. 163
 William 62
Nuttsell, Margaret E. 123
Nye, Iram 71

O

Oak, David F. 115
O'Bannon, Annie P. 203
 Elijah 73
 Minor 82
O'Brien, Robert 57
Oden, Jane 53
 Elizabeth 141
O'Fallon, Benjamin 34
 John 48
Offcut, Ezra N. 88
Offutt, Angelina 172
 Ann Eliza 113
 Annie M. 178
 Azra 51
 Caroline 156
 Charlotte 23
 E. F. 143
 Ezra N. 88
 Henry C. 104
 James L. 133
 Laura R. 209
 Maria 175
 Mary Ellen 157
 Nathaniel 59
 Rebecca A. 82
 Varlinda 16
 Varoline 156
 Z. C. 91
Ogg, William 205
O'Hara, Miss 32
Ohaver, Joseph 178
Oldham, Fatura W. 65
 Henry B. 61
 Jos(eph) C. 177
 Louisa 143
 N. A. 207
 Russia 31
 Samuel G. 96
 Sophia 54
Oliver, Nancy 7
 Philadelphia 32
 Rhoda H. 65
O'Neal, Elijah B. 199
 Jane Ellen 97
O'Niel, Mary D. 166
Oots, Emma 186

Oots, H. C. 205
 Mary E. 187
 Virginia 198
 William 115
Orear, E. J. 172
 Julia E. 172
 Wesley R. 143
O'Rear, Thomas C. 42
Orkiess, Mary Jane 116
Ormsby, Robert 66
Orr, Mary B. 24
 Samuel P. 19
Orrick, John C. 74
Osborne, Ephraim 68
 Kitty 175
Osburn, William A. 158
Ott, Jacob 192
Otwell, Emily 153
 John F. 110
Outten, Celia 111
 Margaret A. 152
 Mary 164
Overstreet, Flora 207
 Martha A. 181
 Smith F. 146
 W. C. 139
Overton, Ann 43
 Charles T. 110
 Frederick H. 208
 John B. 33
 Kate S. 165
 Lucy 8
 Susan Mary 33
Owen, Nannie C. 174
 Susan D. 44
Owens, Cynthia W. 87
 David 150
 Maximilian W. 12
 W. J. 179
Owings, Deborah 16
 Eliza 39
 Francis M. 161
 Thomas D. 6
 Thomas W. 136
Owins, Conquest W. 73
Owsley, Almira 46
 Amanda 34
 Amelia 36
 Bryan Y. 121
 Drusilla 144
 Elizabeth 52
 Erasmus Boyle 69
 John E. 109
 Martha Susan 109
 Mary 109
Oxley, Clear 32

P

Packer, Belverd D. 116
Padgett, Lucinda 78

Page, Ann Eliza 108
 Eliza 77
 Jacqueline 190
 James R. 191
 Thomas B. 142
Pahrish (Parrish?),
 E. H. 185
Paine, Sebastian C. 160
Painter, John 27
Palmer, Ann 16
 C. A. 118
 Charlotte 150
 James W. 19
 John 63
 Nelly 43
 Robert C. 60, 126
 Thomas 27
 Thomas A. 22
Parisa, J. B. 195
Parish, James 60
 Letitia 114
 Mary 25
 Mary D. 18
 Samuel 48
Park, Amanda M. 146
 Benjamin 9
 Solomon 56
Parker, A. T. 198
 A. W. P. 67
 Alley 56
 Amanda 81
 Annie M. 155
 Arzelia 147
 Elizabeth 150
 Elizabeth J. 149
 Georgia 178
 Jacob 87
 James Madison 42
 James P. 52
 John 117, 154
 John T. 155
 M. H. 204
 Margery 22
 Mary 173
 Mary Ann 15
 Nancy 14
 North 105
 Richard N. 73
 Thomas H. 186
 Wilson 22
Parkes, Joseph 39
Parkhill, Charles C. 129
Parmele, Edward 123
Parrish, Eliza A. 189
 Howard Ellen 156
 James 60
 James W. 123
 Joanna T. 11
 Letitia 114
 Lucy V. 192

Pike, Eliza 46
  Mary Ann 29
Pilcher, Henry, Jr. 162
  William 162
Pilkington, Catharine 85
  Joseph M. 137
  Mary Jane 101
  Samuel C. 108
Pillow, Amanda 96
Pinckard, Marianne W. 166
  Mary Ann 90
  Thomas B. 47, 104, 107
Pinckner, Charles E. 89
Pindell, Henry C. 118
Pinkard, Augusta W. 58
Pinkerton, C.H. 127
Piper, W.C. 177
Pirtle, Henry 55
Pitchford, Margaret 99
Pittman, Edward F. 196
  Frances S. 97
  Richard A. 205
Pitts, Cassa 28
  Pamelia 62
  Sophia E. 188
  Younger R. 79
Planck, Jacob 45
Platt, Joseph 105
  Louisa 10
Pleasants, Ann 25
  John H. 59
  Peyton R. 17
Plough, Eliza 56
Plummer, Susan 46
Poage, Ann 55
Pogue, Jane 34
  John C.D. 96
  Rosanna 94
Poignand, Eliza 129
Poindexter, Julia 102
  Laura C. 185
  Maria 140
  Zerilda B. 124
Pointdexter, Sarah 155
Polard, John 45
Polk, Ellen M. 187
  J.J. 33
  Jefferson S. 160
Pollard, J.D. 188
  Joseph 32
  Maria 52
  Nancy 28
Pollock, William 9
Poor, Mary 165
  Robert 19
Pope, Curran 95
  Eliza 7
  Elizabeth T. 54
  Ellen 192
  Hamilton 172

Pope, Hester 11
  John 11, 25
  Martha Ann 126
  Pendleton 76
  Sallie 181
Poppuck, Mary M. 83
Porcher, Elizabeth 115
Porter, Benjamin 84
  Caroline 65
  Elfrida D. 115
  George 72
  Nathaniel P. 111
  Peter B. 20
  Samuel S. 41
  Sarah Ann 147
  Thomas, Jr. 158
  Thomas P. 117
Porwood, Sidney 148
Posey, Fayette 9
  R.T. 183
Postelle, Charlotte 159
Postlehwait, Mary S. 65
  Emily 21
  Harriet 21
  Martha Ann 17
  Mary S. 65
  Samuel 7
Postlethwaite, Eliza 25
  Emily 48
  Nannie 151
  Sarah D. 53
Poston, Charles 116
  Elizabeth 131
  Henry G. 76
  J. 15
Potter, Christiana 141
  Harriet 90
  R.G. 208
  Ruth 96
  Sarah 74
Potts, Catharine 105
Poulter, John C. 153
Pountz, Sarah Bele 164
Pouzee, Samuel 121
Powell, Charles H. 177
  Chester B. 23
  Cuthbert 183
  John 87
  John B. 149
  Josiah 156
  Thomas W. 90
Power, John W. 161
  Reuben 88
Powers, Thomas 126
Poyntz, Ann E. 149
  Sarah Belle 164
Praigg, John G. 88
Prather, Henrietta 172
  J.V. 119
  James N. 192

Prather, Maria Julia 72
  Mary J. 54
  Mary Jane 115
  Matilda 55
  Telitha 151
Pratt, G.A. 174
  William W. 117
Prentice, George D. 83
Prentiss, Harriott 9
  Nancy 98
Prescott, Anna E. 135
Preston, Mr. 84
  Alexander M. 79
  Ann Sophonisba 32
  B. Howard 104
  Emily 189
  Francis 73
  Gertrude V.L. 76
  Henrietta 53
  Isaac T. 53
  Josephine 69
  Margaret 95
  Mary 73
  Sophronisba S. 166
Prevost, Frances C. 35
Prewett, Mrs. 75
  Levi 113
  Pamelia 34
Prewitt, Agnes 48
  Ann 177
  Ann M. 93
  Courtney H. 177
  H. Clay 205
  Henry P. 179
  John W. 99
  Laura 206
  Levi 46
  Martha C. 79
  Nelson 54
  Price 17
  Robert 176
  William F. 192
Price, Mr. 44
  Andrew 7
  Anne F. 138
  Belle 198
  Cosby 100
  D.L. 161
  Eliza 55
  Eliza P. 16
  Elizabeth 8, 26, 31
  Elvira 40
  Fannie 170
  Florida M. 201
  Helen B. 111
  James 73
  James C. 143
  James W. 161
  John 5
  John A. 151

Price, Joseph C. 108
Louisa 130
Margaret 26
Maria Louise 173
Martha 42
Martha B. 104
Mary 146
Mary Ann 135, 203
Matilda 80
Miriam 12
Philemon B. 6
Pugh 8
Richard M. 179
Rosette 14
Sally Maria 47
Samuel 11
Sarah A.H. 88
Tabitha 9
William 36
William H. 205
Willis 7, 164
Pritchard, Elizabeth 70
Probert, Thomas 124
Proctor, Mrs. 26
James 40
Pruden, Mahlon 179
Pruitt, William 11
Pryer, Catherine 149
Pryor, Lea 55
Samuel 137
Pugh, Fanny 158
George E. 171
Pullem, Ida 204
Letitia 32
William F. 181
Pulliam, Laura 201
Pullum, William A. 159
Pully, William 45
Purdom, Elizina Jane 110
Purnell, Julia Ann 94
William 173
Purviance, Henry 5
Margaret 16
Puthuff, Margaret A. 179
Mary 173
Putman, Joseph W. 112
Putnam, Virginia 143

Q

Qarner, Alfred 121
Qheat, Z. 182
Quarles, Susan E. 92
Quarrel, William 162
Quilling, Fannie 207
Quin, Charles 98
Quinn, B.T. 158
Quinton, Philip 12
Quisenberry, Colby T. 142
John 64
Thomas E. 138

R

Rabourn, Amanda 116
Radcliff, William 128
Radford, Elizabeth 115
Ragan, Ann 165
Levy 62
Mary 85
Ragland, Nancy 87
Ragsdale, Sarah 40
Railey, Ann M. 170
Emma S. 198
Lavinia H. 65
Randolph 21
Sarah 14
Thomas 14
Rainey, Ann E. 100
Elizabeth 97
Margaret Jane 98
Nancy H. 85
Nancy M. 52
William 6
Ralston, Eliza J. 149
T.N. 179
Ramsey, H.E.A. 114
Randall, Brice C. 181
Burton 136
Charles M. 100
Susan 89
Thomas G. 151
Randolph, _____ 27
Eliza 37
John H. 60
Margaret 141
Mary 25
Rankin, John 40
Paul 129
Samuel 52
Susan 29
Thomas 28
Rankins, Lizzie 208
Rankle, Susan 35
Rannels, Martha G. 65
Ransdell, Ann 75
Ratcliff, Robert F. 142
Ratcliffe, James W. 171
Rathvon, Jacob 140
Rawlins, Nancy E. 99
Ray, John D. 157
Raymond, Clara M. 180
Rea, John M. 191
Reading, Sarah 88
Ready, Henry H. 62
John M. 158
Sarah Ann 112
Rear, Thomas C. 42
Rector, William 29
Redd, Ann Catharina 77
Anna E. 124
Mary A. 208

Redd, Samuel 8
Samuel J. 151
Thomas 7
Thomas M. 165
Thomas S. 170
Redhead, Wesley 195
Redman, Arminta 169
Mary 148
William J. 146
Redmond, Elizabeth 158
Reed, A.J. 205
Emeline 57
Isabella Eliza Jane 51
John 158
Maria 152
Mary 49
Mary Jane 76
Narcissa A. 184
Rees, Angeline 145
Arthur 94
Sidney F. 186
Winchester E. 147
Reese, Jane 30
Reid, Charlotte 55
Elizabeth 48
Joseph 208
Louisa 92
Thomas W. 152
Reiley, James P. 82
Reineking, John W. 178
Rennick, Louisa 140
Matilda 56
Renton, Mary Ellen 112
Renwick, Allisonia 127
Louisa 140
Reordan, Patrick H. 151
Resor, Susan 23
Respass, William 45
Reville, Ann T. 21
Reynes, Joseph 43
Reynolds, Benjamin 9
J.A. 205
L.H. 76
Louisa 202
Mary E. 148
Nancy 70
S.W. 206
Samuel W. 160
Thomas 33
Rhodes, Mrs. 12
Belle 156
Rhorer, Henry C. 164
Rhoten, Eliza Jane 91
Rice, Allen T. 175
Eliza 73
John B. 160
John M. 16
Julia Ann 166
Lucy 30
Mary Ann 148

253

Wood, Robert A. 108
  Ruth 64
  W.G. 166
  William 18
Woodburry, Mary E. 119
Woodford, Elvira 117
  Lucy 126
  W.T. 126
Woodhouse, William 153
Woodrow, Joshua 115
Woodruff, Catherine Ann 38
  Ezra 13
  Ichabod 14
  James B. 157
  Jesse 143
  Mary 148
Woods, Eliza P. 113
  Joseph 9
  Mary Ann 62
  Merritt 124
  Nathaniel G. 140
  Robert 18
  Sarah D. 136
  Thomas 50
  William 50
Woodso, Samuel H. 6
Woodson, Elizabeth M. 99
  Polly 8
  Robert E. 106
  S. 94
  Samuel H. 6
Woodward, George 16
Woodyard, Charlotte 104
Wooley, Aaron K. 50
Woolfolk, Eliza 15
  Joseph S. 189
  Mary B. 19
  Thomas 37
Woolford, Eliza 15
Woollen, L.J. 186
Woolley, Charles W. 173
  Margaret H. 173
Woolridge, C. 24
  Edward 129
  Nancy 9
Woolums, William H. 180
Wooly, Thomas 19
Wooren, Kitty H. 15
Woorley, Margaret 21
Work, Sarah 53
Worley, Caleb Thompson 172
  Maria E. 124
Wormsley, John 196
Wornall, John T. 175
  Nancy 90
Worsham, Fountain 174
  Susan 176
  W.S. 140
Worthen, George A. 121
Worthington, Isaac 61

Worthington, James 151
  Marie 185
  William H. 128
Wrenn, Woodson 8
Wrigglesworth, Mary 24
  Sarah 68
Wright, Miss _____ 92
  Dorothy 202
  James W. 116
  Maria 181
  Maria Jane 167
  W.H.H. 90
  W.P. 40
Wyatt, E. 139
  James 18
  James F. 192
  John 17
  Lucinda 147
Wykoff, Anna 32
Wyne, Benjamin 14
Wynkoop, Susan 86

Y

Yancy, Mrs. 79
Yarbough, Gustavus 163
Yates, Elizabeth 162
  James M. 138
  Lucy Ann 101
  Susan 87
  Thomas 45
Yeates, R.M. 204
Yeatman, Angelica 200
  Jane 84
Yeiser, Frederick 26
  Frederick 169
  Margaret 58
  Philip D. 129
  Phillip E. 90
Yellot, George 7
Yoder, Mary 85
Young, Adaline K. 57
  Adelaide L. 173
  Alfred M. 119
  Ann 94
  Ann F. 133
  Benjamin 13
  Caroline J. 177
  Catharine 89
  David W. 209
  Eleanor E. 105
  Eliza 40, 193
  Eliza Ann 33
  Ephraim 184
  George C. 175
  Jane R. 192
  Jessamine 106
  John 70
  John C. 58, 102, 116
    142
  John R. 9

Young, Louisa Ann 25
  L.P. 127
  Malinda 93
  Malvina 123
  Marian 57
  Martha F. 200
  Mary 43, 177
  Mary B. 82
  Mary C. 172
  Mary T. 196
  Moses G. 192
  Nancy 77
  Paulina L. 172
  Richard B. 148
  Samuel A. 83, 103
  Susan 42
  Walter Carr 93
  William D. 12
Yulee, David 118

Z

Zake, Sophia 51
Zanone, John H. 200
Zeumar, George 69
Zimmerman, B.T. 207
  David L. 85, 163
  Eliza 55
  Mary F. 187
  Thomas J. 155, 194
  William W. 100
Zook, Elizabeth 54